◆ **Afro-Cuban Religious Experience**

University Press of Florida

Gainesville Tallahassee Tampa Boca Raton Pensacola Orlando Miami Jacksonville

Eugenio Matibag

Afro-Cuban

Religious Experience

Cultural Reflections in Narrative

Copyright 1996 by the Board of Regents of the State of Florida
Printed in the United States of America on acid-free paper
All rights reserved

01 00 99 98 97 96   6 5 4 3 2 1

Library of Congress Cataloging-in-Publication Data
Matibag, Eugenio.
Afro-Cuban religious experience: cultural reflections in narrative / Eugenio Matibag.
p. cm.
Includes bibliographical references and index.
ISBN 0-8130-1431-X (alk. paper)
1. Blacks—Cuba—Religion. 2. Cuba—Religion—20th century. I. Title.
BL2566.C9M38   1996
299'.6897291—dc20   95-46559

The University Press of Florida is the scholarly publishing agency for the State
University System of Florida, comprised of Florida A & M University, Florida Atlantic
University, Florida International University, Florida State University, University of
Central Florida, University of Florida, University of North Florida, University of
South Florida, and University of West Florida.

University Press of Florida
15 Northwest 15th Street
Gainesville, FL 32611

For Karen

◈ Contents

◈ Illustrations

◈ Preface

Sociologist Fernando Ortiz, in numerous studies, discovered the African contribution to Cuban culture in the island's art, religion, and language and "in
the tone of the collective emotionality." Writer and folklorist Lydia Cabrera
would later ask, not waiting for an answer: "What piece of our soil is not
saturated with secret African influences?" Fidel Castro would more recently
declare, "We are Latinoafroamericans!" In the structures of perception and
discourse, in the everyday language of thought and feeling, Africanity runs
through and colors everything that can be called uniquely Cuban. The process of cultural transplantation, diffusion, and synthesis of course is not
unique to Cuba but exemplifies what has occurred generally throughout the
Caribbean since the colonial period. African culture, observes Dathorne, gave
the region "an air of new cultural autonomy" and new patterns of culture,
especially where the absence of indigenous culture was most strongly felt
(1). Indeed, as developments in religious forms have perhaps most clearly
demonstrated, the amalgamation, synthesis, symbiosis, or crossing of diverse West African and Hispanic cultural elements in the American setting
produced a new religious culture. In Cuba as elsewhere in the Antilles, the
"peculiar institution" of slavery made possible the birth of this distinctly
Afro-Caribbean culture. And religion, as I hope to demonstrate, has functioned in Cuba as elsewhere in the Antilles as a social subsystem that gave
form and unity to the insular culture. The present study is intended for an
audience of literary scholars, cultural historians, and critics as well as those
simply interested in the printed literature on Afro-Cuban religion. It approaches a number of modern narrative texts that address themes and symbols of the Afro-Cuban religions with the premise that those texts provide

keys to unlocking some of the mysteries of Afro-Cuban religions and their cultural context.

Afro-Cuban religions—especially the ones known as Regla de Ocha, la Sociedad Secreta Abakuá, Palo Monte, and the Regla Arará—are those Cuban systems of faith and worship that originated from transcultural processes by which elements from West African and Catholic belief systems were combined and transformed; from preexisting rituals, doctrines, mythologies, and cosmologies, new religions were assembled and reconformed. Afro-Cuban religions therefore, as the hyphenated denomination indicates, were religions that were originally reinvented by African peoples who were transported to Cuba during the period of colonization and forced to labor as slaves for the benefit of the Spanish, and later the Creole, plantocracy. In creating new, semicovert religions out of the components of preexisting religions, the transplanted Africans forged a source of identity, an arm of psychic resistance, and a medium of social cohesion to the extent that it could exist under the dehumanizing conditions of slavery.

Beside the transculturative processes by which they developed, other characteristics common to these religions mark their distinctiveness within Cuban culture. Those characteristics include polytheistic and animistic beliefs; rituals mediating between humans and divinities—such as initiation, possession, sacrifice, and divination; magic, in the form of spells or ethnomedicine; and the central importance of music and dance in religious ceremonies. A little more than a century after the abolition, Afro-Cuban religions continue to fascinate, and they continue to gain believers and practitioners throughout the two Americas despite numerous distorted or oversimplified representations of those religions in the mass media. The body of Afro-Cuban literature is substantial, and its systematic study, to which this book aspires to contribute, is only just beginning. That literature will impress generations of scholars not only with its beauty and evocative power but also with its intellectual challenge to Eurocentric modes of reading culture.

This book is an examination of the treatments that Afro-Cuban religion has received in Cuban narrative during the period extending from the middle of the Republican era (from the late 1920s through the 1930s) to the contemporary period of the Revolution and the so-called Second Diaspora of African culture. My approach to the subject includes a reading of Afro-Cuban religious signs and discourse incorporated into the systems of that narrative in works by both major and lesser known authors associated with the movement called *el afrocubanismo*. Afro-Cuban religious motifs in the texts of that literary movement often refer to the subtext of West African myths in which the principal actants are the gods, variously called *orishas, ochas, dioses, santos, espíritus, mpungus, ngangas, loas, mystères,* or *vaudoux.* As literary texts reveal, the deities populate the religious subtexts of mythical storytelling and divination rituals, which maintain their own archive of narrative knowledge.

As if the connection between literature and popular culture did not give reason enough to embark on this study, the list of major Afro-Cubanist authors concerned with religious issues reads like a who's who of Cuban letters. That list includes such names as Fernando Ortiz, Rómulo Lachatañeré, Alejo Carpentier, José Antonio Ramos, Lydia Cabrera, Nicolás Guillén, Dora Alonso, Nancy Morejón, Miguel Barnet, Guillermo Cabrera Infante, Antonio Benítez Rojo, and Manuel Cofiño. As will be evident in our reading of these and other authors, the texts of Afro-Cubanism have from the movement's inception signaled the effort to redefine the "Cuban national identity"—and often at the same time to redefine the very concept of "identity"—with a language cognizant of the African contribution to that identity. And from its own beginnings, as we will see, that African contribution to Cuban identity has been preserved and passed on in the wealth of Afro-Cuban religions whose beliefs and practices continue to give form and coherence to the Afro-Cuban legacy.

Yet since this dimension of Latin American literary culture has been ignored or subject to frequent ethnocentric misunderstanding, I hope that my account will clarify the nature of Afro-Cuban religion both as background or subtext to literary texts and as itself a repository of narrative discourse. Chapters 2 through 7, following an introductory chapter, are thus devoted to readings of a range of twentieth-century Cuban authors who either have written down versions of the Afro-Cuban religious texts or have incorporated ritual, mythological, or doctrinal elements of the religions into their writings. In addition to literary, mythological, and folkloric works, these texts also include manuals and Afro-Cuban "hagiographies," which provide additional materials and interpretations for commentary, analysis, and further interpretation. Recent theories of narrative will illuminate the use of Afro-Cuban religious sign systems (including myth) in fictional narrative, whereas ideas from performance and folklore theory suggest ways in which ritual processes may be reconstructed for an ethnologically informed understanding of the literary text.

In examining the aspects of Afro-Cuban ritual revealed in and by literary narratives, I will also consider the paradigmatic role of narrative in Afro-Cuban rituals of divination and especially the divination narratives known by the Yoruba-Lucumí designation *patakís.* The pataki is the recited or cited narrative of the diloggún or Ifá ritual; as a part of that ritual, it functions variously, by modeling behavior, offering counsel, and serving as a mnemonic device for conserving, organizing, and transmitting cultural information. Various series of patakís discussed in the present study have been transcribed or summarized in printed form, where they signal the transition from an oral to a written or "print" culture. Once these narratives have been thus conserved and fixed as literary texts, they become available for a formal and narratological analysis.

In addition to the published patakís, printed collections of Afro-Cuban myth, folktale, and testimony also demonstrate the way an oral culture undergoes a process of textualization in "becoming literature" and enters into another order or "economy" of signification, one that profoundly overdetermines the reception of that oral culture's artifacts. From the viewpoint of this second order or economy, however, a dialectics of inscription is shown to be already implicit within "oral literature" of the Afro-Cuban tradition, with the possibility that that oral literature's "transcription" into print, with its narrative refunctioning, may contribute to the undermining of the theocentric authority credited to sacred verbal utterance. By so fixing and objectifying sacred discourse, the transculturation process of literary narrative subjects that utterance to contact with the viewpoints, languages, and ideologies of other discourses and signifying practices, promoting in effect a dialogical relationship with other perspectives. In short, the language of religion as inscribed in literature becomes recoded, often for the sake of nonreligious ends. This asymmetrical dialogization between writing and sacred speech occurs most saliently, as we shall see, in the documenting and recontextualizing of Lucumí and Abakuá liturgy in the nationalist narratives of the 1930s, in the neutralizing conversion of religious myth and doctrine into "folklore," and in the related portrayals of African-based religion for the end of affirming the goals and values of the Cuban Revolution after 1959. The signifiers of Afro-Cuban religion are thus dismembered, remembered, and transmuted with every literary reinscription.

At the same time, a conservative countertendency within this transculturative process must be noted as well. A religion is an institution, and one of the functions of institutions is that of conventionalizing signification, of reducing ambiguity and checking the slippage of signifiers by establishing frames of reference and the protocols of reading. Such conventionalization encodes the institution's version of the real, constructing the *Lebenswelt* of its participants in that fashion. As they draw from real religious ritual, myth, and doctrine, Afro-Cuban literary narratives evoke the concentrating focus that religion creates in its discourse practices, practices that give form and sense to the experience of those who profess belief in Afro-Cuban religion. Yet because not all readers are familiar with the signs of Afro-Cuban religious culture, literary interpretation must for their benefit reconstruct the ritual, mythical, doctrinal, and social contexts that made the signs meaningful in performance. If it reads and explicates religious signs as much as possible from the viewpoint of their institutional contexts, interpretation may on occasion speak out of the silences imposed by the dominant viewpoints of the incorporating narrative or out of the gaps of the master narrative that has authorized the use of Afro-Cuban religious discourse for other, more classically rationalist or statist purposes. In reading against the grain of the text, or in expropriating the expropriating reading, Afro-Cubanist interpretation produces something "new": namely, a sign of internal difference that challenges and subverts the apparent, "authorial," or official meaning of the text. Or, to cite one of Lydia Cabrera's collected Afro-Cuban proverbs, interpretation may see and acknowledge that even textually, *una cosa piensa el caballo y otra el que lo ensilla*: the horse thinks one thing and the one who saddles him another.

Many are those who along the way have given me the means—intellectual, material, and oftentimes spiritual—to write this book. My gratitude goes to Christiane von Buelow and John Carlos Rowe, great advisers. Lucía Guerra-Cunningham taught me Latin America's connection to theory. María Antonia Carrillo in Havana opened my eyes. Diana K. Metz's analysis of syncretism in Cabrera set me on Elegguá's crossroads.

Julie Minkler discussed many of this book's ideas over coffee and ŝarbos. Patrick Taylor, in writings and personal communications, has bottled the wine of astonishment like no other. Antonio Benítez Rojo and William Luis guided me like mentors, both through their writings and through their comments on the manuscript. Emilio Bejel, Delitta Martin-Ogunsola, and Eduardo González also read considerable portions of the manuscript, as did my friend and colleague Robert Bernard. Encouragement and counsel also came from Nancy Morejón, Manuel Zapata Olivella, Charlotte Bruner, Norma Wolff, David Roochnik, Berardo Valdés, José Rodríguez, and Susana Sotillo. Jorge Sánchez's tireless searching and typing provided the critical mass. Elías Miguel Muñoz continued our never ending discussion on *la cubanidad*. Alex Leader and Michael Senecal at University Press of Florida contributed their invaluable editing skills. I thank all these friends, colleagues, and readers, acknowledging that any errors appearing on these pages could be only my own and would bear no reflection whatsoever on their own considerable knowledge and high standards.

Portions of my article, "The Yoruba Origins of Afro-Cuban Culture," from *Journal of Caribbean Studies* 10, nos. 1–2 (Winter 1994 and Spring 1995), have been incorporated into chapters 1 and 2 of this book. A portion of another article, "Self-Consuming Fictions: The Dialectics of Cannibalism in Recent Caribbean Narratives," from *Postmodern Culture* 1, no. 3 (May 1991), has been incorporated into chapter 5.

To my parents, Ramona and Dalmacio Matibag, and to my brothers, José and John, and my sisters, Leticia and Julie: *maferefún e ibae*. And the love of Karen Piconi, Cris, and Tessa sustained me throughout the process by which this book was written.

Abbreviations

Abbreviations in the parenthetical notes refer to specific works, listed below, by frequently cited authors or editors, or by authors of two or more works cited in the present study. Unless an English translation of a work is cited, the translations of passages in Spanish are my own.

AP   Guillermo Cabrera Infante, *Así en la paz como en la guerra.*
APA   Julia Cuervo Hewitt, *Aché, presencia africana: tradiciones yoruba-lucumí en la narrativa cubana.*
AVL   Lydia Cabrera, *Anagó: vocabulario lucumí.*
BH   José Antonio Portuondo, *Bosquejo histórico de las letras cubanas.*
CA   Castellanos, Jorge, and Castellanos, Isabel. *Cultura afrocubana.* Vol. 1: *El negro en Cuba, 1492–1844.* Vol. 3: *Las religiones y las lenguas.*
CBA   Carlos Moore, *Castro, the Blacks, and Africa.*
CN   Lydia Cabrera, *Cuentos Negros de Cuba.*
D   Jacques Derrida, *Dissemination.*
DALC   Benjamin Núñez, with assistance from the African Bibliographic Center, *Dictionary of Afro-Latin American Civilization.*
DI   Rogelio Martínez Furé, *Diálogos imaginarios.*
EQT   Isabel Castellanos, *Elegua quiere Tambo: cosmovisión religiosa afrocubana en las canciones populares.*
ES   Julio García Cortez, *El Santo (La Ocha). Secretos de la Religión Lucumí.*
EYO   Alejo Carpentier, *¡Ecue-Yamba-O!*
FS   Robert Farris Thompson, *Flash of the Spirit.*
FV·   Miguel Barnet, *La fuente viva.*
ID   William Bascom, *Ifá Divination.*
IR   Antonio Benítez Rojo, *La isla que se repite.*

KI	Lydia Cabrera, *Koeko iyawó: aprende novicio.*
ISD	Migene González-Wippler, *Introduction to Seashell Divination.*
LB	William Luis, *Literary Bondage.*
LSÑ	Lydia Cabrera, *La Lengua Sagrada de los Ñáñigos.*
M	Lydia Cabrera, *El monte.*
MC	Alejo Carpentier, *La música en Cuba.*
MS	Rómulo Lachatañeré, *Manual de Santería: El sistema de cultos "Lucumís."*
NNH	Salvador Bueno, *El negro en la novela hispanoamericana.*
OC	Natalia Bolívar Aróstegui, *Los orishas en Cuba.*
OMY	Rómulo Lachatañeré, *¡¡Oh, mío Yemayá!!*
P	Julio García Cortez, *Patakí.*
PQ	Lydia Cabrera, *Por qué . . . (Cuentos negros de Cuba).*
RA	Mercedes Cros Sandoval, *La religión afrocubana.*
REM	Alejo Carpentier, *El reino de este mundo.*
RNV	Lydia Cabrera, *Refranes de Negros Viejos.*
RR	Kenneth Burke, *The Rhetoric of Religion.*
RSD	Tomás Fernández Robaina, *Recuerdos secretos de dos mujeres públicas.*
RSS	Roberto González Echevarría, *La ruta de Severo Sarduy.*
S	Migene González-Wippler, *Santería.*
SAS	Joseph M. Murphy, *Santería: African Spirits in America.*
SC	William Bascom, *Sixteen Cowries.*
SE	Migene González-Wippler, *The Santería Experience.*
SMD	Joel James Figarola, *Sobre muertos y dioses.*
SP	Jacques Derrida, *Speech and Phenomena.*
SR	Migene González-Wippler, *Santería: The Religion.*
SRL	Rómulo Lachatañeré, "El sistema religioso de los lucumíes y otras influencias africanas en Cuba."
SSA	Lydia Cabrera. *La Sociedad Secreta Abakuá.*
TC	Antonio Benítez Rojo, "La tierra y el cielo."
TO	Migene González-Wippler, *Tales of the Orishas.*
TOM	"Thunder over Miami: Changó in a Technological Society."
TÑ	Fernando Ortiz, "La tragedia de los ñáñigos."
TTT	Guillermo Cabrera Infante, *Tres tristes tigres.*
VU	William Luis, ed., *Voices from Under.*
WD	Jacques Derrida, *Writing and Difference.*
YM	Ulli Beier, *Yoruba Myths.*
YO	Lydia Cabrera, *Yemayá y Ochún.*
YSN	William Bascom, *The Yoruba of Southwestern Nigeria.*

1

⊕ Afro-Cuban Religion in Narrative

> . . . una multitud presentándose en su misteriosa unidad
> [a multitude presenting itself in its mysterious unity].
> José Lezama Lima, Paradiso

At 9:00 P.M., when the cannon of La Cabaña Fortress was fired, as it has been every evening since colonial times, many Havaneros would throw a bit of water out the front entrance of their homes and knock loudly on the door three times. The knocking was to drive away evil spirits, for everyone knew, and knows today, that the cannon belongs to Santa Bárbara, the protectress of artillerymen and the double of Changó, the Yoruba-Lucumí god of fire and thunder. This and other accounts of African-based custom appear in Tomás Fernández Robaina's *Recuerdos secretos de dos mujeres públicas* (Secret remembrances of two public women, 1983), in which the personal histories of two former prostitutes suggest the extent to which religious belief and practice have given form to Cuban experience since before the Revolution.

Throughout Fernández Robaina's *testimonio*, the "public women" of the title make other references to the signs of Afro-Cuban religion encountered or exchanged in daily experience, in particular the signs of Regla de Ocha (Santería) and spiritualist occultism. The women go to *santeros* and *cartomanciers* for advice on their daily affairs; they read horoscopes in *Carteles* or *Bohemia*; they pray to the Yoruba-Lucumí god Elegguá for protection. Consuelo la Charmé's devotion to Elegguá also includes lighting candles to him on Mondays, giving him caramels and cane liquor or *aguardiente*, and wearing his amulet or *resguardo*, which Consuelo "feeds" from time to time with sacrificial blood. When on one occasion Jehovah's Witnesses condemn the "images and objects" of the religion as "instruments of the devil," the women reply that they could not abandon their religion for without it they "would die." Consuelo adds, referring to the prostitutes who believed as she did, "We always flushed out the business house with purslane, *abrecamino*, white flowers

1. **Elegguá by the door at Casa del Caribe, Santiago de Cuba, 1991.**

and essences of every kind; nor did we fail to put out glasses of water for the dead of our families and, especially, for our protector-guides, whether these be Francisco the Congo, the Indian, the Gypsy, the Nun or the Priest" (RSD 55–56).

In another personal narrative recorded by Fernández Robaina, a certain prostitute named María, nicknamed la Canosa, recalled opening up a restaurant as a cover for her brothel. Good times come to María's business, and at the height of her prosperity María buys the gold jewelry that adorns her person as it honors the goddess Ochún, the deity who loves precious metals and revels in sensual pleasures. In yet another account, Consuelo describes a *comparsa* religious procession called La Sultana in the barrio carnival. That procession includes a Queen of Italy played by "very well-known santero," a Regla de Ocha priest, masked and dressed for the part (RSD 46–47, 63).

These and other examples given in Fernández Robaina's *testimonio* illustrate the quotidian presence of Afro-Cuban religion in Cuban social life before 1959. The practice of this religion, the examples show, was not reserved exclusively for holy days and places but formed a part of the fabric of everyday life. It has had, and continues to have, a "fundamentally immanent character," as Isabel Castellanos characterizes it in her study of the Afro-Cuban "cosmovision" and popular song lyrics: "These are not religions of the 'beyond' but of the 'over here,' there is no aspect of earthly life that is not permeated by the active presence of the supernatural" (EQT 28–29). The "más acá" and the "más allá" of the quote—that is, the natural and the supernatural, the human and the divine, the temporal and the eternal—interact and communicate normally in the world of Afro-Cuban religious experience.

This book is a study of the treatments that Afro-Cuban religious experience has been given in modern narratives. Here we will explore the ways in which the signifying systems constitutive of that experience have been reenacted, recodified, analyzed, critiqued, and otherwise represented in Cuban stories, novels, and, to a more limited extent, poetry and drama. In this exploration, I will establish, in a series of analytical and interpretive readings, some analogies between Afro-Cuban modes of religious discourse and the representational strategies of narrative, especially prose fiction. The method I have chosen is to elucidate the religious content of Afro-Cuban narratives and articulate the function of Afro-Cuban religious elements in each case, while taking into account the forms and functions of literary elements specific to those narratives. In dividing my subject into chapters, I have classified its matter under headings that correspond to each of the major Afro-Cuban religious traditions.

The very concept of "experience," I realize, has, like the related concepts of "subjectivity," "consciousness," and "perception," come under the postmodern suspicion cast upon all phenomenological postulates based on the desire for a metaphysical "center." This desire would overlook the signifying, constitutive, differential, and mediatory activities of a structure while putting faith in an immediate act of making the center present in perception or thought. Yet experience, on the contrary, is constructed in the production and transmission of signs, which substitute themselves for any center. In his critique of Husserl's phenomenology of signs, Jacques Derrida tenders the neologism *différance* to denominate the process of difference and deferment inherent to signification and to what is experienced as "meaning." Language and other sign systems effect "meaning" not by immediate or vertical relations of signifier/signified and sign and referent but by différance, the horizontal transfer-displacement of meaning from signifier to signifier. This semantic necessity, produced by radical differentiation and deferment of signs at the origin of perception or experience, puts in question the assumption that either a noumenal referent or an ideal signified exists as such. Among the many implications of this anti-idealist, anti-empiricist theory of signs, cultures can be said to "mediate" reality by in effect creating it, producing perception and experience in the very cross-referencing of signs that makes use of consciousness as a personal nexus of apersonal semiosis (SP 88, 90–93).

And yet, for all that, there is something that undeniably "feels like" experience, something I experience as experience even as I put in question this "I" that experiences. While putting such subjectivist categories within brackets (or quotation marks), we must acknowledge too that the "subject" who "experiences" does not disappear altogether under the postmodern theoretical construct. Rather it finds itself situated, positioned, in particular signifying systems that constitute the relationships of both the subject with the world and the subject with other subjects. Because there is paradoxically no immediate presence of things or meaning to the perceiving or thinking subject except through the mediating languages of culture, the "living present" of consciousness and perception depends on a "reading" of traces of past and future significations: the *retensions* and *protensions* of signs, as explained by Husserl's theory and Derrida's grammatology (SP 142–43). Religion offers itself as an example of a signifying institution that constructs the subject's experience as such by situating the subject—conceived as a "grammatical function"—in the chains of signifiers that relay meaning (through retentive memory and protensive anticipation) and mediate the encounter of the subject with the object world inclusive of other subjects. Religion's own systematicity and relative autonomy make it, among other things, a complex machine for producing significations and for constituting the subject as a sign-processing, focalizing "function." The postmodern deconstruction of the subject and experience of religion does not annul them, but it discredits the assumption that they originate meaning and perception, precisely by situating them within systems that produce, authorize, and organize signification.

The present study proposes a poetics, or systematic literary study, of the modern Cuban narrative texts, both fictional and nonfictional, that incorporate signifying elements of Afro-Cuban religions. References to textual segments will serve to exemplify Afro-Cuban religious ideas but with the understanding that the literary texts in question belong to a different order of discourse altogether, constituting what Rimmon-Kenan calls "junctions of various compositional principles" (*Narrative* 4). In consideration of this difference and construction, it will be acknowledged that the literary system or subsystem to which texts belong sustains relationships with a varied and heterogeneous sociohistorical context: that is, with the system's "outside," which is also, for the sake of knowledge, constituted textually, grasped as a series of junctions of compositional principles. It is Tynjanov who describes a "literary system" as "first of all a *system of the functions of the literary order which are in continual interrelationship with other orders*" ("Literary" 159). Engaged in such interrelationships, the orders of Afro-Cuban religion present themselves as a multitude of functions susceptible to being incorporated into and refunctioned in the heteroclite unity of Afro-Cubanist narratives. Those narratives may in turn be subsumed again within the broader literary and cultural system that recontextualizes and refunctions elements, aspects, and motifs of the religious system that have been reworked in literature. In the light of these considerations, the present text will focus on three interrelated questions: In what distinctive ways have modern Cuban narratives addressed each of the major Afro-Cuban religious traditions? Which elements of Afro-Cuban religion have been incorporated into modern Cuban narratives? And, assuming those elements and these orders originate in other signifying systems, what sort of refunctioning do those elements undergo within their new narrative orders?

In attempting to answer these questions, this study will trace some of the reflections, refractions, and rarefactions that Afro-Cuban religion has undergone in its literary recodifications, not only in folkloric transcriptions and versions of myths and *patakís* but also in the narrative fictionalizations of the novel and short story genres. This effort is guided by the homology between reading fiction and reading signs of the culture-world that Tzvetan Todorov formulates in his *Introduction to Poetics*; that homology, I believe, both illuminates the nature of religious representations and clarifies the approach of this study. And although Todorov's assertion misleadingly suggests an unproblematic correspondence between narrative and experience, or between reading and perception, his homology nonetheless indicates a fruitful direction for collating and connecting signs across literary and religious spheres. Todorov writes, "Just as we engage in an effort to construct fiction starting from a discourse, in exactly the same way the characters, elements of the fiction, must reconstitute their universe starting from the discourse and signs that surround them. Thus every fiction contains within itself a representation of this same process of reading to which we submit it. The characters construct their reality starting from the signs they receive, just as we construct the fiction starting from the text read; their apprenticeship to the world is an image of ours to the book" (*Introduction* 55–56). In fiction, the subject apprenticed to the world of Afro-Cuban religion would construct a sign-universe in a manner that has similarities to the way we, delivered unto literature's form-giving language, construct a world in reading. By means of its synthesizing figures, in other words, Afro-Cuban fiction may reconstitute, within its own order and in an idiom proper to itself, a religion's prayers, myths, rituals, music, icons, dances, and associated lore and superstitions. Todorov's homology also suggests that, like literary fictions, religious images and practices signify by virtue of a willing suspension of disbelief on the part of the participating subject.

The schools of critical theory issuing from the intellectual cultures called structuralism, poststructuralism, and narratology, to which Todorov has contributed significantly, have given much credibility to the notion of reading reality as a text and indicate a method by which Afro-Cuban religion—a cultural system, a discursive field, a space of semiosis—can be read as having made the text of itself into a reality, a simulacrum of a universe that replaces, for the subject's practical and cognitive purposes, the universe "itself." This method would be a tropological one for which the figures of a text are to be isolated and read as epistemological motifs as well as syntactical organizers. Joseph Murphy's study *Santería: African Spirits in America* has already presented a suggestive "way to organize the many different *metaphors* of divinity in Yoruba religion" (my emphasis). Murphy's major metaphors are initiation, sacrifice, possession, and divination, and within Santería they serve above all to honor the ancestors, to worship the *orishas,* and to order life (SAS 8). Religion's metaphors of divinity, as well as the "social dramas" (Turner) that are raised into religious ritual, serve to codify experience in a manner susceptible to textual recodification and interpretive decodification. Narrative texts, both within religion as myth and doctrine and outside religion as Afro-Cuban literature, participate of course in this recodifying and decodifying activity as they reinscribe, examine, critique, and reinterpret Afro-Cuban religion. A few definitions will help to delimit our subject matter.

Religion is a cultural universal, a multiform human activity and institution, by which humans hold intercourse with the divine. It is a complex of collective beliefs and behaviors engaged in the worship of what is designated as "the holy" or "the sacred," always and everywhere distinguishing this designatum from what is considered "profane." Religion commonly addresses the mystery surrounding birth and death and usually teaches something about supernatural beings and a transcendent realm, bringing humans, through this process, into communication with gods or God, with the cosmos, and with one another.

Religion also consists of instituted forms of worship that mediate the experience of humans with the divine, the cosmos, and other humans. From the perspective of cultural anthropology, moreover, a religion appears as a system of knowledge, or *epistème,* and as a complex set of patterned behaviors. Among its other functions, it gives a sense of meaning to its believers. It unites them into a community. It rechannels or sublimates instinctual drives into socially acceptable form. These functions are congruent with the schema of the six "dimensions" of religion outlined by theologian Ninian Smart. Smart's dimensions or categories comprising the key aspects of religion, which have helped to organize the argument of the present study, are the ritual, mythological, doctrinal, ethical, social, and experiential dimensions. To these I also add a seventh aspect or category, namely, a semiotic dimension, in which religion is constituted in and as a system of signs that produces experience, mediating the individual's encounter with the world as those signs refer to one another within a more or less coherent and self-referring discursive universe. Religion most clearly appears in this aspect as a language—that is, as a mode of expression, communication, and aesthetic creation. This is not to say that religious phenomena themselves may be finally reduced to their linguistic or semiotic dimension as material signifiers but that at least their "principles of verbalization" may be recodified as discursive paradigms and decodified in interpretation (RR 1). In this framework and perspective, what obtains for the informed reader holds true for the Afro-Cuban officiant as well: working inside the Afro-Cuban religious system, the babalaos or iyalorishas are hermeneuts who have the will and possess the competence to read signs generated by this system and to carry out interpretations and appropriate responses based on their knowledge of the system's codes.

Studies in cultural anthropology and folklore have revealed that religion functions as the central, binding force of Afro-Cuban culture. Yet "religion" in the normative Western sense of the term does not do justice to the complex system of systems that is Afro-Cuban religion, a comprehensive system that syncretizes, articulates, and reproduces extensive orders of knowledge in the areas of psychotherapy, pharmacology, art, music, magic, and narrative. Numerous twentieth-century works of Afro-Cuban literature, appearing before and after 1959, refer specifically to the beliefs and practices of the major Afro-Cuban religions that will be considered in this book. Those religions are Regla de Ocha, known popularly as Santería; la Sociedad Secreta Abakuá, often called Ñañiguismo; Palo Monte, or la Regla Conga; and la Regla Arará, the Cuban variation on Haitian Vaudou. Such Cuban writers as Alejo Carpentier, Lydia Cabrera, Miguel Barnet, Manuel Cofiño, and Severo Sarduy have sought to recodify the texts and rituals of these religions in narratives that, in effect, have contributed to the literary redefinition of a national identity, which is a principal obsession even of Cuban authors who have relocated themselves, for whatever reason, outside of Cuba. For all Cuban writers, Afro-Cuban religions have constituted a field of cultural subtexts; for the readers of those writers, a knowledge of that field is indispensable to making sense of a significant body of Cuban narratives.

As a special category of discourse that assimilates other "languages" or cultural codes into itself, literature defamiliarizes—by its own "literariness," that is, by the mediation of its particular form—the modes of signification of those other languages. Through its literarization (and concomitant aestheticization), religion is made to lay bare the functioning of its unifying, universalizing, absolutizing principles—what Kenneth Burke calls the "thoroughness" of religion's rhetoric of persuasion—at the limits of language (RR vi). Two complementary processes come to bear in their mutual interillumination: religious rhetoric, relying on its figures of divinity or transcendence, comes to reveal a striking "literariness," whereas literary language comes to reveal the often muted assumptions of a theological nature implicit in its own forms of absolutization, either linguistic or metaphysical. This latter insight recalls Nietzsche's observation, in *Twilight of the Idols*, to the effect that even if we have eliminated God, we still believe in grammar (483). Yet as the signs signifying God are taken up into new discursive contexts, they are remotivated by new "grammars": that is, they take on new and multiple significations within other frameworks, signifying not just "God" but "gods," but also not just words but the Word.

Contrary to its own unifying, absolutizing tendencies, religion is also a diverse and sometimes divisive issue, motivating group differentiation and dissension. William James's pluralist reflections on the "varieties of religious experience" include the observation that the universe is "a more many-sided affair than any sect, even the scientific sect, allows for." Since a comprehensive examination of different religious experiences would demonstrate the unavoidable conclusion that "the world can be handled according to many systems of ideas," we would do best to respect that diversity by practicing a scholarly eclecticism in studying them (*Varieties* 120). In examining the varieties of experience associated with the aforementioned set of Afro-Cuban religions (Regla de Ocha, la Sociedad Secreta Abakuá, Palo Monte, and Regla Arará) in twentieth-century Afro-Cuban literature, I elaborate, following Edward Kamau Brathwaite, the premise that religion provides a unifying focus to Afro-Cuban culture, a culture in which the texts of symbolic performance play a central role in storing and transmitting knowledge, creating consensus, forging identity, and forming community. As illustrated in the references made by Fernández Robaina's informants at the outset of this chapter, the unifying discourse of the supernatural in Afro-Cuba has undergone a double cultural reprocessing. In the course of its evolution, African-based theology has availed itself of metaphors drawn from the everyday realm. The things of quotidian reality provide the language that makes the metaphors of divinity: segments of reality become *realia*, which evoke a transcendent realm of essences and archetypes. Once they are sufficiently formulated, the now divinized metaphors of this theology sooner or later enter into the talk and thought of Cuban peoples, in Cuba and abroad, becoming a part of that culture sometimes called "folklore" or "subculture." This reciprocal movement of signs continues in the circulation of empirical terms that come to serve religious purposes and in the secular use of religious terms that become common currency in Cuban speech.[1]

The Afro-Cuban Palimpsest

In "The African Presence in Caribbean Literature," Brathwaite challenges the Eurocentrist assertion that the Africans brought to the New World in the slave trade lacked any culture that was not imposed by the slaveholding colonizers. Far from being, as was believed, too primitive or dependent on the dominant culture to develop its own languages of custom, African culture, notes Brathwaite, underwent a process of "transference" to a new setting and "adaptation" to a new environment. The integrity and vigor of that culture owe much to its particular "culture-focus," its "distinguishing style of characteristic": African culture is above all *religious,* and "it is within the religious network that the entire culture resides" ("African" 104). That network is an entire "cultural complex" in which religion is inextricably interwoven as a centralizing and foundational construct. Brathwaite's religiocentric concept is also organicist: with everything tied to religion, no discipline within this culture is separate from another. Religion, art, and practical sciences, conceived in other social spheres as distinct forms of cultural expression or disciplinary technology, are considered in Afro-Caribbean culture to take part in the same activity.

Brathwaite's general theory of African religion in the Caribbean suggests a useful framework for organizing more specific knowledge about the subset of Afro-Cuban religion. Brathwaite distinguishes five "interrelated divisions" or aspects of religion, all of which will be reiterated in my treatments throughout this book. Those divisions are worship, *rites de passage,* divination, healing, and protection. In defining the first category of "worship," Brathwaite negates the Euro-Christian assumption of a congregation's passive, "monolithic relationship" with God. He valorizes in its stead the African concept of celebration, in song and dance, of the *orishas* or gods. That is, the African and Afro-Caribbean practice a social, physicopsychical, interactive form of worship often involving vigorous bodily movement and possession. Healing and protection as *obeah*—magic—means more than "mumbojumbo." It involves a profound knowledge of the medicinal qualities of herbs, plants, and foods and an understanding of "symbolic/associational procedures" by which the causes of disease may be identified and eliminated (Brathwaite, "African" 105). Antonio Benítez Rojo in *La isla que se repite* (The repeating island, 1989) echoes Brathwaite's view in asserting that "the influence of Africa in the nations of the Caribbean is predominantly religious in the totalizing sense" (162). That is, African-based religion there functions in "totalizing" by gathering, involving, ordering, translating, and mastering the disparate phenomena of existence and experience into a more or less cohesive system.

At the same time, the African influence in the Caribbean and particularly in Cuba is varied and multiple. Robert Farris Thompson, in a suggestive passage of *Flash of the Spirit*, characterizes Afro-Brazilian religious history in Rio de Janeiro as a "palimpsest marked by Kongo, Yoruba, and Roman Catholic infusions" (FS 77). If a palimpsest is a document, inscribed on vellum or parchment, that contains several messages—the earliest of which have been imperfectly erased—then Thompson's metaphor perfectly describes the situation in Cuba, where, as in Brazil, religious history is a layering of superimposed markings left by distinct religious traditions. In Cuba as well, the infusions come from a variety of cultures: Kongo, Yoruba, Calibar, Dahomeyan-Fon—and Roman Catholic–Spanish, among others. The challenge for any reader of that multiply inscribed parchment is to recover the texts of those overlaid, partially erased, partially reconstituted and recombined religions. In approaching the strata of religious sedimentations in modern Afro-Cuban narrative, one must also consider the manner in which that narrative itself adds yet another layer to the Afro-Cuban palimpsest. One peculiarity of this layer would have to consist in what could be called its metareligious viewpoint: that perspective of a writing that reflects and comments on the means of religious signification. The religious culture-focus manifests itself even in those texts in which religious belief and practice are not dominant concerns, in which references to characteristics of Afro-Cuban religion may stand as the hallmark of authenticity or seriousness.

Jorge Castellanos and Isabel Castellanos identify the characteristics shared by Afro-Cuban religions in their comprehensive *Cultura afrocubana* (vol. 3), on which I base much of the following presentation of Afro-Cuban religion's identifying features. The list below, in addition to defining the characteristics fundamental to the major Afro-Cuban religions—Regla de Ocha, la Sociedad Secreta Abakuá, Palo Monte, and the Regla Arará, among others—also provides some theoretical considerations under each heading. In all Afro-Cuban religions, then:

1. Monotheism and polytheism are combined. Gods—they include orishas, *santos, mpungus, ngangas, vaudoux,* and *espíritus*—are genealogically or ontologically linked with a supreme god. William James provides a clarifying note here in his definition of polytheism as a pluralistic vision of a universe, one "composed of many original principles," as long as those principles are seen as subordinated to the principle of the divine (Idowu 58). All orishas are emanations of Olodumare or Abasí or Nsambi or Mawu. More on specific conceptions of the gods in this book will come under each chapter's section on the religious pantheon.

2. An active supernatural power comes from a divine source and can be invested into objects. This power is called *aché* in Lucumí, and the name roughly translates as grace, virtue, spirit, power, cachet, and sometimes luck. "Through the consecration," writes Cabrera, "which is to say, through the transfer of a superhuman force to an object, the latter takes on personality, acquires the power, the *aché* of the god or of the spirit who pays attention to him" (YO 156). Aché, similar to the impersonal *mana* of the Polynesians, works according to the belief that objects may be animated with a force that gives them sentience and personality. When the Yoruba religious system, under the conditions of slavery, was made to coalesce with the Catholic religious system, the resulting Reglas Lucumís retained the notion of aché as that metaphysical substance inspiriting and consecrating matter in accord with ritual properly carried out. Such investment of powers, marked by the appropriate signs, plays its part in determining the critical difference between the sacred and the profane. Aché corresponds to a creative notion of language as well: the imperatives "Be" or "Come to pass" are implicit in the word, more literally translatable as the "power-to-make-things-happen." In saying "Aché," one says the equivalent of "So be it," "May it happen" (FS 7). Aché is also regarded as an ontological foundation. In Pierre Verger's description of aché in "The Yoruba High God," it is "Power itself in an absolute sense, with no epithet of determination of any sort. The various divine powers are only particular manifestations and personifications of it" (SAS 147n. 7). Aché thus names a monistic, unifying principle underlying the multiplicity of forms.

As personifications of this unifying, energizing aché, the orishas of the

Lucumí tradition inhabit the sacred stones or *otanes*, and for that reason one must wash the stones and feed them a regular diet of blood or the herbal mixture called *omiero*, both of them rich in aché. The preparation of eggshell, boiled and ground up, becomes *cascarilla* or *efún*. This efún, its whiteness symbolizing purity, is "the universal conductor of *aché*," used in many Lucumí rituals (SAS 41, 79, 80, 83).

3. Rituals, numerous and complex, mediate relationships between humans and gods. These rituals are performed in ceremonies of initiation and in divination, spiritual trances or possessions, sacrifices, cleansings or *limpiezas*, healings, and thanksgivings. Subsequent chapters will include expositions on the varieties of Afro-Cuban ritual, but here I would like to elaborate some key notions for the explication of its symbolism.

Victor Turner's conception of a "syntax" organizing symbolism in African religion suggest a method for explicating scenes of ritual such as those depicted in Afro-Cuban prose fiction. In his article "The Syntax of Symbolism in a Ndembu Ritual," Turner finds three "major dimensions of significance" in ritual symbols: the exegetic dimension, or explanations of symbols by informants; the operational, which consists in their use by participants and their associated affective states; and the positional, reading off the symbol's placement within the series or cluster of other symbols in the same structure. Furthermore, Turner elaborates the three bases he attributes to the symbol's exegetic significance, namely: the nominal basis, or "the name assigned to the symbol" both within and outside the ritual context; the substantial basis, consisting in the material and natural aspects of the symbol; and the artifactual basis, involving the manner in which the symbol is worked upon in the culture ("Syntax" 125–26).

Sacrifice is one ritual readily explicable by the exegetic, operational, and positional dimensions of its symbols. To speak exegetically, sacrifice feeds the divinities, releasing the aché of the sacrificed animal and gaining the favor of the orisha to whom the petition is made. A subtext of tradition and myth determines the nominal, material, and artifactual bases of the sacrifice: only the prescribed animals, agents, instruments, and procedures may be employed, often denominated with their West African (for example, Yoruba, Efik, Kongo, Dahomeyan) names. Operationally, the symbolic act of sacrifice puts life into an abstract schema of the petition to the god. It simultaneously binds the community together by staging an act of violence that averts violence among members of the community, assigning a scapegoat value to the sacrificial offering. The sacrifice inspires the participating subjects through a histrionic sense of seriousness and perhaps also by clarifying guilt and carrying out expiation. Positionally, or in terms of the syntactical significance proper, the symbolic acts of ritual take place in their proper sequence, an invariant temporal order whose ritual repetition harks back to an original instance of the ceremony.

4. Divination is one privileged ceremony practiced as an integral part of the Afro-Cuban religious culture, with diviners consulted for all major junctures and events of the lifespan. The major oracles are the *obí* or *biagué*, divination with four pieces of coconut; the *diloggún* or sixteen-shell divination; Ifá divination, which uses either the *ikine* palm nuts or the more common *ekpuele* chain, cast only by the babalao; and the *mpaka* horn of Palo Monte, with its smoked mirror of revelations. In operational terms, divinatory practices can be called subsystems of symbolic reproduction, manipulating combinatory schemes by an aleatory procedure for producing and organizing information. That information is given in the form of counsel, which typically includes diagnostics, prescriptions, and prognostications. In giving counsel, diviners retell indicated sacred narratives selected from a body of narratives belonging to the particular divination system. The divination ceremony thus brings believers together with the personnel of the religion for the purposes of communication and in so doing gives coherence and significance to the rituals, doctrine, and mythology of the religion as well as to other aspects of its encompassing culture. In Afro-Cuba, the most popular oracle is the sixteen-cowrie divination, or diloggún, on which I will comment at length in chapter 2. A sort of mediumistic divination also takes place in the ritual of possession, where the possessed subject speaks with the voice of the possessing god or "saint."

5. Magic, which includes conjurations or spells and herbal or ethnomedical therapies, is practiced to solve problems or to secure some aim desired by clients, in whom a magical predisposition toward the universe is produced by the myth, ritual, doctrine, and social structure of the religion. "Magic is the great preoccupation of our blacks," writes Cabrera in *El monte* (1954), "and the obtainment, the control of powerful occult forces that obey them blindly has not ceased to be their great desire" (16). The magic of spells, called *ebbó* in Lucumí and *mayunga* in Congo, which control events by means of sacrifice and the use of charms, seems to work toward gaining the love of another or for repelling another; for inflicting harm; for attracting luck; for achieving success in business; for cursing another's business enterprise; and for curing disease.

In the light of semiotics, such magical operations work in accordance with a logic of rhetorical tropes, according to their own figural "language." That language is constituted in detours or deviations from ordinary language use that effect a shift of meaning away from the literal, denotative significations of words. More specifically, magic operates in a manner analogous to the literary significations organized by the master tropes of metaphor and metonymy, along with what is sometimes called the subclass of metonymy, synecdoche. This poetic substructure, of identifying one thing with a similar thing (metaphor) or one thing with a related thing (metonymy) or the part with whole (synecdoche), constitutes the hidden logic of spells and charms. Roman Jakobson, following Frazer, synthesizes this tropological system in his influential essay "Two Aspects of Language." For Jakobson, metaphor and metonymy vie for dominance

> in any symbolic process, either intrapersonal or social. Thus in an inquiry into the structures of dreams, the decisive question is whether the symbols and the temporal sequences used are based on contiguity (Freud's metonymic "displacement" and synecdochic "condensation") or on similarity (Freud's "identification and symbolism"). The principles underlying magic rites have been resolved by Frazer into two types: charms based on the law of similarity and those founded on association by contiguity. The first of these two great branches of sympathetic magic has been called "homeopathic" or "imitative," and the second, "contagious magic." ("Two Aspects" 80–81)

Jakobson could be faulted for placing only "similarity" in the camp of "identification and symbolism" since metonymy or displacement can function to identify or symbolize as well. Yet Jakobson's association of metaphor with similarity on the one hand and of metonymy and synecdoche with contiguity on the other holds up as a useful distinction for classifying forms of symbolization.

In Afro-Cuban religious practice, homeopathic or imitative magic works by way of analogy or resemblances under the law of metaphor (or simile—a metaphor using "as" or "like"): performing a ritual on a portrait or effigy of a person amounts to performing an operation on the person so represented. Contagious magic works by way of contiguity or imputed causality, under the law of metonymy (or synecdoche): performing an operation on a person's belongings or even the person's name also signifies the will to do the same to the person so represented. Synecdoche in particular functions by treating a part of a person as representative of the whole person; this part could be some strands of hair, fingernail clippings, or blood. In the Palo Monte *nganga*, or cauldron-charm, a skull often represents the dead spirit controlled by the charm and thus draws in that spirit's power for use by the *ngangulero*, or Palo Monte priest.

In the logic of narrative itself, both metaphor and metonymy perform analogous symbolic operations in the formation of utterances and in the organization of narrative functions. Metaphor, obeying the law of similarity, is the trope of selections, substitutions, or condensations; metonymy, working by virtue of contiguity or contagion, is the trope of displacement or combination. The operations of these master tropes—metaphor, metonymy, and synecdoche—thus account for the "magic" of narrative causality and symbolization as well.

6. Music and dance have a prime importance in the liturgy. They function, over and above the role of providing ambience or background, to supply a language of worship, a form of prayer, and a vehicle for entering into the state of consciousness that allows an extraordinary mode of perception. The protagonist Menegildo of Alejo Carpentier's ¡*Ecue-Yamba-O!* (1933) is described as singing the *yambú* or the *sones* of the famous Ñáñigo Papá Montero during the *toques de tambor*, or drum-playing parties, also called *güemileres*, that he frequents. Repetition in the verses of the sones creates "a kind of hypnosis"; the drums in the battery form a "magnetic circle," producing what the narrator calls a "[p]alpitating architecture of sounds" (EYO 50).

In *La música en Cuba* (Music in Cuba, 1946), Carpentier gives a more analytical characterization of Lucumí and Ñáñigo singing. A soloist leader and chorus or two semichoruses sing antiphonally, the chorus(es) doubling the part of the leader. Each chorus sings in unison or octaves in long notes extended against the busier polyrhythms of the drums. Often the melody is based on one of various pentatonic scales, lacking in semitones (MC 296).

Rhythmic percussion, dance, and repeated chant-formulas in the güemileres, by modifying the frame and focus of consciousness, produce a new organization of perception and signification, an altered state of consciousness that recenters thought and feeling. In his "Deauto-matization and the Mystic Experience," Deikman finds that a "deautomat-ization of cognitive structures" takes place in the altered state. Cognitive hierarchies are reshuffled, "sensory translations" occur, for "the undoing of automatic perceptual and cognitive structures permits a gain in sensory intensity and richness at the expense of abstract categorization and differentiation" (Deikman 224). Normative ratiocination cedes to the language of the unconscious. The psychological operation of deautomatization found in musical activity, I would add, bears much in common with Viktor Shklovski's formalist notion of *ostranieni*—"estrangement" or "defamiliarization"—as the operation specific to literary art, that of making things appear as new by "creating a particular perception of the object, creating its vision and not its [mere] recognition" (Shklovski 65).

Music and dance are furthermore the vehicles for bringing on the state of consciousness propitious to possession by the initiate's orisha. The relationship of the dynamic arts to worship is based accordingly on the coding of musical rhythms and danced gestures to the identities of each of the gods.

7. The worship community is a dispersed collectivity whose members consider themselves members of the religion but not of any church. There is no central authority ruling over the Regla de Ocha: as one informant tells Cabrera, "We have no Pope!" (YO 132). Although Afro-Cuban religions display defining characteristics of religious "institutions" (in purposive organization, "clergy," customs, gatherings, sites), believers do not constitute a "homogeneous community." This is because worship is individualized, subject to endless reinterpretation, and community-centered rather than ecclesiastical, that is, taking place at homes and in other spiritual gathering places, with active participation of members (CA 3:16–17). Authority is nonetheless invested in the spiritual leaders: *santeros, santeras, iyalochas, babalaos, mayomberos, paleros*; all the *plazas* of the Abakuá society; the *houngans, bokors, mambos,* and *hounsis* of the Vaudou-Arará society.

In addressing these seven broadly defined categories of Afro-Cuban religious belief and practice, this study employs a semiotic approach to studying Afro-Cuban religious experience and its discursive-practical foundation. Semiotics, the science of sign systems, follows the structuralist model of Ferdinand de Saussure's synchronic analysis of the language system. In that analysis, the principle of difference is regarded as that which determines the values of individual functions in any symbol system, both among the functions themselves and with relation to what is considered outside the system. Difference is inherent in all the systemic characteristics of the above list, predicated as they are on the exegetical and operational distinction between the supernatural and the earthly, the sacred and the profane, the true and the false, the inside and the outside, the authentic and the inauthentic. Such characteristics, occurring in all the distinct Afro-Cuban religious systems as so defined by differences, must also be produced and reproduced: ritual, myth, doctrine, and even experience viewed as "within the religion" must be repeated in order to exist as such. Repetition and reproduction, inherent in any symbol system, thus underwrite the apparent uniqueness of any artifact, symbolic act, experience. For the symbols, motifs, and figures of Afro-Cuban religions, signification means not only repetition but also repeatability:

all signs "written" and "read" in religious practice are so executed within the structure of reiteration, in a process that recognizes as authentic what is an imitation or repetition of an original or primordial act remembered in the religion's mythology.[2]

A method that accounts for signifying structures and processes in Afro-Cuban literary narratives must "read" them as texts that reiterate or interpret signs from other texts written in the varied languages of religion, culture, and literature. Literary semiotics would thus produce an interpretation of what are already interpretations: a reading of previous readings. In assuming that reading "reads" what others have read and "written" in various socio-cultural codes, the semiotic notion of the language system and reiterable discourse practices guides us in regarding theology as a field of knowledge "of god" or the divine, a field consisting in a study of the repeatable figures organizing and reproducing the text of worship. And although the mystery of religious experience may never be illuminated in full by such a reading of the conventions on which that experience depends, the informing rhetoric of mystery can certainly be read and analyzed in its verbalizations or figurations of the divine. The figurations of Afro-Cuban religion refer us back, let us recall, to its beginnings in the slave experience in colonial Cuba. A partial overview of the history of that experience will help to contextualize subsequent readings of Afro-Cuban religious phenomena.

Origins: Geographical, Ethnic, and Social

Sylvia Wynter situates Caribbean religions in a continuum whose two extremes represent the predominance of either European or African elements and whose middle represents an amalgamation of elements from the two continents (cited in Lewis 189). Castellanos and Castellanos' model of Cuban culture in particular also projects a continuum stretched between the two extremes of European and African cultures. Between these extremes lie the intermediate "poles" of Euro-Cuban culture and Afro-Cuban culture (CA 1:12–13). This gradient of cultural difference is useful for identifying the origins and degrees of cultural influence in phenomena that include religion. Martínez Furé writes that the African slaves, by their "fidelity to the ancestral" (the expression is Roger Bastide's) successfully resisted assimilation into the white Creole culture of, first, the colonial slaveholders and, later, the national bourgeoisie. In keeping alive an ancestral culture through the semi-covert practice of their religions, the slaves and their descendants preserved a source of resistance against the humiliations of forced labor, prejudice, discrimination, and other forms of oppression. It was in the process of cultural mixing that this resistance occurred, precisely by taking objects, terms, practices, and narratives identified with European and African ethnic groups and making them over into ingredients of a "national culture" (DI 208–9).

The area between Senegal and Angola yielded the most *piezas de Indias* or slaves to the prosperous slave trade, and among them the Yoruba exerted perhaps the most pervasive influence on the slave groups and their descendants in the Americas (YSN 1). Other vigorous traditions beside the Yoruba took root in the Americas, however, sometimes grafting their beliefs and practices onto the trunk of the Yoruba tradition. The following brief overview of the ethnic composition, historical background, and social organizations of the African peoples brought over to Cuba in the nearly three hundred years of the Atlantic slave trade will provide a useful background for mapping the multiple origins of Afro-Cuban religion.

The African slaves brought to Cuba represented more than twenty tribal groups, and the peoples of at least four African regions were substantially represented in the Cuban slave population. The six principal groups came to be known by the names Lucumí, Mandinga, Arará, Gangá, Carabalí, and Congo. The classifications and profiles in the following list are drawn from Castellanos and Castellanos (CA, vol. 1), Bolívar Aróstegui (OC), Cros Sandoval (RA), and others. There seems to be some disagreement over the categorization of certain groups, and keep in mind also that many slaves were named for their port of departure rather than according to the name of their geographic origin. The six principal slaves groups, then, include:

1. The Lucumí. They proceed from the Yoruba of southwest Nigeria and the so-called Slave Coast and from Dahomey, Togo, and Benin. In Nigeria, the Yoruba states include Oyo, Ondo, Ogun, and Lagos as well as part of Kwara state (Eades 1). Culturally similar but not politically united, the Yoruba included peoples known as the Agicón, Cuévano, Egba, Eguadó, Ekiti, Fon, Oyó, Sabalú, and Yesa (OC 20).

2. The Carabalí. These were the peoples of the Calibar in what is today southeast Nigeria and southwest Cameroon, among whom the Efik and the Ibibio stand out. The Carabalís also included the Ejagham—Hispanicized as Abaja or Abakuá—the Bras, Bríkamo, Efor, Ekoy, Ibo, and Oba (OC 20).

3. Those who trace their origin to Dahomey and the western part of Nigeria, including the Ashanti and the Fanti. They are grouped together as the Arará, whose name originated in the kingdom of Arder or Ardra, today known as Benin, home of the Ewe and Fon peoples (CA 1:31). From the west and northwestern parts of the Ivory Coast came the Bámbara, Berberi, Fulani,

Hausa, Kissi, Kono, Mani, and Yola. Díaz Fabelo's list of the Arará includes groups that Bolívar Aróstegui calls Lucumí, namely the Agicón, the Cuévano, and the Sabalú (Díaz Fabelo 24).

A people associated with the Dahomeyan-Fon were called Mina because they were passed through the station of San Jorge de Mina, in Fanti territory on the Gold Coast. They were also related to the Ewe peoples called Popó (CA 1:31).

4. The Congos. Originally, they were slaves drawn from the Congo Basin, which extends through present-day Congo-Brazzaville, Angola, Cabinda, Bas-Zaïre, and Gabon (RA 19–20). From the Guinea Coast down through to the former Belgian Congo, those who would come to be called Congos or Bantus in Cuba included the Ashanti, Fanti, and Mina Popó. From the Congo Basin came the Agunga, Banguela, Bisongo, Cabinda, Mayombe, Mondongo, Motembo, and Mucaya (OC 20).

5. The Mandinga, grouped in Cuba with the Bambara, Diola, and Yola peoples, inhabited the upper Niger and the Senegal and Gambia valleys. The Islamic Mandinga showed an Arabic influence in their syncretic religious beliefs and in the ability of some to write (CA 1:30–31). Carpentier attributes Mandinga ancestry to Mackandal, leader of the slave revolt in El reino de este mundo (The kingdom of this world, 1949).

6. The Gangás. From the coastal and interior regions of Sierra Leone and northern Liberia, the Gangás were further designated by the name of their "nation," such that the subgroups of those called Gangá were called Gangá-cramo, Gangá-quisí, Gangá-fay, Gangá-gorá, Gangá-bandoré, Gangá-yoni, Gangá-ñongobá, and the Gangá-tomu. Their origins since clarified, these peoples have been divided into the Gangás associated with the aforementioned Mandingas and the Gangás called "Bantoid," from the Nigerian plateau (CA 1:32–34).

Cabrera identifies the Yoruba and the Bantu, as do Bastide and other authorities, as the two most influential African groups imported in the slave trade from the sixteenth to the nineteenth centuries. These peoples were known in Cuba respectively as the Lucumí and the Congo (M 8).

Martínez Furé has noted and cataloged the African languages that have survived and been disseminated into the Creole speech of Cuba up to the present. The languages in question fall primarily into two families: the Sudanese, spoken primarily in the western part of the island, and the Bantu. Belonging to the first of these families, Yoruba or Lucumí (also called Anagó) is spoken by the practitioners of Regla de Ocha or Santería. Efik is spoken by those of the Abakuá or Ñáñigo society; Fon or Arará by the groups known as Araráz. The second language family, Bantu, is that of the Congo or Palo Monte cults. Many Cubans are capable not only of reciting but of holding conversations in one of these African languages. Martínez Furé adds that although it is in these languages that one speaks to the orishas in Cuba, many words and expressions have filtered down into the common idiom (DI 203–4).

As Castellanos and Castellanos point out, no one is sure whether Africans first came aboard the caravels on which Columbus and his crew crossed the Atlantic, but black servants probably accompanied the hidalgos who arrived in 1493 with Columbus's second expedition and most likely came with Diego Velázquez in his conquest of Cuba in 1510–11. It is more certain that Portuguese slavers first landed in Guinea or at the Gold Coast of western Africa in 1510. They soon began exporting slaves, mainly through the port of Lagos, with Cuba and Brazil as principal destinations (CA 1:19).

Carpentier's researches find that blacks were transported to Cuba since at least 1513. Two Genoese sailors brought 145 Africans from Cape Verde, and by 1534, there were already about a thousand on the Caribbean island (MC 37). In 1531, the Spanish crown increased the demand for African labor by decreeing, first, the end of Indian slavery; then, in 1532, the release of Indians who had earned their freedom; and finally, in 1552, the release of all the Indians commended to the haciendas. The freedom of the Indians in Cuba, many of whom were to die of mistreatment or European diseases anyway, created the need for a labor force coming from elsewhere (Fagg 16). The slaves were purchased in Africa with money, or with goods, *géneros*, such as sugar, tobacco, rum, guns, gunpowder, beads, cloth, machetes, or iron bars. Once they arrived in the Caribbean, they were traded for sugar and rum, which were transported to Europe so that the entire cycle of a "triangular trade" route could begin again (CA 1:22).

The European slave trade with West Africa increased dramatically with the growth of the American sugar plantations. Once this industry took off, demand for African labor skyrocketed in Brazil after 1550, in the Caribbean and South America in the seventeenth century, and in North America in the eighteenth century (Eades 28). Cuba along with other colonies underwent a process that has been called *amulatamiento*, or "mulattoization," with the arrival of hundreds of thousands of slaves between 1517 and 1873. The Cuban census of 1774 reported a population of 96,430 whites and 75,180 *pardos* or blacks. Out of that last number, 44,300 (or 59 percent) were slaves. From 1819 to 1850, blacks in Cuba would outnumber the whites by about 100,000 (MC 89; DI 207–8; Curtin 34). Fagg asserts that in 1817, out of some

552,000 inhabitants in Cuba, 313,000 or 57 percent of them were non-white (Fagg 27). Philip D. Curtin estimates that out of his calculated total of 9,566,000 slaves transported during the Atlantic trade, some 4,040,000, or 42.2percent, were destined for the Caribbean islands, and that some 702,000 of those, or 7.3 percent of the worldwide total, were taken to Cuba (Curtin 88–89). Castellanos and Castellanos estimate a higher minimum of 850,000 slaves brought to Cuba in the three and a half centuries of its existence.[3]

Some five hundred ingenios or sugar mills were in operation on the island in 1790. Then, with the outbreak of the Saint Domingue Revolution in Hispaniola in the 1790s, the price of sugar shot up. The market was ready for a new producer, and Cuba was there to supply the demand. Entrepreneurs invested in the construction of new mills and in the importation of new slaves from Africa. To fill the demand in the booming industry, Knight reports, Spanish traders brought some 75 percent of the slaves to the colony in the nineteenth century, when most other nations had ceased to participate in the trade. Cuba's monocultivational sugar economy began to boom only in this period, for it had previously been more a "colony of settlement" than of "exploitation," although that fact certainly changed with the accelerated importation of slaves in the eighteenth and nineteenth centuries. Ferdinand VII, under pressure from the British, decreed the end of the slave trade by 1820, but a clandestine trade continued until 1886 (Fagg 25, 27, 30, 41; Knight 66). Although the British outlawed the transport or landing of slaves in their colonies in 1808, and although the trade was in fact officially terminated in the Spanish colonies in 1821, at least 436,844 bozales or new slaves entered the island between 1790 and 1875, during the height of the island's agricultural development. This traffic went on despite the protests of the British and the emancipations in French territories (SRL 36).

Whereas the American South could rely on a self-reproducing slave population, the Caribbean region generally depended on the continual importation of new Africans for labor power up past the mid-nineteenth century. The constant influx guaranteed that new infusions of West African language, folklore, customs, liturgies, and art forms would arrive to enrich and strengthen the life of slave religion in the islands (Lewis 189). Slaves in Cuba, and especially in the urban concentrations, could find a degree of comfort and relief from the rigors of forced labor in certain refuges within slave society, sites where they could practice their neo-African religions under a façade of Catholic orthodoxy. In this infrasocial space of circumscribed freedom, the slaves could associate with their fellows, communing and communicating in the unique Afro-Cuban cultural dialect of a "nation" refounded.

The Cabildo

Several aspects of colonial society promoted the transplantation and growth of Yoruba, Congo, and Ñáñigo cults in Cuba. A first contributing factor was the founding of numerous settlements known as *palenques* by the runaway slaves, known as *cimarrones*. In the palenques, located in the hills of the Escambray or the Sierra Maestra, the cimarrones built up their own syncretic, neo-African microsocieties. In these precarious and embattled redoubts, the runaways, banded together, conserved and reconstructed an African cultural legacy that sustained an oppositional sense of identity. Second, the large number of slaves concentrated in the cities could be hired out or employed in trades or industries such as shipbuilding, carpentry, or smithing. Such work gave some slaves the opportunity to earn and save the means to buy their freedom through the practice called *coartación*, or manumission, which consisted in the paying of a preagreed upon and published price. By the middle of the nineteenth century, a sizable urban population made up of slaves and former, or manumitted slaves, known as *gente de color* (people of color), could freely gather in the *cabildos* and develop their vital culture, complete with rites, indoctrinations, and celebrations reconstituted from the surviving remnants of a shattered African legacy (CA 3:110–15).

In Hispanic culture, the word *cabildo* usually denotes the municipal council or its meetings; it also refers to a cathedral "brotherhood" chapter. Cros Sandoval traces the institution back to the time of Alfonso el Sabio (1042–1109), who required all members of the Sevillian population, including African slaves, to group together in guilds and fraternities (RA 44). An *agrupación* (group, chapter) or *cofradía* (confraternity) of free blacks of Nuestra Señora de los Remedios was founded in 1598 in Havana (MC 290). Ortiz writes that such cabildos were organizations of mainly freed blacks of the same *naciones* or ethnic groups, and that the oldest member was often the leader, the *capitán de cabildo* (or cabildo captain), although in Cuba some of the more organized societies met in houses outside town under the rule of "kings" and "queens" ("fiesta" 6–7). In Cuban societies as well, assemblies made collections to pay for funeral expenses of members and at times for the manumission of aged slaves. It was often in the *comparsas*, or costumed parading groups, that cabildos carried out street celebrations devoted to the patron saints (SAS 30–31). Amidst the festivities of carnival, dances and processions dedicated to particular orishas further contributed to the survival and dissemination of a neo-African culture in the bosom of a colonial Catholic society. The names of these societies attested to their founders' African origins.

Carpentier lists the following cabildo names: *"Arará, Apapá, Apapá Chiquito, Mandinga, Oro, Lucumí, Carabalí Ungrí, Nación Mina Popó de la Costa de Oro, Arará tres ojos,* etc." (MC 290).

While bringing the benefits of security, association, and entertainment into its marginalized space within Cuban society, the cabildo, it should be noted, served the purpose of the colonizers' "divide-and-rule" policy, providing a means of diversion and thus averting revolt by grouping members in these self-regulating organizations (Bastide 9). Yet as the *cabildos de negros* gained in familiarity and numbers, they also gained some clout in local government. In 1573 in Havana, cabildos had a voice in the municipality (L. Foner 148–49).

Measures taken by the Cuban church further promoted the religio-cultural evolution of the cabildo blacks. The *Constitución Sinodal,* promulgated by the Havana diocese in June 1680, required the instruction of all slaves in Catholic doctrine, their baptism within one year of their arrival in America, and that baptism as the prerequisite to marriage by a priest. It also required that marriages outside the church of people baptized afterward be ratified in *facie ecclesiae* (DALC 99, 141–42; Klein 94). These requirements further encouraged the founding, growth, and limited empowerment of cabildos and cofradías in the major Cuban cities.

The members of each cabildo were normally *negros de nación,* blacks of the same ethnogeographic origin who in their mutual propinquity could keep alive not only some of their African traditions but their own language as well. What the church unintentionally made possible by organizing the slaves into cabildos was therefore a combining and transformation of cultural beliefs and practices: a synthesis and hybridization proper to Creole social groups that, after the pioneering work of Fernando Ortiz, has come to be widely called "transculturation."

Transculturation: Syncretisms and Syntheses

Fernando Ortiz is referred to as "the third discoverer of America" (after Columbus and von Humboldt). He followed the lead of nineteenth-century writers such as José Antonio Saco and Domingo del Monte in investigating the blacks in Cuba: their history, art, religion, livelihood, and language. The result of Ortiz's labors was to make what was once scorned and dismissed as a bastard culture of a downtrodden people into an object deemed worthy of intellectual scrutiny (VU 7). For Ortiz, the process of transculturation was typical of all Cuban culture and essential to an understanding of cultural change. In his *Contrapunteo cubano del tabaco y el azúcar* (Cuban counterpoint of tobacco and sugar, 1940), Ortiz defines that process to which the lives of millions of African slaves were subjected on American lands:

> We understand that the word *transculturation* best expresses the different phases of the transitional process from one culture to another, because this consists not only of acquiring a different culture, which is what the Anglo-American word [acculturation] strictly indicates, but rather that the process also necessarily implies the loss or uprooting of a preceding culture, which could be called a partial *deculturation*, and in addition, signifies the consequent creation of new cultural phenomena that could be denominated as *neoculturation*. Finally, as the school of Malinowski well sustains, what happens in every embrace of cultures is what happens in the genetic coupling of individuals: the offspring always has something of both progenitors, but is also always different from each one of the two. (*Contrapunteo* 134–35)

Transculturation names the process by which a culture constitutes itself as a crossing, combination, fusion, and mutual transformation of two or more preexisting cultures. In the process, cultures are uprooted and new cultures are formed. The concept repudiates the tracing of cultural descent to any one nation or ethnia, questioning previous notions of cultural superiority based on racial "purity." For Ortiz, the African contribution to Cuba was present in the island's art, religion, and collective temperament ("factores" 32).

The New World in general was a place where traditions would combine and transform one another. To give one example of a religious tradition that underwent transculturation: in Nigeria, the association and the family lineage are traditionally identified with the particular orisha regarded as the "ancestor" of the group, revered by generation after generation. When slavery shattered the African family structure, however, only the basis of worship in associations survived. The structure of this worship changed as well, for no longer could a fraternity devote its cult to a single *orisa*, as in Nigeria, for the association or "nación" felt obliged to worship all the orishas, and all in a hierarchized sequence of rituals. Cabrera confirms that in Cuba, unlike in Nigeria, one worships "all the Orishas," starting out with the *Santos de Fundamento* or *Santos de Entrada* (Saints [Orishas] of Fundament or Saints of Entry). Worship is therefore not strictly limited to the orishas of one's lineage, although there will be one or more saints to whom devotion is concentrated for different purposes on different occasions. The distribution of worship to all the orishas within each of the associations makes each association a mi-

2. "Changó/Santa Bárbara." Oil on canvas, 1991. Collection of María Antonia Carrillo, Old Havana, Cuba.

crocosm of a nation. Furthermore, that worship is not restricted to the temple, the *ile ocha*, but extends into the home, with its domestic shrines (consisting of *asientos* or ritual settings devoted to particular orishas) and altars (YO 130–31).

The African nations, now gathered into the Cuban cabildo associations, indeed kept alive the Yoruba, Mandinga, Carabalí, and Bantu gods, but these underwent further modifications in Cuba (Bastide 94, 116). In the Yoruba-Lucumí tradition, to give one example, the orishas became reduced in number, took on the characteristics and identities of minor Yoruba gods, transmuted themselves in symbiotic connection with their Catholic doubles, and developed new family ties among themselves (CA 3:22–23). Since the syncretism of Yoruba-based representations meant not only the joining of orishas with saints but also the gathering of the orisha-saints into a single practice of worship, Cuba became a space of narrative transformations and iconic evolutions, as the *ile ocha*, "home of the orisha," took the place of the Yoruba holy grove, the *igbodu* (SAS 52, 113).

We should recall at this point the political origins of the word *syncretism* in *synkretismos:* the Greek word designates the federation or union of Cretan cities against a common enemy. There is a defensive and even militant strengthening implicit in the word that continued on into the dynamics of slave ideology and Creole culture, since it formed a defensive and consensual basis for communication across cultural boundaries. Cabrera quotes one of her informants, called "the mother of Omí Tomi," as saying, "Lucumí, Arará, Dahomey and Mina, all are akin. All understood one another although their languages were different. But their Saints are similar. They would go from one land to another" (M 26n. 1). We should keep in mind that there was already a syncretizing transculturation taking place in African mythology even before its Cubanization. The Yoruba Ogun had already become the powerful Zarabanda among the *mpungus,* or Kongo deities. This Zarabanda gives his name to the most powerful of magic charms, the aforementioned nganga or *prenda* made of bones, cemetery dust, blood, sticks, and other powerful objects kept together in a metal cauldron (S 132).

The specific courses of this transculturation invite closer examination. In the matching of a Yoruba with a Catholic, Bantu, or Ewe-Fon equivalent, a transfer of qualities may also take place, as in the way Babalú-Ayé takes on the humility and gentleness of the Saint Lazarus with whom he was conjoined. On the other hand, the two sides of the equation may maintain their separate identities for the most part, as in the case of Changó and Santa Bárbara. The coupling of these figures from distinct traditions does not require that they interact very much: not so much a blending as a juxtaposition or imposition of appearances takes place. Such adjacencies or layerings allow "the African elements to impose themselves with an extraordinary purity in the initiation, divination or funerary rites" (FV 138).

Diana K. Metz explains these alternative processes as the branching out of cultural *mestizaje,* or mixing, into two contrasting forms designatable by the terms "symbiosis" and "syncretism." Whereas both terms name modes of cultural convergence, symbiosis consists in a heterogeneous combining that respects the separate identities of the participating elements—a "striping." Syncretism would amount to a blending and refounding that transforms the elements so that often in the process they become less recognizable—a "graying." Following Metz's definitions, one could impose on symbiosis the law of *juntos pero no revueltos:* together but not "mixed up." The syncretized orisha-saint on the other hand is neither one nor the other but an alchemical combination, "una deidad novísima" ("a brand-new deity"; MS 13). Metz also suggests that the very syncretic character of Santería and of a Cuban Creole culture demands a strategy affined to that of Derrida's différance in order to track its shiftings and readjustments.

This syncretizing process may also engage other cultural systems besides the African and the European. Benítez Rojo traces the multiple vectors of the myths that became the Virgen de la Caridad del Cobre, Cuba's "patron saint." As Benítez Rojo's analysis explains, the Virgin's wooden statue, discovered in the Bahía de Nipe by the "Three Juans" and giving rise to the legend, was not only the Cuban icon representing the Spanish Virgen de Illescas but also the Yoruba Ochún Yeyé Moró and the Taína goddess Atabex or Atabey, who derived previously from the Arahuacan goddess Orehu, "Mother of the Waters." These three divine personalities did not however merge into one but maintained their separate identities as three-figures-in-one-entity. Deducing from this Cuban archetype, Benítez Rojo correctly concludes that "*A syncretic artifact is not a synthesis, but a signifier made out of differences.*" Precisely because the Virgin was discovered in the Bahía de Nipe by the "three Juans"—Juan Criollo, Juan Indio, and Juan Esclavo—she "belonged" to the three ethnic trunks of the Caribbean genealogy and thus "represented a magic or transcendental space" of their meeting. In essence, la Caridad "mythologically communicates the desire to attain a sphere of effective equality where the racial, social and cultural differences created by the conquest could coexist without violence" (IR xvi–xvii, xxviii, 27). The Afro-hispanoamerican myth offers a symbolic resolution of social contradictions.

The same Virgen de la Caridad del Cobre occupies the transcendental and maternal space of the Creole image in Lezama Lima's *Paradiso* (1966), in which protagonist José Cemí's mother is remembered as one who "jumped from dreams to the quotidian without establishing differences, as if she would to go off by herself, walking on the water." In this Creole space of fluid symbolic metamorphoses, the Catholic quotidian is permeated by the magical, and the magical is saturated with Afro-Cuban motifs. Before a small altar set up in their living room, señor Michelena and his wife Juana, of the same novel, pray to the Virgin to give them a child, for, after all, "to whom but to the Order of la Caridad, foundation of all our religion, can one beseech superabundance?" The supplication itself takes the doggerel form of a thirteen-syllable couplet (a *trecisílabo*) asking for fecundity: "*Virgen de la Caridad, de la Caridad / dadnos la fecundidad, oh fecundidad*" ("give us fecundity, oh fecundity"). Later, la vieja Mela tells her son that señora Munda will cure her asthma by the agency of the same virgin and a seahorse (Lezama Lima 27, 53, 54, 120).

Devotion to the saints, spirits, orishas, mpungus, and *egunguns* (Lucumí for "the dead") constitutes a practice of centering a personal system (or "economy") of signs around the image of a transcendental signified, itself susceptible to displacement by other signs. The self consecrates and thus defines itself on the altar of this devotion. Thanks to the Catholic contribution, the virtue of "saintliness" meant that slaves could find happiness not in "comfort," to quote William James again, but in "a higher kind of inner excitement" leading to tranquillity, such that "when we are in need of assistance, we can count upon the saint lending his hand with more certainty than we can count upon any other person" (James 361). A Catholicism mixed with African beliefs and practices thus earned the name of "afrocatolicismo."

These transcultural aspects of slave religion, we should recall, had their practical function in a sociohistorical context, for it was slaves—considered by their masters to be no more than chattel, labor, property, and investment— who practiced it, finding in their worship the means to compensate or even to negate the negations of their dehumanizing enslavement.

Slave Religion as Ideology

In the preface to the 1993 edition of his historically based novel The African (1967), Harold Courlander explains that religious beliefs have given blacks in both Africa and America "a sense of relationship to the world around them and to the unseen but living forces of the universe" (ii [unnumbered]). This sense of relationship, as numerous writers have observed, has profoundly shaped the nature of black participation in the politicosocial process—and with mixed results.

Anticipating his own critique of rationalism in future narratives, Carpentier in ¡Ecue-Yamba-O! pits the Afro-Cuban worldview against the Cartesian method and attitude. The opposition in Carpentier's text makes historical sense: although the typical Caribbean planter in the time of the colony was no philosopher, as Gordon K. Lewis points out in Main Currents in Caribbean Thought, the planter shared with the Cartesian mind a certain "religious indifferentism" or secularizing disposition that produced the peculiar forms of individualism, voluntarism, rationalism, and hubris characteristic of his class. The subject/object relation may have confirmed in his mind the legitimacy of the master/slave relationship. Different foundational assumptions underlie the contrasting worldviews as well. Whereas the Cartesian mind, finding only clear and distinct perceptions to be truthful, values conclusions arrived at empirically and experimentally, the Afro-Caribbean mind finds the truth in oral narratives.[4] Lewis elaborates these contrasting notions of knowledge: "The one perceives the universe in terms of scientific laws, the other sees it in terms of laws that can only be apprehended by means of therapeutic or redemptive episodes in ritual and ceremony that constitute, as it were, scenarios of the transformation, in essence magical, of personal states." Lewis's dichotomization emphasizes "Cartesian man's" tendency to abstract, divide, and compartmentalize the phenomena and institutions of the world. "African man," however, has never renounced an experiential, ritual, and subjective involvement with the life of the world, for which everything fits into a single design—possibly a cosmological ecosystem—such that "life and experience are unified in one domain of knowledge and understanding in which past, present, and future fuse into the awful mystery of things" (Lewis 196).

Bolívar Aróstegui describes the traditionalist and animist assumptions of this unifying, magical thought: each corner of the universe is infused with personalizing spirit responsive to the appeal of magic; all things are alive and sentient, imbued with aché; and yet every thing is unique, with its own "individuality." Every locality and time has its own particular character within the "subjectivized," non-Newtonian cosmos: "The sensual experience of space and time reveals them to us as heterogeneous and discontinuous: there exists the space of the valley and that of the cave, the time of happiness and that of joy and sorrow, there is no equal time nor identical spaces for the subjective experience." Bolívar Aróstegui affirms the distinction between modern scientific thought and "primitive" magical thought in declaring outright that magic "bases itself in purely fictitious relations" and that it "elaborates its illusory technique and its mythical dominion upon a fictitious knowledge" (OC 26–27, 29).

Others have held that this knowledge has more than a compensatory or illusional importance. For Zapata Olivella, Afro-American religions have functioned as cultural expressions directed toward emancipation. They express the "creativity of the black under oppression," as the title of one of the chapters of Zapata Olivella's *Las claves mágicas de América* (The magic keys of America) proposes. The Afro-Cuban comparsa, the carnival street procession presided over by an elected king and queen, manifests the Africans' custom of making of their "body, mind and shadow a living temple erected to their Ancestors and Gods." Afro-Caribbean cults, Zapata Olivella points out, united and emboldened blacks in the Saint Domingue revolts and in other countless anticolonial uprisings. Such examples illustrate that in a hostile American environment, where identity has meant not only to be somebody but to survive, African slaves had these psychospiritual resources, "religious arms," to rely on, and they relied especially on those resources that drew strength from the deified Ancestors. Even the frequent acts of suicide among Carabalís, Fantis,

Sereres, and Ibos can be accounted for as acts of resistance in obedience to ancestral codes that valued an honorable death over the ignominy of slavery. The African saw himself or herself as a "depository of the life of the ancestors" and struggled against every kind of "infrahuman exploitation" because the offense of slavery was an offense not only to the individual but to all the individual's ancestors (Zapata Olivella, *claves* 117, 145, 60).

Confirming Zapata Olivella's vision of Afro-American religion as manifesting creativity under oppression, Lewis finds in slave religion an "ideology" that negates the masters' ideology. The culture of the African slave in the New World was "denied expression in either economic technology or political structures," yet it "found its classic, architectonic expression in the proliferating secret Negro religious cults." In their war against such cults, which they considered to be forms of idolatry and paganism, missionaries throughout the Caribbean attempted to instill their doctrine in the name of Catholic proselytization, usually in support of the proslavery ideology. The same missionaries did not by and large realize how slaves could appear to embrace the dogma and lore of the church by adoring Changó in the red robes of Santa Bárbara and Obatalá in the white robes of the Virgen de las Mercedes. Colonial officials learned, however, that the cults would die hard and that efforts to suppress the practice of their rituals would provoke resentment and revolutionary backlash. The alternative was to allow a coexistence of religions, such that the blacks could continue celebrating in their comparsas (processions) or *batás* (fiestas with drumming). Tolerance for some degree of religious diversity became the unwritten policy (Lewis 188, 195).

Lewis, citing J. N. Figgis's *From Gerson to Grotius*, a study of church/state conflicts in the Middle Ages, asserts that political liberty in the Caribbean "was the inheritor of an unofficial concordat between the Christianity of the slavocracy and the neo-African belief structures of the slave populations." The antagonism between proslavery and antislavery ideologies ceded to this cold war accommodation between African and European worldviews. Lewis perhaps overstates the case for an "Afro-American religious ideology" in the Caribbean, with the exception of Haiti, in claiming that it was engaged in "mortal struggle" with European ideologies, "waged as bitterly as any war of religion," for outside of Haiti religious ideology has tended to serve more as a compensatory philosophy than as a call to arms, more as a restorative adhered to covertly, leaving the fundamental life conditions of the slaves unchallenged (Lewis 196, 190). This was especially the case in Cuba, where practices of Santería, Ñañiguismo, and Palo Monte never led their believers into a full-scale anticolonial war. This absence may in part have induced Carpentier, still regretting the youthful errors of ¡Ecue-Yamba-O!, to choose the colony of Saint Domingue as the main setting of El reino de este mundo. For in Vaudou, slave religion has had a more direct, although varied and problematic, relationship with historical change, an issue I will address in chapter 6.

It would seem that Cuban culture in the first half of the twentieth century could accept and assimilate African-based mythical and religious thought in its collective representations. In Walterio Carbonell's view, it was the inherent weakness of the dependent Cuban bourgeoisie, due to the imperialism that forced a change from the colonialism of the Spanish to an economic neocolonialism of Wall Street during the early years of the Republic, that made the middle class susceptible to the influences of the African culture that had survived since the slaveholding colonial days. "The savage gods, the eaters of children, Changó, Obatalá, Yemayá, were civilized and took possession in the spirits of the well-to-do, not in order to eat them up nor to cohabit with them, but in order to try to solve their amatory problems, their aspirations to occupy a high government position, or to pull them out of business difficulties."

This sentimental dependence on black mysticism is reflected in Benítez Rojo's satire "El escudo de hojas secas" (The coat-of-arms of dry leaves, 1969) in which a middle-class Cuban couple relies on the advice of a babalao to make their fortune, precisely by winning the national lottery. In Afro-Cuban religion prior to 1959, the "nongoverning" bourgeoisie could find the compensations and assurances that their economic situation could not afford them. Even before this prerevolutionary period, however, the bourgeoisification of Afro-Cuban myth was an ongoing process that involved the translation into Castillian of West African narratives. Parallel transculturations occurred in music and dance (think of the mambo, rumba, and son) once those art forms were mainstreamed and then internationalized, and the new Cuban culture ended up becoming more openly "una gran pachanga" (a great party) with the blessings of the Cubanized African gods (Carbonell, Crítica 24–25).

The sign systems of what originated as slave religion, and certainly much of those systems' imagery and language, carried over into another transforming context, that of the literary movements known as negrismo and its particular Cuban variant, afrocubanismo. I turn to these in the chapter 2, after examining some of the semiotic and phenomenological implications of Afro-Cuban sign systems in the following sections.

Afro-Cuban Religion in Narrative

The signifying systems of Afro-Cuban religions, codifying the cultural world for and of their subjects, have also provided terms for reinscription into literary language. As I proposed earlier in this chapter, when literature reinscribes ritual, myth, doctrine, and the personal experience originally "scripted" by those religions, it offers a phenomenologico-semiotic reading of signifying mechanisms engaged in the shaping of that experience. For the healing arts, a symptom is a metaphor that the *curandero* (healer), santero, babalao, iyalorisha, houngan, mayombero, or palera—all semioticians after a fashion—may read. Myth serves as the narrative foundation of ritual and doctrine, as symbolic charter for the ethical and template for the personal.

In Frye's illuminating theory, *mythos* as narrative "involves movement from one structure to another." This movement is a process of formation, maturation, conversion, or transformation, and it corresponds analogically to the cyclical pattern of development, death, and rebirth or its analog in the yearly progression of the seasons (Frye 158). Afro-Cuban narratives imitate this movement between structures in portraying ritual and in retelling myth, reinscribing both into narrative prose, thus providing a subtext upon which the idioms of novels and short stories—other layers of the palimpsest—acquire the depth of stratified and mutually cross-referencing levels.

In reconstructing an architectonics of each religion in later chapters, I schematize the systematic arrangement of its knowledge and "technical arts," emphasizing above all the agency of language in constituting religion as a transcendent realm or a world apart. The primacy of language, or the privilege of that which is accessible and intelligible by transposition into language, becomes evident in the multilingual order of Afro-Cuban narrative texts: texts that typically take pains, as it were, to teach the reader—through appositional definitions, footnotes, glossaries, and translations—the sacred language of the religious tradition in question.

Previous discussion of Afro-Cuban religions, even in anthropological treatments of the subject, has often devolved into a vocabulary of essentialist assumptions, hypostatizations of abstract or immaterial entities, and uncritical descriptions of mystical phenomena. It is natural for the analyst's writing to identify, even if ironically, with the believer's language of faith, but previous summaries of and commentaries on magical narratives nonetheless have often produced the effect of affirming their referentialist illusion. What is needed is a metanarrative of that illusion, one that examines the springs and levers of its referentialist machinery. This approach calls for a supporting theory of narrative structures—a narratology.

I have suggested in the foregoing discussion that methods available to literary analysis and interpretation may suffice to render comprehensible the ritual, myth, doctrine, institutional structure, and experience of Afro-Cuban religions. My explications will be aimed at reading the signs, scenes, agents, agencies, and acts of the Afro-Cuban religious world constructed in Afro-Cuban literature. My approach accordingly relies on quotation, definition, comparisons, and translation, and consequently the rhetorical devices of parenthesis, apposition, pleonasm, and antithesis will figure prominently in the study. I will admit at the outset that this assertion of "readability" relies upon sort of a circular logic, but I incorporate into the method a certain interdisciplinary approach that includes the interpretive use of findings in recent cultural anthropology and folklore studies. My critical tendencies, informed by the above mentioned disciplines, lead me to read Afro-Cuban religious experience as a heterogeneous set of sign-producing and sign-interpreting "performances" actualizing an archive of narrative knowledge.

The oral folktales gathered and retold by Cabrera, Barnet, Alonso, Martínez Furé, and the Castellanos may be analyzed with the methods the Herskovitses used to analyze Dahomeyan narratives, methods outlined in Herskovits's "The Study of African Oral Literature." The study of Afro-Cuban narratives finds hidden regularities in the appearance and reappearance of motifs throughout the multigeneric corpus of these narratives. The same elements resurface in diverse contexts and fulfill distinct functions conditioned by those contexts. The act of a Yoruba deity may be worked in the plot of a divination narrative, the pataki, and reworked in the secular context of a folktale or a children's story. The motif or function, retaining its distinctive features, can be recognized within each new frame, but its meaning must be construed in the contextual reading (Herskovits, "Study" 363). This recontextualizing and refunctioning is at least doubled when a motif originating in Yoruba, Dahomey-Fon, or Calibar culture is reset and remotivated in a framework dominated by traditions alien to the motif's original setting. The connection of the pataki with the diloggún or Ifá divination, for instance, associates the narrative with that specific ceremony but does not anchor it forever to that operational dimension nor fix its significance as would sacred convention. The literarization of the pataki breaks it loose of this context and its "enclosing phenomenon" and in effect desacralizes it, aestheticizes it, frees its elements to combine and recombine in other narratives with other forms of discourse.

Orishas, mpungus, loas—all deities worshipped in Afro-Cuban religions—appear frequently in Cuban poetry and narrative. Such texts include: the aforementioned transcriptions or retellings of the myth, legend, fable, or divination narratives, which are rewritten as folktales and short stories (in Lachatañeré, Cabrera, Ortiz, Barnet, Martínez Furé, Alonso, and others); narrative or poetic reenactments of the ritual and other practices expressive of faith and worship in the African-based religions (as in Carpentier, del Valle, Ramos, Cabrera Infante, Granados, Cofiño, Sarduy, Hernández Espinosa, and others); and the narratives of personal spiritual or social experience taking place within the context of the subcultures associated with Afro-Cuban worship (as in Fernández Robaina, Isabel and Jorge Castellanos, González-Wippler, and others). Mythical narratives are common to all the Afro-Cuban religions and translate readily into literary text. With the possible exception of the Regla Arará, where the function of myth is minimized, myth, as stated earlier, generally serves to provide a precedent, a background, a subtext, and a charter. In literary form it continues to give reasons for ritual, doctrine, social relations, custom, and even personal experience, for what is personal may conform or respond to the archetypal paradigm. Whether patakís of the Lucumí tradition or kutuguangos of the Congo, mythic narratives so recontextualized continue to play their part in preserving and transmitting the knowledge of the group, most formally in depictions of divination rites, most informally in inclusions of anecdotes and scenes of storytelling. Despite their status as sacred stories, patakís and kutuguangos, I hope to demonstrate, are susceptible to narratological analysis and interpretation.

By reducing sacred narrative to the "spheres of action" defined by Vladimir Propp in his *Morphology of the Folktale* (1928), we may construct a model that isolates and then integrates their "functions." Propp's functions are so conceived that a particular character may take on several functions either simultaneously or consecutively; that several characters may comprise one actant (for example, the "town" or "townsfolk"; the *omordé* or women all taken together); and that representations of animals (Chameleon, Guinea Fowl, Sheep) or other creatures (Stick, Cotton) may be incorporated into narrative as actants. A. J. Greimas's reduction of Propp's thirty-one actants to six, in *Structural Semantics*, helps to organize the analysis of other narratives such as patakís.

Adapting Greimas's practical schema of six actants to the narrative analysis, one grasps an underlying framework of functions and recurring patterns. The Subject seeks an Object: for example, the Hero seeks the Grail, Changó seeks control over the *Tabla de Orula* (the Ifá divining board), Elegguá seeks to test and then chastise Obí for his arrogance, the calabash seeks the favor of Ochún, and so on. Another narrative opposition exists between the Sender

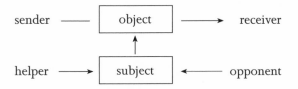

3. Binary oppositions in narrative (from Greimas).

and the Receiver in communicative or transferential propositions: God sends the Grail to humanity; Obatalá sends the Ifá to humanity; Aganyú Solá sends his son, Changó, to his mother, Yemayá; Obbá sends the amalá stew with her ear to Changó; Elegguá sends the *aleyos* or non-initiates away from Orúmila's *ile* and to another Elegguá ready to read the diloggún, and so on. A Helper and an Opponent enter the picture and readjust the power relations between antagonists. The Helper, the ally who facilitates communication and mediates desire, may be a god. The Opponent, who places an obstacle in the path of the Subject, is sometimes concretized as the mischievous Eshú-Elegguá (see Greimas, *Structural* 207–8).

Some of the complexity of narratives on and of Afro-Cuban religious discourse resides in their implicit notion of the author as the voice of a collectivity. In the system of Afro-Cuban literary production, the author appears not so much as an original creator or receiver of divine inspiration as compiler, mythologic polymath, ethnologist, and reporter: Lydia Cabrera anticipates a Miguel Barnet and carries on the work of Ortiz before her in collecting and transcribing the testimonies of many participants in a set of related events. As Cabrera puts it in the preface of *El monte* (The mountain), *"The only value of this book . . . consists exclusively in the very direct part that the blacks themselves have taken in it. It is they who are the true authors"* (M 10).

Cabrera's role as transcriber and literary artist also has had a reciprocal impact on the religious culture she depicts in writing. As Joseph Murphy states in his article discussing Regla de Ocha in the United States, Cabrera, "by her transfer of the oral wisdom of the elders into print, . . . has participated in the transformation of the religions themselves" ("Lydia Cabrera" 246). Cabrera's classic *El monte* presents us with related special problems of generic classification. Reading it, we pause to ask: what is it? It is only in part a collection of testimonies, a kind of Afro-Cuban anthology. One is tempted to put it into the category of folkloric literature, but its prescriptions and narratives of beliefs, practices, and ritual remove it from the category of the purely aesthetic: this is a book to be used. *El monte* seems at times a work of cultural anthropology due to its wealth of pharmaceutical and therapeutic information. It is a classic sourcebook of folk medicine, as Morton Marks notes in his article "Exploring El Monte: Ethnobotany and the Afro-Cuban Science of the Concrete." Cuervo Hewitt confirms that many have come to consider the book to be "the Bible of Afro-Cubanism" and likens Cabrera's myth and folklore-filled stories to the Yoruba oracle. Furthermore, continues Cuervo Hewitt, "the work of Cabrera is a mythopoetic, mythical and historical charade, which breaks with the traditional seams that hem it in in order to hurl itself into a wild race through the vast field of the literary imagination" (APA 7, 8).

One of the most appealing aspects of Afro-Cuban religions, grounded in the centralizing symbolicity manifest in their narratives, is their unifying, holistic vision of nature, culture, and the divine as harmoniously interactive and mutually supportive. Religion establishes a human and cultural relation with the supernatural, that which is seen as above or superior to the natural yet immanent within the natural as its potential for fulfillment. Lezama Lima conceived of a nature that must "attain supernature and counternature" (350). Since religious language and other signs mediate that impulse to transcendence, one must account for the principles of those religions' internal organization and coherence as sign systems directed toward attaining supernature and counternature.

Systems Centered and Recentered

All Afro-Cuban religious systems share a supernatural vision of the world that accepts the life of divine beings and their interactions with the living. Also common to all of these systems is what James Figarola calls the "principle of multiple representation": that is, their semantic tendency to signify the same referent or signified by varied symbols, objects, names, or figures. Such manifold representations include the different names of a mythic element or ritual or the "plural crystallizations" taken by a supernatural force or deity in the mind. Multiple representation accounts for the different "modalities" that representation takes: Yemayá has sixteen caminos (literally roads) or avatars, Elegguá more than twenty; Changó appears as female or male, and so does Obatalá. Divination performances in Cuba often refer to religious figures by their hagiographic counterparts. Multiple representation also functions as an articulating subsystem within magic-religious systems, connecting what would otherwise appear as disparate elements (SMD 13–17).

The notion of "multiple representation" conforms to C. S. Peirce's concept of "limitless semiosis," by which the "interpretant"—roughly, Saussure's "signified"—must refer to a second signifier that must be interpreted by a third signifier, which yet must be interpreted by a fourth, and so on *ad infinitum* (see Eco 133). Yet multiple representation maintains the operation of a unitary principle, a centering function that draws the shifting signifieds toward a privileged signifier. The concept of the *fundamento* provides this centripetal function, a nucleus for gathering together heterogeneous elements within each of the varieties of Afro-Cuban religious experience. In normal usage, *fundamento* means foundation, basis, grounds. In the Yoruba-Lucumí tradition, the word designates the collection of stones, otanes, in which the aché of the orisha is absorbed and held. In the Abakuá tradition, the fundamento is the sacred drum called Ekue; it holds and releases the voice of the Supreme God Abasí. For the Mayomberos, the fundamento is none other than the spirit-controlling cauldron called the nganga or prenda. For the *serviteurs* of the Arará, the same foundational function could be fulfilled by the stones or by altars consecrated to specific loas, or by the central post, the *poteau-mitan*, that holds up the peristyle dance area of the houmfort temple and connects this earthly stage with the divine realm. The fundamento is not in itself a center but a centering device, a focal point or bridge through which the subject is brought into the "presence" of the mythic and divine source (SMD 56).

As I have previously argued, the specificity of each Afro-Cuban religion as a system of signs arises from extrinsic and intrinsic processes of differentiation: the religious system, like a language, differentiates itself from other systems; the religious system, like any dynamic structure, constitutes itself by internal differentiation. Saussure asserted that in language there are no substances, but that the differences between phonemes, their negative relations with one another, assign them a place in the system. Consonant with Saussure's seminal insight, the concept we may apply here is that all Afro-Cuban religions are readable synchronically as different signifying "systems of functions."[5] James Figarola's semantic analysis thus contributes an inventory of the traits that differentiate the Afro-Cuban religions or reglas. To touch on one example that I will discuss at length in chapter 5, the Reglas Congas (such as Palo Monte Mayombe) stress the relation of the priest or initiate to the "center of magic power," which is identified as the nganga cauldron-charm or the cosmogram inscribed at its bottom. This centering feature, James Figarola points out, makes the Reglas Congas distinctive within the Afro-Cuban cultural universe, indicating the necessity of this particular system to "fold in on itself [*plegarse a sí mismo*], in order to prevail, given certain adverse circumstances, with its own profile within the Cuban religious spectrum" (SMD 56, 58).

Figures of centering abound in other discourses on and about Afro-Cuban religions, and here I would like to address two of the forms it takes: the centering that has posited the Yoruba-Lucumí religious system as the paradigm for organizing Afro-Cuban religions in general and the positioning of the subject and the organization of consciousness with relation to a center in the religious sign-world.

Lachatañeré, Cuervo Hewitt, and others have stressed the predominance of Lucumí religion over other Afro-Cuban religions by virtue of its popularity and its role in providing mythical and ritual structures to other religious traditions. Bastide concurs with Lachatañeré's notion that the culture of a particular African ethnia may predominate in a given area. This phenomenon has taken place in the Brazilian Bahia state, where the theology of the Yoruba-based or Nago religion called *Candomblé* has prevailed over all other religious systems by providing the framework for the syncretization of Dahomeyan, Gêgê, Angolan, and Kongo traditions. As in northeast Brazil, Yoruba culture in Cuba and in Trinidad exerts a "determining influence" and "dominates all the rest" of the transplanted African cultures, including the Calibar and Kongo. A similar conformation to the pattern set by Dahomey-Fon culture took place in Haiti (Bastide 11–12).

The Yoruba-Lucumí element in Afro-Cuban religion has arguably constituted an architectonics of cultural signs: a totalizing symbolic order suggested by Adebayo Adesanya's characterization in "Yoruba Metaphysical Thinking." In that article Adesanya states, "from the Olodumare an architectonic of knowledge was built in which the finger of God is manifest in the most rudimentary elements of nature. Philosophy, theology, politics, social theory, land law, medicine, psychology, birth and burial, all find themselves logically concatenated in a system so tight that to subtract one item from the whole is to paralyse the structure of the whole" (Adesanya 40). The concatenations or interrelations of the disciplines in the Yoruba system have carried over, albeit in attenuated form, to Afro-Cuban religious cultural systems. The notion of architectonic unity does not however account for the complications that arise in the process of Afro-Cuban syncretism, by which religious systems tend to be supplemented or reconfigured with elements from other systems. Lucumí religion or Santería is not reducible to its own "system" because it came into being as an amalgam of different components from different systems. James Figarola corroborates this point in stating that none of the Afro-Cuban religious systems can be found "in its pure form" due to "crossing and mixing" (SMD 54, 68). In effect, the interrelationship of the Yoruba system with other systems decenters its mythology and doctrine. To counteract the "Lucumí chauvinism" that has prevailed in Afro-Cuban religious studies, we must account for the welcome encroachments of other religious traditions into what has been called the "orisha tradition" (compare TO 12). The Lucumí predominance has obscured the vital contribution of other West African religious traditions transported into its architectonics, especially the Bantu-Congo, the Calibar-Abakuá, and the Dahomeyan-Arará.

Afro-Cuban narrative, in view of this intrinsic otherness within Afro-Cuban religion(s), promises to reveal a cultural dynamic that cannot be reduced to the structuralization of the Yoruba-Lucumí system.

With various relations to the Yoruba-Lucumí paradigm, each Afro-Cuban religious system differentiates itself internally and externally by its selection and constitution of figures, motives, and symbols. Each religion accordingly presents its own dominant modality of symbolization, the systemic regularity that will be elaborated in each of the following chapters. With each dominant modality of representation, as indicated in multiple representations centered on the fundamento, goes a specific attitude toward the supernatural. James Figarola, in *Sobre muertos y dioses* (On the dead and gods), charts these different attitudes in the following manner. Regla de Ocha emphasizes the believer's affectionate relation of devotion to his or her orisha, the orisha who has chosen him or her. The Vaudou practiced in Cuba, called Arará, encourages a fearful attitude toward the loas, for whom one strives to fulfill obligations (formulated as taboos or promises) or against whom one seeks to obtain the assistance of other loas. Palo Monte, more than Regla de Ocha and Regla Arará, is centered on the cult of the dead. One's dead, if properly approached, will bring life and power. James Figarola explains that the dead in Palo Monte constitute "the point of support, or that in which the forces of everything that exists join together; the catalyzing factor that opens the life, the closed-up life, which was dead until this moment, of the most diverse materials" (SMD 81–84). Such identifications of dominant traits are useful in making broad distinguishing characterizations of the three listed religions, but we must also recognize that, upon closer examination, each of the three reveals traits similar to those attributed to the others. Similar to Palo Monte, orisha worship has its cult of the ancestors, the *egún*, who often become orishas themselves. Additionally, one orisha may be invoked to defend against the harm inflicted by another, as happens in Regla de Ocha, and the serviteurs of Vaudou may establish close, often affectionate relationships with the loas or gods they serve. The devotees of Palo Monte would never forget their obligations to the mpungus or spirits, each one associated with a corresponding orisha. James Figarola also overlooks the persistence in Cuba of the Abakuá religion, whose pantheon of spirits is virtually the same as that of Regla de Ocha with the exception of the central Ekue.

Of course the motifs or figures of religious representation function in organizing the perceptions and thoughts of the religious subject, situating that subject in a readable world, at home in a signifying cosmos. Behind this process lies an unconscious awareness of an otherness that the ego must control in some fashion or another, a not-self that the ego must either master or resolve into sameness in order to find order outside itself. Locating this unifying process in religious symbolization, Zuesse writes that "[o]nly a genuinely transcendental center organizes the preconscious disposition and sensory symbols in a secure order." The center will hold: it makes things over into the signs of its system and gathers them into its fluid architecture. It is precisely religion, continues Zuesse, that "aligns the passions with the consciously known structures of the universe" (Zuesse 176). The Spanish expression "Estoy en mi centro"—"I'm right where I belong"—sums up the feeling of centering achieved through the use of religious symbolism.

The forerunner of the phenomenology of religion, William James, defined "mental field" as "the total mental state, the entire wave of consciousness or field of objects present to the thought at any time." The field of consciousness in this conception undergoes recentering shifts of mental energy that succeed one another in the course of an individual's life. Movable shifting centers accordingly orient action like a compass in a magnetic field. The process of conversion can be explained as one that relocates the subject's "habitual centre" of "personal energy" whereby contents that were once peripheral, on the fringes or margins of the field, "now take a central place" (James 226, 227, 193). James's concept of centering within the mental field lends support to James Figarola's arguably "pluralistic" theory of the fundamento. James's limitation lies in his disregard of questions of language, representation, and signification in general. In assuming the pure interiority of some prelinguistic mental activity, similar to the "authentic cogito" or "transcendental ego" of phenomenology, James, despite his dynamic view of consciousness, retains a metaphysical belief in the subject as origin of meaning and foundation of personal identity. A salutary alternative would be to see a centering active in the selection and repetition of figures that organize the systems of each religion; the fundamentos of each religion, we should stress, not only focus signification but ground a sense of selfhood as defined within the matrix of the religion's beliefs and practices.

Transported to America, the slaves could carry with them nothing but

their languages, their beliefs, their gods, and their religions: the broken main-
stays of their identity, recreated in the face of an institution that destroyed
their familial organization and the coherence of their belief systems (SMD
23). As the violence of the transplantation required that the shattered systems be recomposed and regenerated in Cuba and elsewhere, African-based
religions accordingly reiterated the desire for reunion or for a return to the
center identified with the "homeland." As belief systems incorporating elements of Hispanic Catholicism, Afro-Cuban religions can be said to preserve
and enrich the image of Christianity that Kenneth Burke describes in *The Rhetoric of Religion*: "It is seen as a unifying principle, the vision of an original Edenic
one-ness, with endless varieties of action and passion deriving from it somewhat as the many languages that came to beset the building of the Tower of
Babel eventually followed expulsion from the Garden" (v). The study of religion is pluralistic, but the study of the religious system should account for
its utopian impulse for unification. Yet because Afro-American religious systems did not come across the Middle Passage whole and intact—families and
worship communities were divided, officiants and devotees separated in the
African diaspora—those religions could be practiced only after being recomposed, restored unto themselves as religions, by devotees who reunited
the remembered fragments of myth, doctrine, and ritual from their own
tradition and from the traditions of other slaves from other parts of Africa.
Paradoxically, then, the system of belief put in practice by a heterogeneous
mass of slaves in a plantation area bound them "back" into a community that
never was before, and it bound them "again" to an African center of myth
and legend that did not previously exist. For the slaves, there is no pure
and original religion, no simple "return to Africa." On this premise, the notions concerning religious syncretizations, semiosis, and multiple representation that I have elaborated will come into play in the chapters that follow,
which address each of the major religious traditions in various sociohistorical
contexts.

In order to contextualize a large corpus of Afro-Cuban literary texts, chapter 2 provides an overview of Yoruba-Lucumí religious manifestations in
Cuba. The mythical, ritual, doctrinal, social, and experiential dimensions of
Regla de Ocha will be addressed as will Santería's claim to a dominant status
on the island.

Chapter 3 develops more literary-interpretive readings of Afro-Cuban narratives appearing during and after the period of Machado's dictatorship in
the 1930s, when Lucumí motifs were incorporated into works that sought

to define a distinct national identity and a postcolonial culture. During the early Republican period, I argue, Afro-Cuban myth, doctrine, and ritual were called on to participate in the project of redefining and revitalizing a national culture, in part as a reaction to foreign cultural impositions. A brief history of *el afrocubanismo* will present the contours of the new culture of nationalist resistance. The authors subsequently examined in this chapter will include Alejo Carpentier, José Antonio Ramos, and Rómulo Lachatañeré. Afro-Cuban religion especially enters into the nationalist allegory of José Antonio Ramos's *Caniquí* (1936), in which the runaway slave protagonist becomes a symbol of protest against neocolonialism. In that novel, Caniquí's African-based religious beliefs define his rebellious character and furthermore frame a critical interpretation of traditional Catholicism as a repressive religion in complicity with colonial domination. Lachatañeré's primitivist narrative preserves a number of divination narratives, patakís, and folktales in a sequence that projects a primordial world of mythical gods for its readers.

Chapter 4, "A Is For Abakuá," reflects on the significance of the Abakuá Secret Society or so-called Ñáñigos in the literature of the first half of this century. After summarizing its principal beliefs and rituals, which involve faith in the Lucumí orishas, I will turn to the "futurist" discourse of Abakuá religion in Alejo Carpentier's *¡Ecue-Yamba-O!* The Ñáñigo stories of Gerardo del Valle's *1/4 fambá* (1938) evoke a world of secret rites, arcane myth, intergroup rivalries, and the kind of brutality that Ortiz described in his *Hampa afrocubana: los negros brujos* (Afro-Cuban underworld: the black sorcerers, 1917). In del Valle's stories, group formation leads to intergroup aggression and violence. Although del Valle's use of Abakuá and Lucumí myth does not always square with versions provided by more ethnologically minded authorities, his inconsistencies and inaccuracies, I hope to show, help to underscore his apparent aim of demonstrating the atavistic nature of the Ñáñigo subculture in Republican Cuba.

Chapter 5 shifts the focus to the Congo-Bantu heritage with its discussion of Palo Monte. Although this much discussed heritage relies on Yoruba-Lucumí tradition for much of its structure, I argue that Palo Monte also affirms its own idiosyncratic significations in its recurrent metaphors of centering and circling, its magic inscriptions, its nganga charms, its repertoire of spells or *bilongos*, and its mythology of non-Yoruba gods and devils in the oral tradition of kutuguangos and in the literary tradition of Kongo-based folktales.

Chapter 6, "Versions of Vaudou," examines the reasons why some Afro-Cubanist authors have turned to the Dahomey-Fon-Haitian tradition as a textual source. Transported to Cuba through migrations of Haitians to Cuba at the end of the eighteenth century and, at several times, during the twentieth century, the magic, ritual, and myth of Vaudou, as will be seen, have supplemented the Afro-Cuban religious system and provided a counterexample of religion's role in Caribbean history and politics. A history of Vaudou and an overview of its myths, rituals, and metaphysics will precede readings of two Cuban narratives concerned with the Vaudou heritage, namely, Carpentier's *El reino de este mundo* and Benítez Rojo's "La tierra y el cielo" (Earth and heaven, 1969).

Chapter 7 examines the Afro-Cuban novel and short story in the context of the Cuban Revolution. In that narrative, the themes of social consciousness and solidarity are juxtaposed with varied visions of Afro-Cuban religion. In the first section of the chapter, an account of the Revolution's cultural policy toward literature and Afro-Cuban religion will prepare for a reading of Guillermo Cabrera Infante's story, from *Así en la paz como en la guerra* (In peace as in war, 1960), "En el gran ecbó" (In the great Ecbó), which, as will be shown, offers an ambiguous reading of Afro-Cuban religion but employs its motifs in a critique of bourgeois culture under Batista. Carpentier's *La Consagración de la Primavera* (The rite of spring, 1978), representing Afro-Cuban religion in a more affirmative light, traces the alternative process by which Afro-Cuban myth and ritual, especially those of the Abakuá Secret Society, become positively refigured as metaphors for political struggle and historical destiny. A subsequent reading of Manuel Cofiño's *Cuando la sangre se parece al fuego* (When blood looks like fire, 1977) will explicate the manner in which a more exclusivist politics of culture became textualized in novels that, while respecting the beauty and complexity of Afro-Cuban religion, nonetheless justify the suppression of that religion in what the state determines to be the interest of the collectivity. In this case, fiction attempts to rechannel and thus manage the desires and energies awoken by Afro-Cuban religion. In so doing, it also explores the way that motifs of religion break out of the marginalized category to which the overt narrative would confine it and thus overturn the dominant message of the text.

The next section of chapter 7 elaborates the thesis that a process of "folklorization"—involving the containment, marginalization, and aesthetizing secularization of Afro-Cuban religion by the agencies of official culture—can be traced in works of Afro-Cuban narrative by Cabrera, Miguel Barnet, Martínez Furé, and Dora Alonso. The final section examines texts that view the Afro-Cuban sign-world as a compilation of "local narrative" available for redefining—and de-defining—the Cuban national identity. Sarduy's

De donde son los cantantes (Where the singers are from, 1967) is read as a post-modern ludic attempt to reincorporate a decomposed Afro-Cuban religion into a dynamic, nonessentialist definition of Cuban national identity. That attempt, I argue, ignores the official categories of "inside" or "outside" the Revolution in the name of affirming the freeplay of signification inherent in Afro-Cuban mythopoetics. On the other hand, a reading of Hernández Espinosa's drama *María Antonia* (1979) unravels a text in which divination, possession, dance, sacrifice, and conjuration function in producing a sign-world that gives coherence to experience, restoring a sense of how Afro-Cuban religion constitutes the mysterious unity in which a multitude—consisting of the heterogeneous artifacts of various literatures and cultures—presents itself.

2

⬦ The Lucumí Sign System

*The gods are naturally fond of expressing themselves
in proverbs and metaphors.*
Lydia Cabrera, "Introducción," *Refranes de Negros Viejos*

In *The Rhetoric of Religion*, Kenneth Burke proposes a theory of words about words—that is, a "logology"—that identifies three classes or empirical orders of language. These classes include words referring to nature, words referring to the sociopolitical realm, and words referring to other words. These empirical terms serve as analogies constituting an additional fourth order, one in which those terms can name the supernatural. Elaborating a Platonist, upward/downward dialectic in his own rhetoric-based theory, Burke finds that the supernatural order, as it relies on the empirical orders to provide it with recognizable signs, recurs back upon those empirical signs to condition or modify them according to its transcendent perspective. Such is the case, to cite Burke's premier example, when "supernatural personality" is said either to exist prior to the empirical personality or to contain its center or core; such is the case, more generally, when the transcendent realm becomes the "ground" or essence of the other three terms (RR 14–15, 36).

This dialectic of terms can be observed in the genesis of Afro-Cuban religious signs. All are founded on the orders of natural things, sociopolitical entities, and other signs (including words, to semiotize Burke's schema a bit). And the transcendent order symbolized by empirically based metaphors turns back to invest those metaphors with a meaning founded on metaphysical grounds so constituted. Divine signification and exegesis both operate on the assumption of these translations between orders of terms.

The Lucumí system, on which Regla de Ocha or Santería is based, centers representation on the orishas or on their concrete signifiers: on the one hand, iconic images and identifying objects called *atributos* and *secretos* (attributes and secrets) function as their metaphors and metonymies. González-Wippler appropriately calls Santería "a system that seeks to find the divine in the most common, ordinary things" (SR 23). That is to say, the religion identifies a divinity in natural and artificial objects. In the mode of iconic representation, on the other hand, correspondences or parallelisms between saints and orishas signal an identity with a difference; an equivalence but not an equality. Given their difference, the match between saint and orisha within Regla de Ocha constitutes an originary displacement of meaning. Mostly of Yoruba origin, the orishas furthermore model the personality of the omo-orisha or "child of the orisha," most visibly in the ritual of possession, as they personify the divine forces of nature.

The orishas thus perform multiple symbolic functions in providing a focus to the cult. According to González-Wippler, "The orishas are the very soul of Santería. The central aim of the santero is to worship the saints, to observe their feasts, obey their commands, and conduct their rituals" (SE ix). The orishas are archetypes, primordial beings, magical agents, the receivers of prayer and sacrifice. Syncretized with the santos católicos, they acquire qualities consonant with William James's characterization of saints as "authors, auctores, increasers, of goodness," those whose symbolic presence actualizes the potential and "essential sacredness of everyone" (James 350). Murphy uses a dramatistic metaphor in saying that in the relation between believer and orisha, "The world is revealed as a theater for the interaction of invisible powers, and the orisha within is an infallible guide to worldly success and heavenly wisdom" (SAS 143).

The interdependence and intimacy between humans and gods forms the axis of worship in Regla de Ocha, whose name translates as "religion," "order," "law," or even "rule" of the orisha (ocha). As the deities of what began in the Americas as a "slave religion," the Afro-Cuban saints have played a central role in the evolution of a unique Creole culture and an Afro-Cuban identity through the process of transculturation.

In the theater of the world, the orisha acts in a variety of archetypal dramas in which he or she displays diverse personalities. As mentioned earlier, these sometimes contradictory personalities or avatars are called caminos, "paths" or "roads," suggesting the manner in which the orisha's identity may shift completely with each distinct manifestation. Saldaña defines the avatar as "one of the moments in the life or in the trajectory of an orisha. It could be defined," she adds, "as an aspect of the 'theopsychical' personality of the deity, like a fact [or action, event, hecho] or an anecdote" (122). Elegguá and Oggún, two eminent and popular orishas, have about twenty caminos

4. Ritual setting and attributes of Obatalá. 1991. Museo de Regla, Old Havana, Cuba.

each. And to each camino corresponds a number of mythical narratives featuring the orisha as protagonist. Some individual orishas will have different genders in male or female caminos, as is the case for Yemayá and Obatalá. Yet all the avatars of the orisha contribute to making up one multifaceted mythical character associated with the aforementioned set of identifying objects or themes. These objects and themes considered collectively are called the "universe" of an orisha; the universe of Babalú-Ayé, for instance, is that of skin diseases, wounds, and pustules, and includes miniature representations of crutches and other things that signal his syncretization with San Lázaro.

Identified with the orishas, the objects called atributos function as metonymies of the orishas themselves within each orisha's universe, inasmuch as the object is invested with significance by an equivalence drawn between the thing and the deity to which it is adjoined. To prepare to invoke the orisha, it is necessary to gather together the particular attributes of the deity into the ritual asiento or setting that will be placed on the worshipper's altar. The dialectical principle works here again as we go from orisha to attribute and back again to the transcendental referent. A series of equivalencies will illustrate the Burkean analogy between natural phenomenon and divinity: Changó is the thunder (and the thunder is Changó). The wind is Oyá. Ifá (the divination system) is Orúmila. Elegguá is the mound of earth, cement, blood, and cowrie shells that stands watch behind the front door of the house. The orishas, by these correspondences, double as anthropomorphic symbols of natural forces as they objectify human character types or obsessions. González-Wippler is correct in defining Santería as "an earth religion" in the sense that "nature is a manifestation of God's will" (SE 199, 201).

Ritual operations with the attributes call the orishas into presence or represent the orishas in devotion. As stated in chapter 1, the foremost representation of those deities are the otanes or stones sacred to a particular orisha. These stones are the fundamento, the fundament that centers signification, comparable to the Ekue drum in the Regla Abakuá and the nganga-cauldron in Palo Monte. In Regla de Ocha, the sacred stones are ritually placed in a soup tureen, the *sopera*, then fed with sacrificial blood and washed with omiero, a sacred mixture of herbs and liquids, then bathed in palm oil, so that in and through the otanes the orisha can drink up nourishment in the form of aché (PQ 253). As transmitters of aché, the sacred stones call to the gods, inviting them to come down and take possession of their omos, to give the sign that they accept the sacrifice and feel strengthened by it.

Into the sopera or tureen of each orisha also goes, alongside the otanes, the orisha's personal set of cowries for the diloggún divination, a ritual I will explain in detail toward the end of this chapter. The practitioner uses each set of cowries for communicating with the orisha in question, with the exception of the shells assigned to the individual's tutelary or protecting orisha, which another believer may throw and read on that individual's behalf (SR 21). Other signs invested with sacred significance enter into ritual. A color code comes into play in the beadwork, flags, and dress of believers: red and white for Changó, green and black for Elegguá, yellow for Ochún, white for Obatalá, blue for Yemayá (see Argüelles Micet). Specific numbers belong to an orisha. Favorite foods, dance patterns, herbs, plants, and fruits also identify the orisha in question. The manner of placing attributes in the ritual *canastillero* or storage cabinets symbolizes the hierarchy of orishas, with Obatalá, venerable god of wisdom and tranquillity, often occupying the top shelf (SAS 60). The ritual asientos may also include effigies, soil, metal sculptures, roots, sticks, and bones (RA 121). Flowers, too, correspond to the orisha who owns and favors them, and the orisha's preference tends to match the color of the favored flower. The lyrics of Jully Mendoza's "Flores para tu altar" (Flowers for your altar), recorded by Celina and Reutilio, name the flowers and the orishas that claim them: the yellow sunflower, *girasol*, for Ochún; the *rosa nacarada* for Obatalá; the white gladiolas for Babalú-Ayé. The *príncipe de pura sangre*, "pure-blood prince," belongs to Changó, Yemayá, and the rest of the most popular orishas (EQT 24, 58).

Once natural, cultural, and "metalinguistic" terms have been directed "upward" to signify the holy, the holy word may then, as the foregoing nature-divinity equivalences have suggested, be turned "downward" to identify qualities in the "lower" sociopolitical order. Miguel Barnet in *La fuente viva* (The living fountain, 1983) acknowledges the naturalness with which Cubans accept mythicopolitical identifications, such that the creator-deity Oddudua has symbolized not only life and death but also government, bureaucratic organization, the Revolution, and Fidel Castro himself (157–58). Some expatriate believers have reported that Castro performed devotions to the warrior Elegguá when he lived and trained in the *manigua* or jungle of the Sierra Maestra. El Comandante himself supposedly wears two watches to hide his initiation bracelet, and he gains power and protection by bathing in a tub full of sacrificial blood. Batista before him was rumored to believe in Santería, and "allegedly owed his miraculous escape from Havana to the protection of the orishas." Finally, "[l]ike many other Latin-American musicians," to give another example, "Tito Puente is an initiated santero" (SE 108, 114).

Filtering down into popular myth and imagination, Santería signs continue to contribute their combination of elements drawn from a variety of preexisting African religions and the kind of baroque Catholicism practiced by the Spanish colonizers. Cros Sandoval attributes the predominance of Yoruba-Lucumí elements in Santería not only to the fact that the majority of Africans brought as slaves to Cuba were Yoruba but to "the greater organization and structuralization of their religion" (TOM 2). In an influential article published in 1938, Rómulo Lachatañeré previously accounted for the family resemblances among Afro-Cuban religious systems by claiming the tendency of non-Yoruba groups, such as the Congo-Bantu, to adapt their beliefs to the Yoruba system. The famed Afro-Cuban scholar judged that the Yoruba element in the Afro-Cuban cultural amalgam set the norm and operated as a catalyst for the transmission and adaptation of African religion in Cuba, especially in the western part of the island where the Yoruba-Lucumí were gathered in the greatest numbers (SRL 42–43). The dominant Yoruba-Lucumí cults have provided an analytical framework for Afro-Cuban religion in general, in the view of Lachatañeré and other investigators, who thus, perhaps prematurely, oversimplified the task of analyzing the heterogeneous phenomena known together as "Afro-Cuban" religion, as the following excerpt from Lachatañeré's article suggests. According to Lachatañeré,

> If we examine the Bantu traits, for example, and with regard to the identities between the saints of the Catholic pantheon and the deities of African origin, we will be able to see that the latter evolve toward the original deity utilizing the Yoruba characteristic as the norm. In this way, it seems that such Bantu beliefs have had need of Yoruba mythology and its other religious essences in order to match the Catholic saint and the deity. . . . [T]he sum total of all the cults shows a major percentage of Yoruba influence, [and] one could judge that in the Afro-Cuban Religious System there has existed the tendency among the varied African cultures to nucleate their religious elements in accord with the Yoruba pattern. (Quoted in Cuervo Hewitt, APA 16)

The systemic, integrative aspect of Lucumí religion and the availability of its orishas as models for refashioning deities from other traditions indeed made it available to serve as an infrastructure for evolving syncretic religions. Yet the Yorubo-centric bias of Lachatañeré's hypothesis runs the risk of overlooking the specific characteristics of other classes of religious phenomena, such as those belonging to Congo, Calabar, and Ewe-Fon cultures. The thesis of the Yoruba predominance and the visibility and preeminence of its religious pantheon among Afro-Cuban subcultures indicates a synecdochic treatment of Lucumí religion as representative of Afro-Cuban religion in general. Given the prevalence of transculturations, that treatment in effect overlooks the free play and transfer of signs across the borders between religious systems whose elements would supplement the Lucumí system. Because Santería is already heterogeneous in its composition and dynamic in its adaptation to a new settings, "it is always open to new reinterpretations and innovations" (TOM 2). Other corpi of belief and practice, including complementary or competing pantheons, were always at hand to provide supplements of "foreign" mythemes, figures, and motifs to the syncretizing process, as an overview of Yoruba-Lucumí history should make clear.

Historical Backgrounds

The Yoruba of the Guinea Coast do not comprise a single "tribe" but rather consist of numerous and varied tribal groups only loosely unified by common language, mythology, history, dress, and ritual symbolism.[1] The name *Yoruba* serves to distinguish the Oyo Yoruba as the "Yoruba proper"; the Fulani or Hausa gave that name to the inhabitants of the Oyo kingdom, and it also served to differentiate Yoruba-speaking peoples from other ethnias such as the Hausa, Nupe, or Tiv (YSN 5; Eades 4). Internecine warfare, migration, and external conquest fragmented the region and did their part in creating what Lloyd calls "a kaleidoscopic pattern of culture" and in "differentiating throughout what appears only superficially as a political unity" (551). That these more than fifty subtribes or subgroups did not share a common sense of identity, however, is confirmed by the fact of their various alliances with non-Yoruba peoples for warfare with other Yoruba subgroups. The Yoruba subgroups, all told, occupied a land of forests and savannas extending from the Gulf of Guinea in the south to the lower Niger River. These kingdoms included Ijebu, Oyo, Ijesha, and the holy city of Ife, among others. The most important subtribes are the Oyó, of the northwest, and the Nagos, or Lucumí proper, in the west (YO 20n. 11). The Yoruba living in southwest Nigeria, the region of highest concentration, and in the area of the so-called Slave Coast included the Ekiti and the Fée as well. From the westernmost part of Yorubaland came the Sabalú, the Agicón, and the Cuévano (RA 20). Yoruba also inhabit a part of eastern Dahomey, and they also live in Benin, Ghana, and Togo. The provinces of Ibadan, Abeokuta, Colony, and Ondo occupy the western part of Yorubaland and Kabba and Ilorin the northern part.

Predominantly agrarian before colonization, the Yoruba were nonetheless by tradition "the most urban of all African people," their concentration in towns and cities "dating back well before the period of European penetration" (YSN 3). Three factors allowed the development of Yoruba kingdoms in the Guinea forests. The first factor was the development of a kind of sustaining cultivation whose produce would come to include yams, plantain, banana, maize, cassava, kola trees, and oil palms. Second, Yoruba subgroups found support in commercial relations with European traders on the coast and with central and east Africans, especially those from Sudan. The development of markets and export trade encouraged the growth of handicrafts and plastic arts, in which Yoruba artisans and artists would excel. Third, cultural influences from western Sudan and possibly from as far away as the Nile

Valley through Meröe may have transmitted knowledge of such arts as iron working to the Yoruba, although the veracity of this influence and its extent are still disputed (Smith 5–9).

The origin of the Yoruba is said to be the sacred city of Ile-Ife, and as the focus of the Yoruba "reference myth" it provides a charter for their culture, a basis for self-identification, and a validation for other Yoruba myths, orisha names, taboos, and ritual. As Robert Smith asserts, "the primacy of Ife in the life of the Yoruba—their religion, their political system, their culture—is unlikely ever to be contested" (35). In archaeology, it was Leo Frobenius who first called attention to the art of ancient Ife. While researching the sacred groves of Ife in 1910 and 1911, Frobenius came upon a now famous bronze head of Olokun, as well as a number of terra-cotta heads and stone monuments. Yoruba art drew further international attention with the discovery in 1919 of a bronze Obalufon mask (representing the third or fourth Oni, or king, of Ife) and a terra-cotta head representing the would-be usurper Lajuwa. The seventeen bronze heads discovered in the Wunmonije compound in 1938–39 represent what is perhaps the most "spectacular" find, according to Smith (27). In cosmogonic myth, as I will discuss later, not only are the Yoruba as a people said to have originated in Ile-Ife, but the earth and the human race began there as well.

The Yoruba peoples were once a nomadic tribal group, but settled in the southwest portion of what is today Nigeria in the early 1700s. It is then that the old Oni of Oyo named Katunga consolidated his subjects into a powerful and industrious nation. Katunga's successor, Ajagbo, divided the nation into four parts: the Yoruba, the Egba, the Ketu, and the Ijebu. From that time onward, all the Oba ruling Ile-Ife have claimed their descent from the founding father (Idowu 14, 22–23). The traditional Yoruba political order indeed mirrors the cosmic hierarchy: Ijimere in the didascalia of *The Imprisonment of Obatala* describes the Supreme Sky God Olodumare as seated upon a throne in the fashion of an Oba. Olodumare wears the appropriate beaded crown and veil of beads, all in white; he carries the *ada*, the ceremonial sword that is *"symbol of the power over life and death"* (47). The leader Ajagbo was succeeded by Abiodun and Abiodun by Arongangan in 1800, under whom the Yoruba empire began to disintegrate due to the pressures of intertribal warfare. The Vaíz nation was largely responsible for delivering the Yoruba to the slave traders who transported them to the Americas (ES 15).

The descendants of the Yoruba in Cuba are often called Lucumí, their language Anagó. References to the tribe of the Ulkumí date back as early as 1728,

and some say the name became corrupted as lucumí and generalized to denominate all Yoruba slaves brought to the island (OC 21). Others say that
lucumí is an altered form of akumí, which referred to the Aku region of Nigeria
from which many of the Yoruba were taken into slavery. The name is also said
to originate in oluku mi, Yoruba for "my friend." Yoruba-based religion thus
became the Regla Lucumí (SAS 27). Anagó or Nagó is the name for the Ifonyin
subgroup that was generalized by the Dahomeyans to refer to all Yoruba-
speaking peoples and by Cubans and Brazilians as a synonym for Yoruba or
Lucumí (YSN 5). Today, the more than ten million inhabitants of Yorubaland
approximate the total population of Cuba. (That of Nigeria is over 65 million.)

As in the derived Lucumí culture, religion plays a central function in Yoruba
life. Each Nigerian town typically has its personal deity: in Abeokuta, it is
Yemayá; in Oshogbo, Oshun. Shangó comes from Oyó; Obatalá and Ogun
from Ife, and Elegguá from Ketu. In Lloyd's account, the worshippers of a
particular orisa in a representative Yoruba village, Ado, belong to the same
lineage and live together. The myths of their founder will provide the charter
defining the position of the lineage and its food taboos (560–61). This exclusive worship helps to explain the high number of orishas in Yorubaland
since each town has its local deity. Fewer orishas came to be worshipped in
Cuba, it will be recalled, because there the orishas were worshipped together
in private practice or in the cabildos (TO 14).

In Cuba and Brazil, the relocation of those from Oyo and Ketu led to an
American resurgence of the cults of Obatalá, Eshú, Ifá, Osanyin, and Oggún
and to a revitalized worship of such river goddesses as Yemonja—rechris-
tened Yemayá in Cuba and Xêmanjá in Brazil—and Oshun, the Cuban Ochún.
Murphy's ethnohistory of Santería emphasizes that it was the nature of the
Catholic church in Cuba, mediated by the cabildos, that allowed both the
flourishing of a "mosaic syncretism right beneath its ecclesiastical noses"
and the refunctioning of the church's signs into the service to the orishas.
Catholicism in Murphy's view was open to reverse co-optation by Lucumí
culture because it valorized ritual and iconology, in contrast, say, to the in-
ward-directed, anti-iconological denominations of Protestantism. Catholicism's distant and impersonal God furthermore bore a resemblance to the
Supreme God Olodumare and also had need of intermediaries who would
act on His behalf: divine power was invested in the corporate body of saints,
Virgins, angels, and even in the personnel of the religion, with its priests,
bishops, cardinals, and infallible Pope. And the Catholic notions of ritual and

self-abnegation dovetailed quite well with the santero's beliefs and practices surrounding the Lucumí rituals of purification. Like Catholic ritual, Lucumí ritual is sacramental, communal, and mystical (SAS 114).

Whereas in Africa, orisha-worship tended to be directed by the imperatives of lineage in social groups devoted to a single deity, in Latin America the violence of slavery disrupted the ties of kinship and generational continuity, preventing the formation of groups overtly devoted to the worship of orishas (APA 42). Back in Africa, the forced relocation of entire villages also caused the exclusive worship of particular orishas to die out. The cult of Ochosi underwent this complete deracination and transplantation (SR 15). Yet Yoruba-based religion in Cuba succeeded in building ties of solidarity and communication that the dispersive violence of slavery otherwise denied the slaves. For the syncretism of Lucumí religion in Cuba produced not only the conjoining of orisha with saint but also the gathering of the orishas and saints into a single practice of worship (SAS 113). The Cuban equivalents of the Yoruba lineage-based shiré would then reappear in the Afro-Cuban religious associations—cofradías, potencias, or agrupaciones—of the Regla de Ocha. Members in the cofradías, or religious brotherhoods, attended the same church and often hailed from the same geographical origin (or nación). True to the Spanish tradition, the cofradías sponsored or participated in carnivals and parades. The popular character of Afro-Cuban worship combined with the democratizing tendency of worshipping all the important orishas together has allowed diverse elements of the Lucumí religious system to trickle down into popular speech and culture in the form of folktales, proverbs, exologisms, dance, music, painting, beadwork, and other kinds of artistic expression. This religion was a indeed a "popular" religion—of and by a people—and yet, to be a religion at all, it had to reserve for itself at the same time its own sacred space of ritual drama and representations, removed in principle from the profane and empirical orders.

The Order of Mysteries

After entering the "Lucumí home" you may see an altar in one of the rooms. The altar is covered with a mantle on which wooden or plaster-cast figures of saints and virgins are set, alongside candles, plates of food, bells to call the spirits, cigars, and other offerings. On the walls of the altar room are usually hung lithographs of the saints. This altar is also called a bóveda espiritual—literally a spiritual "vault," even "burial chamber" or "crypt"—before which the misa espiritual, the spiritual mass for the dead and the orishas, is celebrated (MS 15, 42; CA 3:201–2).

In Cuba (and in Miami too), the Santería temple is the ile ocha or *casa de santos*—"house of the orishas"—usually the house of the santero or santera, priest or priestess of the religion. Three spaces of worship are kept within the ilé ocha. In the igbodu or inner sanctum, the more esoteric rites of the cult, such as initiations, are carried out. The *eya aranla*, which is often the living room of the house, is reserved for semiprivate meetings of the devotees. Public ceremonies are held in the *iban balo*, which is often the patio (TOM 3).

Once inside the home or temple, you may see, hanging from a rafter, the feathered birdlike amulet called the *niche osain*, constructed with the requisite prayer and ritual, possibly containing a turtle's head, pieces of turtle shell, wine, and needles from the *zarza* bush. These ingredients are dried and crushed before they are placed into their little gourd container, into which are inserted the tips of buzzard feathers. Strings are attached to the osain, and it is then ready to hang in its position of flight from beam or ceiling. From there it brings protection and security to the household (MS 71). On a high surface or shelf set into the corner stands a silvery bell-ringed cup, topped with the figure of a rooster: it is the *osun*, which symbolizes the life of its owner. If that cup should fall, it forbodes imminent disaster (FS 48).

The community that congregates in the ilé ocha includes fellow initiates, the spiritual guides known as iyalorishas or *babalorishas* (santeras and santeros), those of the diviner caste known as babalaos, and the anthropomorphic orishas themselves (SDM 79–80). Following its precedent in the cabildos of the colony, the worship community of Santería makes the religion "a cultural and social support system" (Castellanos, "Commentary" 224). As will be seen later, that support system creates its own spiritual and social world through the inculcation and practice of its symbol systems.

Lachatañeré once judged that the santero is neither mystic nor charlatan but "a realistic character with active participation in the life of the community," one who "performs according to the economic uncertainty in which the community lives" (MS 50). Responding to the real problems of the community, the santero is priest, diviner, and healer of the cult. He officiates in the ceremonies of initiation, cleansing, propitiation, and burial; he reads the life condition of the client and the course that his or her future will or should take; he prescribes or obtains the herbs, plants, and other medicines of the *manigua* or "wild" parts of the city and knows how to apply them for a cure (see Lewis 193).

Despite the leadership provided by its santeros, no central authority rules over the Regla de Ocha; as one informant told Cabrera, "We have no Pope!" (YO 130–32). Yet an authority invested in the religious personnel does regulate and order the life of the community. Santeros and babalaos enjoy a high degree of autonomy in interpreting doctrine and guiding practice, and this free individualism does in effect decenter religious practice (RA 48). Members of the society or the particular ilé ocha group will nonetheless recognize a ranking of members according to the degree of their knowledge and their progress through the scale of rituals through which they pass. Julio Sánchez's study of the Afro-Caribbean orisha tradition presents the hierarchical model of the group based on the image of a pyramid. On this pyramid, each ranking of humans is based according to a corresponding ritual stage in the process of acquiring and mastering the arcana of the religion. The model, explains Sánchez, appropriately represents the largest group, that of the nonbelievers, at the lowest of the eleven levels, the pyramid's base. Those possessed of the maximum degree of knowledge and occupying the top of the pyramid are the omókoloba, those of "long experience and prestige" who have been consecrated in Ifá divination and have received the Supreme God Olofi (30). This Lucumí hierarchy of course remits to the authority of the orishas, who together form the transcendental center of the Lucumí sign system.

"Scattered Divinity"

In the Yoruba language, the word orisha was not originally synonymous with the word for deity (ebura) but referred to the more than fifty gods subordinate to the God of Whiteness, Orisanla (Obatalá). The word orisha, González-Wippler proposes, may be traced back to the root ri, meaning "to see" and sha, "to choose." Or, alternatively, to asha, "religious ceremony" (SE 2). The total number of orishas depends on the informant. One Ifá verse collected by Bascom in Nigeria refers to the four hundred deities on the right and the two hundred on the left. García Cortez reports that as few as 201 to as many as 600 have been counted (ID 103–4; P 35).

In Cuba, the orishas are worshipped not only in the Lucumí cult, but also in the Abakuá Society, and conjointly with other, sometimes "overlapping" deities in Regla Arará and Palo Monte. At the heart of Regla de Ocha, the narratives in which the orishas appear as characters form the foundation for beliefs and practices of that religion. It is important to keep in mind that all orishas, in all their incarnations, monistically partake of the divine substance, which is immanent in the very elements of nature: "As Oggún is the hard strength of iron, Ochún is the yielding force of water. Each is a different refraction of Olodumare's aché" (SAS 12).

Whatever their ontological status, the orishas are indeed integral to the Cuban imaginary, manifesting the existence of a sort of social or collective unconscious. The following section is intended to serve as an introduction to the nature and character of the orishas, whose pantheon forms the focus of worship in the Yoruba-Lucumí religious traditions. A few explanatory notes will precede a series of orisha profiles.

In Cuba, one begins to worship all the orishas by first approaching the *Santos de Fundamento* or *Santos de Entrada,* "Saints of Foundation" or "Saints of Entrance": Obatalá, Changó, Yemayá, and Ochún. Of these *santos,* the orishas Changó, Ochún, and Yemayá enjoy the greatest popularity among Cubans and for that reason are fondly known as *Los Niños de la Simpatía,* The Children of Sympathy (MS 29). The orishas collectively known as "las Siete Potencias Africanas"—the Seven African Powers—are Obatalá, Elegguá, Yemayá, Ochún, Changó, Oyá, and Oggún (Canizares 49).

Certain alterations occurred in the names and identities of the orishas as they survived the Middle Passage from Africa to Cuba. In a perceptive study that compares the West African and Cuban pantheons, Cros Sandoval explains that since the artificially formed communities of slaves in Cuba tended to worship all the orishas rather than those of a single family lineage (as noted earlier), the number of orishas declined, from hundreds to around twenty. With this reduction, the more widely known divinities lived on in Cuba, with many of the lesser deities being assimilated into the major ones, the former sometimes becoming caminos of the latter. Such is the case with Obatalá, who absorbed both Obalufon, ancient god of peace and giver of language, and Nana Burukú, the Dahomeyan creation goddess. The local Yoruba gods of rivers, trees, or hills simply did not survive the passage. Due to separation and dispersion of families, neither did the Egungun cult of the ancestors cross intact (RA 122–24).

In Cuba, furthermore, the Yoruba Shango merged with the Kongo Kanbaranguanje, just as he had beforehand among the Yoruba with the god Jakuta (APA 40). To the believer's mind, this merging of gods, added to their syncretization with Catholic saints, presents no distortion of their "true" identities but rather successive variations on the same theme of the caminos, paths, or avatars that the orisha takes up in certain life stages or incarnations. The manner of syncretization may display this successive character even after the orisha's arrival in the Americas. In Brazil, for instance, Changó or Xangó is not Santa Bárbara but San Miguel; Oggún or Ogum is not San Pedro but rather San Jorge (S 134).

The syncretization of orishas with Catholic saints in Cuba effected a transmutation in their personalities as well. It has been noted that the vengeful Babalú-Ayé took on the humility and mercy characteristic of San Lázaro. Oshun, like her sisters Oyá and Oba, owned and inhabited a particular river while in Nigeria, but in Cuba she became the orisha of all fresh waters. Yemayá underwent a similar process in becoming the goddess of the sea or salt waters. Certain of Oyá's qualities were amplified in Cuba, so that she became the goddess and personification of wind, lightning, and the cemetery; Obbá's fluvial association was neutralized in favor of her paragonization as the loyal, self-sacrificing wife (RA 124–25). The Virgen de la Caridad del Cobre, Ochún, became Cuba's patron saint by decree on May 10, 1916, under Pope Benedict XV. She is celebrated on her feast day, September 8, in Santiago de Cuba (YO 56–57; CA 3:50).

Not only did syncretization produce alterations in the identities of individual orishas but it strengthened relations among them to the extent that they came to be regarded as belonging to one family. Changó, for example, became brother to Orúmila, Oggún, and Babalú-Ayé; adoptive son to Yemayá; godson to Osaín. A redistribution of roles also took place between the members of the extended family. In Cuba, Eleggúa sometimes assumes Oggún's role of cutting roads through the forest, and Ochún, instead of Aye Shaluga, becomes the goddess who owns and loves money (RA 125–26; compare Canizares 45).

The series of profiles that follows may serve as a useful vade mecum for quick identifications. Bear in mind that the same profiles will tend to gloss over the numerous caminos or avatars of the orishas, their varying relations with one another, the complexities of their attributes, and the catalogs of their associated herbs and plants. These identifications include only the deities that figure in the works examined in this study and will be discussed in greater detail as appropriate in explications of specific texts. For a more complete account, see Cabrera's El monte, Bolívar Aróstegui's Los orishas en Cuba, and Cros Sandoval's La religión afrocubana—all principal sources of the following discussion.

First among gods, Olorun-Olodumare is the "Great Benefactor," the "Creator." Olorun means "Owner of the Heavens." Olodumare is composed of ol, meaning "owner of," and either ódu, great, or odu, meaning "he who carries the scepter"; mare means immutable, unchanging. In this aspect the Supreme God is regarded as the creator of the universe. One of Olodumare's names, Oba Airi, means "the invisible king who sees and judges all things, is everywhere, but can be seen by no one." He is a wise judge when he has to be: he knows all things and all thoughts and often settles disputes among the subordinate orishas. Omnipotent and eternal, Olodumare on one occasion put down a revolt of the gods by stopping the universe altogether, not setting it back into motion until the defeated divinities agreed to recognize the authority of the Almighty. Another common name of the Supreme Being is *Olofi* or *Olofín*, "the supreme sovereign." As befitting his name, Olodumare governs all that goes on in the natural world, and he dwells immanently in all creation and in all creatures. The orishas are but emanations of Olodumare's aché (RA 102–7; SAS 7–8).

García Cortez, a Cuban babalocha who researched his book *Pataki* in Nigeria, also finds a pantheistic principle in Olodumare: "'The Maintainer of Harmony' maintains the harmony between all living things, not only the already animate, but also the so-called inanimate, for all is a part of the great energy that makes up the universe, for them nothing is dead, death, as such, does not exist. . . . In the rivers, in trees, in rocks, in the seas, in the earth; in everything that surrounds us vibrates the spirit of God" (36). To say it in another way, all creation signifies Olodumare, the transcendental center of centers removed from the "system" of divinities. Often considered too remote and indifferent to concern himself with human affairs, he is invoked but usually not worshipped directly. The Supreme God nonetheless has his own triplicate form, taking on three aspects that correspond to his three names and liken him somewhat to the tripartite Christian God. Olorun is the creator and origin of being; Olodumare seems to represent a more withdrawn will; Olofi, often presented as a character in legend and patakí, personifies of the divine essence in the actively intervening will or law, and many of those narratives depict him as taking an active part in earthly dramas (SR 24–25). He is called *Padre* or *Babá* in Cuba. The Anagó saying *Kosi oba kan afi Olorum* applies to him: "There is no god but Olorum." Olorum or Olorun, Olodumare, Olofi is the only one—yet his energy, grace, personality, and aché flow out into all beings (SAS 8).

According to Cros Sandoval, the abstractness and aloofness of Olodumare, the lack of any cult or priesthood dedicated to the Supreme Being, and the greater accessibility of the orishas all contributed to weakening Olodumare's presence in the New World. The sovereign deity has become more human, shrinking in stature and tending to appear as a tired, gray old man who often finds himself entangled in situations in which he requires assistance from lesser deities. Because Olodumare distributed his aché among all the subordinate deities, his power diminished among the Afro-Cuban believers, who at any rate could more readily communicate with the orishas (RA 108, 111). The orishas embody the force of this Lucumí equivalent of God the Father. Yet they are different from the Father.

The name of *Obatalá* means "King of the White Cloth," and he is the dignified, pure, and just god sent down by Olodumare in the beginning to create the dry land of the earth and to mold the human race out of clay. This primordial Obatalá is Olofi's son, named Orichanla or Obatalá Alafunfún. Owner of the head (*orí*) where spirit dwells, he also owns thought and dreams. His attribute is the white *iruke*, the horsetail switch symbolic of royalty. Obatalá is danced either as a tired old man or as a vigorous young warrior, depending on his camino. He is syncretized with the Virgen de las Mercedes. The origin of human speech is attributed to a very old Obatalá and one of the avatars of Orichanla, the aforementioned Obalufon, "he who gave man the word" (YO 142, 113). In another version of this genesis, Olofi created the first orisha and named him Obatalá. It was Obatalá who created human bodies out of clay but Olofi who breathed life into that clay (CA 3:26). We will return to Orichanla momentarily.

Oddudua is an androgynous god, lord of the underworld who owns solitude and the secrets of death, sometimes appearing as the husband of a female Obatalá and sometimes receiving credit for creating human beings. Jetstone and mother-of-pearl are among Oddudua's attributes; his colors are white, red, and black. In the Catholic Church, Oddudua syncretizes with San Manuel or the Holy Sacrament. All the Yoruba peoples descended from him or her, according to one popular belief (Lloyd 567). Other versions present Oddudua as the female consort of Obatalá. As the first man and the first woman created by Olofi, they are the equivalents of Adam and Eve. Oddudua gave birth to Aganyú and Yemayá, and the latter, violated by her son, gave birth to the fourteen orishas: Changó, Obbá, Ochún, Dada, Olokun, Olosa, Ochosí, Orún, Oggún, Chankpana, Oko, Oke, Oyá, and Aye-Shaluga (CA 3:28, 54; Canet 29).

The myth of Obatalá as *Orishanla* tells a different story of the origins of the orishas, a genesis in conflict and death. Orishanla had "a faithful slave, who cooked his food and looked after him in every way." One day the slave decided to revolt and set an ambuscade for his master in the form of a huge boulder that rolled over and smashed the god. "Orisha was crushed into hundreds of pieces and they were scattered throughout the world." Orúmila goes about the world picking up pieces of the original orisha, putting the fragments he finds into a calabash he calls *Orisha Nla* and installing the calabash in a shrine in the first city, Ile-Ife. The myth concludes: "But hundreds of fragments are still scattered throughout the world today. And this is why Orishanla (i.e., the big *orisha*) is the most important and senior of them all." All "401" original deities owe their being to the same pulverized and scattered archdeity, and the same goes for all the humans, animals, and other creatures: all manifest a bit of this "scattered divinity" in their own being. This genetic myth also explains and facilitates the susceptibility of human believers to "ownership" and "possession" by a particular orisha (YM 6–7, 62–63).

The messenger of the gods, the orisha of thresholds and crossroads, is *Elegguá*, the powerful deity who, after the dead, must be propitiated at the beginning of every ceremony before the ceremony may proceed. The initial greeting and offering made to him at that point constitute small bribes to keep the trickster god from sabotaging the work of the sacrifice. Owner of the "keys of destiny," Elegguá is the one who opens doors and roadways to those who earn his favor (Canizares 48). From the Dahomeyan Elegbará comes Eshú, the originally syncretic incarnation of the Elegguá who, for many in Cuba, doubles the Christian Devil himself. One honors Elegguá first among the orishas by pouring out three spills of water before his image or by spraying out a mouthful of rum spiced with chewed black peppercorns, once tribute has been made to the *egungun* or dead (SE 158–59). The prayer to Elegguá contains the plea, "Accept what we give you separately, be benevolent, we ask you not to obstruct what we do" (YO 143–44n. 117). Elegguá—in Haiti known as Papa Legba or Papa La Bas—is the interpreter of the orishas, hermeneut god or go-between who makes communication between gods and humans possible. In all orisha-centered religion, according to Sánchez, the three Eshús said to be allied with the babalao are called Agunacue, Vivakikeño, and Kikeño Laroye. One of Elegguá's attributes is the hooked tree branch or *garabato*, which he uses to open the way through the wilderness. The knife blade often found encrusted in the top of the orisha's head in busts and statues indicates his prowess as a warrior and his virtue as a "cutter of spiritual paths" (SAS 71). Bascom calls the Yoruba Eshú "the divine enforcer," and Idowu calls Esù a "special relations officer" whose duty it is to visit misfortune upon those who disregard the command of Olodumare, delivered through the Ifá oracle (ID 105; Idowu 80). For Murphy, Elegguá "does resemble the Advocate of the book of Job, restlessly overturning human complacency" (SAS 46, 71). Most Lucumí households have an Elegguá made of earth from a crossroads mixed with concrete, with cowrie shells for eyes and mouth, who sits right behind the door that opens to the street. This Elegguá requires regular presents of pastries, the herbal omiero water, sweets, and tobacco. He also likes plums. In his Catholic syncretization he is the Niño (or Christ child) de Antocha, San Antonio de Padua, and the *Anima Sola*, the Wandering Soul in Pain. His day is Tuesday; his colors are red and black; his sacred number three (CA 3:29).

Agallú or *Aganyú Solá* is a giant, the owner of the river and the plain, and, like his (now discredited) Catholic counterpart Christopher, the patron saint of Havana, he is patron of travelers and friend of children, depicted iconographically as carrying a child on his shoulder across a river on his shoulder. By some accounts he fathered Changó and like his son claims the phallic *oché* or two-headed hatchet among his attributes, along with the *oggué* or calf's horns. "Agallú," according to Núñez, "dances with large strides, lifting up his legs as if he were getting over obstacles, and picking up children and carrying them away" (DALC 15).

Yemayá is goddess of salt waters and maternity, the Great Supernal Mother. She loves children and has adopted many. Her color is the blue associated with the sea, and her dance imitates the fluctuating movement of the waves. Yemayá likes to eat maize, pigeon, cock, and castrated he-goat. She carries a sword and a fan as her insignia. A marine shell serves as her fetish. Yemayá is syncretized with the Virgen de Regla, patron saint of the Bay of Havana. "The stars," writes Cabrera, "are the jewels of Yemayá's mantle," and according to one of Cabrera's informants, Yemayá is "the Blessed Mother and the Wet Nurse of the World" (YO 116, 121).

As mentioned earlier, the same goddess gave birth to all the orishas and to the sun and moon as well. Notes Cabrera in *Yemayá y Ochún*, it is this Yemayá, known widely in Cuba as Yemú, whom Oggún violated, thus committing incest with his own mother (25). Yemayá makes an androgynous appearance when she is seen cutting through the thicket with her machete: "In this path she is mannish [*marimacho*] and dresses as a man." She transforms into a man another time when she fights alongside Changó, for she is "an *Obini ologún*, a woman who knows how to fight like a soldier." In one of her oldest aspects, Yemayá is a mermaid, a *sirena*: "she has pearly scales from the waist on down, fishtail, white bulging eyes, round and very open, 'the pupils black, eyebrows like thorns and the bosoms very large.'" Yet for all the goddess's multiplicity, Cabrera's informant reminds us, "there is no more than one Yemayá. A single one with seven paths" (YO 23, 45, 31, 30).

Olokun, called the most ancient avatar of Yemayá, is the amphibious, androgynous denizen of the deep waters. Cabrera in *Yemayá y Ochún* calls Olokun an androgynous god: *okobo*—"[o]f amphibious sex." As Cabrera's informant Omí Dina explains, "Fundamentally [Olokun] is male. So you say El Mar.

5. Ritual setting and attributes of Olokun. 1991. Museo de Regla, Old Havana, Cuba.

And female, *La Mar*, in other aspects. Therefore, when you enter the sea you should say, Papá, Mamá, Yemayá-Olokun." Half human and half fish, Olokun dwells on the ocean bottom, "next to a gigantic marine serpent that they say shows its head during the new moon." It is to Yemayá-Olokun that one makes tributary offerings of seven centavos when crossing the Bay of Havana by ferry. Animal sacrifices to the androgynous deity are also placed in the sea (YO 28, 26, 18). And s/he is considered magnificently rich in this aspect, for s/he owns all the sea's treasures. Murphy identifies Olokun as "the orisha of the sea depths who protected [the Afro-Cubans'] ancestors on their terrible journey from Africa to the New World" (SAS 2).

Fire and thunder are the possessions of the virile *Changó*. He is a womanizer, probably the most popular of orishas in Cuba, and the passionate fiesta-loving warrior god of storms who gives license to his "children" to do what feels good. The neolithic hatchets called *piedras celestes* or *piedras de rayo*, "thunder stones," are thought to belong to Changó and adorn the altars of Arará and Lucumí alike (M 249). Handsome and seductive, Changó wears bright red (*punzó*) and white, especially on a sacred garment called *banté*, which resembles an apron. Changó's other attributes are the sword and cup. Changó gladly accepts sacrifices of *ayapá* or tortoise, *quimbombó* or stewed okra, *akara* or bean fritters, and *eco* or cornstarch gruel (Simpson 87).

In ceremonies dedicated to him, Changó is said to sit atop a sacred mortar-stool carved out of wood, the *pilón*. His Catholic double is Santa Bárbara not only because she is the patroness of artillerymen but also because the orisha in some accounts had to disguise himself in woman's clothing loaned him by Oyá in order to escape his enemies. No one plays the drum in the güemilere or drum party better than Changó, who traded the Board of Ifá with Orúmila for the ability to play and dance. Changó has an almost obsessive fear of death, the Ikú, and for that reason Oyá could defeat him on one occasion by frightening him with a human skull (S 111; CA 3:44). Yoruba myth frequently contrasts the passionate Changó with the cool-headed, pacific, and good-natured Obatalá, the artisan of the human species. One well-known myth, restaged in the play by Ijimere, tells of how Changó as the Oni of Oyo, due to the machinations of Eshú, wrongfully imprisoned Obatalá, the wise king of Ife, for the apparent theft of Changó's favorite horse.

Obbá symbolizes marital devotion and fidelity. She is considered a minor orisha, associated with a river in Nigeria. Cabrera among others presents a version of the patakí in which Obbá prepares a special kalalú, a vegetable stew also called amalú in Anagó, for her husband Changó. This amalú is special because Ochún has fooled Obbá into cutting off her own ears and adding them to the stew, claiming that this is the way to "bind" (amarrar) her philandering husband (YO 79–80). Obbá is accordingly portrayed as wearing a scarf or cloth on her head to hide her mutilation. Her attributes include a wooden anvil adorned with implements—and the ear. Her colors are pink and yellow. With Oyá and Yewá, she guards the cemetery. In the Catholic Church, she is Santa Rita and/or Santa Catalina (CA 3:48).

The warrior goddess Oyá consorts with Changó and often fights at his side. In addition to the cemetery, she owns the lightning and the wind. As Changó's female companion and another of the climatological orishas, Oyá like Changó has been known to have lightning shooting out of her mouth. She dances in a frenzy, waving the iruke, the horsetail switch that is her attribute, whirling about with her colorful skirt ends flying. She is identified with the Catholic Virgen de Candelaria and also, in some locales, with Santa Teresa (APA 171–74).

Ochún has been called the Yoruba Aphrodite: goddess of the Oshun river in West Africa and sister to Yemayá, in Cuba she owns the fresh waters, beauty, love, and sexual desire. Cabrera in Yemayá y Ochún writes that Ochún is "the Lover, the personification of sensuality and love, of the force that drives the gods and all creatures to seek out one another and to unite with one another in pleasure" (89). Coquettish, seductive, irresistible, she gives her love freely, often to other women's husbands, capriciously taking it away. Her attributes include mirrors and coral. She loves honey, pastries, and cala-

6. "Obbá." Oil on canvas, 1991. Collection of María Antonia Carrillo, Old Havana, Cuba.

bash. She also owns *albahaca*, or basil, which is used in many magical and medicinal mixes. Her color is yellow; her number five, and five are the diaphanous scarves she wears around her waist. Ochún is considered to be Changó's favorite *apétedvi* or concubine. In the Catholic Church, look for her in the Virgen de la Caridad del Cobre, patron saint of Santiago and all of Cuba. The *omo-Ochún* or child of the goddess prepares for her a favorite dish called *ochinchín*, made from shrimp, watercress, and almonds. Other favorite foods include she-goat, fish, hen, and beans. The otanes of Ochún are the smooth round stones of riverbeds. She also likes small bells (FS 79–81; CA 3:50–53).

Inle, Ile, or Erinle is the nature god who hunts, farms, fishes in rivers and dispenses medicine; he knows the sciences of extracting the bounty of the earth and even symbolizes the earth itself for some. Because he spends six months of the year in the water and the other six on land, Bastide calls Inle a "double deity" (117). Yellow and blue are his colors. His Catholic equivalent is San Rafael. He is danced with the zigzag motion of one who harvests a crop.

Cabrera tells the story of how one day Yemayá conceived a wild passion for the amphibious Inle. She abducted the youth and brought him down to the depth of the sea, where she made love to him to the point of weariness. Desiring to return to the world and to the company of the other orishas, Yemayá abandoned Inle but not without eliminating one problem her passion had created: since Inle had learned secrets both earthly and divine, she cut out his tongue. "Note that it is Yemayá who speaks through Inle in the Diloggún" (YO 45). His pataki bears certain similarities to the Greek myth of Endymion.

The orisha of hunters and the hunt, *Ochosí* is the archer whose attribute is a metal bow and arrow and who, as one of the "warriors," is said to "walk" with Elegguá and Oggún. In Catholicism, this forest spirit corresponds to San Norberto. When he dances, he carries his weapons and moves like a hunter after his game. That creolization modified the pataki was evident when the runaway slaves, who "went for the mountain," invoked him for their protection from recapture or imprisonment (P 17–18). Barnet writes that the popular expression "to have the letter of Ochosí" means "to be on the way to jail, or that some problem with justice approaches the believer." The metal bow and arrow charm, often worn in necklace chains, thus signals Ochosí's desire for justice (FV 182).

Orisha-Oko is the orisha of farming and agriculture, the normally chaste and hardworking god whom Obatalá commissioned to cultivate yams. Yet Yemayá seduced Orisha-Oko one day in order to procure the secret of the yams from the ingenuous youth. Of Orisha-Oko's starchy tuber, which is

7. Attributes of Oggún: rake, spike, shovel, and other iron implements. 1991. Old Havana, Cuba.

considered sacred, Cabrera reports, "it speaks at night and makes sleepers talk in their sleep" (YO 37). A pair of oxen pulling a plow symbolize this orisha, to whom one would offer sacrifice to ensure a good harvest. Orisha-Oko's Catholic double is San Isidro Labrador, but his cult fell off early in Cuba because the first harvests of Cuban agriculture were undeniably the bitter fruits of slave labor (CA 3:61–62).

One-legged and one-eyed Osaín or Osanyin is the Lord of the Forests, typically depicted as hopping on his one foot. He is called ñoco, one-armed. He has one overlarge ear that is deaf and one tiny ear that hears acutely well. Symbolizing the forces of vegetation, his color is naturally green. To this god of medicines, patron of the curanderos (healers) called osainistas, one must render tribute before taking away any of his plants and herbs, essential ingredients in the ebbós and cures of Regla de Ocha. Osaín loves to smoke, and this habit compels him to appear at night before travelers, asking them for a light.

One story explaining Osaín's mutilations has it that Changó, angered at Osaín's attempts to violate Oyá, blasted him with a lightning bolt, destroying one of his eyes, one of his ears, one of his arms, and one of his legs. In another version of the myth, Orúmila has just learned from Changó the preparation of an ebbó using twelve torches and twelve odduarás, or flintstones, resulting in a lightning flash that sets fire to the woods. Osaín is burned and maimed in the conflagration. Thus originates the continuing enmity between the god of the forest and the god of lightning (SE 94).

Oggún is orisha of metals, mountain, and forge; a mighty warrior, another rival to Changó, and sometime archdenizen of the forest. He was originally associated with the town of Badagri situated near the mouth of the Ogoun River on the Nigerian coast. Called Ogun in Nigeria, Papa Ogoun in Haiti, and Oggún in Cuba, he is doubled by the Catholic Santiago or Saint James the Elder. Although revered as a patron by some West African hunters, in Cuba he receives more recognition as the archetypal blacksmith. Like Changó, his brother and rival in arms, Oggún likes to wear the color red and loves to eat red cocks and red beans with rice. All keys and chains belong to him, which explains his alternative syncretization with San Pedro as the heavenly gatekeeper. A machete, brandished in his dance, also symbolizes him. The fundamentos of Oggún's asiento consist of miniature iron implements kept in a small cauldron: a rake, a sledge, a sword, a pick, a hoe, a machete, a pike, a spade.

Babalú-Ayé is the crippled orisha who, like Lazarus, his Catholic double, goes limping about on a crutch, accompanied by a pair of dogs who lick his open wounds. Babalú-Ayé is owner of epidemics and diseases, especially skin

8. Ritual setting and attributes of Babalú-Ayé. 1991. Museo de Regla, Old Havana, Cuba.

diseases like smallpox and leprosy, and his own skin is broken out in pustules. Afraid of flies, he both infects with disease and cures it. The *ajá* is his attribute, a bundle of coconut or corojo palm sticks. The Yoruba-Lucumí Babalú-Ayé derives from the Dahomeyan Chankpana or Shonpona, called by the Yoruba honorific *Obaluaiye*: "the king who hurts the world" (YM 45). Desi Arnez, it will be recalled, made the Afro-Cuban name internationally famous when he sang "Babalú" on the television comedy *I Love Lucy*. In Lucumí ceremony, when Babalú-Ayú comes down to possess, his omo-orisha is wont to start licking the wounds of the sick. Embodied in such human guise, he wears a placard around his neck warning others of his illness.

One prays to Babalú-Ayé, the diseased and ragged one whom Jesus resurrected, for protection against disease and want. In diloggún divination he speaks through the odu configurations Iroso (four mouths up), Ojuani (eleven), and Metanlá (thirteen). The god has many caminos or avatars and numerous genealogies. Due to the absence of smallpox and other serious epidemics in Cuba, and because his image mellowed somewhat through his syncretization with the other Lazarus who came to be the Bishop of Marseilles, Babalú-Ayé took on a more benign and gentle aspect than he had among the Yorubas (OC 142–46).

The *Ibeyi* are the mystical twin children, *jimaguas*, of Ochún and Changó. In myth they live in the palm tree, often keeping company there as elsewhere with their prodigal father. As in the typical Yoruba fetishization of twins, the Ibeyi or Obeyi symbolize immortality and bring good fortune, perhaps by their metaphorical doubling of human life (DALC 239). Cuervo Hewitt emphasizes their symmetrical symbolism of cosmic order, balance, and harmony. Yemayá is said to adopt "the twins of Heaven" as her wards or grandchildren. The Kaínde and Taewo of Lucumí myth are equivalents to the gemini Castor and Pollux, the Catholic Cosme and Damián, and the Marassas of Vaudou. Their fetish is a pair of hollow wooden dolls that are often painted black, dressed in Chango's red, and connected by a cord representing the umbilicus. Inside the hollows of their dolls, devotees put such aché-charged particulars as human hair and nails, bones, dust, needles, and stones. The typically cheerful twins are wise beyond their years but love sweets and mischief (APA 182, 248).

Orúmila or Orúnmila or Orúmbila is the owner and master of Ifá, the Yoruba oracle and divination system, and therefore considered patron of babalaos. Idowu writes that the name of Orunmìlà is the contracted form of Orun-l'-o-mo-à-ti-là: "Only Heaven knows the means of salvation" (75). Also called "Ifá," perhaps by metonymy, Orúmila is the mediator between humans and gods: purveyor of wisdom, reader of destiny and prescriber of sacrifices necessary for solving problems or achieving aims. Called Kisimba in Kikongo, he is syncretized with Saint Francis of Assisi or San Francisco, most likely because the ekpuelé or Yoruba divining chain resembles the rosary of the Catholic saint. The beads in his eleke necklace are green and yellow and his attribute is the Tablero or Tabla de Ifá, the divining board that symbolizes the world. In the liturgical calendar, the date of the orisha's remembrance falls on October 4, on which day it is appropriate to utter, Maferere Orúmila, "Thanks be to Ifá" (S 52; CA 3:38–39).

The centrality of divination in Afro-Cuban religion explains the importance of Orúmila's figure throughout the narrative tradition. According to the myth recorded by Abimbola, Olodumare sent Orúmila "to use his profound wisdom to put the earth in order" (Ifá 9). Members of Lucumí society consult Ifá at the outset of every major event in their lives. At the birth of a child, Ifá will identify that child's orisha, his or her future prospects and problems, and the steps the parents should take to bring aché and good fortune to the child. Ifá can also extend advice on finding a partner, on undertaking a journey, or on making decisions at all the critical junctures. Abimbola characterizes Ifá's knowledge as that which gives order to everything: "Without Ifá, the importance of the other Yoruba gods would diminish. If a man is being punished by the other gods, he can only know this by consulting Ifá. If a community is to make sacrifice to one of its gods, it can only know this by consulting Ifá. So that in this way, Ifá is the only active mouthpiece of Yoruba traditional religion taken as a whole. As a mouthpiece, Ifá serves to popularize the other Yoruba gods; he serves to immortalize them" (Abimbola, *Ifá* 3–4). As in all Afro-Cuban religions, the practices of sacrifice, initiation, and possession depend on divination for instructions on proper procedure and prayer. Orúmila thus mediates between gods and humans and between humans and their ancestors. With his ally Eshú-Elegguá to enforce the divine will, Orúmila and his followers are considered the interpreters of that will for all intents and purposes. Yet the Ifá system is not the sole source of counsel, for at least another system of divination, the diloggún, is considered the more popular and accessible oracle in Afro-Cuba. I will discuss this oracle after examining the Lucumí rituals of initiation and burial of the dead.

Initiation

The diviner, through casting the Ifá necklace or diloggún shells, may determine if a client should be initiated. That is, the client's personal *eledá* or orisha guardian, may require initiation or the diviner may prescribe it as the cure for a chronic illness. Initiation, a measure not taken by the majority of devotees, would also be the first step toward priesthood (TOM 2).

To become initiated, the neophyte or *iyawó* must in fact pass a series of initiations culminating in the ritual called the *asiento*. The following summary outline of the complex initiation process will serve as an introduction to a ceremony that Castellanos and Castellanos, after Van Gennep and Turner, have rightly described as "liminal" insofar as its rites signify a passage through transitional stages or "thresholds" (CA 3:91).

The initiation consists of about a week of prayer, sacrifice, and other rituals. During a period of intensive training, the *iyawó* or novice is placed under the care of the *padrino* or *madrina* (godfather or godmother), who isolates the iyawó from the outside world, dresses him or her in white, and teaches the novice the mythology, doctrine, and rituals of the cult. The rituals that follow in the preparatory stage, together with the indoctrination, prepare the mind and body of the iyawó for eventual possession in the state of trance by the orisha. The asiento rituals, or the initiation ceremonies proper, conclude the weeklong preparation.

The asiento, which "makes the saint," is held inside the igbodu or inner sanctuary of the ile ocha temple. For this the iyawó's head is shaved, and on it the madrina paints concentric circles of yellow, blue, red, and white dye—

an invitation for the orisha to come in. The padrino or madrina takes care to save the hair and remnants of the dye so that they may one day be buried with the initiate after his or her death (S 36). Before undergoing the actual asiento, the novice receives a *revocación de cabeza*, a ritual cleansing of the head. In the revocación, the madrina anoints the novice's head with a paste made with coconut pulp, coconut butter, and cascarilla (powdered eggshell), and she calls on the novice's protecting orisha, also called *ángel de la guardia*, to purify and protect the neophyte from evil. The padrino or madrina then gives the iyawó a name in the faith, a baptismal gesture in recognition of putting on the iyawó's "rebirth." Next comes the ceremony of the eleke necklaces, the *imposición de los collares*. The iyawó receives these elekes in the colors of the orishas Obatalá, Ochún, Yemayá, and Changó, in addition to those of his or her special protector, the aforementioned ángel de la guarda or eledá. Next, the iyawó receives the *guerreros*, the warriors Oggún, Elegguá, Ochosí, and Osun, manifested by their attributes and their necklaces in their characteristic colors (TOM 2–3).

On the third day of the asiento, as explained by Cabrera, the diloggún shells are consulted in the meeting of babalaos called the *itá*, which will serve to inform the novice about the past and the future as well as about dangers to guard against. In this context, the diloggún ritual begins with the babalocha or iyalocha requesting permission and blessings from Olodumare; then he or she greets (*ayuba* or *moyubba*) first the dead and then the padrinos. The sign of sixteen cowries with their mouths turned up, if it appears, will indicate that the iyawó will become a diviner and thus receive the otanes or stones of all the orishas, begin apprenticeship in the Ifá, and learn the secrets of Osaín and *ewe*, herbs and plants (YO 179, 184).

The day called the *ka ri ocha* ("putting the orisha upon the head") or *lerí ocha* ("crowning the orisha") is a birth day, the day the iyawó, if the preceding ceremonies have gone well, dies to the old life and person and is born into a new life in the saints. The ritual bathing, changes of clothing, isolation, and other treatments suggestive of birth or infantilism on the part of the iyawó have indicated that this ceremony is indeed a liminal rite of passage. The novice then passes into the new life of the omo-orisha or child of the orisha once, or if, possession takes place. In possession, the initiate, "mounted" by the orisha, or "making" the saint, will also become the orisha's "horse" (*caballo*) and act, dance, talk, and otherwise move in the manner characteristic of the possessing orisha. Orisha and iyawó are also said to form a contract in the asiento. The term *asiento* itself proceeds from the language of jurisprudence and the history of the conquest; one of Cabrera's informants recalls its special meaning of "annotation of a shipment, entered so it isn't forgotten." The obligation suggests mutuality, for it is by serving the orishas that the omo-orisha benefits, living by the words "to worship is to give in order to receive" (YO 128). The asiento is therefore also a settling, a stabilizing and seating of another "consciousness" into one's own, and the marking of a penetration into the mysteries of the cult (SAS 16).

At the end of the initiation rituals, the novice finishes by gathering the attributes and paraphernalia of his orishas, thus performing the act called "levantar santo" (raising or gathering up the saint), and then goes home to add those sacred objects to his or her domestic altar. One year and seven days after the asiento, the sponsoring madrina or padrino will pass on the libreta or notebook, where information essential to practice the religion has been noted down, to the iyawó (SR 16).

As previously mentioned, not all believers in Regla de Ocha are initiated, but initiation is a mark of seriousness about the religion. Some initiations can be very costly if the sponsors command a high esteem in the community and if expensive animals such as sheep or bulls are required for sacrifice. (Cros Sandoval reports that the "initiation cost" in the United States, due to these factors, "might fluctuate from a modest $3,000 to $6,000 or more" [TOM 2]).

Ituto: Passage into Death

Among the Yoruba, death marks the beginning of a journey into another life (Idowu 190). Afro-Cubans continue the Yoruba ritual of ituto, which amounts to a send-off ensuring the comfort and well-being of the deceased on that journey.

To give an idea of the funeral rites identified with the Regla de Ocha, I will summarize the mortuary ritual of one kind of ituto, the burial of a babalao, as Gabriel Pasos described it to Lourdes López (López, Estudio 42–45). On the day of his funeral, in the house where he lived, the deceased is dressed in the clothing and beads of his kariocha, for as he entered this life in the faith, so shall he leave it. The babalao in charge of the ituto sits upon a mat and produces nineteen ikines or palm nuts, removing three of them to stand as "witnesses" and going on to perform a registro or divination reading with the remaining sixteen. The reading gives information and instructions concerning the funeral of the deceased babalao. Then, to mark the passage through the threshold separating this world from the next, the presiding priest either breaks the warriors—Elegguá, Oggún, Ochosí, and Osun—that the babalao received as an iyawó in his initiation or keeps those warriors with other artifacts for burial with the body of the deceased. A cleansing ceremony or limpieza follows, which includes an aspersion with dried okra and poplar leaves. Animals are then offered in sacrifice: a rooster goes to feed the four warriors, but first it is passed over the body of the deceased to remove—*despojar*—any evil influences remaining there. Two hens go to feed the stones in Orúmila's sopera or tureen, but after the hens are killed, the nineteen palm nuts from the divination ritual are inserted through the anus of one of the hens. The two hens are placed in the sopera, and this, with its voluminous contents, is placed behind the body of the deceased, to be emptied into his grave just before he is buried. Another procedure, notes Sánchez, is to "erase," *borrar*, from the head of the deceased what was put there in the asiento; another is that of combing his head with the comb from the same initiation and dressing him in the same clothes he wore in the beginning of his life in the religion (139).

Once purification and the final dressing have been carried out, the babalaos in attendance light sixteen candles, place them around the corpse, and walk around it, intoning the special funeral chant. The leader then sacrifices a dove and extinguishes the candles with its blood. All participants rap on the coffin in a rhythm with three beats and a pause. The obí or coconut divination is performed to inquire if anything else needs be done. Before the coffin is closed for the last time, the deceased is placed inside with the dove, the candles, and the coconut pieces used in the ceremony, alongside the personal artifacts of the deceased, should the divination indicate that these be included. The deceased's eledá, now made tranquil, can go to render accounts to Olodumare (López 45).

Divination and Narrative: The Diloggún

As the preceding accounts of the asiento and ituto illustrate, the myth, ritual, doctrine, institutional codes, and experience of Lucumí religion have entered literature in recodified form as narrative texts, constituting new transculturations and reinterpretations of the Afro-Cuban tradition. Other, more literary texts that recodify the texts of Lucumí religion, as readings in subsequent chapters will demonstrate, often draw on Santería's body of sacred or mythical narratives containing etiological, cosmogonic, and moral messages. To understand the uses of those sacred narratives, it is essential to know the place and function of divination in Afro-Cuban religion since divination consists in a practice of a narrative-based knowledge that mediates between earth (*aiye*) and heaven (*orun*).

In pragmatic terms, divination offers counsel and guidance to believers, who consult it at all critical transitions in the life cycle. Of the three principal methods of divination practiced in Cuba—the coconut or obí, the sixteen cowries or diloggún, and Ifá—the third one, Ifá, which only babalaos are permitted to practice, seems the most prestigious. Barnet, comparing it with the other two, calls it an oracle of "greater rank but not of greater efficacity" (FV 173). The obí, on the other hand, can be practiced by all believers and the diloggún by all santeros and santeras.

The divination narratives called patakís, also called historias (stories, narratives) or caminos (paths or roads), are recited or at least recalled during the diloggún and Ifá ceremonies. The system of patakís preserves and organizes the bases of Afro-Cuban religious practice; the babalao Julio García Cortez assures that "the root of conduct" is found in the patakís (ES 137). Versions of patakís have been collected and published by García Cortez, Cabrera, Rogers, Cros Sandoval, de la Soledad and Sanjuan, González-Wippler, and Castellanos and Castellanos. Collections of patakís—in texts that now have served as guidebooks to the method of the oracle—afford a unique opportunity to see how the narratives of an Afro-Cuban divination corpus function in the production of counsel and knowledge.[2] In the following I will outline an isagogic, or an introduction to exegesis, of the diloggún ritual and narratives, drawing on examples from the above mentioned writers. My thesis here is that the texts of the diloggún not only preserve the narrative discourses central to the oracle, but they participate in a specific kind of intertextual activity. Even when the diviner recalls preformed interpretations attaching to indicated figures and narratives, divination consists in the diviner's reading of a destiny into the gaps between texts, signs, and symbolic acts that together constitute the divination event.

For Jules-Rosette, whose commentary suggests a useful frame of reference, African divination in general is a self-validating system of thought offering "strategies for handling problems in daily life" and which therefore must be understood as mediating between the client's misfortunes and the social structure (551, 557). Similarly in Afro-Cuba, the oracles are consulted not only during initiations and other important ceremonies, as noted in my preceding accounts of the asiento and the ituto rituals, but on every important occasion involving crisis or transition in the client's life (see ISD 5–9, 111–15).

As a self-validating system, divination is an art of producing significations for making sense of life; in other words, divination is an art that, as Pierre Guiraud states in his study of semiology, "projects upon the signified universe the shadow of its own structure" (82). As interpretive revision and verbal performance, divination consists not so much in "seeing into the future" as in inscribing, reading, and rewriting the signs of a futurity imbricated with the present—that is, a present re-presented by the signs of the oracle. In ritual practice, divination involves recalling and reinterpreting the prayers, proverbs, and patakís that make up the intertexts of the diloggún ritual. Narrative knowledge on which the ceremony depends is therefore not fixed into a static structure but rather continually reproduced in the divination ceremony.

The ceremonial art of the diloggún is known by several names: *echarse los caracoles*, "casting the shells" (the word *caracol* having this sense in Cuba); *hacerse una vista*, or, roughly, "taking a look"; *registrarse*, meaning "register" or "search"; and *bajar el caracol*, casting (or dropping) the shells. The shells are also called *elifás* (MS 60; ISD 13).

Perhaps because it is more commonly used in the Americas than Ifá, the diloggún, rather than the Ifá practiced exclusively by the babalaos, tends more often to provide the Afro-Cubanist writer with ritual narrative sources. Bascom attributes the diloggún's greater popularity in the Americas to several factors: to its greater simplicity, to the popularity of such orishas who are associated with the diloggún as Changó, Yemayá, and Ochún, and to the fact that both men and women can practice sixteen cowrie divination (SC 3).

There are in fact eighteen or twenty-one shells included in the whole divination set, but two shells, called *adele* or *edele*, are separated from the sixteen actually thrown in the divination procedure, and those two are assigned the task of "keeping guard" and watching over the session. The sixteen shells that are cast form the centerpiece of the *registro* or consultation. Each shell is the *boca del santo*, "mouth of the saint," through which the orishas speak (de la Soledad and Sanjuan 96). The cowrie shells, of the species *Cyprea moneta*, have themselves been opened and filed down on their backsides so that they will lay flat when their "mouths," the dentated natural openings, are turned upward. Such shells are also called *ayé*, a name translated as "contestón" or "ser de otro mundo," suggesting that they answer from another world. As befitting their use and value, the diloggún shells are washed with omiero and fed with omiero and sacrificial blood (Cabrera, YO 181; Rogers 4–9, 11).

With each throw of the sixteen shells, it is the number of shells with their mouthlike "speaking" side facing up that determines the figure—*odu* or *letra*—of the cast. Cabrera defines *odu* as "'The siblings of Orúmila' . . . Sign or situation of the shells and seeds in divination" (AVL 236). For Canet, "the sixteen original odus correspond to the first sixteen narratives told to Ifá" (57). Each odu figure corresponds to a particular set of patakís (somewhat as a book title heads its chapters) along with the set of associated proverbs, ebbó (or magic-sacrificial formulas), and orisha names. Each odu moreover bears its own proper name, which is often the name of a character appearing in some of its patakís.

In the following list of odu names, each one corresponding to a number of cowries with their mouths up, the first column comes from González-Wippler; the second, from García Cortez; the third, from Cabrera (ISD 17; ES 139; KI 48ff.). The names in the three columns also exemplify some of the variations found in spelling and pronunciation of the odu names.

1. Okana Sodde	Ocana	Okana
2. Eyioko	Eyioko	Eyioko
3. Oggunda	Ogunda	Ogunda
4. Eyorosun or Iroso	Ollorozun	Eyorosun
5. Oche	Oche	Oche
6. Obbara	Obara	Obara
7. Oddi	Ordi	Odi
8. Eyeunle	Elleunle	Eyeúnle
9. Ossa	Osa	Osa
10. Offun mafun	Ofun mafun	Ofún
11. Ojuani chober	Ojuani Chober	Ojuani
12. Eyila chebora	Ellila chebora	Eyilá
13. Metanla	Metanla	Metala
14. Merinla	Merinla	Merinla
15. Manunla	Marula	Manula
16. Mediloggun	Medilogun	Meridilogún

It should be noted that the odu with numbers higher than that of Eyila chebora (twelve) are not normally read by diviners who are ranked lower than the babalao. When figures thirteen through sixteen appear, the diloggún remains silent, and the client may be sent to Ifá for further consultation. The more experienced *oriaté* or *italero* priest presiding over initiation ceremonies may however read off the odus above twelve by referring to the odu, along with corresponding texts, from which the former are derived or "born" (ISD 17).

The diviner's paraphernalia supporting the sixteen cowrie shells includes the five tokens known collectively and individually as *igbo*. The igbo-supplements are called *otá, ayé, ewé ayó, ero aworan,* and *efún*; they are, respectively, a small black stone, a white shell, a seed, a doll's head, and a piece of *cascarilla* or pulverized egg shell. Prior to each casting, the diviner gives the client the stone and the cascarilla to hold, one in each hand. After casting, the diviner asks to see the token in one of the hands, and that particular igbo will decide the direction of the oracle's message (YO 181–82; Rogers 11–12; CA 3:118–19; ISD 83, 154).

Having surveyed the procedure of the diloggún ritual, we now turn to the function of the patakís in the system. The patakís of the oracle fulfill their role as the textual grounding of diagnosis and prognostication. A number of writers on the diloggún observe that the babalocha or iyalocha reads into the pataki narratives a certain comparison with events in the life of the divination client. Canet refers to the santero's procedure of comparing the odu's narrative with "what's happening" (37). García Cortez remarks on the uncanny correspondence of the narrative with the client's personality and situation (ES 137–38). For Rogers, the letra selects a "mythology": "its story always compares the character of the other world with that of this one" (18). The diviner, writes Cros Sandoval, must know these narratives by memory and "should be capable of choosing that one that relates best to the life and problem of the client" (RA 82). De la Soledad and Sanjuan underscore as well the method of comparison in a passage in which the authors liken the letra, or the pataki itself, to "a fable that also has a moral, [to] these mythological stories that compare the characters of that other world with this one, or that place the consultant in [the role of] protagonist of these stories assuring them, through the same, of the response that they seek in life" (98). Much of the registro thus consists in a personalizing interpretation of the pataki, focusing on the narrative's semantic level, making the client over into the character of a new narrative. González-Wippler confirms the unique character of each reading as determined by the particular odu interpretation: "Each individual interpreter adds his own definitions as he desciphers [sic] the oracle, but the meanings given here form the basis of the registro." In addition, the "interpretations given here do not apply to every consultant, and it is up to the santero and his understanding of the odu to determine which of the admonitions attached to a pattern apply to his client" (ISD 44). The authority of that interpretation is premised on the idea that the diloggún enables the diviner to read the destiny that the client, and/or the client's ancestor, chose before birth; the oracle does so by putting the diviner in touch with the client's ancestral guardian soul, called the eledá (Rogers 18, 22). In carrying out the sacrifice or ebbó prescribed in the recited narrative, the client cannot change his or her destiny in any fundamental way, but the client can make the best of the situation by increasing the probability of receiving possible benefits (such as long life, money, marriage, children, etc.)

or by averting anticipated evils (such as fighting, sickness, death, want of money, etc.) (SC 8, 33–34).

González-Wippler elsewhere calls the patakís "aids in the interpretation of the oracle" and "a philosophical explanation of various natural laws in parable form," for they "explain why things are the way they are and what is likely to happen according to the immutable cosmic laws" (TO 121). The narratives indeed fit into the generic category of the fable or the parable; that is, into the genre of stories of didactic intent with either an ethical message or an etiological explanation of natural phenomena. Often, though not always, an odu will convey the tale of one or more particular orishas. Other characters may be kings or anthropomorphized animals and plants that play major or secondary roles in the narrative. All these characters belong to a mythical "past" that mirrors the client's present and foreshadows the client's future. The diviner and the knowing client will therefore search out in the mythical stories a precedent that would clarify the problem and guide future conduct. Significantly, the plot of the pataki often involves the protagonist's consultation with a diviner.

The pataki's protensive social drama is framed within the three-part structure common to all the Yoruba *ese Ifá* and the Afro-Cuban pataki. In both narratives, one usually finds the following: a statement of the mythological case precedent, naming diviner(s), client(s), and problem; the outcome of carrying out (or of not carrying out) the prescribed sacrifice, often with an explanation of what remained obscure in the first part; and an application of the exemplum to the present client's situation, that is, the diviner's interpretation of the data for the client (see ID 122–27).

In the Americas, published Afro-Cubanist versions of sacred narratives often provide the "pre-texts" or scripts for ritual recitation. In many cases, those narratives include not only transcriptions from verbal performance but rather genuine rewritings. Due to the obstacles to sustaining long apprenticeships in the art in the Americas, those learning to read the diloggún will commit narrative materials to writing: the myths, rituals, prayers, ebbó, and other liturgical texts go into the aforementioned notebooks called libretas (CA 3:95–96). In the multigeneric format of the libretas, the same materials undergo a textual syncretization, with new juxtapositions, combinations, and valorizations. The patakís, unlike the more stable ese Ifá, learned by lengthy oral transmission in Yoruba society, become more personalized and more concise by this process of individualized recording. Cuervo Hewitt attests that "of the manuscript or copybooks of patakís I have seen, one sees in America a tendency to synthesize the most important elements of each odu in very short anecdotes, with which one loses perhaps the original ese, but on the other hand gains the dynamic vitality of the myth-poetry in a collective, colloquial, and archetypal language of the Cuban people" (APA 77). Having survived the African diaspora, reincorporated in the libretas, the ese of Ifá or the patakís of the diloggún are thereby simplified and reduced down to their narrative prose core. The libreta becomes a practical bible and breviary for the Afro-Cuban believer. Andrés Rogers's practical guide Los caracoles: historia de sus letras (The seashells: story of their letters; 2nd ed., 1973) has the look of a long, well-researched libreta, one that seems to maintain the colloquial expressions, idiosyncratic spellings, run-on sentences, and other ungrammaticalities that could characterize both an awó's (diviner's) speech and the initiate's writing in a private libreta.

Another significant divergence between the African mèríndínlógún and the Afro-Cuban diloggún can be seen in previously mentioned matters of performance. In Nigeria, the diviner will recite the ese or divination verses until the client hears and selects the one that seems most appropriate to the problem to be solved (ID 22). In the Americas, on the other hand, the santeras and santeros who read the diloggún in registros tend, due to limitations of time or resources, to suppress the recital of patakís, limiting themselves to reciting the proverb or to giving the indicated counsel. Diviners in the Regla de Ocha will however recite patakís, including some of the lesser known, on the third day of the initiation ceremony, el día del Itá (YO 203). On other days, the diviner may choose the one pataki appropriate to the client's problem out of those belonging to the set of the indicated odu.

In another transculturative shift, the diloggún as it has evolved in Cuba has emulated the complexity of the Ifá system through the practice of reading pairs of odu together, such that the odus Eyioko (two mouths up) and Osa (nine mouths up), subsequently cast, would combine to form Eyioko-Osa (two–nine). Such a combination of two different odu requires the combining of their two narratives in the same interpretation, although the diviner will emphasize the meaning of the first odu of the pair (ISD 16). The pairing of odus means that the number of figures that could be cast would equal the sixteen possible combinations of mouths up and down for each cast, multiplied by the sixteen possible combinations of a second cast: 16 x 16 = 256 (CA 3:118). (García Cortez does refer to a simpler method, to be practiced only once a month for each client, which consists in throwing the cowries four times and looking up their interpretation in a book [ES 482].) The 256 total possible odu pairs would correspond to all of 256 sets of prayers, proverbs, stories, and sacrifice prescriptions, all of which the serious diviner must memorize during a long and arduous training period. In the absence of opportunities for apprenticeship, written texts naturally supply the apprentice with a study guide and "second memory" for preserving and handling this immense base of information (KI 83–84).

It is important to keep in mind that it is the orishas as well as the dead (egungun) who are said to create the evils or benefits predicted by the diloggún, and that a number of divinities speak through each of the odu figures, as do Changó and others through odu 6, Obara (ISD 56). The "presence" of the orisha's (or ancestor's) voice is one factor that influences the selection and reading of the pataki(s) considered appropriate to the client's situation. To reinforce the divine presence of the sacred voice, the diviner makes a ritual invocation and offering to the orishas in Lucumí. This act, denominated by the verb moyubbar, takes place in the initial stages of the divination ritual (Rogers 13–15; de la Soledad and Sanjuan 96). And since each odu is itself considered a minor orisha, each one requires its own ritual prayers (YO 186–87).

To illustrate the oracle's connection with the orishas: Oggún, truculent god of iron and the forge, speaks through or in odu 3, Ogunda. Because Oggún also oversees or "presides" over Ogunda, its appearance presages that Oggún "himself" may also appear in some form to endanger the client. Ogunda thus forewarns the client against attacking others with weapons of iron, and the client should avoid iron in all its other forms as well. The proverb corresponding to Ogunda is either "Dispute, tragedy for some reason" or "The Dead (One) on foot," and the disquieting patakís of Ogunda all speak ominously of conflict, strife, and attendant dangers. In one of those patakís, the character Erurá hides from his enemies in a large earthenware jug (tinajón), preventing his dog from climbing in with him. Although the dog would prefer to stay with his master, it returns to the village and brings back enemies, who quickly capture Erurá and reward the dog (Rogers 18, 72; de la Soledad and Sanjuan 104; ES 192–93, 486; YO 189, 193–94).

In another pataki of Ogunda, Laquín entrusts to his friend Adofin the safekeeping of some money and merchandise and then goes away on a trip. During Laquín's absence, Adofin throws a party during which his friend's valuables are stolen. Laquín returns, learns of the loss, publicly accuses his friend of the theft, and fights with him. Since the narrative anticipates similar events in the client's life, the diviner forewarns, "Beware that they don't accuse you of robbery," or, alternatively, "Do not trust anyone with your secrets" (Rogers 73; YO 204; de la Soledad and Sanjuan 104–5; ES 207–8; ISD 49).

As the texts of Ogunda exemplify, each odu or letra comes associated with a proverb, the *refrán* that heads the whole set of texts included under the odu. The odu named Osa (number nine) tells the client, "Your friend is your worst enemy," and it follows that betrayal by friends is a theme that runs through Osa's patakís. It should be noted that proverbs enjoy a special truth-value in Yoruba-Lucumí culture, as suggested by Chief I. O. Delano's observation, "A proverb can drive home a point or describe a situation in a few striking words: hence the Yoruba proverb . . . meaning 'a proverb is a horse which can carry one swiftly to the idea sought'" ("Proverbs" 77). In the registro reading, the proverb may be allowed to dominate or frame the global meaning of the reading. It does so in three ways: it "signifies the point of support where rests the letter in question," "the basic points" for speaking from the diloggún; it conveys in moralistic "idiomatic expressions" the messages of the odu; and, corroborating our sense of the proverb's focusing power, it "serve[s] to orient in registros." This orienting function requires an interpretive act of matching, comparing, and combining a proverb with the stories connected to its odu. González-Wippler adds that of the combined proverbs of the odu pair, those of the first odu will carry more weight than those of the second, although the double odu will have a proverb of its own (de la Soledad and Sanjuan 98, 121–22; Rogers 18; RA 82; ES 147; ISD 23).

The Afro-Cuban use of proverbs, let me mention in passing, recalls Kenneth Burke's concept, developed in *The Philosophy of Literary Form*, of proverbs both as epitomes of recurrent situations and as narrative cores of literary works. These works, Burke points out, make sense when considered as "proverbs writ large." The proverb so conceived offers neither truth nor definitive interpretation but a strategy for coping with a situation, or attitudinal adjustments. Literature can be read as texts that are structured on axioms, a feature that qualifies them to serve as "equipment for living" or as "medicine" that changes the reader's epistemological orientation toward a given set of circumstances (Burke, *Philosophy* 293–304).

Another clear correlation between proverb and divination narrative obtains in the case of Odi, odu 7. For Odi melli (7–7) specifically, the proverb goes, "Where the grave was dug for the first time." The proverb alludes to the legendary manner in which the character Mofá instituted the practice of burying the dead: after discovering his wife in an adulterous affair, he buried her—alive. Since this story illustrates Odi's theme of "betrayal between husband and wife, of tragedy and blood" (ES 493), the odu foretells of transgression and terror: "it is death, fear, sicknesses, calumnies, gossip and curiosity. It speaks of vicious people who break their customs and their traditions." It follows that clients drawing Odi may be living in a state of constant fright or alarm, suffering insomnia or dreaming of the dead; they are invited to learn from the precedent and follow the odu's admonition. The clients' initiation into Regla de Ocha may be in order. If they fail to heed the warning, so the logic of comparisons goes, something like the fate of Odi's wife may befall them (YO 189; Rogers 94, 96; RA 88–89; de la Soledad and Sanjuan 115, 116.)

As this reading of Odi indicates, the oracle has a diagnostic as well as prognostic function, by which the iyalocha or babalocha (santera or santero) gains knowledge of the client's eledá or spirit-double and thereby knowledge of the client's life condition. For example, the odu Okana sode, corresponding to one mouth-up cowrie, is a "fearful" sign. Boding ill for the client, it calls upon the diviner to cleanse the room. This limpieza ritual includes taking a piece of meat, smearing it with palm oil, and throwing it into the street for any dog to take away (ES 483; RA 83). For Okana sode says that the client is guilty of impiety, dangerously "backward" in spiritual matters (de la Soledad and Sanjuan 99), "unbelieving and expeditious." A rationale for these conclusions may be inferred from one pataki for Okana sode: there was a man who believed in witches but irreverently mocked the orishas, in whom he did not believe. But down comes Changó to possess one of his omos, and the mounted orisha accurately tells the man the correct number of people (eighteen) to be found inside a house familiar to the man. When the prediction comes true, the repentant man, now a believer, throws himself at the foot of the saint (YO 192, 193, 203–4; Rogers 63–64).

Serving the purposes of prediction, diagnosis, therapy, and conversion, the patakís also serve to orient individual thought and action through a meaningful sign universe that is, in part, a projection of the divination system itself, assuring that natural or social phenomena bear a personal significance for their "readers." The odu Eyioko, two mouths up, indicates the two proverbs "Fight for the obtainment of a thing" and "Ofó, arrow between brothers," both thus foretelling of conflict. These proverbs also link up with the pataki of Ode, one of the avatars of the hunting god Ochosí. On every hunt in which he catches white doves, Ode performs the ritual of leaving the doves next to a silk cotton tree so that Orishanla can drink up their blood. Ode's wife, anxious to know why her husband regularly brings home those bloodless birds, one day follows her husband, hides behind a tree, and spies upon the secret ritual. An angry Orishanla discovers the curious woman and curses her by giving her the blood of the doves, precisely in the form of a monthly menstruation (YO 189, 205; Rogers 70). In de la Soledad and Sanjuan's version, Orishanla curses the wife in these words: "'The blood that the doves, which your husband brought you, did not have, from now on you will see it run from your womb every month'" (103). In the terms of a patriarchalist, even misogynist myth, the odu Eyioko thus "explains" the origin of the menstrual cycle as it warns the client of relatives who will watch for the opportunity to betray him (ES 485).

As the foregoing comparisons demonstrate, the diviner—perhaps like the literary interpreter—looks for a common thread among the narratives, prayers, and proverbs comprising an odu, although such coherence need not be readily apparent.

It is also evident that the inner logic of the divination text, so interpreted, functions to reproduce the coherence of the belief system in which it plays a central role. Cros Sandoval displays this internal validation for the system in explicating the figure Oche, indicated by five shells mouths up. That odu recalls the story of the pig who declines to eat the fattening food the owner brings to the corral but chooses instead to eat only plantain shoots and garlic bushes. By habitually lying next to the fence of the corral and staying slim, the pig avoids butchering and wears out a ditch in the ground through which he will lead all the other pigs to their eventual salvation. Instead of reading into the parable an apparent message concerning the advantages of self-restraint and patience, Cros Sandoval (citing her informant) stresses the analogy that the pataki makes to patrilineal orisha worship: "The needle carries the thread; one makes a hole and the rest escape through the same place. Which of your ancestors made [or became] the saint? You and your family should be initiated too" (RA 86–87).

Counterposed to such references to the Lucumí belief system are narrative reflections on the divination system itself. Self-validating references to the oracle appear in many of the patakís. I have already noted the importance of the divination precedent as an implicit model of behavior, whereby protagonists of patakís often resort to consulting with Orúmila or another diviner before undertaking a major task or project. Frequently, too, the outcome of complying or not complying with the prescription validates the oracle. In Iroso melli (4–4), Obí seeks advice from the diviner that would help him avoid capture by death, la Ikú. Obí dutifully carries out the ebbó-sacrifice, which involves placing animals, palm oil, and his own clothing between the roots of a tree. Orúmila warns that Obí will experience a great fright but tells him to stay in place in order to find out the cause of that fright. True to the prediction, the tree at the foot of which Obí leaves the offering comes alive and makes as if to lunge and seize him in its outstretched branches. The terrified Obí summons up enough courage to stop running and return to examine the tree. The tree, now split apart, reveals a large amount of cowrie money, *owo*, in its interior. The discovery of unexpected fortune concurs with the idea of the wealth of Yemayá, the orisha who speaks through Iroso, and with the matching proverb, "No one knows what is hidden at the bottom of the sea" (YO 188, 207–8). The proverb may allude to treasure, mystery, and surprise; an inheritance may be forthcoming (de la Soledad and Sanjuan 106, 107). The fulfillment of prediction in Obí's salvation and reward also validates the intelligence of the diviners, those who identify themselves as children of Orúmila, owner of the diloggún and Ifá.

Guaranteed as well in such systemic self-referencing is the efficacy of sacrifice, already mentioned as a motivic element in the patakís. The sacrifice prescribed to the client is often identical to the sacrifice performed by the protagonist of the pataki. It is well for the client to remember, as Bascom notes, that "the object of divination is to determine the correct sacrifice, and nothing is gained if it is not offered" (SC 8, 28–29). Obara, in odu 6, gains nothing indeed by failing to carry out the ebbó advised by Orúmila (de la Soledad and Sanjuan 112–14). Obara consequently earns the contempt of his father the Oba, or king, when the elephant he says he killed has disappeared. Exiled from the kingdom for his alleged mendacity, Obara eventually returns to Orúmila. Orúmila prescribes a double sacrifice this time, and remonstrates with righteous indignation: "if you had done ebbó when I told you, you would not have gone through the humiliation, obstacles and misery that you suffer today, and how different everything would have been. Disobedience is a carpenter making boxes for the dead" (YO 209–11).

As Orúmila reproachfully reminds Obara directly—and the client indirectly—the oracle demands respect and obedience. The diloggún authorizes the wisdom that the diviner possesses as it internally reproduces and sanctions hierarchy in the broader social structure. Yet the diloggún is, more than a mere instrument of social manipulation or mystification, "the active 'memory' of a social whole" (Saldaña 132). The diloggún as a social practice assumes the function of what could be called a comprehensive and accessible information recall system, a database organizing and articulating its vast reserve of narrative knowledge for the good of the community.[3]

In a mythological perspective, divination tells us that this world is a reflection of the celestial world whose image is captured in the odu narratives.

"Don't forget," says the narrator of Cabrera's "Se hace ebbó" (One makes sacrifice), "that whatever happens in the world already happened in another time; and first, before time began down here, it happened up in heaven." With implications for divination, the same story refers to the idea of a divine scripture or inscription, for it is through oracles that we find out the history written by Obatalá, Olofi's representative, "about every one of his children—what Obatalá writes every day or at every moment." And it is Orúmila's task to read the divine will written in that "language of destiny" (PQ 204–5, 209).

My readings of the texts and discourse practices constituting Lucumí sign systems, including divination, has assumed the relative autonomy of those texts and practices within spheres of semiotic activity set within the cultures and subcultures of a society. As the order of self-referential signification within the diloggún demonstrates, Lucumí sign systems actuate a systemic principle of negativity, both with relation to the environment external to the system (inasmuch as any "outside" to the whole system can be so identified from the system's perspective) and by internal differentiations among signifiers and their signifieds. Although the system is structured by internal differentiation and supplementation, the metaphysics built into the system sustains a faith in "transcendental centers"—the gods, the ancestors, aché—that would control, from an external position, the processes internal to the system. Yet those transcendental centers are but organizing functions of sign systems whose self-referentiality allows a process of continual combination, synthesis, and permutation at the heart of the system's symbolic activity. The gods of course are fond of expressing themselves in proverbs and metaphors, but these verbal signs, as I hope the foregoing discussion has demonstrated, obey the laws of a complex rhetoric of religion. If, as we will see in subsequent chapters, the structure of the culturally dominant Lucumí system has given form to other religious and textual systems, Afro-Cuban religion has also accommodated, through transculturation, various supplementary figures of centering from other orders and traditions. We will also see how those other orders and traditions have offered alternatives to the rule of the orisha tradition.

3

✦ The Orishas in Republican Cuba

But since the bourgeoisie did not rule, since it became a class ruled
by Yankee imperialism, since the weakness of its economic system
facilitated the survival of African religious beliefs, they survived to
the point of undermining the very religious beliefs of the bourgeoisie.
Its Catholicism became "Afro-Catholicism."

Walterio Carbonell, "Birth of a National Culture"

The anticolonial aspirations of the second Cuban revolution against Spain
were cut short by the U.S. intervention in 1898, when Cuba ceased to be a
colony of one imperialist power only to become the protectorate of another.
The Platt Amendment, ratified in 1902, accorded the United States the right
to send the Marines to safeguard "the preservation of Cuban independence";
the right to ensure "the maintenance of a government adequate for the protection of life, property, and individual liberty"; the right to exercise its veto
in Cuban pacts or treaties with other international powers; and the right to
keep its naval base at Guantánamo. The U.S. occupation of the island had
begun soon after its entry in 1898 into the Spanish-American war ("Remember the Maine and to hell with Spain!") and ended in 1902 with the
establishment of the new republic under Tomás Estrada Palma, but it would
exercise its right to intervene in 1906–9, 1912, and 1917. As Huberman and
Sweezy sum up the U.S.-Cuban relations of the time, "[t]he United States
did, indeed, have the key to the Cuban house; it did, indeed, enter at will;
and the Cuban governments which it supported had, in the nature of the
setup, to be run by politicians who could be relied on to do Washington's
bidding" (14).

At Washington's bidding, the Cuban economy was to become, in effect,
the sugar producer for the United States. This imbalanced relationship meant
that, although sugar brought prosperity to some Cubans, no truly Cuban
national economy existed as such. Cuba's monocultural function, encour-

aged by increased foreign investment and tariff reductions, was carried out in a highly technologized and rationalized manner, but this progress irrationally impeded the kind of development of Cuban resources and industries that other parts of Latin America would enjoy in the second quarter of the century. Moreover, the post–World War I crash in sugar prices would soon allow U.S. investors to take over production on the island, forcing independent farmers to grow sugar for corporate owners. In this period, total U.S. capital investments expanded 700 percent, and already by 1927 some 40 percent of Cuban land was U.S.-owned or controlled (Barry et al. 269). With Cuba so integrated into the foreign-based economy, U.S. patronage, for all its progressivism, would in effect add sixty years of neocolonial economic domination to the island's four centuries of Spanish colonial rule. That latest chapter in the island's history of external control concluded with the expropriation and nationalization, in the early 1960s, of U.S. investments in oil, real estate, sugar-producing properties, hotels, and casinos. It has been said in retrospect that the antagonisms of the 1950s leading up to the Cuban Revolution were a replay of the tensions that produced the popular anti-Machado movement of the 1930s, which was in great part a movement of resistance to the foreign domination of the economy.[1]

In that earlier period, radical Cuban students and rural and urban proletarians were engaged in a mass struggle to overthrow the dependent dictatorship, to open up the economy to new industries, to revive a national consciousness, and to establish national sovereignty. Their political-economic arm was the general strike. Intent on destabilizing a government characterized by its series of U.S.-supported regimes, they took a step toward autonomy by ousting President Ramón Grau San Martín in 1933, with the approval of U.S. Ambassador Sumner Welles, and by pushing the abrogation of the Platt Amendment to realization in 1934, the year in which the U.S. Congress passed the Reciprocal Trade Agreement with Cuba. Grau San Martín's ouster of course allowed Fulgencio Batista to assume power, first as a political force behind a series of weak presidents, and later, with the overthrow of Carlos Prío Socarrás in 1952, as the president himself. Despite the return to dependent dictatorship under Batista, the desire for a national identity and culture that had awakened during the republican era continued on into the period of 1953–59.

Curiously, the cultural forms of expression considered characteristic or idiosyncratic of a national identity in the early years of the Republic would frequently be associated with the African pole of the Cuban cultural spectrum. The affirmation of religion-focused Afro-Cuban culture during the interwar period involved a turning inward to the authentic sources of *la cubanidad*, an introspective process of isolating and promoting what appeared, in resistance to the U.S. cultural invasion, uniquely Cuban. The discourse of Afro-Cuban religion thus entered into a process that could be called, after Fanon, the "racialization of thought," for it asserted an ethnic, color-related identity developed in opposition to the Nordic-pragmatic character of the U.S. hegemony, both cultural and economic (Fanon 212).

Feeling the pressure of historical change, Afro-Cuban religion nonetheless continued to develop according to its own internal, systemic logic. Cut off from the profane world of the political—at least in its ritual, mythic, and doctrinal dimensions—the sign-worlds of that religion constituted themselves in at least momentary insulation from the intrusions of secular institutions. In chapters 1 and 2 I addressed the relative autonomy of an Afro-Cuban religious culture that literature has reconstructed for a variety of purposes. Considered in their aggregate, the figures of Afro-Cuban religion have always constituted their own space of holy representation, a religious semiosphere populated by its hosts of metaphors and metonymies, organized by its sacred ritual and mythic motifs. At its margins, Afro-Cuban religion continued to reproduce the signs that distinguished this sacred precinct by its difference from the profane outside. Within the religious culture itself, an "interpreted world": the collection of patakís functioned as archive, preserving and organizing knowledge. Divination functioned as interpretive paradigm; ritual as social drama; music as a sacred solicitation; possession and dance as languages of worship; sacrifice as a metaphorical statement; magic as a principal of metonymic causality. These relatively stabilized religious functions not only provided their discourse community with a totalizing account of the whys and wherefores of human existence, they helped to "explain" the causes and effects of the general economic instability. In Afro-Cuban literature, however, a profaning politicization of Afro-Cuban religious discourse became a creative and interpretive option: the postindependence Afro-Cuban narratives that incorporated elements of religious sign systems frequently broached politico-economic issues by placing religious discourse in implicit dialogue with the discourses of the reader's historical present.

The "Lucumí religious system," which Lachatañeré described in the seminal article discussed in the preceding chapter, amounted to a subcultural dominant inscribed in the Cuban literary-anthropological discourse of the 1930s. For Lachatañeré, the field of Afro-Cuban religion was organized by that unifying Lucumí system, a structure-in-process. Both that system and

Lachatañéré's 1938 interpretation of it, I would propose, can be read as metaphors of resistance to the pressure of outside forces that threatened to dissolve the community and cultural identity of the Cuban/Afro-Cuban subject. In response to that threat, Lachatañéré's theory offered a literary metaphysic founded in opposition to the modernizing rationalization that made Cuba one big sugar plantation within the expanding U.S. economy. Underlying Lachatañéré's theoretical systematizing of Afro-Cuban religion was the awareness that the forces of modernity were threatening the communitarian unity of Cuban society, such as it existed.

In the transition to modernity, González Echevarría has observed, an imperiled communitarian or even communist unity may be replaced by the refashioned unity of syncretic religions. González Echevarría illustrates this shift with reference to Severo Sarduy's *De donde son los cantantes* (Where the singers are from, 1967), a novel that places the spotlight on the Yoruba-Lucumí stratum of the Afro-Cuban palimpsest:

> The *ad hoc* religions of the post-colonial world . . . arise from the disintegration of the grand religions, devastated by the advance of the western world, with its science and technology. The defense of those religions, of those cultures, will be the preservation of a type of symbolic activity at the margin of the totalizing claims of the Occident and its historicist religions, such as Hegelianism, Marxism or Progressivism. It has to do with a kind of contingent, local transcendentalism; with the recuperation of histories, of texts, of language, that *De donde son los cantantes* should resist global interpretation, and retain something of a pre- or post-modern symbology. (RSS 133)

The alternative of a "contingent, local transcendentalism" in an earlier period, however, could run parallel to and supplement the historicist universalisms of the Occident. Afro-Cuban religions, ad hoc religions, are also complex if supple institutions that made their symbols available to a putative national identity as redefined in literary works. Their worship communities preserved the elements of a shared culture and projected, for the sake of survival, the image of a solidary racial group, an image that could eventually symbolize the nationalist unity and transcendence of a Cuban citizenry.

At the same time, the master narrative of a multicultural nation such as Cuba must confront the heterogeneity of its plural symbologies, those of Afro-Cuban religion included. The elements of such symbologies may provide the components for constructing a national heritage and identity, but that kind of construction requires the kind of mediation or translation that forges a more or less unitary national destiny out of the contradictory experiences of diverse Cuban social groups.

The instrument for creating this national culture had to be, to use Frantz Fanon's terms, a "literature of combat," one that "mold[ed] the national consciousness, giving it form and contours and flinging open before it new and boundless horizons" (Fanon 233, 240). As exemplified repeatedly in Afro-Caribbean writing, the molding of a national consciousness in literature and other artistic manifestations would not only refuse the definition of the colonial subject imposed by European culture. It would also give a people, their identity so redefined, an "international dimension," a profile that linked them in solidarity with other postcolonial subjects, all of whom would inaugurate nothing less than a new history of the local, liberated from the universalist Eurocentric narrative.

Within a process of literary refunctioning consonant with Fanon's call for an anti-Eurocentric and postcolonial culture, the orisha tradition undergoes what could be called a transformative carnivalization in the Cuban narrative of the first half of the century.[2] Lucumí religion takes on new significance in this process of recontextualization: so rewritten, it merges into a discourse of resistance, testimony and validation of the forms of a national community, a "literature of combat." The Burkean-Platonic dialectic that I outlined in the preceding chapter—I refer to the movement of signs upward into the sacred order and then back downward, such that they invest the secular and sociopolitical world with divine echoes—provides a schema for the Afro-Cuban literary act of recodifying religious sign systems into their texts as allegories of a national culture. The Afro-Cuban religious discourse of the 1930s illustrates that dialectic by constructing a multicultural, racialized "dialectic" of Cuban identity. A brief history of the literary movements known as negrismo, afrocubanismo, and négritude will clarify the relation of a syncretic religious heritage to a national culture. This discussion will be followed by readings of Lucumí-related narratives of the 1930s by Alejo Carpentier, José Antonio Ramos, and Rómulo Lachatañeré, the first Afro-Cubanist writers to set forth the terms of a possible postcolonial Cuban identity.

Vindications of Africanity

The term negrismo names a literary movement that involved all the Hispanic Caribbean artists who incorporated aspects of African-based culture into their works and texts. Beginning as a European vogue, negrismo would come to influence the works of Afro-Dominican, Afro-Puerto Rican, and Afro-Cuban artists. Negrismo as an international movement was the Hispanic counterpart of the Négritude movement that, initiated in Paris with the publication of the journal *L'Etudiant Noir* in 1932, took root in the Francophone countries of Martinique, Guadeloupe, Haiti, Senegal, and French Guyana.

It will be recalled that the emergence of Afro-Antillean cultures in predominantly "white" Puerto Rico and Cuba (at least for the main part of Cuba's history) was made possible by the annihilation, soon after the Spanish conquest of the islands, of any indigenous population or legacy of cultural artifacts whose presence could have otherwise supplied the basis of a national culture. In the absence of surviving Taínos, Arawaks, and Siboneys, and especially after the advent of North American imperialism in the Caribbean, black-based nodes of expression became available as the privileged vehicle of protest and national self-affirmation, the "authentic *alter/native*," to use Brathwaite's expression from "The African Presence in Caribbean Literature" (111). In the Cuban context, the Brathwaitean alter/native took the form of a paradoxical, double writing. Representing Afro-Cuban experience and culture in Spanish language, and not primarily in Anagó, Efik, Congo, or Fon, this double writing constituted an ethnic difference disruptive of the normative, colonial modes of narrative understanding, speaking to a Hispanic public and its traditions while celebrating the African otherness within Cuban society.

The negrismo movement affirmed an African heritage in opposition to the prejudices of many Cubans who considered that heritage to be a sign of backwardness and source of shame. José Antonio Portuondo calls negrismo "the Cuban version of the Ibero-American *indigenism* and of *populist* movements throughout the world." Carpentier's ¡*Ecue-Yamba-O!* is a specimen of that movement, as are the collections of stories and "black theogonic legends" of Lachatañeré, Cabrera, Ramón Guirao, and the Ñáñigo stories of Gerardo del Valle (BH 61). In these and other authors, the *negrista* theme takes two main directions: either the historicist approach or what could be called a radicalizing sociological approach. The first looks to the slaveholding past as past and laid to rest, assuming that its problems have been resolved. The second tends to examine the lot of blacks and mulattoes in a contemporary context, denouncing both their victimization by racial prejudice and their common cause with the proletariat under capitalism. Yet, as Bueno has evaluated it, this denunciation would often fall into the "trap of typicism and the picturesque" (NNH 17, 23).

Negrismo, like its French-Antillean equivalent, had found philosophical support in a number of anthropological and historiographical events. In 1910,

Frobenius had published *The Black Decameron*, based largely on the author's archaeological and anthropological researches in Africa. Oswald Spengler explained the malaise of Western culture by the theory of the rise and fall of cultures in his *Decline of the West*, first appearing in 1917. In North America, Vachel Lindsay affirmed the beauty of African-based tradition in *The Congo and Other Poems* (1914), as did the poetry of Langston Hughes (1902–67), and similar sentiments were expressed in another national context, in Blaise Cendrar's *Anthologie nègre* (1927).

Of the poetry of négritude, which influenced negrismo, it is generally agreed that the *Cahier d'un retour aux pays natal* (Notebook of a return to the native land, 1939), by the Martinican poet Aimé Césaire, is the seminal work. In that long poem, which has been called a literary ritual of parthenogenesis or self-engendering (Eshleman and Smith 21), Césaire critiques colonial civilization and its racism, calling for a new beginning to culture while invoking elemental realities, the "fresh source of light," and the "spark of the sacred fire of the world," in which Afro-Antillean identity would be reborn. Césaire declares in his *Cahier*:

> my negritude is neither tower nor cathedral
> it takes root in the red flesh of the soil
> it takes root in the ardent flesh of the sky
> it breaks through the opaque prostration with its upright patience
> (*Collected* 67, 69)

In Césaire and others, négritude expressed the black intellectual's will to build a hybrid sense of identity on a new cultural foundation, out of the motifs of Africa and the language of Mother France. Césaire in particular rejected the violent rationalism of the white European world as it celebrated the instinctual and intuitive life of African-descended peoples. In response to marginalization and alienation, he proposed a vision of liberation and social justice. Yet Césaire's négritude falls short of producing a truly liberating narrative by its exclusive recourse to myth, as Patrick Taylor has cogently argued; that is, it "became a narcissistic contemplation of a contrived self; it reaffirmed the Manichaenism of European racism by romanticizing Africa, glorifying intuition over reason, and proudly presenting itself as the antithesis of European culture" (163). In the end, by celebrating black intuitionism and irrationalism, Césaire offered an elitest oversimplification of African cultures and perpetuated the dualisms that originated in the racism of the colonizers.

Unlike the négritude writers, the Hispanic negristas, as Jahn asserts, drew less inspiration from Paris's vogue of Harlem and Africa than from the German "prophets of decline" (*History* 219). In addition, the negristas seemed more attentive, in their historical and sociological narratives, to the concrete circumstances of black and mulatto characters. Yet like négritude, negrismo combined an African-inspired sense of vitality, naturalness, spontaneity, and exuberance with a radical critique of occidental civilization, whose violent ethnocentrism had sanctioned the institutional practices—slavery and colonialism—that had made it powerful.

What was called the *movimiento afrocubano* (the Afro-Cuban movement) in fact began as a political program of the black rights organization called the *Partido Independiente de Color* (Colored Independent Party or PIC), led by Evaristo Estenoz and Pedro Ivonet from 1909 to 1913, when Gómez was president. As documented by Fernández Robaina, those Afro-Cubanists sought to gain equal political treatment for blacks and to protect the rights of racially based political groups like the PIC to meet and organize. Government acts of repression provoked a failed Afro-Cuban uprising in 1912, in Oriente province, where some three thousand blacks lost their lives (*El negro* 46–64).

With political avenues thus closed off to Cuban blacks, their political aspirations would at least turn inward, to be translated into artistic and literary self-expression. El afrocubanismo would soon begin to designate an artistic movement that flourished in Cuban literature, dance, music, and plastic arts between 1928 and 1940. In poetic and musical works especially, the makers of the movement characteristically featured the onomatopoeic phrasings, phonetic repetitions, and mythological references known to Afro-Cuban peoples, in poems and lyrics featuring a creolized, Africanized Spanish. The narrative of Afro-Cubanism often reenacted aspects of the ceremonials practiced by the descendants of the island's slaves, with sound reiterations emulating the percussive effects that induced trances in initiates during the typical drum-playing parties, the *toques de tambor* or *bembés*. This aesthetic emphasis could suggest that the Afro-Cuban movement was not "anti-European or anti-Christian" but rather "aim[ed] to stress the magical and telluric values of an urbanized black folklore" (DALC 14). Yet a criticism of the European-imposed colonial culture, with its oppressive forms of Christianity, did become part and parcel of the Afro-Cuban revalorization. Often in opposition to the colonial heritage, the movement evolved into a search for unique cultural roots and national themes, aspiring to produce works that could be claimed by a universal literature (see VU 7–8).

The most celebrated negristas in the Cuba of late 1920s and 1930s were white-skinned writers, with the notable exception of the popular and celebrated Nicolás Guillén. What the former saw in the Afro-Cuban presence and often strove to re-create in their poetry, and not without a modicum of persistent ethnocentricity, could be summed up as a cultural primitivity. Many works of Afro-Cuban primitivism appeared for the first time, next to republications of European avant-garde works, in the *Revista de Avance* (Review of advance) founded in Havana in 1927. The *Revista*'s approach to the Afro-Cuban equated it with a new artistic vitality, spontaneity, and sensuality, sometimes exalting the sexual appeal of the rumba-dancing mulatta or other stereotypical images. Nicolás Guillén (born 1902), however, avoided the stereotypes by giving expression to the Afro-Cuban experience in poems written with Afro-Spanish dialect. Guillén recognized the complexity and robust dignity of a culture unknown to many Cuban intellectuals, incorporating elements of the myth and ritual of New World African culture into his poems (see Franco 277–79).

Afro-Cuban literature of the republican years thus appeared and gained popularity in a general climate of disillusionment and frustration, participating in a general artistic push against the intellectual inertia of the period. Of the literary artists caught up in the effort to revitalize the nation, the early José Antonio Ramos belongs to the first generation, associated with lyricism, Americanist *arielismo*, and nationalist sentiment. Both Alejo Carpentier and an older Ramos belong to the second generation, characterized by a certain antiacademicism and an impulse for nonconformity and innovation that took the black theme as its vehicle of artistic and social revolt (Barreda 117). Rómulo Lachatañeré, their contemporary, pioneered the recuperation of the Afro-Cuban oral tradition in his literary writing.

In the narratives by Carpentier, Ramos, and Lachatañeré to which I now turn, Afro-Cuban religion—as social structure, doctrine, slave ideology, mythic archive, transcendence—fulfills its diverse vocations as a signifier of otherness in the bosom of Cuban culture, as its nationalist alter/native. At the same time it offers an image of consensus and organic community that negates the conditions of a capitalism dominated by foreign powers and a stratified society dominated by its dependent and disorganized bourgeoisie. All three writers translated texts of the Lucumí religious system into new, literary-aesthetic idioms; in the process, they redefined the Cuban national culture by reopening the question of identity with a notion of difference.

The Forerunner: *¡Ecue-Yamba-O!*

Some ten years after Fernando Ortiz published *Hampa afrocubana: los negros brujos* (Afro-Cuban underworld: the black sorcerers), a twenty-three-year-old Alejo Carpentier, in the Havana jail for forty days in 1927, began work on his first novel, the first sustained presentation in Cuban literature of an Afro-Cuban belief system based on Lucumí and Ñáñigo elements. Published in 1933, *¡Ecue-Yamba-O!* roughly translates as *Lord Be Praised!*—although "Lord" does not quite convey the sense of the central "Ecue," to be discussed in chapter 4. Although the novel focuses on the experiences of Ñáñigo characters, experiences that will be addressed in chapter 4 as well, here I will discuss the novel's Lucumí religious elements and the sociopolitical implications of their treatment for the period in which the novel was first published. With its observation of ritual and its collation of doctrinal fragments, *¡Ecue-Yamba-O!* is full of the "scenarios of transformation" to which Lewis alludes in his study of slave ideology. In presenting those scenarios, a tradition of postcolonial Afro-Cuban narrative was beginning to create a space for its own unfolding.

Carpentier's novel consists of forty-three chapters divided into three major sections entitled "Infancy," "Adolescence," and "The City." The episodic chapters are fragmentary, some presenting static portraits of rural labor, games, and customs and all loosely tied to the plot of the life of its protagonist, Menegildo Cué. Menegildo is born into a rural black family around the outbreak of World War I ("There's war there in Uropa"), and the account of his early years are dominated by the family's labor for the sugar factory, the *central* or *ingenio*, of the opening descriptions. There is a ritual implication in the cyclical nature of the plot, by which Menegildo, son of a cane laborer, is born, grows up, engenders a child, and dies to be replaced by that child. Brushwood finds in the circularity of *¡Ecue-Yamba-O!* a confirmation of Afro-Cuban culture's "durability" and the hold of its pattern not only on the individual but on his or her offspring. Menegildo's child does not escape the continuing cycle of exploitation, poverty, criminality, and violence that finally killed his father and could eventually kill him (EYO 36, 102–3).

The life of Menegildo Cué and his family is clearly shaped by oppressive circumstances produced by economic rationalization—but it is also shaped by spiritual impulse and religious custom. At the beginning of the story, Menegildo's grandfather is a slave who was freed when Cuba became a republic in 1902, and Menegildo's father is a small landowner who is forced to sell his parcel for half its worth to the North American monopoly that owns the ingenio. The family as a whole struggles to survive financially despite the economic crisis and the hostile environment this has created, which the novel holds responsible for the family's illiteracy and grinding poverty as well as for the racial prejudice under which it suffers. In this marginalized world of underdevelopment and ignorance, the characters seek protection in the warmth of syncretic beliefs and magical practices, especially in those of Afro-Catholic religion. When Menegildo, at the age of three, is bitten by a poisonous crab, the family calls for "Old Beruá, doctor of the family for four generations," who comes to the house "to 'cast the seashells' and apply three ounces of snake butter on the belly of the child with his calloused hands." Beruá goes on to recite a Catholic prayer to the "Just Judge, who would protect him from the persecution of men and beasts of prey" (EYO 42), to complete the cure.

Isidro Salzmann finds a religion-reinforced ideological unawareness and passivity in the characters in Carpentier's novel. Whereas Vaudou in Carpentier's subsequent, more mature *El reino de este mundo* (The kingdom of this world) will have a heroizing, unifying function for the rebelling slave community on Saint Domingue, the religion represented in the earlier novel, argues Salzmann, is shown to foster acquiescence, escapism, and egoistic self-seeking in its believers. The Afro-Cuban religion attributed to the narrative in this view is but one means for accommodating oneself to, or else fleeing momentarily from, a socioeconomic system that offers no means of advancement through education or employment, a system that makes use of dispossession, prison, and religion itself to contain dissatisfaction. Especially because the novel's action is set in a period just before the sugar crisis of the 1920s, the characters seem like blind victims of an economic fate that decides their fortune and survival. Menegildo's religion thus provides no more than a means of rechanneling the frustration of disempowered and marginalized characters into "safe" avenues, giving form to an alienation reflected in the lack of any explicit ideological stance in the novel (Salzmann 77, 82).

Carpentier's novel indeed reflects on the character's passivity with relation to the sociopolitical order, but rather than equating their religion with mystification, one could read that religion as a supplement to the ideological vacuum created by their sociopolitical environment. As the narratorial perspective reveals, the situation offers no viable alternatives, but the consolations and rewards of religious practice provide some symbolic compensation and limited empowerment to the characters as references to this practice help to situate the reader within the narrator's bicultural and antihegemonic outlook. The Cuban interpretation of sociohistorical reality is defamiliarized by this shift in viewpoint. Many descriptions in ¡Ecue-Yamba-O! seemed aimed at indoctrinating the reader into a dual perspective, an analytical-magical worldview—both Afro-Cuban and European and neither—by a process of naming, explaining, categorizing, and analyzing the world in the "Afro-Cubanist" language. Rather than denounce religion altogether, the narrative assumes a perspective in between, where it questions the adequacy for human needs of both the scientific perspective, whose positivistic and progressivist outlook helped to create dependency, and mythical thinking, whose blindness has allowed dependency to continue.

Carpentier moreover suggests that Afro-Cuban religion has uses unknown to Western science. In the novel, it provides something more than an avenue of escape or symbolic transcendence to its characters: it offers a kind of verbal-semiotic "medicine" for healing. For in the same prayer that Beruá recites to the Just Judge as part of his treatment for Menegildo's poisoned crab bite, he delivers a poem with the suggestive, psychoactive power to orient the patient toward recovery and to safeguard him against enemies: "I drink their blood and I cleave their heart." The supplicant then affirms his imitation of Christ by claiming to wear his holy shirt. The Son of God is invoked, as are the holy Gospels and Jesus, Mary, and Joseph. A sort of imitative or homeopathic magic operates in the enumeration of the things the supplicant, speaking for Menegildo, would avoid: prisons, stabbings, "bad tongues" or gossip, animal bites (EYO 43).

The reader's apprenticeship in mysteries follows Menegildo's and continues with other descriptions of sacred scenes. In presenting a young Menegildo's first view of Beruá's altar, for instance, Carpentier lays out a mysterious display of Lucumí signs: "In the center, upon the skin of a low ritual drum, stood Obatalá, the crucified, caught in a net of interwoven necklaces. At his feet, Yemayá, little Virgin of Regla, was imprisoned in a glass bottle. Changó, under the features of Santa Bárbara, second element in the trinity of the major *orishas*, brandished a golden sabre" (EYO 86). The description serves a multiple function. First, the enumeration "fills in" the narrative with some informative background indexes: these function as metaphors of character, creating the atmosphere of "great things" that overawe Menegildo with their otherworldly aspect and contribute to the definition of his identity. Second, the enumeration underscores Carpentier's favorite theme of cultural *mestizaje*, the mixing that brings different cultural forms into juxtaposition and symbiosis. Third, it verbally reproduces the iconic image whose mystery contributes to "mystifying" Menegildo's consciousness and thus obscuring his knowledge of real social conditions. But fourth, the altar as so described offers a vision of symbolic transcendence in religious allegory—a way of reading signs that sees more in them than meets the eye.

Other descriptions of artifacts evoke the figural foundations of religious experience. Menegildo's first narrated encounter with the family altar appears in chapter 4, "Iniciación (a)" (Initiation [a]). On a low table, the infant Menegildo gazes upon little statues of the saints. The initiated reader may recognize their orisha doubles. They include Babalú-Ayé as San Lázaro, "an old man, propped by crutches, followed by two dogs with red tongues"; and Obatalá as the Virgin of Mercedes, "[a] crowned woman, dressed in white satin, with a chubby-cheeked boy in her arms." On the same altar Menegildo sees the elekes, "necklaces of green beads," those of Osaín, and the sopera tureen with its consecrated stones. The narrator comments: "Magical theater." With this informal "initiation," the reader accompanies Menegildo in meeting the orisha-saints for the first time and also learns that one must keep a respectful distance from the altar when Menegildo's mother tells him to let go of its mantle (EYO 40–42). By reminding us that all of this is "theater"—stagecraft, artifice, simulacra—Carpentier switches codes to confirm the analytical perspective that contradicts and demystifies the experiential narrative.

The chapter entitled "Mitología" (Mythology) follows on the episode covering another session of "therapy" with Beruá, this time for knife wounds. Recuperating, Menegildo has recourse to pray to San Lázaro-Babalú-Ayé, the saint who heals with a glass moved in a sign of the cross and with a snakeskin belt, who speaks through a cast of the cowries. Menegildo's free indirect discourse then shifts into the second person to address the orisha-saints directly: "Christ, nailed and thirsty, you are Obatalá, god and goddess in one body, and you animate everything, who spreads out the canopy of stars and carries the cloud to the river"; and to the Virgen de la Caridad del Cobre he mentions the three Juans who discovered her in the Bay of Nipe and the protection she promised to those who believe in her power (EYO 104, 105). These narrated recollections and appellations thus immerse the reader in a world of African mythic thought and the Afro-Cuban synthesis discussed in chapter 1 of this study. The abbreviated retelling of myth in Carpentier's passage expresses Menegildo's belief as it reflects on the uses of myth and mystification in an unconscious process, where mind and body, through a language of wonder, may work together to heal Menegildo's wounds.

Elsewhere, alternative and alternating discourses, either liturgical or analytical, emerge from a chaotic background. On the side of mystery, a passage describes a sacred *Nochebuena*, or Christmas Eve, celebration. The drummers "profane" sacred songs, other members of Menegildo's potencia or Ñáñigo association dance in rings moving in contrary directions, and all sing in unison the repetitive chant, "*Olelí, / Olelá. / Olelí, / Olelá. / Olelí, / Olelá. / Olelí, / Olelá.*" The Ñáñigos mix Lucumí, Efik, and Efor ritual with spiritualist calls to "transmitters" that include Jesus Christ, Santa Bárbara, Allan Kardek, and Yemayá. A circle is drawn and a bottle is placed in the center, as the circle's "axis"; in the midst of rhythmic corybantic dancing, the saint "arrives" and old Cristalina is possessed: "she writhed on the ground, with her eyes open and her mouth full of foam." The drums are silenced, and she is taken to another room, where, transmitting advice in consultations given by the saint, "[s]he was a skylight open to the mysteries of the other world" (EYO 177, 178, 179).

Earlier in the novel, Carpentier allowed a different voice, the voice of analysis, to explain the mystery of possession. After relating one episode of possession there, the narrator steps back to reflect on what has just occurred: "It is possible that, in reality, the saint never talks; but the deep exaltation produced by an absolute faith in his presence ends up endowing the word with its magical creative power, lost since the primitive eras. The word, ritual in itself, then reflects a proximate future that the senses have already perceived, but which reason still gets a hold of in order to control it better" (EYO 67). In this passage of scientific explanation or cant, the narrative voice makes use of the subjunctive "hable" after the phrase "Es posible que" as it searches for a term to name a creative-prophetic power of the word that is as yet "monopolized" or "caped over" (as in *acapara*) by reason. For there are other ways of knowing, there is more to the real than the rational, and the word, called "ritual en sí misma" or "ritual in itself," follows a logic that reason does not govern.

Speaking of "occult forces" issuing from another world, the double-visioned, double-voiced narrator later comments on how the space between humans and between objects and humans carries the magical, but more powerful, equivalent of radio waves: "A wooden doll, baptized with Menegildo's name, becomes the master of his living *double*. If there are enemies who sink a rusty tack into the side of the figure, the man will receive the wound in his own flesh. Four hairs of a woman, duly worked some leagues from her hut . . . can infallibly tie her to a bed. The jealous female succeeds in assuring the happiness of her lover by correctly employing the water of his intimate ablutions." In these measures for securing power over others we recognize practices belonging to Frazer's categories of imitative magic and contagious magic. The baptized doll mimetically represents the man, as does the metonymically related name; the four hairs represent the desired woman by synecdoche, as a part symbolizing the whole. The narrator continues to explain: a gold chain contracts as a sign of danger. Why? "If one accepts as unquestionable truth that an object can be endowed with life, that object will live" (EYO 66, 67). If one accepts the premise, one accepts a personification involved in the magical attribution, as well as the metaphoric mimesis by which a contracting chain makes a gesture of cowering or "shrinking" in the anticipation of harm.

Similar magical mechanisms go into the making of a love charm through the *enamoramiento* or love-securing ritual in the chapter entitled "El embó" (or ebbó, charm or sacrifice). Menegildo, wishing to win Longina's love, arrives at Beruá's hut with a piece of cloth from Longina's dress. To carry out the embó, the brujo would work with the "victim's" name, but Menegildo has only just met Longina and does not know it at this point. Beruá nonetheless goes on with the ceremony, ensuring that the saints are "fed" with aguardiente (cane liquor), yam fritters, cornmeal balls, and a metal heart and hand, all provided by Menegildo. The ritual involves six steps that the narrative represents in sequence.

Carpentier devotes all of chapter 19 (EYO 83–89) to this ritual. The steps for creating an *amarre* or "tying" love charm for Menegildo include the following: the limpieza or cleansing, done by anointing the client with palm oil and casting toasted corn on his back; the invocation; the interrogation regarding the birthplaces of the client's father ("Luis's farm") and the saint ("Guinea"); the call-and-response exchange repeating the information of the interrogation and invoking the name of the one who ties; and the tying of the cloth with hemp into seven knots, during which Beruá calls out in anaphoric incantation:

—With one I tie you.
—With two as well.
—With three Mama-Lola [Ochún].
—With four you fall down.
—With five you get burned.
—With six you stay.
—With seven, tied you are!

After step 7, Menegildo buries the knots in the shade of an aromatic myrrh as Beruá recites the prayer to the *Anima Sola*, thus appeasing the Lonely Soul in Pain (EYO 88–89).

The magic apparently works when, in the next chapter, Longina surrenders herself to Menegildo (EYO 92). How to explain it? A certain *post hoc, ergo propter hoc* logic works in both Beruá's magic and the narrative structure. The ceremony's invocation of supernatural agents, its repetitions, and its rehearsal of the effects intended for Longina produce the attitude of expectancy and confidence in Menegildo conducive to precipitating an amorous union with the beloved. We again recognize a combination of a contagious magic in making the charm with a piece of the victim's clothing and an imitative magic in the knot-tying ceremony and chants. On the level of the story, we know that the charm works simply because the narration tells us it works, and the magic effect can confirm this tautology.

Myth serves an explanatory function in the novel outside the context of religious ceremonies as well. In "Tempestad (b)" (Storm [b]) (EYO 55–57), as the Cué family takes refuge from the familiar tropical hurricane, the whole catastrophe becomes an event with a special Afro-Cuban significance, and so the narration takes on a magical quality. The storm manifests the presence of Changó and turns into a pan-Caribbean affair: "Santa Bárbara and her ten thousand horses with bronze hoofs gallop over a rosary of unprotected islands." Unexpected symbolism occurs spontaneously: "The coffin of a child navigates along the street of Souls"; a sign for CIGARROS [cigars] gradually loses letters until it seems to read "CI . . . C . LO." Such occurrences betoken *lo real maravilloso*, or Carpentier's notion of "the marvelous real," because they serve as portents within the Afro-Cuban sign-universe, in which nothing is purely accident and everything signifies (see Carpentier, *Tientos* 132).

Despite the misgivings on the part of critics and Carpentier himself about the execution of the novel (see Sommers 234; EYO 26), we should give it its due by acknowledging its achievement in incorporating Afro-Cuban religious elements into an avant-garde pastiche that, modeled in part on Dadaism and Futurism, strove to depict a many sided or fragmented reality while foregrounding the side of lived myth. The narrative creates the impression in the reader's mind that Cuban culture itself after the 1920s, during the early years of the Republic, was an analogous collage of heterogeneous and at times contradictory voices. From a double perspective, one which the Ibeyi twins no doubt would approve, Carpentier did not simply portray the *vivencias* or experiences of Menegildo's race and class but attempted to explain that group's collective representations, out of which an Afro-Cuban world that negated the sociopolitical world of the Cuban present was created.

¡Ecue-Yamba-O! deserves the credit for recovering in one presentation both the authoritative voice of Afro-Cuban experience, which recalls Guirao and Guillén, and the authoritative voice of sociological analysis, which recalls Ortiz and Jorge Mañach. Seen from both angles, the narrative takes on the semiotic reading of religious signs as both creative and interpretive venture. The metanarrative comment on the novel's metareligious activity can be found in chapter 38, entitled "Niños" (Children), in which a gang of street boys form a club in a room they call "the Cave of Crabs." In this improvised sanctum, the boys are said to "worship" a print from a French magazine of a naked woman. The narrator underscores the cultish quality of this reverence: "The image came to satisfy a need for religious fervor in them. No one dared to pronounce bad words or urinate in her presence" (EYO 160–61). Whereas the passage may seem like a digression in a chaos full of digressions, it textually reflects the motives and activities involved in group formation as it mirrors, albeit in desublimated and degraded miniature, the impulse to avail oneself of religion's expressive and instrumental means. Carpentier's novel emphasizes the social and semiotic dimensions of Afro-Cuban religion without, for the moment, elaborating their implications for political praxis, leaving that task to his own later works and to those of other authors such as José Antonio Ramos.

Narrative Cimarronage

Ramos's *Caniquí* (1936) is a pluridimensional realist narrative, one that recontextualizes African-based myth within a multifaceted critique of Cuban colonial and neocolonial social structures. The novel represents events set in Trinidad, Cuba, in 1830 and so makes allegorical use of colonial history for figuring the Cuban condition of the mid-1930s. The narrative of *Caniquí* employs Afro-Cuban religion as a mark of character, as an alter/native mode of interpreting experience, and as a symbol for the multiethnic Cuban national identity, as well as a defamiliarizing frame of reference for understanding social reality. With its many references to Afro-Cuban myth and ritual, the novel's allegorical reading of a neocolonial situation through a family chronicle set in colonial times bears out Cuervo Hewitt's assessment that Cuban literature consists of "polysemic" and "peregrine discourses" in which the drift of history rather than Cartesian rationality governs the production and displacement of signifiers within a dialogics of national culture and national identity (APA 27). By examining the function of Afro-Cuban religion in *Caniquí*, one sees how the drift of history carries that system of belief and practice toward a conception of new political possibilities.

Caniquí's predecessor is the antislavery novel *Sab* by the Cuban novelist Gertrudis Gómez de Avellaneda, first published in 1844. The action of *Sab* centers on the love of a slave for his white mistress. This idealized and ill-fated love contrasts favorably with that of Enrique, the novel's avaricious white slave owner, and serves to exemplify, in nineteenth-century Rousseauistic fashion, the greater nobility and morality of the black slave. For Castellanos and Castellanos, the "philanthropic humanism" of Gómez de Avellaneda's novel puts to shame the "deformed and feeble Christianity that was practiced on the Island" (CA 1:307).

Slavery and abolitionism were no longer current political issues in the early years of the Republic, but they served as metaphors for the contemporary political situation in narratives such as Lino Novás Calvo's *Pedro Blanco, el negrero* (Pedro Blanco, the slaver, 1933), which uses the history of the past to remark upon and critique the history of the present. In Ramos's novels and treatises, a certain bitterness over the political decadence of the period leads to a search for alternative cultural origins, and such is the case in *Caniquí*. As William Luis writes in *Literary Bondage*, "*Caniquí's* message is a contemporary call for rebellion, a rebellion that will emancipate not only blacks but the entire society. With *Caniquí*, we discern how the passage of time has allowed the incorporation of a discourse of rebellion that was present in the nineteenth century, as represented, for example, by José Antonio Aponte and later David Turnbull but not included in the early novels of the slavery period." The "discourse of rebellion" that sustained abolitionism will lend its force to a discourse of anti-imperialist nationalism. *Caniquí's* "counter-discourse of power" also adds the text of Afro-Cubanism to that anti-imperialist appeal (LB 8–9).

The full name of the novel's protagonist is Filomeno Bicunia Caniquí, slave of the *hacendado* or hacienda owner don Lorenzo de Pablos. Caniquí's constant obsession is to escape—*hacerse cimarrón*, to become a runaway—which he does repeatedly. At one point, when he has been recaptured, he defiantly tells his master, "Tie me up, master or put me in the stocks, . . . because if not, I'll run away" (Ramos 76). The plot largely hangs on Caniquí's attempts to escape, the last of which ends in his death by the guns of the posse. The narrative also includes the conspicuous subplot of the intrigue surrounding the character Mariceli, don Lorenzo's pious daughter. Obsessed with expiating her sins, Mariceli first strives to become a nun, but when this plan is blocked, she delivers herself to a nightly regimen of self-mortification. Caniquí witnesses one session of flagellation that nearly takes Mariceli's life, and his mysterious complicity in covering up her actions with her thereafter becomes the obscure center around which the subplot revolves. Juan Antonio Luna, the proindependentist and abolitionist lawyer in love with Mariceli, gets caught up in the mystery surrounding his beloved's relationship with the runaway slave. He seeks her love, but she seeks forgiveness; Caniquí seeks his freedom, and don Lorenzo alternately pursues his slave and ever greater riches and power.

The events of the novel thus stage various scenarios of desire played out some thirty-eight years before the first wars of independence. The novel itself, first published in the era of economic dependency, of the *choteo* (mocking humor), demagoguery, corruption, and the relaxation of morals, addresses the present need for emancipation from the new forms of "slavery" that had oppressed the island and stunted its political and economic growth.

Although a slave, Caniquí, the narrative makes clear, is an individual with a uniquely Cuban history. The narration makes this point by recalling his mischievousness as a child and his African-Chinese ancestry. This last quality marks Caniquí as an authentic representative of Cuba's mixed ethnic origins, combining the blood of the two major laboring groups brought to the island in large numbers during the nineteenth century: the African slaves and the Chinese indentured servants. Unlike the passive slaves of abolitionist novels, Caniquí is a restless, vigorous hero who makes a deep impression on the Pablos family and other characters (Barreda 129–31). Cuervo Hewitt points out that Caniquí's Hispanic name itself anticipates the appearance of another slave character of the same name in Cuban literature. Appearing in Carpentier's *Concierto barroco* (Baroque concert, 1974), that character is the music-playing Filomeno, a descendant of the first black hero of Cuban literature, who appeared in Silvestre de Balboa's *Espejo de paciencia* (Mirror of patience) in 1608 (APA 229–30).

Ma Irene is Caniquí's maternal great-grandmother and an iyalorisha. In her role as diviner, she has told her great-grandson the secret of his birth and destiny: "Elegbará—the great god, vindictive and powerful—was angry since his, Caniquí's, birth, because Calixta—daughter of a Mandinga princess— had listened to a man of another race: a Chinese. That was the history of his parents. And so much so, that Bián, the black god of smallpox, had finished them both off immediately after his arrival to the world" (Ramos 161). The references are vague or confused, but it seems that the miscegenation committed by Calixta and the Chinese man brought on the "justice" of the enforcer Elegbará and punishment dispensed by Bián, more commonly known as Chankpana or Babalú-Ayé.

By his crossed lineage and his own defiance, Filomeno Bicunia Caniquí symbolizes a multicultural and oppressed Cuba with a mystical bent. Seeing themselves reflected in Caniquí's otherness, Juan Antonio and Mariceli may grasp the extent of their own servitude to the codes and rules of their colonial society and then evolve their own forms of resistance to its authority: "To liberate themselves, they will find an example and strength in Caniquí. The slave is the inspiration that extricates them from the terrible circumstances in which they find themselves" (Barreda 133). A close reading can establish that the strength of the exemplar derives largely from resources of religion.

The narrator of the novel tells us early on that Caniquí's great-grandmother was Mariceli's black nursemaid; by her nurturing presence as well as by her religious instruction, ma Irene has taught Mariceli to abhor the cruelty of slavery, most visible when her father's slaves are humiliated in the stocks or lashed in the *tumbadero*, a clearing or yard reserved for such torments. The nursemaid's influence explains in part Mariceli's desire to see her father punish the runaway Caniquí with leniency, and her sympathy will win her over to the cause of Cuban abolition. The narrator tells us that the nursemaid "had inculcated in her since childhood a certain absurd notion of heaven and hell. The 'bad' whites, according to ma Irene, suffered after death the same punishments that the blacks had received in life. The latter, in the end, were so [i.e., black] because of their sins, or those of their parents. And if they were good in life, they became white as they rose up to heaven." The passage refers to the belief held by many Lucumís that all humans return to life after they die and that "sin" or its equivalent is punishable by the assignment to a low station in life, such as that of the black slave subjected to a white master. Much later, ma Irene suffers a sickness from which she is thought to die, and yet she miraculously recovers; with her near death and rebirth, ma Irene becomes a symbol of a reborn Cuba that has vindicated the Africanity in its own bosom (Ramos 50, 273).

Due to the conflicting ideological pressures that bear upon Mariceli's tortured psyche, this becomes the site where doctrines and discourses compete for dominance. In addition to alluding to ma Irene's Afro-Cuban teachings, and in proximity both to don Lorenzo's pontificating on the greater good of the slaveholding institution and to Juan Antonio's denunciations of the colonial subjugation, the narrative explicitly cites works of sacred and mystical poetry of the Golden Age, especially that of Fray Luis de León, San Juan de la Cruz, and Sor Juana Inés de la Cruz.

Apart from Mariceli's own Afro-Catholic formation, other religious doctrines and dogma from various traditions meet, contradict, and entangle each other in Ramos's anxious narrative. The epigraph of chapter 3, for instance, is identified as a passage from *The Chariot of Clay*, a Hindu drama attributed to

Prince Zudraka, second century A.D. In that epigraph, a slave named Estavaraka declares, echoing the previously introduced notion of reincarnation: "The gods have already punished me with slavery for the faults of a previous life; I do not want to risk being punished again by being reborn a slave." A different religious tradition is recalled in a later description of the hills and valleys surrounding the Pablos family's sugar mill. The narrator, focused on Juan Antonio's thoughts, mentions that "Close to the Solitario, on very white foam, a black and rotund Buddha was settled." This landscape speaks of "a prehuman and inconceivable God, equally indifferent to all the beings of that penetrating and impenetrable nature, without any relation to the mystical allegation of his cousin" (Ramos 58, 61). The attitude of Buddhistic calm seems removed from the turbulent drama of the novel's characters, but the passage prefigures the pantheistic mood of Caniquí's personal form of worship, soon to be revealed. Texts of other religious and philosophical traditions are cited and interwoven into the narrative: those of African myth, the Bible, Enlightenment encyclopedism, French vitalism, the poetry of Heredia, and, again, the Afro-Cuban discourse of syncretic religion and negrismo.

Although the polyphony of religious texts in the novel does not point to any simplistic relativism or tolerance with respect to religious faith, the novel argues negatively for a dominant viewpoint that is critical of Christianity, implying that it, rather than African-based worship, is the life-denying slave religion. The specific target of critique is the kind of conventional, complacent brand of Christianity that, practiced by the majority of Cuban colonists, sanctioned the institution of slavery. By contrast, the kind of Christianity that Mariceli reads about in the *Leyenda dorada* (The golden legend), for instance, with its history of saints and martyrdoms, provides a model of a more "heroic" and otherworldly self-sacrifice incompatible with worldly existence (Ramos 123–24).

By giving herself over to religious fervor, Mariceli virtually rejects the order of her plantation-owning father once she realizes the priestly complicity of the father-confessor with her own father in discouraging her attempts to become a nun. In effect, in choosing to live in accord with her ideal, she resists "the satanic power of her father and of the men like him." Her violent antipathy against the patriarch only intensifies when she learns of his machinations in the sinking of a competitor's ship, loaded with slaves (Ramos 122, 226). Her self-torment thus symbolizes an attempt to expiate the paternal-institutional crime of slavery, which is shown to epitomize the collective sin of one race's domination of another.

Ramos thus elaborates what could be called a Nietzschean critique of

Christian morality. That critique, as I have suggested, works a curious inversion: Christianity is presented as the "slave morality" that militates against the needs and interests of life, whereas the *slaves'* morality appears as that which promotes a free and ascendant life. As defined or figured by patriarchy, "woman" symbolizes and thus sublimates the subjugation, passivity, and weakness prescribed by Christian morality. Nietzsche indeed asserts in *The Will to Power*, with perhaps only metaphorical misogyny, that woman "needs a religion of weakness that glorifies being weak, loving, and being humble as divine: or better, she makes the strong weak—she rules when she succeeds in overcoming the strong." Mariceli's masochistic practice, although implicitly critical of the colonizers' Catholicism, expresses an extreme of the same kind of weakness made into virtue. On the other hand, the African-based religion practiced by Caniquí is an empowering, celebratory, physical-spiritual faith affirming a personal communion with the natural world inhabited by the orishas. That religion symbolizes an alternative vision of the national destiny as well. Like Ramos afterward, Nietzsche "declared war on the anemic Christian ideal . . . not with the aim of destroying it but only of putting an end to its tyranny and clearing the way for new ideals, for *more robust ideals*" (Nietzsche, *Will* 460, 197). Inasmuch as Christian ideals devalorized the will and favored personal and collective disempowerment, Caniquí's situation—Cuba's situation—called for a new credo of strength, pride, and self-determination: more robust ideals.

At various moments, the novel broaches the topic of a repressed sexual element inherent to religious fanaticism, bringing the debate over Cuban nationalism into the Freudian libidinal arena. In discussing with doña Celia her plans to turn her own nursery into a private chapel, "Mariceli remembered an insignificant fact, perhaps already forgotten by her mother. . . . The year before some pairs of dogs had been enclosed there, to what purpose she didn't properly know." The recollection comes near the end of chapter 5, "Solitudes," and remains unexplained, but the recollection is juxtaposed with Mariceli's expression of intent to use the chapel for acts of penitence. Mariceli also dreams one night that the young Roman martyr of one of her lithographs is embracing her. In the same dream-scene, a tiger positions itself to devour Mariceli and Caniquí, and then the slave offers her a hairshirt of mortification. A mob of slaves is shouting around them, but she hears nothing. Mariceli thus unconsciously identifies herself with the victims and martyrs of her dream, associating them with images of desire and death. Later on, in the chapter entitled "Camino de Perfección" (Road to perfection), we read a mix of religious and sexual signs in learning that Mariceli "[p]laced her candle on the altar and began to remove the melted sperm [*esperma*] from her fingers" (Ramos 119, 134, 148).

The narrative gradually brings bits and pieces of the mystery surrounding this strange devotion to light. Caniquí has hidden the blouse that Mariceli bloodied during her rounds of self-flagellation. We also learn that Caniquí brought the blouse to the *taita* for him to make a *resguardo* or protective charm with it, consistent with the apotropaic logic of a Congo magic that wards off evil. We sense, however, that there exists a secret beyond the secret that Caniquí protects. The scant clues suggest a transgression committed and left unspoken. Could the secret, we ask, be a sexual encounter between the slave and his white mistress? The narrative does not dispel this indeterminacy, but a weary Mariceli, after kneeling for hours in her flagellation chamber before the crucified Christ, reflects on the weakness of the flesh as the narrator's voice blends once again with hers:

> Perhaps in her ultimate yearnings were mixed abominable desires, unextinguished ember of that surrender to the Incubus, on her first night in the chapel! It was better that she find that ember cold, the sinister power of the Incubus exorcised. Caniquí was innocent. And her only desire, now, was that of purging her sins of pride and rebelliousness before the designs of the omniscient power in snatching her mother away from her, the neglect of her faith for so much time, the forgetting of the pristine impulses of her heart: and of the non-fulfillment of her promises. So that the specter of the unhappy slave, delivered by her to the dark powers, could return to the bosom of God as if to bring peace to her mother's soul, she had to carry out her expiatory penance. (Ramos 285–86)

Caniquí thus acquires spectral dimensions in Mariceli's mind to the extent that he himself has become "El Incubo." The narrator reports the rumor running through Trinidad: the slave keeps her "under his satanic power by means of a spell, according to some, or by means of some vital secret, which the less credulous affirm." Caniquí and Mariceli's dark secret thus forms the novel's center of mystery and motivates the pining José Antonio to seek the truth of their relationship (Ramos 281, 291, 296). The incubus that is Caniquí's ghostly presence, symbolizing the African difference that his perspective introduces into the nationalist dialogue, in effect doubles the text of the narrative as it opens up an alternative reading of Cuban history from the runaway's point of view.

In the novel's first extended discussion of Caniquí's beliefs, the narration signals the insistence of African religious figures in the slave's thinking, despite the overlay of Christian symbols and precepts in his consciousness and even despite Caniquí's "mature" skepticism toward African religion. One revealing passage sums up the process of empowering syncretism by which Caniquí has reinterpreted Christianity and Yoruba religion within a dual system of correspondences and differences. Cognizant of incongruities between symbologies, this syncretism produces not syntheses, as would be the case in complete identifications, but heterogeneous combinations or juxtapositions: "Before Christ on his cross—sympathetic symbol for his imagination peopled with analogous tortures inflicted upon the elders of his race— Obatalá had given him the sensation of his infinite power. Truly, God the Father, of whom Rosario had spoken to him, could well be Obatalá. By his order, the terrifying Changó—god of thunder—had made him cry with the dazzling brilliance of his flash, his frightening noise and his fire, which killed blacks and burned trees and houses. That, surely, could not be the work of the poor crucified Christ." As this reference to Changó illustrates, Caniquí finds that the orishas, more than the God and saints of Catholicism, provide a satisfying *ratio* explaining natural phenomena in supernatural terms. In Caniquí's memory, Biri once extinguished the sun; Orúmila brought "an intense happiness" one tropical morning during Caniquí's time in the palenque or settlement of runaway slaves, or cimarrones (Ramos 160). It is in his heroic personal history, moreover, that Caniquí himself will fulfill the requirements of an Obatalá-Christ figure whose example will symbolize the way to redemption.

Such syncretisms and their explanation further illustrate the manner in which African-based religion is compared to its advantage in the novel with the other religions. Not only do its animism and cult of nature expand the individual's sense of self, but its secret languages of myth and ritual bind their speakers into a community of like-minded worshipers—unlike the Western religions of interiority that seem to isolate the individual in a private relationship with God. Whereas Caniquí is more often than not depicted as a lone individualist, descriptions of Afro-Cuban celebrations in the narrative nonetheless indicate their function as forms of ethnic self-identification and symbols of solidarity. During the Epiphany carnival in Trinidad, for instance, "[t]he iron-like collective identity imposed by the whites, with its distorted Christianization, broke itself one more time upon the diverse origins and social categories of faraway Africa. Each one felt something more than black and slave. The Congo, the Mandinga, the Carabalí remembered or discovered precarious differences with which to feed his elemental human yearning for individuation" (Ramos 217). While the carnival provides a release valve for pent-up energies, it also strengthens, by a process of collective individuation, the latent ties of community across the boundaries of distinct African ethnicities. African tradition is tolerated by the whites and embraced by the blacks in the same event.

In addition to forging a sense of identity and ethnic belonging in Caniquí, African-based religion strengthens his will to defy the whites hacendados and slavers. The orishas, appearing ubiquitously in Caniquí's sign-world, are not only the life of nature but the guides of the spirit. To Caniquí's mind, their existence and immanence is not just a question of faith and understanding but of feeling and intuition: "Amidst the mysterious concavities of the hills, . . . as in the enormous treetops of the ancient ceibas, in the fire, in the rain, in the fruits of the earth and in the flowers—which constantly shook their spirits in intense emotions—Filomeno refused to concede that there was no benevolent and protective orisha, the way that in his early youth he had felt it on his own account, before learning it through the traditions of his race." Despite Caniquí's skepticism and Christian indoctrination, orisha worship offers assurance, especially in moments of solitude or despair. In the forest, Caniquí knows that the gods dwell in the sacred ceiba, and that Elegbará opens the paths that lead away from his oppressors; on the seashore, he feels the presence of Olokun and bathes in the exhilaration of freedom. Caniquí's form of worship is indeed not a question of believing dogma, as Barreda observes, but of experiencing the "forces of the universe" (Ramos 160; Barreda 134).

And despite his disbelief in other aspects of orisha worship, Caniquí has no doubt whatsoever that Olokun assists him, having helped him to swim away and escape from his master and the other pursuers. With Olokun's protection, "the sea was his element," and it gave him "an unspeakable happiness" to dive in the water, where no harm would befall him (Ramos 162). Cuervo Hewitt has noted the confidence of Caniquí in Olokun, his protecting orisha, despite the threat posed by the destiny-turner Elegbará. It could be added that Caniquí's faith in the sea god reflects the Cuban identification with the ambisexual Yemayá-Olokun: "Pursued by the whites, the slave Filomeno (Caniquí) reaches the place that he considered the nest of his protection, as if he arrived to a maternal bed: the blue, infinite sea of Yemayá-Olokun." Olokun's syncretization with the patron saint of the Bahía de La Habana, the Virgin of Regla, further places Caniquí at the heart of the evolving Cuban national identity in this recasting of Cuban history from the Afro-Cuban viewpoint (APA 134, 165). This water symbolism not only confirms

Caniquí's identification with the water god but also foreshadows the end of his life in a mountain lake, where, cornered and shot by the posse, he will be reunited with Olokun and the natural world.

Caniquí's communication with the orishas, as suggested earlier, becomes a sort of animistic nature worship in Ramos's text, especially evident when Caniquí arrives at Olokun's sea, but also when the author refers, erroneously by most lights, to Birí as the moon and to Orúmibila as the sun. A sunrise is described in the following unusual terms: "on the rigid horizon of the waters, magnificent Orúmila [normally considered the god of Ifá] began to cast upward the blood of his agonizing enemy, to come up later, gentle and serene, in the luminous and lightening blue of the sky." In Ramos's erroneous reading of West African mythology, the orisha names of natural phenomena mark those phenomena as allies in Caniquí's quest for liberation, for although Caniquí is said not to believe wholeheartedly in the orishas, he worships the personal and impersonal forces they personify and symbolize. To do so is his second nature. Caniquí will save enough from his salary to purchase his *coartación* or manumission and not feel the temptation (*comezón* or *impulso*), inspired by Elegbará, to escape to the forest once again. Here Elegbará appears as the sometimes malicious Eshú, whom Caniquí blames for making him see an undressed Mariceli and because of whom he must undergo a *limpia*, otherwise known as limpieza, or ritual cleansing. Caniquí also carries his resguardos or magic safeguards against Elegbará: a piece of iron, *cayajabos* or jack beans, and a written prayer to the Just Judge (Ramos 158–59, 186–87).

Other characters appearing in *Caniquí* indicate other Afro-Cuban codes of conduct that come to bear on the protagonist's attitude toward his masters and his bondage. The taita ("father") José María, a one-hundred-year-old plantation slave, functions as a helper who aids and instructs Caniquí. After the slave sees his unclad mistress during one of her ritual flagellations, he goes, deeply disturbed, to seek José María's advice. The taita gives him counsel, which in fact refers to the precedent of one "negro spiritualist" named José Gabriel Trelles, who had committed a similar transgression. Because he had seen a white woman "*ejnúa*" (*desnuda*, naked), José Gabriel suffered from an embó that led him to be lynched outside the gate of the village, his body left to feed the vultures. In sum, says the taita, "Naked white woman, even in dreams, was the perdition of a slave" (Ramos 163). Cuervo Hewitt finds in the passage the "transculturation of a concept" related to African divination, for the taita applies a moral lesson from a past precedent to a future action.

Here, the "patakí" is not African myth but an historical antecedent that "now comes to determine the repetition of the narrative denouement" (APA 68–69, 83).

While consulting with José María, Caniquí recalls the precedent of yet another slave named El Chino, whom the taita had accompanied for a reading of the diloggún oracle. On that occasion, the cowries advised El Chino to flee from a certain woman who would otherwise bring him disaster. El Chino's response was to cut her throat and flee, never to be heard from again. To avert the same disaster, José María gives Caniquí the instructions for producing the embó—made of Mariceli's undergarment, corn, and, later, nails—that will rid him of his curse or salación. As it turns out, the prenda or article of clothing that Caniquí obtains for making his safeguard will be Mariceli's blood-stained blouse, taken from the house servant Rosario, to whom it was given for cleaning. That theft will be reported by the envious domestic slave Domingo, who betrays his rival to the owner and overseers (Ramos 164, 166, 174).

Caniquí's eventual self-surrender to the posse led by Captain Armona recapitulates, in a language of gesture peculiar to Ramos's text, the cimarrón's attitude toward nature, death, and life beyond it. Floating face upward in the waters of Olokun, the narrator tells us, "He kept immobile, his arms open, upon the soft bed of the calm waves, as if he heard the voice of a mother in the air, rocking his reverie: mother nature, his only one, like him a slave of the whites and like him rebellious, confident, laughing, . . . Blue! Magnificent Obatalá! Freedom! in the width and breadth of space: in the air, in the sea! Freedom, expanse" (Ramos 317). Although the passage once again misidentifies Obatalá, whose color is normally white, with the blue of the sky, it anticipates the dispersion of Caniquí's mind and body into the freedom of a liberated nature, into the expanse of a space unfettered by irons and the religion of the slave owners. In death he will meet the maternal-paternal embrace of the re-engendered Obatalá, syncretized with the crucified Christ of Catholicism and merged with the indwelling spirit of creation. In the face of death, Caniquí's orisha-worship thus liberates and affirms life, exalts in the beauty of the natural world, celebrates sensuality, and ennobles the individual as it consecrates his example for a community of believers.

Mariceli's silence at the end of the novel, after Caniquí's death, mirrors "the eternity [lo eterno] of the night," a night that serves as the endless ground of peregrine discourses that must collide or collude with one another along the drift of history. As Mariceli tells José Antonio during their last reported exchange, the final dialogue of the novel: "He was a hardened runaway. He loved freedom above all things. It was his religion." (Ramos 332, 327). Which is to say not only that freedom was Caniquí's religion in a metaphorical sense, but that in practicing his neo-African religion in defiance of the Spanish masters Caniquí attained a circumscribed measure of freedom.

A Foundational Folklore: Lachatañeré's Mythic System

Myth supplements history in proposing figures of the self, images of community, and even alternative ways of narrating that history. As a compilation of stories of explanatory power for the speaking community, a mythology keeps alive a cultural unconscious, a collection of archetypes. Seen with the family of narratives, and as differentiated from history, myth exhibits the mode of literary "abstraction" placed at the extreme opposite end of a scale at whose other end we find realist verisimilitude. Caniquí, as a historical novel whose characters engage in myth telling and myth making, explores the way in which the flesh-and-blood slave is transformed into a symbol of the rebellious subject and the forerunner of a new kind of community. In other narratives of the period, however, mythic tales of gods, removed from more historicizing contexts, depict them as beings insured against all contingency, finitude, and doubt. In the narrated exploits and adventures of the gods, we find projected, in symbolic codes, an abstract schema of desire. Frye's characterization underscores this aspect of idealized wish fulfillment inherent to all myth: "In terms of narrative, myth is the imitation of actions near or at the conceivable limits of desire. The gods enjoy beautiful women, fight one another with prodigious strength, comfort and assist man, or else watch his miseries from the height of their immortal freedom. The fact that myth operates at the top level of human desire does not mean that it necessarily presents its world as attained or attainable by human beings" (36). To extend the implications of the connection Frye makes between desire and representation: the world of myth constitutes the vanishing point of signification, delimiting the human world by establishing the unattained or receding goal. Yet as collective fantasy, myth operates at the level of a collective desire, presenting its world as an allegory of an alternative collective destiny drawn to newly conceived and redefined limits.

Two years after the publication of Caniquí, Rómulo Lachatañeré brought out ¡¡Oh, mío Yemayá!! (1938). An exclamation of reverence for Yemayá serves as the collection's title, curiously framed by the unusual double exclamation marks. Four years later, Lachatañeré himself discredited the book, a collection of patakís, in his introduction to Manual de santería (Manual of Santería, 1942), where he admitted publishing the previous work "with a certain irresponsibility" due to his dependence on unreliable sources, namely, youths who too willingly and inaccurately divulged the secrets of the cult (MS 10–11). Yet for all its distortions of or discrepancies from more authoritative versions (wherever they be found), ¡¡Oh, mío Yemayá!! stands as a seminal work of Lucumí myth and folklore. In his "Reference Notes" to the collection, Lachatañeré expressed his desire that it "serve as a stimulus to others . . . for the incorporation of what is black [de lo negro] . . . to the national culture" (OMY xxxi). In the stream of Cuban letters during the 1930s, the book is a heteronomous island inhabited by gods unconcerned with the sociopolitical turmoil of the moment.

Lachatañeré's Afro-Cuban collection affirms the folkloristic and mythological orientation of Afro-Cubanism marked by the appearance of Carpentier's ¡Ecue-Yamba-O! in 1933 and the first volumes of Nicolás Guillen's poetry in 1930, 1931, and 1934. In his prologue to Lachatañeré's work, Fernando Ortiz attempts to "predispose" the reader of Lachatañeré's stories by instilling the notion that they have a religious function, such that "reading will draw out all the value from the poetry and will be able to enjoy the brilliance of its metaphor, the genius of its theologic and cosmogonic philosophy and the artifice of its mythological scheme" ("Predisposición vii). Thus framing the reading by these comments, the preface reminds us that we are dealing with a unique "literary genre" with its own mythicoreligious language.

That is, Lachatañeré's mythic world, enclosed unto itself, features a cast of supernatural characters at the limits of desire. Abandonment, incest, matricide, cannibalism, abuse, fraud, sloth, cowardice, hypocrisy—the gods commit all the deadly sins and some additional ones with impunity. In the primordial world of this text, orishas struggle in armed combat against other orishas. Animals struggle against gods, and even some vegetable characters, including calabashes and yams, know how to assert themselves. They all squabble, members of one big dysfunctional Afro-Cuban family. The revitalized myths of Lachatañeré's story cycle offer the etiological legends, cautionary tales, and cosmogonic narratives characteristic of an ethnic group's mythology. Their archetypes, consisting of "motifs" or "[i]dentical elements" of an oral tradition that are "worked and reworked," which Herskovits finds in African oral literature, give the transcultural model and pattern for subsequent narrative imitations ("Study" 363). The self-enclosed world of myth projected by Lachatañeré's stories can be opened to various allegorical interpretations, including a "nationalist" reading that construes it as defying the norms of Western (or colonial) civilization while preserving an ethnic subculture's narrative tradition. Its innovations include the introduction of Yoruba-Lucumí terms into the literary lexicon.

Many of the orisha narratives in Lachatañeré's work are recognizable as patakís, which, as will be recalled, function as repositories of counsel and knowledge in Afro-Cuban divination systems. In Lachatañeré's retellings, the patakís reveal a further, dreamlike function, that of wish fulfillments that perform symbolic reconciliations of social contradictions through the agency of fiction. A reading of a few representative and connected stories from Lachatañeré's collection will unfold some of their allegorical dimensions, including the nationalist ones.

The first paragraph of the collection's first story, "El río" (The river), marks out the narrative's "terrain" in several senses of the word. The "avalanche of men," it begins, entered the forest and trampled the herbs of the paths and "made the roads." In this manner, "man constructed his means of communication and extended the limits of the villages, establishing new relations and taking possession more and more of the secrets that the forest jealously guarded." The opening of the story thus refers us to a literal opening in the "dense forest" where culture meets with and masters the natural. The river is described metaphorically, as "winding snakelike [*serpenteando*] through the mountains," "contorting itself like a wounded serpent, showing and hiding its back in the convulsions of death." The river, so metaphorized, also "howls lugubriously" (OMY 35, 36). Reading the description makes us animists, present at the (mythical) beginnings of civilization, preparing us for the appearance of Agallú Solá.

Agallú Solá, a laborer who is "strong and vigorous like a young warrior," one embodying the civilizing will to conquer nature, takes up the challenge to conquer the river. We know that he is also San Cristóbal, the patron saint of Havana. Agallú Solá builds a boat in which he crosses the mighty river, and then recrosses it again and again until it settles into a "gentle and calm current." His labor has in this way connected a society across the waters and set the pattern for an economy based on commerce and transport between peoples (OMY 38). The master of the river will then accumulate great wealth in transporting passengers from shore to shore. The myth thus recollects, in narrative time, the birth of navigation in the origins of business.

But one day one of Agallú Solá's passengers does not pay, or rather pays by removing her dress and offering herself sexually to the boatman. Only after completing their intimate commerce does she reveal her identity: "You have had the high honor of lying down with Obatalá" (OMY 39). One wonders why the first story stresses the concupiscence of a *female* Obatalá. Here, the

Yoruba god of whiteness and purity has been syncretized with the Catholic Virgin of Mercy and will perform the function that Yemayá more commonly fulfills in other narratives from the Yoruba. In joining his line with Obatalá's, Agallú Solá gains the privilege of knowing the name and origin of his clients and the right to demand prepayment for all he carries across the river. Lachatañeré named the chapter "Aché," for it is grace, power, or blessing that the boatman receives as a consequence of his fortuitous union with the goddess.

Changó is born of that union, but it is Yemayá, the great maternal orisha, who raises him. Changó's illegitimacy is problematic precisely because the narrative treats it as unproblematic. Emblematic of Cuban writing's alter/native origins—repeating perhaps the motifs of the Cuban populace's mixed or confused heritage—Changó's bastardy becomes a source of perverse pride, for the god is conceived much in the manner of Afro-Cuban writing, as illegitimate, mulatto, orphaned, and culturally displaced. We will return to him shortly.

It happens that one day a different child arrives at Agallú Solá's dock, pleading for transport but without the means to pay the boatman. The child convinces Agallú Solá to carry him on his shoulders. The orisha does so, only to find that the child grows heavier and heavier until Agallú has no choice but to let him drop in the river. Looking at the child, he realizes that he was carrying none other than Oduddua, who in exchange for his efforts gives possession of the river to Agallú Solá and then disappears. Unbeknownst to the boatman, he has carried the cocreator of humanity, the (mythical) first king of Oyo, dispenser of justice and guide of babalaos (OC 74–75).

Throughout the stories of ¡¡Oh, mío Yemayá!!, as Agallú Solá's cycle exemplifies, the constant element is the transfer of a value from one character to another. The subject seeks to obtain an object over and against the wishes or efforts of (an) opponent(s), often turning to helpers for assistance.

The pattern is further exemplified in the section of the book entitled "The Ekuelé Board," a section appearing second among those of Lachatañeré's stories. The plot revolves around Changó's acquisition of Orúmila's coveted ekuelé board, the *Tablero del Ekuelé* (Table of Ifá). On that board, divination readings, *registros*, are made with the cast of the special necklace, consisting of a string of eight coconut shell pieces, called the *collar*, or ekuelé (also *opele*, or *epkuele*). Narratologically speaking, the narrative tells of a subject, Changó, who desires the object. Surrogate mother Yemayá, and later on Elegguá, are the helpers (agencies, powers) providing the means to realize that aim. The obstacles or opponents are those parties who would withhold the board or prevent Changó from obtaining it—including, at least early on, Obatalá, the first owner (see Bal 26–31).

During a thunderstorm, Yemayá finds to her surprise that the child Changó has appeared before her, cast out of the heavens by his mother, Obatalá. The maternal Yemayá delightfully regards him as a gift and takes him in, but Changó soon demands that his adoptive mother take him to a güemilere, or drumming party with religious significance. He then orders her to serve him his amalá, or stew made with lamb and vegetables, and demands a sleeping mat that is not as dirty as his mother's (OMY 54–55).

Changó continues to abuse Yemayá, calling her "criada" (maid) and abusing her motherly generosity to the point of telling her to stop dancing to his wild drumming and go to a mountain to find him bananas, oguedé. Eager to please, she leaves immediately. In a little while, Changó, god of fire that he is, sets the ilé (house, hut) aflame. The solicitous mother returns to save her adoptive son but comes back empty handed. Changó upbraids her but gives her a second chance by sending her to Obatalá's ilé to procure the ekuelé board.

Exhausted, her feet transformed into bloody masses by her long journey to the ilé, Yemayá finally arrives at the doorstep and faints. When she recovers, Changó is standing before her, the Tablero del Ekuelé in his hands. He has taken away the board when Obatalá, in her camino as Olofi (sic: "with all the attributes of Olofi upon her") returns home and detects the attempted theft. For her crime of aiding and abetting, Yemayá must labor for forty days in Obatalá's house. At the end of the sentence, the god of whiteness grants the maternal goddess her liberty and the ekuelé necklace to give to Changó. Changó receives the necklace and begins immediately to cast it "on the polished surface of the board, and in accord with the different positions taken by the beads, explains to Yemayá what has happened to her and gives her formulas to resolve her difficulties." Yemayá now understands that Changó is "thrower of the ekuelé," which is the reason why he will not allow her to raise him (OMY 58, 59).

That story line continues in the chapter "Olvido" (Forgetfulness), in which Changó has become a successful soothsayer but longs to return to beating the drums at the güemileres. He therefore gives the divining tray to Orúmila but not without asking him to pay a regular percentage to Elegguá. In the story "Codicia" (Greed), Orúmila runs a thriving business disentangling complications in the lives of the aleyos, or noninitiates, who come seeking a consultation. Elegguá as his assistant receives his assigned portion of profits, and all is well—until Orúmila's consultations earn him more money than he needs. Then Eleggúa offers one hundred coins to become Orúmila's partner. Orúmila refuses Eleggúa, puts him off, tells him to come back, and then refuses to pay him altogether.

An angry Eleggúa devises a plan to make Orúmila pay up. He goes out and splits himself into three beings. The first Eleggúa he commands to stand out in the savanna and tell all comers that Orúmila has lost his skill, thus defaming the diviner's hard-earned reputation. He assigns the second one a position at Orúmila's doorstep and orders him to tell the clients that Orúmila is just fine, he still knows how to cast the ekuelé, but that he is out at the moment and the clients may, if they so desire, obtain a reading at the house of Orúmila's "substitute." The third Eleggúa plays the role of that substitute with his own board and ekuelé necklace. Siphoning off Orúmila's clientele in this manner, the old man's business withers away. To make a living, Orúmila at the end has no choice but to pay Eleggúa as a partner (OMY 64–69).

As we follow the passing of the divination board from Obatalá to Changó, and later to Orúmila and Eleggúa, we (re)learn the rationale behind elements of the Ifá ritual. The story of Changó's acquisition of the Ifá presents, in Ortiz's words, a certain "astute mystification" of the requirement to pay the Ifá diviner for his services, and thus serves as a narrative confirmation of the oracle's veracity and value ("Predisposición" xxv). The story also indicates how, by guile and cunning, Eleggúa earned the right to become the intermediary between the orishas and humans, the hermeneut as messenger and nemesis who must be propitiated at the beginning of every rite. Eleggúa as the purveyor of truth may resort to duplicity, even "triplicity," in performing his go-between role.

Lachatañeré's "Incesto" (Incest), within the series entitled "Changó," confirms the structure of Lucumí myth as a family "romance" situated at Frye's top level, or extreme, of desire. Yemayá Saramaguá, the maternal one, is one day taken with a sexual desire for her adopted son. Changó, waking up from a nap, rejects her advances and scrambles up a palm tree. "But Yemayá, recovered from the humiliation produced in her flesh, pursues him and runs wildly and her exuberant breasts sing in incessant pealing the lust of the omordé [woman], who has let herself be dragged by the impetuous force of her sex" (OMY 101). Yemayá's incestuous lust knows no restraint, and the story becomes pornographic. She cries, "Obiní, satisfy me!" He responds, "Omordé, look for a beast like yourself!"

As its transgression in this narrative reveals, the universal taboo on incest delineates, as Lévi-Strauss has reasoned, the very boundary between nature and culture (46, 51). Yet the more-than-human orishas both precede and follow the establishment of the nature/culture dichotomy; that is, they may act as if no taboo existed for them. At the same time, they are anthropomorphic projections of a human desire cognizant of human limitations. Despite his misgivings, Changó weakens and gives in to temptation: "Their inverted bodies roll in confused movements and for a long while they possess each other contra natura" (OMY 102). "Contra natura" in this context paradoxically refers to that which goes against universalized social convention and not simply to that which "goes against nature." The orishas in their multiple caminos are free to define and redefine what is natural. Cros Sandoval retells the same patakí of Yemayá's consummated desire for her own son and follows it with yet another narrative, one in which it is Changó who makes the sexual advance. This time Yemayá disabuses him of his lustful illusions by taking him out to sea in a boat; out there, she saves him from drowning (RA 219–20).

From the social criticism of *¡Ecue-Yamba-O!* to the mythical enclosure of *¡¡Oh, mío Yemayá!!*, passing through the historical allegory of *Caniquí*, we chart the course by which selected elements of Afro-Cuban religion have been incorporated into the narrative of a nation and the multiethnic reidentification of a people. All of the texts from the 1930s examined in this chapter have demonstrated how the narrative of nationalist allegory, seen from the critical perspective of postcoloniality, make use of the propositions of a popularized religion for arguably nonreligious ends. Cuban writing in the republican period, to be Cuban writing, included its component of sociopolitical critique. But that writing also needed a mythological base like that of Lachatañeré's collection, a self-contained system of myths of no certain genealogy and with no immediate value for praxis, a textual foundation to which a properly Cuban culture could refer and by which that culture could refer, perhaps "incestuously," to itself. At the mythical level of desire, that orphaned writing aspired to become a heteronomous universe—negating something in affirming its own right to be—of which Lachatañeré's article on the "Lucumí religious system" may have been the apologia and theoretical mirror of patience.

4

◈ A Is For Abakuá

Nyuao manga tereré [What is written cannot be erased].
Lydia Cabrera, *Refranes de Negros Viejos*

In Miguel Barnet's poem "Ceremony with a Rooster and a Fish," from *La sagrada familia* (The holy family, 1967), the sacrifice of a black rooster in an Abakuá ceremony serves "to preserve the scene / the splendor in the pitcher of Sikán / her cursed tongue." The lyric speaker observes the ceremony and imagines a transformation: "listening to Ekue who roars and swells / and stamps / because he wants to be a fish and not wood behind a curtain / because he wants to call himself Tanze and go away slowly / in the hard tide."

The poem's proper names, its elliptical allusions and unexplained prosopopeia belong to an insider's language, a language that can only seem opaque to the uninitiated reader. The narrative of and about the ritual doubles that ritual, in effect doubling the ritual's metonymic displacements by the poem's modalizing propositions, such as "he wants to call himself Tanze." Ekue—the wooden drum that roars like a bull—desires a transmutation into the fish Tanze, but the fish is already substituted by the sacrificed rooster, which at the same time signifies an "image" of the rooster, an ideal that is "intact in heaven" (*sagrada* 171). For, in the beginning, issuing from heaven, the voice of the Supreme God Abasí, it is said, was transferred to the fish in Sikán's pitcher and then displaced into the Ekue, the original drum of the original secret society. In the beginning, that drum stood in for Sikán's earthen jar, but now the goatskin membrane of Ekue's successors commemorates the use of Sikán's own skin as a drumhead in the original scene of sacrifice.

As this series of transmutations suggests, the desire for metamorphosis conjures a complex phantasmic presence: in the founding myth and in the ritual of the Abakuá, the roaring sound is a voice that speaks for Abasí. A multiple sacrifice (of fish, woman, and rooster) is condensed into one symbolic act, and the splendor of the original sacrifice catechrestically amounts to a "cursed tongue" or to a cursed "language" (*lengua*), a pun drawing attention to the poem's own construction in language as memorial and echo of the sacrifice's inaugural speech. Yet the voice of Abasí itself is also a construction, one built of negations and differences: it manifests itself as the fish that would swim away but doesn't, becoming a memorial of self-difference or impossibility.

By these tropological operations, and especially by metaphorical substitution, the assumed presence of Abasí in the voice of the drum is produced as an interplay of presence and absence. Although Abasí would speak, that interplay suggests not so much the fullness of the voice as the hollowness of writing. The quotation that serves as epigraph to this chapter, *Nyuao manga tereré*, is rendered, "Lo que se firma no se borra": that is, what is signed, what is written or what is inscribed within the religion—like the cult's ground-signs called *firmas*, *grafias*, or *anaforuana*—cannot be erased. Cabrera glosses the translation in this way: "The commitment to which a Ñáñigo is solemnly sworn (or obliged) cannot be refused" (RVN 59). Writing—considered as an inscription on a surface, as a psychosocial contract among members of a fraternal order, or as a mnemonic prop substituting for the full presence attributed to the voice—provides a key for unlocking the sign-world of the *Sociedad Secreta Abakuá*. In the Abakuá Secret Society, "writing" is a function of a whole institution, produced by the machinery of the institution's special language, laws, tradition, psychology, ritual, and, now, its literature.

The Afro-Cuban symbol systems that concerned the preceding three chapters have exhibited the analogical thought that equates the word/thing relation to that of aché/nature, or in Kenneth Burke's terms, spirit/nature (RR 16). This metaphysical relation notwithstanding, the nature of language as system consists in a radical negativity toward reality; that is, in language's essential heterogeneity with respect to the noumenal world. The rhetoric of Afro-Cuban religion displays the labyrinthine complexity and self-referentiality by which the act of using or making of symbols negates both naïve linguistic naturalism and the nomenclature theory of correspondence. The arbitrary or unmotivated relationship of language and reality, or the variable relation of signifiers with signifieds and referents, is precisely what allows symbol systems to produce relatively autonomous spheres of signification.

The self-referential enclosure of language suggests an analogy for characterizing other cultural systems and subsystems. The common name of the Ñáñigo institution—the Abakuá Secret Society—indicates the greater emphasis it puts on clannish sociality than other Afro-Cuban religions known in the national literature. Such sociality frames the production of secret signs whose operation obeys a strict logic internal to and consistent with the context of the fraternal order. Those practices and traditions, when experienced from the inside, or emically, by the believer, seem natural and right. Yet that inside is constituted by a language of symbols, such that knowledge and "possession" of those symbols earns one the right to belong to the society and communicate according to its conventions.

The popular designation of Ñáñigos for the members of the Abakuá fraternal associations originally named the Abakuá figures called íremes, ñañas, diablitos, or ñáñigos. These íremes are the street dancers of the society, and they symbolize the spirits of the dead or the spirits of the society's founders. They are especially famous for coming out in the carnival on Epiphany, January 6, the Day of the Three Kings, when they can be seen running and dancing along the streets. Wearing masks that conceal their human identities, the íremes dress in multicolored or checkerboard costumes complete with conical headpieces topped with tassels, and they may also wear a big hat behind the headpiece, a raffia skirt, raffia cuffs, and a belt hung with bells. In festivals, the íremes dance to the beating of *encomo* and *boncó* drums with frenzied movements. In this way they pay homage to ancestors whom they revere in a

9. "Día de Reyes," by Federico Mialhe. Lithograph, c. 1850. Museo Nacional de Cuba, Old Havana, Cuba.

10. "Día de Reyes," by Víctor Patricio Landaluze. Oil on canvas, nineteenth century. Museo Nacional de Cuba, Old Havana, Cuba.

manner bearing similarities to that of the Yoruba Egungun cult (Ortiz, "Fiesta" 9, 11–12; CA 3:211; Simpson 92).

The accounts of Ñañigo belief and practice in Cuban literature date back to the beginnings of Afro-Cubanism, and that literature has often revealed the way in which a body of religious myth, doctrine, and ritual has entered into the forms of popular culture. Especially in the history of the Abakuá in Cuba, esoteric ceremonies and in-group narratives have entered into a public language, where it is used to describe an otherness residing in the heart of society. In the sections that follow I will introduce some of historical, social, mythological, and ritual dimensions of the Ñañigo world. This extended introduction will give a context to readings of the Abakuá sign system in narratives by Ortiz, Carpentier, Cabrera, and Gerardo del Valle.

The Abakuá Society

In the popular Cuban imagination, the Ñáñigos are surrounded by the aura of magic and interclan violence; they were once the talk of the town. In Fernández Robaina's *Recuerdos secretos de dos mujeres públicas*, the former prostitute Consuelo speaks of the "epoch of Yarini," that is, the time of the Ñáñigo celebrity Alberto Yarini y Ponce de León. Yarini was also the notorious pimp or *chulo* who attained a legendary status during the first years of the Republic. It was Yarini who gave Consuelo the name *la Charmé*; he was also a conservative political leader and a high official in a Ñáñigo *agrupación* or association. Yarini, Consuelo recalls, was shot to death by a certain Lotot in connection with the rivalry between the *guayabitos* and *apaches*, pimps from Cuba and France, respectively. The memorial for Yarini in the barrio of San Isidro, on October 24, 1910, together with his burial in the Colón cemetery, was a grand event: "There wasn't a whore, guayabito, Ñáñigo and people of all classes who didn't go to the funeral and burial," and the press reported an attendance of some ten thousand. Why the adulation? Yarini's mourners remembered his generosity; his largess seemed limitless, for he gave assistance in the form of money and influence with the police not only to his *ecobios* or comrades but even those who were not of his agrupación. Yarini's funeral brought out the "espíritu del compañerismo"—the spirit of camaraderie, and of "honor" and "manliness"—that prevailed in the politics, both the public and the clandestine, of the epoch (RDM 32, 34–35, 49, 45–46, 50).

Miguel Barnet's informant "Rachel," a nightclub star or *vedette* from the prerevolutionary belle époque, also speaks of Alberto Yarini: Yarini the cruel, the mysterious, the popular, the irresistible. Chulo and Ñáñigo, surrounded by an aura of power and violence, "Yarini had his harem. Woman were really crazy for him." Rachel tells of Yarini's knife fights, his part in the "black slavery" (*la trata de negras*), and his death during the fearful time when Halley's comet passed over (*Canción* 33–36).

These and other testimonials confirm the mystique that *el ñañiguismo* has held in Cuban culture. Long associated, often prejudicially, with the image of intergroup warfare and with an earthy, lumpen kind of spirituality, the name of Ñánigo for some has meant a sort of bogeyman and for many has connoted criminality, violence, and political intrigue, all belonging to the dangerous Afro-Cuban underworld, *el hampa afrocubana*.

The Ñáñigo or Abakuá religion traces its origin back to the Calabar region of western Africa. An animistic cult devoted to ancestor worship, it sprung from the Efik and Ekpe or Ejagham tribal groups of Calabar, in what is today southern Nigeria and Cameroon. The peoples who accepted their artistic and religious forms include the Ibibio, the Igbo, the Bras, the Koy, the Abakpa, the Bríkamo, and the Oba (RA 20). The origins of the Ekpe or Ngbe, meaning "leopard society," are found in the Ejagham (in Cuba, Ekoi) and the Efik, for the Efik word *ngó* leopard, forms part of the etymon *ñañ-ngó*—"leopard men" (TÑ 100). The name *Abakuá* is the Cuban Creole version of "Abakpa" (in Spanish, "Abaja"), by which the Ejagham are called in Cameroon. Thompson observes that the woman Sikán took the place of Ebongó, the Ngbe mother of the leopard among the Ejagham (FS 236, 248).

According to Valdés Bernal, the Abakuá group comprised of "Appapa" slaves from Calabar established the first cabildo in Havana in 1834–36—the "Apapa Efó" (128). Cabrera in *La Lengua Sagrada de los Ñáñigos* (The sacred language of the Ñáñigos) writes that early Abakuá societies were formed in Havana, Regla, Guanabacoa, Matanzas, and Cárdenas. The first groups were generally referred to as potencias, naciones, agrupaciones, *partidos, sitios, tierras,* or *juegos,* and the first to be founded, according to Cabrera, were the Akua Bután in Havana and the Efik Bután in nearby Regla (13–15). In El *monte,* however, Cabrera cites an old Ñáñigo "genealogy" of the potencias founded during that period: "Appapa (Efó), the foundation of Abakuá in Cuba, authorizes Efik Bután, who authorizes Efik Kondó, Efik Ñumané, Efik Acamaró, Efik Kunakúa, Efik Efigueremo and Efik Enyemiyá; Eforí Isún, Eforí Kondó, Eforí Ororó, Eforí Mukero, Eforí Bumá, Eforí Araocón. These are the seven branches of the two founding *potencias,* Efí y Efó" (196). Especially in urban settings with high concentrations of slaves, the Ñáñigos established their cabildos and in them kept alive the music, song, rituals, dance, and language they had carried with them in the crossing (TÑ 79). In addition to gathering its members together for purposes of religion and entertainment, the Ñáñigo cabildo could offer them relief for unemployment and sickness and for paying the cost of burials from a fund collected for those purposes (LSÑ 14).

In another of Cabrera's accounts, the members of the early Ñáñigo group called the Potencia Abakuá, with its seat in Guanabacoa, worshipped the patroness of the bay, la Virgen de Regla, who is doubled in the orisha Yemayá-Olokun (YO 18–19). The ceremonies of Ñáñigos thus combined Catholic and African, especially Lucumí, liturgical elements with those of Calabar (Bastide 114). This multicultural symbiosis of symbols can be observed throughout the religious art, ritual, mythology, doctrine, and ethics of the Abakuá cult.

The Abakuá societies had already fallen into disrepute in the popular imagination of the Republic prior to the period of the Machadato. Eager to make Cuba over into a modern society, the Cuban bourgeoisie deprecated the Ñáñigo cabildos as atavistic remnants of African institutions. Their comparsas and güemileres were outlawed in 1913. Police targeted the Abakuá babalaos as perpetrators of crimes that included alleged acts of human sacrifice. Fighting between rival agrupaciones provided jutification for harassments and raids against all practitioners.[1] Yet despite this state repression, in 1914 there were, according to Carpentier, some 107 Abakuá agrupaciones active in Havana and its outlying districts and in Matanzas (MC 286, 291).

Meanwhile, within the potencia's cabildo, Ñaniguismo had a different look. There, the plazas or leaders of the Abakuá hierarchy would hold court and preside over activities and ceremonies. The great priest is the isué, sometimes called by the Bantú name mkongo, "jefe militar" or military chief. The isué presides over the initiation ceremony or rompimiento. It is he who holds the head of the sacrificed cock between his teeth and places it atop the sacred drum. Other plazas include the obón iyamba, the king and keeper of the Ekue and second in command; the nasakó, or hechicero, sorcerer; and the ekueñón, priest or mystagogue (LSÑ 15).

The aberisún, executioner of the sacrifice, takes charge of killing the he-goat. He slits its throat and feeds the Ekue with some of its blood, "charging" the drum already filled with the presence of the sacred voice. Then the initiates and ecobios or brothers of the potencia, as recorded in Ortiz, drink some of that blood, "in the manner of a sacramental communion so that [the Ekue] may renew its vitality." This rite, claims Ortiz, had its antecedent in human sacrifice and ritual anthropophagy, and it was the blood of a Kongo that made the Ekue speak until the time when a goat would be substituted for the man (TÑ 88, 100).

Other plazas and priest-officiants of the society are as follows:

The embákara, an assistant priest, has the duty of untying the male goat and handing him to the main priest for sacrifice (CA 3:36).

The embríkamo (or nkríkamo) plays the drums during the procession of priests and attendants, his steady pounding building to the climax at which the he-goat is killed. The embríkamo is also chief or foreman of the íremes, the one who calls them and leads them in their dancing (SSA 197–200; Hernández Espinosa, 114–15).

The empegó draws the trazas or magic signs on the floor or walls of the cuarto fambá—the Ñáñigo igbodú or inner sanctum. These signs resemble somewhat the vèvè of Haitian Vaudou. Their functions, which I will elaborate on later, are to identify groups and members and to help direct the power of the sacrifice toward specific ends (SSA 177–79).

The enkandemo prepares and serves the sacred meals to the orishas; he also prepares the meat, full of magic, of the sacrificed animals (SSA 224–26).

Before the ceremony can commence, the eribangando dances around the cauldron with the offerings of food and purifies the temple and takes charge of carrying the ceremonial offerings to the river (SSA 208–9; CA 3:234, 236).

"Ireme of the Consecration," the enkoboró dances ahead of the priests and scares off the hostile spirits (TÑ 90; SSA 215–16). The organization of these plazas is structured on the narrative of the founding group of Efor priests. The initial sacrifice by the priests, constituting the central secret of the Abakuá society, amounted to an act of unitive violence at the origin of the cult.

The Secret

The Ñáñigos tell a complex foundation myth from the Efor, alluded to in the poem by Barnet discussed at the beginning of this chapter. That myth has numerous variants, some of them contradictory, all of them commemorating an originary act of violence by men against a woman and establishing the divine principle she was made to symbolize. In the beginning, the great god Abasí gave his chosen people, the Efor, the secret of the magic fish Tanze and its mysterious voice. By a process of shifting significations, the fish, Tanze, stands in place of the leopard, the Ekpe or Ekue, whose Efor name continues to be borne by the central object of the cult (CA 3:220). The name of Tanze derives from the Efut Ta, lord or father, and the Ejagham nsi, or the fish that is doubled in the spirit of the leopard (FS 242).

It happened one day that Sikanecua, or Sikán, remembered as the daughter of Mokuire, king of Northern Efut, discovered the fish by the creek known by the Abakuá as Odán, in Calabar as Ndian. The sorcerer Nangobié placed the fish in the drum called Ekón for safekeeping. Some time after the fish had died, the voice was heard every time the sacred drum was played. Nangobié then initiated his seven sons into the secret (FS 236, 237–38, 241). Nasakó, delegated to skin the fish, inscribed the skin with the marks of the leopard and stretched it across the mouth of a calabash. In this receptacle would reside the Voice. At a later time, Sikán committed the indiscretion of disclosing the secret of the fish. For this reason, the sons of Nangobié, led by Nasakó, ordered her sacrifice. On the instructions of his divining instrument, the mañogo pabio, Nasakó strengthened the drum with the blood of the sacrificed Sikán (CA 3:217).

Initiated into the secret of that drum, Nangobié's sons, the seven chiefs of the Ejagham (Ngbe) and Efut hierarchy came to be remembered in time as the founding priests of the Abakuá Secret Society (Bastide 112–13). The seven plumes adorning the silent drum match the seven chiefs and correspond to the hierarchy of plazas presiding in the lodge: the ekueñón, isué, mpegó, iyamba, nkríkamo, and nasakó.

After the initiation of the first seven chiefs, Sikán's body served as a source of magic power. Sikán accepted her fate and now welcomes the souls of initiates after their deaths, helping them to escape the cycle of reincarnations and gain immediate entry into heaven (APA 48). In this function, she has become a figure of the feminine that eccentrically centers a masculinist religion. Her inaugural transgression, it turned out, set the Efik on the path of divine revelation, precisely through a violent objectification-fetishization of the feminine (CA 3:219). Thompson explicates the Ñáñigo symbolism in somewhat mystical terms: "it came to pass that through this orchestrated union, skin on skin on wood and other media, male and female valences fused within a single object and Tanze's mighty voice—'the fish that thunders like a bull'—returned. The accomplished miracle assured the moral continuity of the Ejagham and the Efut and, centuries later, the Abakuá" (FS 243).

The incarnation is, to reiterate, an inaugural displacement: the life force of Tanze merges with the body of Sikán in the figure of the silent ritual drum, called Seseribó (SSA 88). The cost of the male drum's "speech," in other words, is the silence of the female drum during the Abakuá ceremonies, since that plumed drum, mediating male and female orders, is not for playing but for "display." Seseribó is the sacred "mother" drum that, unlike the Ekue, can be taken out of the sacred cuarto fambá and looked upon. As Cabrera explains, "The Sese Eribo, Akanarán, mother of all the Ñáñigos, is a soundless and most sacred drum in the form of a cup with two handles whose skin is sewn on the borders and stuck with glue" (LSÑ 480–81). The drum manifesting the presence of Sikán bears the signature of the isué whose sacred duty it is to hold and carry it. This unplayed instrument has entered into the national mythology, as suggested in the poem by Teófilo Radillo entitled "Bembé," which describes the "Senseribó" as a silent drum in the form of a large feathered cup (Morales 336–37).

As Cuervo Hewitt explains it, the cult of death surrounding the ur-sacrifice of Sikán, represented in the sacrifice of a goat or rooster and emblematized in the silent drum, has a metaphorical significance that goes beyond a ritual sanction of male domination: "The sacrifice reiterates the link through which a complex mythological labyrinth of desire, rivalry, conquest and salvation is edified. The expiatory death of the woman at the beginning was not brutal, senseless murder, but rather remembrance and reintegration with the femininity of the earth, the gentle, undulating and firm movements of the trees, of the flora, of the water, and of the leopard, sacred animal, a marriage of death with life. In short, a metaphysical orgasm, an imaginative one, of man with the indecipherable omnipresence of existence" (APA 49). This is a violent non-violence at the beginning, a reintegrative "metaphysical orgasm" that killed a female but saved feminity for all time. The gesture of this loving murder repeats itself throughout the narratives of Ñáñigo ritual and Ñáñigo narrative revisions that I will address in the following readings of works by Cuban authors.

In Cabrera Infante's *Tres tristes tigres* (Three sad tigers, 1967), the book section entitled "Seseribó" begins with an italicized epigraph, a little over a page in length, of the Sikán and Ekue myth. The epigraph, complete with humorously irreverent commentary, includes the story of how Sikán trapped Ekue in a water gourd in order to bring the fish before her incredulous father. Despite her good intentions, Sikán, because she was a woman, committed sacrilege in hearing the Voice. Cabrera Infante's parodic retelling continues:

Sikán paid for the profanation with her skin. She paid with her life, but also with her skin. Ekue died, some say from shame of letting himself be trapped by a woman or from the mortification of traveling inside a bowl. Others say that he died of suffocation, in the rush—he was not, definitely, made for running. But neither the secret nor the habit of meeting nor the joy of knowing that it exists was lost. With his skin was the *ekue* covered, which speaks now in the fiestas of the initiated and is magic. The skin of Sikán the Indiscreet was used in another drum, which bears no nails nor ligatures, because she still suffers the punishment of blabbermouths [*los lengua-largas*]. It has four plumes with the four oldest potencias in the four corners. Since it is a woman it is necessary to adorn it beautifully, with flowers and necklaces and cowries. But on its drumskin it wears the rooster's tongue as an eternal sign of silence. No one touches it and it alone cannot speak. It is secret and taboo and it is called *seseribó*. (89–90)

Despite the comic deflation of mysteries surrounding the sacred drums of the cuarto fambá, the strain of Afro-Cuban mysticism in the experience of Cabrera Infante's protagonists provides a holdfast against the undertow of time, a fragment of solidity amidst the phantasmagoric spectacle of a prerevo-lutionary society in rapid dissolution. The Seseribó thus forms a part of the shifting mosaic of Cuban identity and a fleeting symbol of transcendence in the popular mythology. Negatively, by its silence, it also spiritual-izes the idea of the feminine voice developed elsewhere in *Tres tristes tigres*.

Introduced by Cabrera Infante in the first of several chapters entitled "Ella cantaba boleros" (She sang boleros), Estrella Rodríguez is the mulatta night-club singer whose music allows her to rise above the baseness connoted by her physical enormity and inspires the personal cult of La Estrella among Arsenio Cué, Silvestre, and their friends. "We will adore her," declares the seriously joking narrator, "like the saints, mystically, in the ecstasy of re-membrance" (TTT 85). One could say that the narrative of *Tres tristes tigres* expresses a will to restore a voice to the silenced Sikán by allowing her to be reborn in La Estrella, the star whom the "twins" ("jimaguas") Arsenio Cué and Silvestre "adore" with personal, half-ironic devotion. This activity, it should be noted, parodies as it recalls the studies of cult formation in Carpentier and del Valle.

On one occasion, someone puts on a record of the mulatta singer, and "the song of the sirens came forth and we, every one of her public, were Ulysses tied to the mast of the boat, enthralled by this voice that the worms will not devour because it is there on the record now, in a perfect and ecto-plasmic facsimile and without dimension like a specter, like the flight of an airplane, like the sound of the drum: that is the original voice" (TTT 115). By conflating mythologies, the passage equates the voice in the Abakuá drum with the voice of the Homeric sirens. So doubled, the voice of divinity is a telluric, chthonic presence that a masculine perspective identifies with the feminine. Cuervo Hewitt rightly notes that "the myth of the rivalry and of the expiation of Ekue constitutes the narrative axis" of Cabrera Infante's novel, although its treatment of the founding myth is not as explicit as in more realist works of Afro-Cubanism. Cuervo Hewitt continues: "the beating of Ñáñigo drum is heard again, no longer in the temple of initiation, but in the very beat of the text, in the hidden voice of the characters, the secret, the silence and the rivalry of the masculine world of Havana, specifically be-tween Arsenio Cué the actor and Silvestre the writer." We can hear Sikán's voice interwoven into the uneven fabric of the Cuban text, with the sacrifice of Sikán—of the feminine principle—signifying the gift to the gods that sustains world of the masculine. At the same time, the phonographic record-ing indicates a repetition of the simulacrum: endless reenactments in a sym-bolic order, "keeping alive the memory" of a violence that inaugurated that symbolic order. The running about of the two *habaneros* mirrors the antics of the Ibeyis or twins of Yoruba mythology, Kaínde and Taewo, and thus rein-forces the thematics of doubling through a mythic and experiential repro-duction (APA 48, 52). By symbolic reproduction, the original and founding sacrifice can initiate a ritual by means of which a society of men can set aside their rivalry and aggressivity, a woman's sacralized and reiterated punishment serving as the means by which individuals identify themselves as a group and communicate as a group (see Guiraud 120).

What Is Written

The Ñáñigo rites take place in the cuarto fambá, the inner sanctum in which the mystical signs—*anaforuana*, also called trazas, grafias, firmas, or *nsibidi*—are drawn on the floor or ground. So inscribed with such trazas, the cuarto fambá encloses the stage for worship in the form of music, dance, chanting, sacrifice. The anaforuana resemble the *pontos riscados* of the *candomblé* dance rituals in Brazil as well as the aforementioned vèvè of Dahomeyan-Haitian ceremonies. Such graphic designs assumed specialized names in the Ñáñigo context: anaforuana are signs; *gandó*, chalked signatures; *ereniyo*, "revelations" (SSA 68, 178).

The anaforuana constitute a conventionalized pictographic writing with several functions. One function is to convey messages. A pictogram, for example, may be written on a piece of paper and passed to an ecobio to inform him that he has, say, committed an offense against the statutes of the society. Another sign could notify him that he is to be poisoned as a punishment for revealing secrets. The signs are also indexes that focus religious power. The marks "affirm the past," for they carry the authority and power of the society's elders and forefathers. Calling them "arcane signs of sacred presence and recollection, luminous ciphers of the founding rulers and most important women," Thompson refers to a certain black stevedore of Havana by the name of Margarito Blanco, the would-be founder of an Abakuá lodge, whose papers were confiscated by the police in 1839. Planning to call himself "monkongo" or Abakuá keeper of justice, Blanco had refashioned nsibidi signs in his search for an emblem of priesthood (FS 227–28, 260).

Prior to the initiation ceremony, or rompimiento, the isué will draw the schematic map of anaforuana signifying initiation with white chalk on the floor of the cuarto fambá. For a funeral ceremony, on the other hand, he draws with yellow chalk the same grafias on the dead ecobio's body, but with a significant difference. Whereas the arrows in the initiation signs point downward, the arrows on the deceased's body will point upward, toward the sky of Sikán to which the ecobio's soul will ascend (Bastide 114–15; CA 3:305–11).

As the power of the anaforuana and the founding myth suggest, signs of the past maintain a connection with ancestors and predecessors and serve as the subtext (a literal one, in the case of the ground-signs) for ritual. Yet other myths beside that of Sikán and the Ekue are signified in Abakuá ceremonies. Castellanos and Castellanos have noted that both the Calabars of southeastern Nigeria and those brought to Cuba, called Carabalí, opened their beliefs to Yoruba and Congo influences. This is true in the composition of the Abakuá pantheon. As mentioned before, the Ñáñigos call their supreme god Abasí, the creator who prefers not to meddle in human affairs. Roughly equivalent to the Lucumí Olodumare and made present in the sound of the Ekue, Abasí could be called, after Kenneth Burke, the "ideal audience" of Ñáñigo rites: He whose voice gives the meaning that returns to their source through those rites (see RR 35). The proverb *Ekué úllo akanón Ekué úllo Abasí bon* sums up the relationship between the supreme deity and the drum: "Where there is God, there is Ekue, and where there is Ekue there is God" (RNV 59).

With the accommodation of the Lucumí doctrine, the match between Abakuá deities and Lucumí orishas is a fairly close one: the Lucumí Obatalá or the Catholic Virgen de las Mercedes is nearly identical to the Abakuá god Obandío; avatars of the same Obandío are Obebé and Eromina. Babalú-Ayé is Yiniko—or vice versa—and similarly, Changó is Okún, Oyá is Onifé, Yemayá is Okandé, and Ochún is Yarina Bondá. Oggún corresponds to Sontemí, whereas Elegguá is either Obiná, as the Soul in Purgatory, or Efisa, also known as San Juan. In addition to this pantheon of deities, the Abakuá maintain a Bantu-reinforced belief in the opposition between Abasí, as the good god, and his evil brother, Nyógoro, the *Diablo* or Devil. This dualism may refer back to Biblical or Christian influences in the Bantu-Kongo culture that preceded the transplantation and transculturation of the religious through the slave trade (CA 3:220–22). In addition, Omalé Efor is the spirit of the first forest god, Nkanima, comparable to the Lucumí Osaín. Nkanima is assigned the special task of taking the testicles of the sacrificed goat to the mountain and leaving them under a tree as an offering to the dead (LSÑ 456, 397).

The Body of Ceremony

As in the Reglas Lucumís, the Abakuá rituals conform to the pattern of *rites de passage*, complete with the display of liminal or threshold symbolism appropriate to the transition of the initiate from one stage to another. Ritual agencies—equipment and paraphernalia—play their part in the process. A stretched-out goatskin mounted like a flag, the *sukubariongo*, represents Sikán's skin, which covered the first drums of the confraternity. This sukubariongo is carried in rituals by a sorcerer wearing women's clothing. The *itón* is the sacred staff with which the priest kills the he-goat in ñáñigo rituals. Among the musical instruments of the rites, the *encomo*, a small drum constructed of a trunk hollowed out with fire and covered with parchment, serves as a means of communicating messages. On the parchment of the silent Seseribó, the priest lays the sacrificed rooster or *enkiko* (TÑ 90; EYO 187; CA 3:391).

Ortiz gives an introduction to Ñáñigo ritual and its mythical significance in his informative study "La tragedia de los ñáñigos" (The tragedy of the Ñáñigos, 1950), to which I have already referred in this chapter. Affirming the noble descent and dignity of the Abakuá culture in that study, Ortiz alludes to deep spiritual roots connecting the Ñáñigo rites with the mysteries of ancient Egypt, Thrace, Eleusis, and Crete. A summary of some of the points covered in that article, complete with the analogies made by Ortiz to Greek mysteries, will serve to summarize the Abakuá ritual activity. As in the satyr plays of ancient Athens, the "theatrical" *ebori mapá* consisted in the ritual sacrifice of a goat. The Ñáñigo "tragedy" takes place in the *isaroko* or *plazuela*, a patio serving as stage or site for the performance, in which stands a holy ceiba or a bush substituting for it. The *mystikos sekos* or inner sanctum of the Abakuá is the cuarto fambá; in it dance the aforementioned íreme or írimi devils, who carry the itón scepter, the *ifán*, branch of bitter broom, or some other phallic symbol. Those diablitos, like the plazas and props, have their specific names: enkandemo, enkanima, enkoboró, amanaguí (TÑ 79, 81–82).

The ceremony may be part of a fititi *ñongo* or fiesta; or it may be a *baroko*, the ceremony of "fraternal alliance" or initiation. Whatever the ceremony, the hieroglyphic anaforuana are traced in yellow chalk or plaster, recalling the aforementioned nsibidi of the Ekoi and the pictographic origins of writing. The ritual candles are lit: the *enka-uke-Eribó*, the *enka-lú-man-togo*, and the *enka-lú-mape*. At the culminating point of some ceremonies, the "Great Mystery," the Ekue, becomes present in a "voice" whose sound resembles the growl of the leopard (TÑ 83–85).

In underscoring the affinities of the Ñáñigo rites with those of classical antiquity—Afro-Cubans have their own Eleusinian mysteries—Ortiz points out the commonalities of the two symbologies: in both, the spiritual cycle is considered analogous to the life cycle. "In Cuba as in Greece, the lustral bath of the neophyte, the simulation of his death, the resurrection, the vision of the ancestors and his communication with them [are] equivalent to the Greek mysteries of the *katarsis*, the *paradosis*, the *epopteya*, and the *purification, the revelation of the great secrets* and the *enlightenment of the initiates*" (TÑ 99). It was especially the rites of the Ñáñigos that impressed Lydia Cabrera too with their complex mixing of memory, ritual, myth, and desire. For Cabrera, "the Ñáñigo 'juego' is an imitation, a repetition of situations, copy of the acts that took place in the origins of the society," and ritual repetition evokes the time of the origin: "When the Ireme Aberiñán holds the hoof of the holy goat of the sacrifice, he is executing the same act of the first Aberiñán who accompanied the first Mocongo at the first consecration" (M 286). The initiation ceremony, displaying these elements and qualities, will be discussed at length in connection with specific literary exegeses to come.

The funeral ceremony, which will also be discussed at a later point, has its own symbols and sequential operations. On that occasion, the ecobio's basin is inverted and plantain fronds are cut to signify the negations of death. The plate of the deceased ecobio is lifted from his place in a ritual (called *levantamiento de plato*) marked by its own elaborate anaforuana. The ceremony continues in the procession called *beromo*. Ecobios marching in the beromo raise up the sukubariongo (goatskin flag) representing the spirit of Sikán. The Sikán's Seseribó is held high atop a pole by one brother, and all the ecobios, carrying the articles of faith to the music of claves and bongos, follow the dancing íremes, who lead them to the cemetery (FS 257, 269).

In Praise of Ekue

Much of what I have summarized in the preceding discussion of the Ñáñigo institution—its myth, doctrine, and ritual—appears in some form in the works of Afro-Cuban narrative. In an early literary precedent, Morúa Delgado's *Sofía* (1891), the Ñáñigo character Liberato has his brother-in-law, Nudoso del Tronco, killed in the manner customary to the secret Abakuá societies, making his murder an execution. This act symptomizes a violent political brand of Ñáñiguismo that the reformer Morúa Delgado found to be among the "social factors" responsible for the blacks' backwardness in his decadent society (LB 144, 160).

As remarked earlier, the first significant treatments of Afro-Cuban religion in twentieth-century literary narrative, beginning with Carpentier's ¡*Ecue-Yamba-O!* (1933), are concerned not only with the Yoruba-Lucumí tradition but with the Abakuá. The two volumes of Ortiz's sociological *Hampa afrocubana—Los negros esclavos* (Afro-Cuban underworld—the black slaves, 1916) and *Los negros brujos* (The black sorcerers, 1917)—present much information on the Abakuá associations. In those works, the Ñáñigos's social reputation for intergroup rivalry and violence is confirmed. In later, more literary works, the Ñánigos are identified with the knifings and murders narrated in ¡*Ecue-Yamba-O*¡, Gerardo del Valle's *Cuarto fambá* (1951), and Manuel Cofiño's *Cuando la sangre se parece al fuego* (When blood looks like fire, 1977). Fitting in with this image, the machismo of the Ñáñigos, the manly style of behavior and demeanor known in Cuba as *guapería*, is shown in those works to provoke the violence that often broke out between rival potencias (Cuervo Hewitt and Luis 34).

It is interesting to note how the construction of Abakuá-related narratives evidences a repeated effort to teach the reader an insider's vocabulary, essential for understanding the words and deeds of their Ñánigo characters. Glossaries, parentheses, appositives, footnotes, and intercalated definitions guide the uninitiated reader through the texts of Abakuá religion and history. Such features characterize Carpentier's groundbreaking first novel.

The title of Carpentier's first novel has been translated as *Lord Be Praised* (literally, "¡Señor, Loado Seas!") but the original title of course refers to a central object of worship in the Abakuá cult, the sacred Ekue drum. Because I have discussed some of the Lucumí-related themes of the novel in chapter 3, I will only address its Abakuá dimensions here. For the black Ñáñigo characters of Carpentier's novel, it will be recalled, Afro-Cuban religion offers a refuge for the damaged psyche and a sign of difference on which to base a cultural identity.

At the same time, as I argued in chapter 3, Menegildo's participation in the Ñáñigo practices serves as an escape valve and a form of self-expression, a means of creating solidarity, and a mode of resistance to economic exploitation. Although Salzmann correctly observes that liberation through the rhythms of African music and dance is no more than a "merely physical liberation that only from an ingenuous point of view could be considered whole" (98), his view does not explain the whole appeal of the Abakuá society for Menegildo nor does it do justice to the significance of the society's ritual, myth, and doctrine as they are reworked and reexamined in the novel.

Dathorne has pointed out that the initiation ceremony depicted in ¡Ecue-Yamba-O! embodies the African legacy in Cuba, affirming the connection of Afro-Cuban identity with ancestral myth and ritual (114). The Ñáñigos, furthermore, in calling their initiation a *rompimiento*, refer to a breaking or breaking off. To undergo initiation into a new phase of personal evolution is to create a rupture or break in the course of one's life. Within the rompimiento ceremony itself, the individual undergoes a transformation, turning from the status of *amanisón*, uninitiated believer, to *abanecue*, initiate. To actualize this transformation means to identify with a character in myth, to play a role in an archetypal narrative that restores at least in part one's sense of personhood in a dehumanizing social environment.

The following summary of the distinct actions in Menegildo's rompimiento will reduce it, on the analogy of the sentence, to its simple propositions. The propositions, each indicating if not actually consisting of an actant and a predicate, all add up to a ritual sequence. I have also added transitional propositions to frame the narrative subsequences and included the embedded propositions that refer to the Sikanecua founding myth within brackets. The exegetical and operational dimensions of Turner's analytic of ritual are implicit in the action presented by each proposition. Specifically in the sequencing of propositions, we discern Turner's positional or syntactical dimensions ("Syntax" 146–58). Menegildo (M) and his helper-friend Antonio (A) are readable as functions in the ritual syntax, which unfolds according to a temporal organization. The chapters analyzed are 35, 36, and 37, respectively titled "¡Écue-Yamba-O!," "¡Ireme!," and "Iniciación" (EYO 146–58).

1. A takes M to the *batey* (sugar mill grounds)
2. Ecobios greet each other ("Enagüeriero")
3. M hears drumming of the *llanto* (lamentation for the dead)
4. Ecobios approach *bohío* (hut) of the iyamba
5. M reads the firma of the juego: the cuarto fambá
6. Padrino brings in the enkiko (black rooster)
7. M takes off shirt and rolls up pants
8. A marks M with chalk crosses
9. A blindfolds M
10. Ecobios kneel
11. *Famballén* (doorman) beats on empegó drum
12. Nasakó chants invocation
13. Ireme dances purification
14. Ireme throws rooster to road
15. *Munifambá* (dignitary) spins ecobios around
16. Iyamba introduces ecobios into cuarto fambá
17. Ecobios kneel before altar and Seseribó
18. Ecobios hear the roar of Ekue
19. Remembrance of Sikanecua and Tanze
20. With the fish, three obones become four
21. Iyamba moistens ecobio's head with *mocuba* (ritual liquid)
22. Isué administers the oath
23. Ecobios led out of cuarto fambá
24. Blindfolds taken off
25. Clothes put back on
26. Ecobios presented to the potencia

27. Fiesta begins
28. Ecobios play drums
29. Ecobios drink aguardiente (cane liquor)
30. Ecobios eat the *iriampo* (ritual food)
31. Ecobios compete in lengua (exchanging proverbs)
32. Iriampo offered to dead in *emgomobasoroko* circle
33. Ireme dances again
34. Nasakó ignites powder crosses
35. M seizes pot and hurls it
36. Ecobios, in procession, sing

Passing through the ritual sequence, the ecobios are prepared and then introduced into the mystery of the Ekue, the centering symbol of the Abakuá cult. Nakedness connotes the birthing process and the baby's helplessness, infantilist associations that identify the would-be initiate prior to transition into full membership in the association. The passage of the neophytes into the state of the abanecue is accordingly symbolized by the action of putting on clothes. Ritual acts of disorientation—the blindfolding, spinning around, the drinking, the long periods of dancing—prepare the subject for reorientation as one who will enter the group.

The entire ceremony emphasizes the dependence of the neophytes on the elders in the faith for instruction and guidance. With the elders in charge, the initiation transforms the outsider into insider and the ignorant into a possessor of the gnosis that is the privilege of the cult. The mechanism of consecrations and substitutions described with references to Barnet's poem at the opening of this chapter is reiterated as a process by which the ties of a group are forged and strengthened.

Another rompimiento is described in Manuel Cofiño's *Cuando la sangre se parece al fuego*, in a manner that reveals other exegetic and operational features of the initiation ritual. The protagonist Cristino's introduction to the Abakuá mysteries takes place in a toque de tambor, or drum-playing ceremony, where Cristino watches the dance of the íremes, learns some Efik, and sees the feathered Seseribó drum. At a later date, he will be initiated into his potencia, the Ubioco Sese Eribó. The ceremony requires a rooster, a bottle of aguardiente, and the customary fee or *derecho*. As he arrives at the site of the rompimiento, Cristino sees a rooster and a male goat, both tied to the ceiba, both of which will be sacrificed. He confronts the *kiriofó* or group of potencia leaders, the plazas of the potencia: the isué, iyamba, isunekue, ekueñón, empegó, mosongo, abasongo, and nkríkamo. Cristino is marked with the symbol or traza of his potencia in white chalk, then cleansed with basil; the rooster is passed over his body; he is taught laws and doctrine (Cofiño 86, 94–96, 241). At the end of this process, he is led into the climactic part of the initiation, which takes place in the chamber of mystery, the cuarto fambá. Cristino tells of being blindfolded and hearing the drumming while awaiting the moment of revelation: "I heard a prayer and after a while distant thunder, a sound that grew for seconds. It seemed that I had a savage bull on top of my head, a furious roaring lion. It was the Ekue. I had him in my head and they were rubbing him [lo fragallaban] to make that sound. I couldn't bear the noise and trembled, I shook to my bones. That hoarse sound, unbearable, penetrating, intense, was the voice of Tanze, the sacred fish, of Abasí, of God. The voice of the god was entering me through the head to stay inside me like a roar of fury" (Cofiño, Cuando 96). The climax of the ceremony sends the participants, all ecobios and neophytes, back into the past and the time of myth. Or it gives them that impression, for the passage also describes the elements that would produce the state of excitation conducive to a mystic encounter. Isolation, darkness, anticipation, suggestion, rhythmic drumming, fatigue, and the whole symbol-filled setting prepare for the ecstatic moment of a ritual recentering of consciousness focused on the penetrating and mysterious sound of the Ekue.

In a jarring return to sociohistorical reality, Carpentier's last chapter concerned with Menegildo's initiation ends with a description of a barbershop with an upholstered barber's chair from North America. As this image connotes, the initiation has not changed the socioeconomic circumstances that limit his life chances, nor has it equipped Menegildo and his ecobios with the means to critique or change it. Add to Menegildo's ignorance his brutish indolence and his subscription to the Ñáñigo's macho code of conduct and Carpentier's skeptical profile of an Afro-Cuban life seems complete. Menegildo is ready to be killed quickly and senselessly in the intergroup warfare between the Efó-Abacara and the Enellegüellé (EYO 104–5, 135).

Popular talk or gossip and narratorial observations in Carpentier's text metaphorize the rivalry between the Enellegüellé and the Efó-Abacara associations as an antagonism between the Toads and the Goats. The narrator makes it clear that theirs is a feud of signs, at least up to the point where the fighting breaks out. Drum-playing, firmas written in yellow "chalk" (or "plaster," yeso), gourds of brujería or sorcery sent by one group to the other—all these signs work hostile magic against the signs sent by the enemy. Reading such signs is risky business: "A slight 'bad interpretation' would suffice to provoke encounters" (EYO 169). The rivalry anticipates del Valle's depiction

of conflict between the potencias in his story "Cuarto fambá" (to be discussed shortly), wherein the semiotics of group formation and antagonism
are studied in greater depth.

Carpentier's novel concludes with an account of Menegildo's violent death
at the hands of a rival Ñáñigo group that attacks Menegildo's group in a fiesta
celebrating the initiations. His death leaves his lover, Longina, alone and dependent on the mercies of Menegildo's unsympathetic family. When Longina
gives birth to a son, also named Menegildo (EYO 183), we know that another Afro-Cuban and future abanecue will continue the cycle of poverty,
ignorance, mystical rites, and violence past the novel's ending.

Inside the Cuarto Fambá

He who comes to inspect it
will only find
the sacks, canes and roosters
in the *cuarto fambá*.
And on the altar
our insignias
he will see.
And if you want to mock me,
four will come, a few,
since the *encorocos* can
close in on me.
He who becomes *paluchero*,
at once they'll bury him
because I beat the drumskin
quickly with the "*itón*."
Come on, *negros*, don't butt in,
'cause I'm from the *Sitos*,
and die if you don't respect
the *juego* "Betango."
(Báez 384)

The anonymous Ñáñigo song titled "El cuarto fambá," reproduced in Báez's
Enciclopedia de Cuba, describes for us once again the sacred room of Abakuá
ceremonies, a site of mysterious signs. The lyric speaker is probably the
Abakuá singer called the *moruá yuansa*, charged with the responsibility of an-
swering, with a mortifying comment, any disrespectful comments made
about the sanctum sanctorum of the Abakuá society (see CA 3:236). The

moruá yuansa's song is called a *puya*, a jest, literally a goad or prod, that taunts the uninitiated viewer, possibly a hostile intruder ("que venga a inspeccionarlo"), with the claim that he does not know how to read those sign-objects inscribed in italics in the poem, nor even knows the Efor or Efík words that name them. For that outsider, a rooster is only a rooster and not the enkiko, specially prepared for the ritual offering.

At any rate, only initiates, the abanecues, are permitted entry into the *fambá*, the sacred room of Ñáñigo rites. Those who come to mock will have to confront the *encorocos* or *ekuruku*, the congregated group of abanecues, who can be called immediately with a beating on the drumhead, or the "cuero," with a stick or scepter called itón or itán (M 209, 211, 214). At the last, the singer calls out a final challenge: "de los Sitos soy yo," which translates as "I come from [or belong to] the *Sitos*"—the Ñáñigo associations or potencias, "sitios" (sites)." Intruders may pay heavily if they do not respect the Betango, also spelled Betongó, a juego of Havana, named after a territory of Efor (LSÑ 195, 224, 263, 109). (It is generally acknowledged that the Efor—or Efut—belongs to the oldest Abakuá lineage, that of the Calabar Ekoi; the Efík branch, on the other hand, proceeds from the Ibibio line [CA 3:212]).

Let this anonymous poem serve to frame the treatment of Abakuá themes in a story collection whose title, or the main part of it anyway, sounds like that of the poem—"cuarto fambá"—but is written 1/4 *famba y 19 cuentos más*. Midway into the period between the publications of *¡Ecue-Yamba-O!* and Cabrera's *La Sociedad Secreta Abakuá* (1970), Gerardo del Valle's Abakuá stories first appeared in an anthology entitled *Retazos*—a word meaning remnants, scraps, or fragments—in 1951 (Bueno, *Historia* 416).

Born in Venezuela of Cuban parents in 1898, Gerardo del Valle lived in Havana since the age of four. There he observed and recorded the legends, superstitions, beliefs, and practices of the blacks of the hampa, especially of those belonging to the Abakuá society, by now in a period of decline. Del Valle participated in the same movements of the *vanguardia* as did Carpentier, including participation in the *Grupo Minorista*, and like Carpentier manifested an early interest in the Abakuá society. Like Carpentier as well he was jailed in 1927 for anti-Machado activities. As Salvador Bueno has observed in his dustjacket notes for the 1967 edition of del Valle's anthology, the Maracaibo-born writer's narratives do not exhibit the same rigor and ethnological accuracy as those of other Afro-Cubanists but offer instead a "literary elaboration" of African motifs found in a Cuban culture. It is on the dustjacket of that edition where the title of del Valle's book is announced as 1/4 *fambá y 19 cuentos más*. The fraction designating "one fourth" (*cuarto*) suggests the use of a secret code or inside joke, as it plays on the name for the sacred room (cuarto fambá) in which the sacred drum is kept while referring at the same time, metonymically, to the exclusive group that meets in the room.

Some stories of the collection depict scenes of the kind of violence associated in the popular imagination with the Abakuá potencias, tracing the origins of that violence, as did Carpentier, to the dynamics of group formation and rivalry. In all the Ñáñigo stories of 1/4 fambá, narration and dialogue showcase the Afro-Cuban argot of Ñáñigos—often used and then defined in parentheses—to give an impression of the insider's experience of the religious culture and the whole atmosphere of camaraderie, secrecy, danger, and violence surrounding the potencia abakuá. More hospitably than does the poem that opened this discussion of del Valle's works, the stories beckon the reader to enter into the cuarto fambá and into the Ñáñigo's daily struggle for identity, recognition, power, and life, in a universe ruled by the laws of Abasí, the codes of the potencia, and the politics of the hampa. The stories tell us: learn the mysteries of the Ekue and the Seseribó, and beware the evil eye and the icua rebenesiene (the Ñáñigo's knife).

Del Valle evokes these particulars of life in the potencia as well as its ceremonies, its "executions" of rival gang members, its bachatas and bembés (religious parties)—and all the erotic and bloody attraction it had for Cubans after the 1930s, when avant-garde writers continued to search through Afro-Cuban lore for the bases on which to redefine a national culture. Frequent digressions interrupt del Valle's narrative in order to describe ceremonials, explain symbols, and fill in historical background, as if to ensure that the noninitiated reader can acquire enough competence in the reading of the Abakuá sign-world to understand what is going on. A glossary at the end of the text, perhaps hastily composed by the look of its sometimes unalphabetical ordering, provides more definitions. From an often analytic and critical perspective, the narratives draw out connections between religious belief and criminal behavior, again with resemblances to the way Fernando Ortiz characterized the hampa in Los negros brujos.

The stories also depict the involvement of Ñáñigo groups in the politics of a time when politicians, such as Menocal in his 1920 campaign, sought their support. That such politicians solicited Ñáñigo support was evident in the fact, noted by Martínez Furé and the Castellanos, that many of the electoral materials of the time were printed in Efik (DI 205; CA 3:304–5). Several of del Valle's Afro-Cuban characters are shown to consort with local politicians, who in some cases hire them as guardaespaldas, bodyguards, or as outright hit men.

Whereas the Ñáñigo stories of 1/4 fambá also outline the cosmology and mythology of the Abakuá society, their principal focus is on the sociopsychology of group formation. The characters, subject to a determinism they only dimly understand, demonstrate the thesis that the fault for the ills of Cuban society in the period is not in the orishas but in those who rule the little world of the hampa.

To a greater degree than in Carpentier and Cabrera, who attempted to evoke the aura of mystery surrounding depicted rites and symbols, del Valle's narrator takes a skeptical approach. A philosophy of literary form takes priority over a philosophy of divine intervention and mystical power in 1/4 fambá. The Ñáñigo content in some stories appears marginal or superadded to the main action of the narrative, as local color or exotic backdrop to the action. In addition, some of the specifications concerning ceremonies or Yoruba hagiography do not agree with more authoritative accounts in Ortiz, Cabrera, the Castellanos and Thompson. Yet with all their superficialities or distortions, and because of them, del Valle's stories reveal much about the place of the Abakuá societies and their role in the Cuban imaginary.

In the collection's title story, we read of four old ecobios who decide to start up their old fambá, called the Molopo Sangañampio, again after its dissolution fifteen years before. The whole business starts when the old ecobios hear that two Ñáñigo groups, on the point of engaging in a fight and armed with their icuá rebesiene, or knives, have been arrested by only four policemen. The narrator exclaims, "What a humiliating way to run down the name of the glorious institution, and what cowardice [valor más enano] of the encurís (youths), to the extreme of forty men letting themselves be led away by four munipós (policemen)!" (del Valle 82).

The "king" of the Molopo Sangañampio, its Efimeramaetacua, has called on his companions to vindicate the "glorious institution" by forming a potencia strong enough to stand up to the police, unlike the groups of the encurís who bring shame upon all Ñáñigos. This narrative, we pause to note, is replete with words in Efik and Hampa slang (Trobocó Irén, ñampeado, Erenobón, apapipio, eronguibás, abanecues, and so on), and thus constructs a verbal universe of its own. Using such language, Efimeramaetacua proudly recalls his torture in the Castillo del Príncipe at the hands of a young official of the Guardia Civil, to whom "The King" refused to become an apapipio and inform on his ecobios. He also recalls killing that officer with a well-directed knife in the chest, a punishment the officer "deserved" for trying to force the Ñáñigo to break the unwritten law against informing. Nostalgically, Efimeramaetacua recalls a Golden Age of the Regla Abakuá: "What times! What heroism! Ñañiguismo was invincible, and when you agreed to kill a man, it was not to rob him but for very just motives. Its ends and programs were as good as those of any white fraternity formed for mutual protection. One fought for the emancipation of the slave and one worked ardently for the independence of Cuba. Nevertheless, always, in every moment *guarandaria, guarandaria, guarerí* (To a friend as to a friend and to an enemy as to an enemy)." To bring back the heroic days of the Ñáñigos, the potencia reassigns the plazas or offices of its chiefs (in descending order, with del Valle's spelling): *insué, illamba, mocongo, empegó*. The ecobios buy the materials for the diablitos' costumes, along with paraphernalia and cocks for the Seseribó altar of the cuarto fambá, which now has a membership of seventy (del Valle 84–85).

Yet group formation again means group rivalry. The ruling potencia of the Gumanes, one of the modern associations composed of young thugs at the service of a local politician, challenges the Molopo Sangañampio to battle. Meeting on a bare plot of land, the two groups face each other, dancing to the sound of bongos. The ecobios of the Molopo seem to disappear in the shadows, then suddenly reappear "as if from the center of the earth," their heads covered with handkerchiefs and shouting in Carabalí. Twenty Gumanes are killed or "cleaned," *limpiados*. Three of the remaining youths challenge the chiefs of the Molopo to one-on-one combat, but the *jefe máximo* or insué of the old-timers, Erenobón, takes on the three of them single-handedly. Erenobón, armed with his icuá rebesiene, knows how to use it: El Negro is slashed in the chest; Enano, stabbed in the groin. Trompeta, injured, tells his adversary to kill him, but Erenobón will let him live, and he does, momentarily, until the victim catches a bullet shot by the police (munipós), who have arrived to break up the rumble. The fambá Molopo Sangañampio escapes, no one informs on them, and it is "installed in another place in greater secrecy and . . . recognized, by all the potencias of Havana, Marianao, Regla, Matanzas, Guanabacoa, and Cárdenas, as the first of all times past and present" (del Valle 86, 88).

Unlike the title story, Lucumí elements predominate in the story that is placed first in del Valle's collection, one that establishes an ironic perspective toward Afro-Cuban religion. In "Ella no creía en bilongos" (She did not believe in bilongos), descriptions of the *solar* or tenement named "La Casa de Lola" (Lola's house), where a bembé will take place, evoke Africa in Havana. Papá Casimiro throws the elifás, the cowrie shells of the diloggún, which tell him to advise a suspicious Candita to "[b]e extremely careful with light cinnamon, because it was going to darken the greatest thing in her life." That greatest thing is Candita's husband Paulo, obsessed with another woman, a cinnamon-skinned mulatta named Chela. Chela is a *quitada*, one who has "removed" herself from the cult, no longer a believer. The jealous wife commissions Papá Casimiro to produce a bilongo to do harm to her rival, and the ceremony will involve Candita's participation in the rite of the limpieza or spiritual cleansing. Del Valle describes the homages rendered to "Echó" (sic), said to have "influence over Elegguá." Consistent with the Christianized simplification of the orisha tradition, the narrator also calls Echó "the devil himself, who poured so many troubles and misfortunes on decent people" (del Valle 9, 11).

In the room of the bembé, the babalao prepares the limpieza that should rid Candita of Echó's evil influence: "she began to receive, from the iyalocha and her helper, the rubbing with the blood of the black rooster, the feathers of the same, almost turned to dust and overturned on her head, falling to her feet, *chumbas* [baskets] full of grated coconut, dried corn, and a preparation with fresh basil water, mint and some of the flowers of the *Sacramento jubilar*." When Candita disrobes for the herbal bath, the ceremony becomes a virtual striptease, momentarily rekindling Paulo's interest in his wife. Candita's rival watches on, but she is not to be outdone. Since "modern" Chela does not believe in bilongos, she can interrupt the ceremony to put in practice her own "sistema" (system): she opens up her night gown, revealing her own body, "bronze, triumphant and provocative, tremulous with desire and anxiety, fixing her ophidian eyes at Paulo, who, ecstatic, trembling and yearning, contemplated her as well." The husband and his lover leave the Casa de Lola together. The babalao explains the outcome to a disconsolate Candita in these closing words of the story: "The two are prisoners of Echó and it is to be expected that the evil fire that envelops and guides them will be consumed. We are going to evoke the powerful beings that will save them and then restore peace to this afflicted home" (del Valle 12–13, 15, 16). It would seem that old "black magic" is defeated by plain old lust in the end, but the babalao's consoling words hold out for a happier resolution in the future.

The sociological aspects of Ñáñiguismo are emphasized in the incidental details of del Valle's "La majagua nueva" (The new jacket). It tells the story of Cheo, an *agenciero* or furniture mover who suddenly receives a hundred pesos for an unspecified job he did the night before. With the money in hand, Cheo decides to buy a *majagua*, a linen jacket, because "[a]lmost all his ecobios owned at least one and the modern *negritas* were going more and more for *los hombres chéveres* [elegant, "cool" guys]." In his new majagua, the tall and muscular Cheo ought to make a big hit at the party held at the Solar de los Mosquitos, where the famous Sexteto Lucumí will be performing. But there's going to be trouble at the solar. Members of the potencia Embrilló are wait-ing nearby, enemies of Cheo's own *Chequendeque tongobá balle*, a potencia of which he is the *iyamba* or second chief. Cheo has not brought his icuá rebesiene, but he carries his *cocomacaco* or cane-truncheon under his arm. Besides, he can take care of himself, he has known the inside of a jail (*embocobí*) and prison (*barancón*) for having fought for his own group (del Valle 35, 36).

The narrative presents other signs related to Abakuá culture that motivate the actions and reactions of the characters. Cheo believes that the owner of a house into which he and his ecobios are moving furniture has meant to jinx them—the verb is "*basiliquiarles*"—with his evil, "basilisk" eyes. A Virgin of Regla, to whom he lights candles, adorns his apartment and brings him luck. The *bachata* or fiesta at the solar is celebrated by the political boss of the neigh-borhood in honor of "one of the more 'consequential' [members] of the party," exemplifying the manner in which politicians would court the Ñáñigos of their district (del Valle 32, 33, 37).

Into the tension-filled atmosphere of the Solar de los Mosquitos steps Cheo, wearing his new majagua. The members of the rival potencia are there to meet him. With tragic consequence, one of them calls him by a word that Cheo does not understand, "¡Pepillito!," which del Valle's glossary defines as "*Youth, of either sex, who goes overboard and thinks himself a refined and irresistible Don Juan, and who dresses outlandishly.*" Sensing an affront despite his incomprehension, Cheo raises his cocomacaco to strike back; the ensuing chain reaction of blows leads an enemy to stab him with his icuá rebesiene, making Cheo a "victim of his *majagua nueva*" (del Valle 38, 209, 39). A jacket conjoined with a single word, one sign plus another, suffices to bring down disaster.

Politics and Ñañiguismo appear both together and mixed up in "Para consejal" (For councilman). The news is going around the potencias: the municipal assembly of the Palotista Party has nominated the Ñáñigo Eduviges Ramos, also known as Candela, for election to the council. The behind-the-scenes handler responsible for Candela's nomination is one Mano Abierta (Open Hand), president of the Comité Palotista of his *barrio* or neighborhood district. A smooth operator who knows how to "work politics," the white Mano Abierta has joined the Ñáñigo branch of the Efó in Guanabacoa: "he was 'sworn in and baptized with cemetery dirt,' he danced like the best 'moruá' and he understood the language of drums and bongos" (del Valle 94–95).

The nominee Candela, on the other hand, is a black man with a history of *tánganas* (fights) who has done time in the embocobí (jail) and the *cufón eñongoró* (prison). He presides as insué or first chief over the Abatangá Efó; Mano

Abierta belongs to this potencia, which is affiliated with the Partido Palotista and closely connected with the other potencias of the same Efó branch. The enemies and rivals of the Efó are the potencias of the Efí branch, which opposes the initiation of whites. The narrator describes Candela as "intelligent," one in whom "the fanatical ceremonies of the Ñáñigos did not produce much religiosity in him. But he was aware of what it meant politically to count on a secret and offensive force among numerous elements of the people." With an eye to advancing his political ambitions, Candela has learned to manipulate the languages of both Abakuá and civil society. The narrator confirms "he had educated his beak [pico]," and he is quoted later as invoking the names of Martí and Maceo (del Valle 95, 97).

Yet the campaign to build up support among the Efó has backed Mano Abierta into a corner. Knowing that the Efí are planning some tángana at the next Efó meeting, the white representative finds that he cannot hire bodyguards, who would make Candela look cowardly; yet a confrontation between the rival potencias could get ugly and bear out, once again, the truth of the proverb, "guarandaria, guarandaria, guarerí (to a friend as to a friend and to an enemy as to an enemy)." Mano Abierta also knows that asking the government to intervene and maintain order would also bring on disfavor among his Abakuá constituency, reluctant to rely on any "outside" protection (del Valle 96, 97).

Into this perilous situation steps an ancient woman by the name of ña Julia, and she will bring down disaster upon the nominees. She is "an apparition arisen from a medieval witches' sabbath," a woman feared by all as a bruja (witch) responsible for powerful registros and bilongos, keeping close ties to "Echó, called "el Diablo." It turns out that ña Julia has an old score to settle with Candela for his having withdrawn support from her grandson, and Candela, despite his "freethinking," fears the old woman. Sent by the potencia Efí, ña Julia approaches the podium, scares Candela into silence, and then, with a frightening curse, throws a bag containing a red mixture in his face. The magic attack overcomes Candela, who faints on the stand, and later on succumbs to a painful possession by Echó. Mano Abierta finds his political hopes dashed as well, his nomination for representative now "in the vulture's bill" (del Valle 99). The conclusion demonstrates how the privileges of Abakuá membership may come at the cost of vulnerability to the same powers in which the individual has invested.

Other stories in del Valle's collection appear less like fictional narratives than Afro-Cuban scenes or portraits. The narrativity they do exhibit consists in their representation of ceremonial events. In two stories in particular, ritual provides the syntax of the narrative construction. The first story, entitled "El tata," tells of an unnamed brujo's activities during the *ojo-shangó*, the fourth day (Changó's) of the Lucumí week. The Tata (or "taita," meaning *papá*) leads a special bembé called a *batucafu* in which he attempts to induce Changó to send Batalá (Obatalá and/or Babalú-Aye) to remove the "Elegba" that has entered and sickened the body of one of the women of the cuarto fambá. He then invokes the god of fire and thunder but fears that the violent Oggún will displace Changó, who is Oggún's traditional rival. This is exactly what happens: "Elegba helps Oggún and multiplies; the saint goes into all in attendance. Oggún wants war and loses patience. The Tata, knowing that it's very dangerous to fall out with the orisha, changes the tone of all his chants, goes down on all fours and imitates the roaring of a lion. And like a lion he rushes at all those in the way who, for their part, also possessed by the spirit of belligerence, strike out against one another" (del Valle 111–12).

By all other accounts, Oggún would not enter into everyone at the bembé in such a way. Possession occurs in individuals under specific psychophysical conditions; the subject must be prepared and predisposed in just the right way for the orisha's "personality" to take over. But in del Valle's story, the possessed, all mounted helter-skelter by Oggún, fight among themselves. Then, suddenly, they hear the sound of distant thunder: Changó is approaching, so everyone calms down and starts to look for something to offer him. The Tata shouts: "*¡Arangullón, atachanamé! ¡Eudofia aguareque abasi Efí!* (Hear what I say: God in Heaven and I on Earth!)" (del Valle 112). With its inaccuracies of content, "El tata" broaches the topic of possession by constructing a case for abnormal (or animal) psychology. The narrative at least conveys a confused sense of the mythical dimension of worship and suggests the cathartic possibilities of possession.

Because "La muerte del ecobio" (The death of the ecobio) relates the sequence of events in a Ñáñigo funeral, it lacks the elements of choice and confrontation generally present in literary prose fiction. However, it offers a quick, detailed study of the ritual procedures included in the Abakuá ceremony to which I referred earlier. Other than the figure of the deceased, no one single character stands out in the narrative, a fact that gives the story an impersonal feeling, for the center of interest is the funeral ceremony, the itutu itself. The preparations for the funeral give the narrator occasion to rehearse some of the tenets of Ñáñiguismo. First, we read that the deceased ecobio is Endilló, insué or first chief of the Usagara, one of the potencias of the Efí branch. Adding to his distinction, the wise Endilló descends from Nasakó Namoremba, who was high priest of the Guanabecura Mendó potencia in western Africa and one of the ancestors who, beneath the palm tree next to the river "Oldán," received the revelation of Dibó. In other words, Namoremba resembled the receivers of the fish Tanze, those who founded the first potencia in building the first sacred drum of the Abakuá lineage, the Ekue. Dynastically, then, Endilló has received the secrets handed down by the Namoremba and upheld the ideals of the potencia. Ritual once again recalls the origins of the cult and reaffirms the claim of the origin on the members' lives. Accordingly, Endilló has taught that the neophyte "should embody the essential conditions of courage, loyalty, perseverance, unbreakable faith to carry out the will of his cuarto fambá and a firm hand to grasp the icuá rebesiene (knife), ready to be plunged into the enemy" (del Valle 113–14). Since the sacrifice of Sikán and the fish, as it was in the beginning, the code of honor is a code of brotherhood, and of blood and vengeance, to the death.

The funeral preparations follow a standard sequence, and some steps, the narrator explains, repeat those of the initiation ceremony. With great seriousness, twelve nasakó (sic) clear out two rooms and perform a limpieza in them, cleansing the four corners of each room with a rooster held by the legs, waving the tail like a broom. Trazas or ritual symbols are drawn; the rooster is released into the street. The nasakó beat the walls with basil (acamererurú). A woman designated as the cascanecua—representing Sikanecua or Sikán, the only female allowed into the cuarto fambá—brings black cloth to cover the table. With a silver cross and two long candles, the capilla or chapel is ready to admit the coffin of the revered ecobio (del Valle, 115).

Later, when the funeral party is walking to the cemetery, the twelve nasakó carrying the ñampé (deceased) murmur a first Abakuá prayer of mourning, then a second prayer, one of "resignation and submission to the laws of Destiny," and then a third, advising "patience." Inside the cemetery, the burial rites begin. Into the tomb the nasakó sprinkle a bottle of icó, aguardiente, and an herb and plant mixture identical to that used in the initiation ritual. The narrator lists the ingredients of the mixture: "bananas, yam, Guinea pepper, peanut, sesame, incense, dry wine, aguardiente, sugarcane, ginger, salt, star thistle, little pieces of firewood, yellow plaster, a bit of smoked hutia, white powder, holy water, basil, feverfew and charcoal." The ingredients together carry many and various connotations: the plaster is used in drawing the anaforuana ground-signs, the holy water signifies adherence to Catholic belief, the basil recalls the purifications or limpiezas; the white powder could be the eggshell (cascarilla), used to attract aché; the incense, aguardiente and hutia (an indigenous rodent, jutía) are frequently offered to the orishas. After a final responsory, the ceremony is ended and the ecobios disperse, each one thinking on the revered ecobio's teachings on loyalty and honor (del Valle 116, 117, 118).

The code of honor among the members of an Efí potencia is once again examined, and this time critiqued, in "El ecobio traidor sería castigado" (The traitor would be punished). The story contains a lengthy, general history of the Abakuá cult. Of ethnological interest as well are the details of another funeral ceremony, including songs and ritual. We read a detailed inventory of drums—including the bencomo and the cosilleremá—cataloged with their ceremonial functions and other instruments: the ringing llaibí llenbí, the maracas called eridundi, and the bell-like ecón. All of which the protagonist Muñanga can play with skill and style (del Valle 102, 105–6, 104).

Muñanga has been chosen by his cuarto fambá in Matanzas to punish the betrayal of Abasongo. The story builds suspense not only by posing the question of whether and how Muñanga will carry out his mission but also by establishing the enigma of what it is that Abasongo did to deserve such a punishment. In narrative retroversions, we learn that a red cowrie shell has identified Muñanga as the agent of the Ñáñigo "justice." Muñanga will challenge the betrayer to a fight with the icuá rebesiene, for Abasongo has earned the right to defend himself by his past service. The formal challenge to Abasongo will turn the encounter into a test of manliness, for Muñanga will say, "Amicha urquiriquiqui chancobira masongo. That was the phrase that he would throw in the ears of that despicable eronquibá (effeminate) when he met up with him: 'You have to go with me because I'm a man'" (del Valle 101).

Muñanga has searched now in Havana for twenty days without finding the traitorous ecobio, and he has just received a piece of paper with drawings on both sides. In the description of the drawings we recognize the look of the trazas, used for sending messages: "a triangle was drawn with yellow pencil, cut through by three arrows that divided the triangle in four parts and in each one of them was a circle; it represented obedience to his cuarto, the rubric of the insué or first chief; on the other side of the paper was the terrible symbol, warning him that the time limit for his mission was about to close: the grotesque skull with the bones partly bound up: Ñampe! Death . . . ! with the number five: the days remaining" (del Valle 101). The Ñáñigo symbols hold a mystical authority over Muñanga, reinforcing the fear for his own reputation, manhood, and even life should he fail in his mission. The first grafia in the drawing is a signature, identifying the leader as representative of the agrupamiento or association, the divided triangle symbolizing individuals in a group hierarchy. The other sign—part icon, part convention-alized symbol, recalling the pirate's skull-and-crossbones—reminds the ex-ecutioner of the deadline. And what is written cannot be erased.

But what was Abasongo's transgression? Muñanga recalls an aforemen-tioned *fiesta de muerto*—funeral fiesta—for the deceased insué of the Ebión Efó potencia. When the time came to pour the *macumba* into the grave, Abasongo, it was discovered, had drunk the whole bottle of the secret liquor, and it is of course unthinkable that one would "profane and betray the terrible insti-tution" in such a manner. Fearing the consequences of his indiscretion, Abasongo took the first bus to Havana. Eventually, Muñanga does catch up with the "traitor" in a bar in Marianao; to Muñanga's astonishment, a smil-ing, elegantly dressed Abasongo tells him he makes a living dancing for the tourists in a cabaret. Muñanga recalls his crime to him and the fight to the death; Abasongo replies, "Cut it out, Muñanga. The times change and the two of us can live like the rich whites." Abasongo even offers a cash repara-tion. An outraged Muñanga, true to the code of the cuarto fambá, stabs the traitorous ecobio in the heart and escapes (del Valle 106, 107, 108–9).

The last story of 1/4 *fambá* begins by relating the arrival of the giant black man named Seboruco, whose name gives the story its title, at a solar where women are washing clothes. Seboruco has returned from *la chirona*, prison. Looking for his former mistress, La China, he forces La Abuela ("the Grand-mother") to tell him with whom La China has taken up. La Abuela tells Seboruco, "She lives with rich white in Almendares district" (del Valle 195).

Having established the story's enigma with that scene, the narrative takes the reader back to a time when the *licenciado* Angel Gutiérrez—a university graduate or lawyer—nicknamed Seboruco ("Dolt") was a feared and dan-gerous personality known throughout the "popular masses" of Havana. He is "[u]gly as a gorilla," and a Ñáñigo: "The *potencia ñáñiga* of which he was *insué* or first chief, was proud of his command; he performed wonders with the *icuá rebesiene*, liquidating a Christian as quick as a rooster can crow. . . . He was familiar with jail and with the Island of Pines. . . . A stab-wound, given without a second thought, more or less consequential, always turned out to be the reason. He owed his recent sentence to a punishment inflicted on an iyamba or second chief of the fambá 'Ecorio Efó' for opening his beak too much in a matter of daring" (del Valle 196). With this background, del Valle once again links a protagonist with Ortiz's Afro-Cuban hampa and the Abakuá code of conduct.

After an angry meditation in the room in which he used to make love to La China, Seboruco, with revenge on his mind, arranges for his clothes to be retrieved from the *casa de padrino* or pawnshop, and goes to the chalet where La China lives with Seboruco's rival, "a councilman of Havana, very fond of 'cinnamon' [*canela*]." From outside the chalet he sees her—but wait, there's something wrong: instead of dancing the rumba as she did so well with Seboruco, La China is dancing the mambo, a dance that rumba lovers consider to be "stiff and unspirited." That, and La China's modern dances, would make Seboruco the laughingstock of his friends, were they together again. Here, in Seboruco's judgment, the rumba has a positive value ("only the rumba interpreted the soul of the race") and the mambo a negative one. Having suddenly lost his interest in La China, Seboruco spits, lights a cigar and leaves, "completely at ease, whistling his favorite tune" (del Valle 197–98). The conclusion of del Valle's last Ñáñigo story thus frustrates our expectation of a bloody encounter as it suggests the obsolescence and irrelevance of a Ñáñigo society that continues to live in the past.

With this last satiric rendition of life in the hampa, the Abakuá cycle in Afro-Cuban prose narrative closes with a last depiction of the Ñáñigo culture as a macho world of slang, sex, mysticism, vendettas, superstition, fashion, and barrio politics, all reminiscent of Ortiz's and Carpentier's earlier studies. Following Ortiz and Carpentier, del Valle has drawn the myth of Ekue out of Barnet's "heaven" and preserved it in scenes of ritual sacrifice and violent talk and even more violent action among the sons of the seer Nasakó: he who ordered the sacrifice of Sikanecua and inscribed the marks of the leopard on the skin of a talking fish.

5

⟐ Re-marking the Bantu Center

Cotorra vití colorá pá afamá a su padre [*The parrot dresses in red to bring fame to his father*].

Lydia Cabrera, *Refranes de negros viejos*

In the preceding chapters I have advanced the thesis that religious belief and practice rely for their form and meaning on systems of symbols, signifying matrices each focused on the privileged metaphor(s) that are "written" or "read" under the assumption that they manifest the presence of the divine, personified as God or gods, spirits or ancestors, the force of aché or the forces of nature. Afro-Cuban literature, often reiterating and reelaborating the centering "metaphors of divinity" (SAS 8), has displayed the discursive, ritual, and institutional operations that organize and produce religious experience. My analyses of Afro-Cuban and Afro-Cubanist texts have moreover considered the manner in which symbolic centers are elaborated and over-determined by other symbols within the discursive space of a religious culture's communicative practices and how those centers are subject, in the evolution of Afro-Cuban religious culture, to displacement by other centering figures. The center will hold, it has an ordering function, but the semiosis of transculturated systems themselves necessitates that certain decenterings and reorderings occur in the normal operations of each religion's culture.

Disquisitions on the "Lucumí religious system," above all those of Rómulo Lachatañeré, have proclaimed the centrality of that system as a structuring paradigm among Afro-Cuban religions, as providing a ritual and mythological framework for all Cuban religions of West African origins. This has not been entirely the case for alternative Afro-Cuban religious traditions, however, which present "subcountercultural" responses to what they regard as a Lucumí orthodoxy and which offer what they consider as more effective

11. A nganga from Old Havana. 1991.

means of spiritual development. Indeed, the earliest extended treatment in narrative fiction of Afro-Cuban religion, Carpentier's ¡Ecue-Yamba-O!, depicted a subculture whose system was not so much Lucumí as Abakuá, revealing the manner in which the Ñáñigos placed not the orishas at the center of their worship but rather the Ekue, the silent drum fetish, symbolic of the origins of the cult. Also in the mid-1930s, Lydia Cabrera was writing the stories that would comprise her *Cuentos negros de Cuba* (Black stories of Cuba, 1938), stories that told not only of Changó, Yemayá, and Ochún but of spirits and demons from the Kongo mythologies. In the Cuban version of the Bantu religions, known by the names Regla Conga, Regla de Palo, or Palo Monte Mayombe, the privileged object of worship, or its dominant metaphor of divinity, is the magic nganga "charm" or *prenda*, by means of which the mayombero priest may communicate with and control a dead spirit who becomes the ghostly agent of magical operations.

The epigraph for this chapter refers to that spirit-controlling, thought-transmitting nganga-cauldron, central and centering symbol of the Palo Monte religion. Possessed through the medium of the nganga, the palero himself becomes a medium through whom the spirit, also called nganga, is said to speak. In a trance, the palero, parrotlike, utters someone else's words,

words he does not necessarily understand. This mystic ventriloquism makes sense of the proverb, translated from Cabrera's Spanish gloss: "The parrot . . . possessed by the nganga, dresses in red to fight and overcome and bring fame to his father." That is, the palero "dresses" in the colors of a language authored by a spiritual "father," the ancestor or nganga-spirit. Since the language of the other speaks through the palero's mouth, his empowerment through the divination ritual entails his very accession to the paternal word: by defeating the father he exalts himself. And yet this psittacine psychology may justify a reading of the proverb against the grain: the metaphor takes on another significance when we recall that the parrot creates no original utterances but only repeats those generated by other speakers. Although the palero feels enlightened and strengthened in his trance, believing himself a channel for the supernatural voice that talks through him, it seems more likely that he, like the parrot, cotorra, mimics the previous enunciations of other speakers, or joins the pieces of other enunciations together into an utterance that is taken for truth. The parroted paternal word is the word of the religion's patriarchs.

Yet this word consists of more than the *doxa* of a religious culture. Religion, by its operation of centering, as William James knew, touches upon the unconscious or subliminal regions of the psyche normally covered over by the "hubbub of the waking life" (237). Unspoken knowledge and internalized, unconscious codes must form the subtext that speaks through the palero medium's word, just as the speaker must produce a meaningful utterance before the parrot can imitate the speaker. On another level, the conversions and realignments by which the "orthodox" Lucumí system is transformed by a Congo supplement are effected by an act of recentering the field of consciousness. This recentering, by the mediation of the nganga, accesses a language of the unconscious into play, but for the end of empowerment in accordance with the codes and constraints of the Bantu-based religious institution. In possession as in dreaming, symbolization both expresses and masks the latent thought, saving the divine word from silence while giving voice to the father's prophetic-authoritative language.

Bantu Background

The name *Palo Monte* in Cuba serves to designate all of the Bantu-derived religions, those also known as the *Reglas Congas*, and its name denotes the "sticks" or "branches" of the "mountain" used in the making of the nganga. Africanist terminologies signal the origins of the religion. The culture of the *Bakongo* people, who speak the *Kikongo* languages, includes *Kongo* art and religion. The

Kongo, spelled with a K to distinguish the nation from the colonial Belgian Congo, present-day Zaïre, are a people who inhabit a broad sub-Saharan area extending from the southern part of Cameroon through northern Angola to Mozambique on the eastern side of southern Africa. *Kongo* once designated as well what is today the modern republic of Congo-Brazzaville, whose non-Kongo peoples include the Teke. Kongo civilization was also established in northern Angola, Bas-Zaïre, and Gabon (FS 103). The Africans taken in slavery from this general region—the Teke, Suku, Yaka, Punu Bakongo, and Angola—discovered affinities among their languages and religious beliefs. The above orthographic and geographic distinctions made by Thompson justify the use I have made thus far of "Congo/a" with a C to designate the Kongo-based religions that have taken root in Cuba, since the Kongo-based culture there is called "conga" or "bantu" (CA 1:129). I will use the terms Bantu, Palo Monte (Mayombe), and Congo/a more or less interchangeably in the discussion that follows.

Records of the Congo religion in Cuba go back before the nineteenth century. In 1796, reports Carpentier, to give only one illustration, a magusking named Melchor ruled the Cabildo de Congos Reales in Havana (MC 290). Reglas Congas have appeared most strongly on the eastern end of Cuba, alongside the Dahomey-Ewe-Fon–based Reglas Araràs, in Santiago and Guantánamo, but their themes and symbols seem to have spread throughout the island. The various Congo religions, commonly referred to under the rubric of Palo Monte Mayombe, comprise la Regla Conga, la Regla Biyumba, la Regla Musunde, la Regla Quirimbaya, la Regla Vrillumba, and la Regla Kimbisa del Santo Cristo del Buen Viaje (that is, "of the Holy Christ of the Good Journey") (CA 3:130; Pérez Sarduy and Stubbs 301). As stated above, the Bantu cults emphasize "working" with a spirit of the dead, denominated, like the container of the spirit-calling medium, the nkisi (plural minkisi), or nganga. In the popular imagination, the Regla Conga or Palo Monte is tied to the idea of "witchcraft," and this *brujería de congo* includes formulas and spells for working with the dead, "*trabajos con muertos*" (MS 14–15). The palero priest is also called *Tata Nganga*, and paleras and mayomberas work magic as well. It is the mayombero or palera who catches and controls the spirit, often called the *nganga-perro* or "nganga dog," in the nganga-receptacle (EQT 7), which will be described and explicated later in this chapter.

Aside from the symbolic paraphernalia of the religion, Bastide has argued, the "cultural focal point" of the Bantu peoples in the New World has been "folklore" rather than religion. The former, reasons Bastide, survived because during the colonial period the Bantu slaves, valued for physical

strength, were put to work on the plantations, out where it was more difficult than in the urban environments to regroup and reestablish the African
cults (106). Yet the widespread continuance of specifically Bantu-based religious practices on the island, recorded by the literature on the subject, would
seem to contradict Bastide's assertion unless his category of religion (as opposed to "folklore") is intended to refer exclusively to a more or less cohesive whole composed of the kind of discourse practices we have been examining thus far.

Bastide's assertion relies on the premise that the cultural deprivation and
underdevelopment imposed on the Bantu plantation slaves disorganized the
system of their religious practice, causing the Bantu-based religions to disintegrate into ritual and folkloric fragments. Consistent with this premise, it is
generally acknowledged that the Reglas Congas have no elaborately developed set of deities that one could call a "pantheon," and that they have therefore looked to the Lucumí religion to give form to their mythologies with its
narratives and iconography of the orisha-saints. Due to their reliance on other
systems, especially the Lucumí, for structural frameworks, the Reglas Congas
are often called *religiones cruzadas*, "crossed" religions (EQT 9, 84). In grafting
their ritual onto Dahomey-Ewe-Fon or Yoruba ceremony since the beginnings of Cuban culture, the Congos and their descendants and followers have
created what Bastide refers to as a "double series of correspondences" (see
106–7). That tendency to syncretizing assimilation, along with the aforementioned conditions of work to which the Congos were subjected and the
pressures under which all neo-African religions were forced to adapt, accounts for the partial disappearance of Bantu sects, at least as cohesive institutions, in the Americas. The Bantu spirits who arrived in the New World
thus fused with the Catholic saints on the one hand and with the Yoruba
orishas and the Fon loas on the other. In the *Mayombe cruzado* practiced in Cuba,
believers chant to the orishas of the Yoruba pantheon, identified either by
Bantu, Catholic, or Yoruba names: Insancio is Changó or Santa Bárbara;
Nsambi, Sambia, or Asambia is Almighty God or Olodumare; Kisimba is St.
Francis of Assisi or Orúmila (Bastide 109, 111). The dead, *los muertos*, are also
called to intervene in human affairs.

There is no clear demonstration of this syncretism in Cuban prose fiction
to my knowledge, but such admixing and amalgamation accounts for Colombian author Zapata Olivella's synthesis of Bantu liturgy and ancestor-wor-
ship with Yoruba mythology in his novels *Changó, el gran putas* (meaning,
roughly, *Changó, the great motherfucker*, 1983), a section of which I will examine
in chapter 6.

Whereas Congo mythology in Cuba assimilated the Lucumí myth, and rivalries between santeros and paleros exist, the Lucumí and Congo religions continue to complement one another in ritual practice, with the cult of the nganga remaining foremost in Palo Monte and often incorporated into the individual practice of orisha followers (Cuervo Hewitt and Luis 9; CA 3:129–30). The crossing of symbolic elements between those religions once again displays a process of decentering and recentering by which the "freeplay" of the symbol system, tending otherwise toward fixity by the reliance on a presumably transcendental center or structure, is set into a course of mutual transformation between religious systems. An Afro-Cuban religious "semiotics" would have to account for this sort of slippage of signifiers from their referents and their tendency to link up with other signifying chains. To employ Derrida's terms, a "process of substitution" subjects deities to replacement or modification by other deities within the same group or from other groups. The lack of referent or "transcendental signified" permits this displacement along the series of signifiers, although it also opens up signification to the violence of religious rivalry and antagonism (see Derrida, D 89). In James Figarola's theory of "multiple representation," which he applies to Regla de Ocha, Palo Monte, and Vaudou, such slippage is considered the norm: "the representations have the capability of free movement, of increasing or of decreasing and of establishing relations with the rest of the exterior world, independently of the behavior of the represented object" (32). This "free movement" of signs that establish relations with the systems external to their "own" system accounts for the transference and translation of signs across systemic boundaries as well as for the adaptability of the systems themselves.

In the light of these reflections on religious sign systems and their mutations, a study of Palo Monte ritual, doctrine, and myth, including their treatment in literary works, reveals the way that Bantu-based religion has enriched Afro-Cuban literature and religious culture with its instrumental and expressive language.

The eminent Afro-Cuban writer of *poesía negrista*, Nicolás Guillén, exploits the onomatopoeic sounds and rhythm of Bantu language in the poem entitled "Sensemayá." This "Canto para matar una culebra"—"Song for killing a snake"—first appeared in *Motivos de son* in 1930 and relies on some of the same imitative magic that characterizes many of the ebbós or spells of Palo Monte. The tradition of the snake-killing dance, performed in the comparsas or street processions of Epiphany, probably originated in the eighteenth century (Barreda 15). The rhythms of the poem rehearse the movement of a dance that imitates as it "invokes" the presence of the snake and at the same time produces a charm to ward off its threat. Whereas the repetitive verses exploit the rhythmic, musical values of the words, semantic values also connect the verses with Kikongo language. A few definitions suggest the potential impression of the poem on a reader familiar with the vocabulary. *Sensemayá:* a spirit represented at times by a snake. *Mayombé:* once, a slave brought from the Kongo region; now, a representative "Congo" religion. *Bombé:* a popular Antillean black dance, such as the *Bombé serré* of Martinique; or, a personalized drum of Ghanaian origin, with female name and sexual attributes; or a dance such as the *bomba* held on Sundays, with rhythm by a lead dancer, with spectators singing responses in chorus, playing on two drums and two maracas, and beating on a bench with two sticks (DALC 424, 310, 81).

The following sample from "Sensemayá" gives a sense of the poem's incantatory effects, produced through rhythmic repetition, as well as its mimetic effects, produced by exclamations and onomatopoeia:

> ¡Mayombe—bombe—mayombé!
> ¡Mayombe—bombe—mayombé!
> ¡Mayombe—bombe—mayombé!
> Tú le das con el hacha, y se muere:
> ¡dale ya!
> ¡No le des con el pie, que te muerde,
> no le des con el pie, que se va!
>
> Sensemayá, la culebra,
> sensemayá.
> Sensemayá, con sus ojos,
> sensemayá.
> Sensemayá, con su lengua,
> sensemayá. . . .
> ¡Mayombe—bombe—mayombé!
> Sensemayá, la culebra . . .
> ¡Mayombe—bombe—mayombé!
> Sensemayá, no se mueve . . .
> ¡Mayombe—bombe—mayombé!
> ¡Sensemayá, se murió!
> (Guillén 68–70)[1]

The ritual act of invoking Sensemayá's eyes and tongue and death in words "means" (or imitates or anticipates) killing the snake in reality. Guillén's poem demonstrates the "magical" power of the word as name or naming, a concept that is signified in the Bantu word *nommo*, which bears certain similarities with the Lucumí aché. The creative nommo literally means "name" in Bantu, but also "word," *verbum*. It connotes the identification drawn between the person or thing and the name of the person or thing (see APA 18). Naming the snake, one calls the snake itself to presence and commands it.

To expand on this point a bit, the Bantu concept of nommo I would add is central to Edward Kamau Brathwaite's theory of African expression in Caribbean literature. The word or name carries a power to change reality, to transform life, for nommo is itself the life force flowing through all things, that effects changes in things in and through the words that name those things (Brathwaite, *Development* 237; see also Tempels 44 and Jahn, *Muntu* 124). Myriad depictions of verbal art as performance in Caribbean literature attest to the power of nommo, whose sacred potency comes across in scenes of courtroom drama, storytelling, political speeches, divination, conjuration, riddling, calypso, and "wordthrowing." Such performances manifest Brathwaite's "magical/miraculous" conception of the word (Brathwaite, "African Presence" 123–26).

To give an impression of nommo's power, but in Lucumí terms, Cabrera records the statement that in order to conquer another person's love, one must steal that person's *angel de la guarda* or protective personal spirit. One does so by intoning that person's real name, which is often secret. "In those names that one does not say," Cabrera's informant tells her, "there is something like the trace, essence of a life. The true name and the person, they are the same thing. The name is something very sacred" (M 506). The magical power of language, especially in naming and in verbal performing, assumes that language and reality are identical or at least coextensive in some sense and that to work upon the name means to work upon the thing or person named.

As these linguistic operations suggest, and contrary to Yorubo-centric stereotypings by Palo Monte's enemies, Congo ritual procedures display an intriguing efficaciousness. Distinguishing themselves from Lucumí practice by emphasizing their magical communication with deceased spirits, muertos or minkisi, the paleros know the right words and ritual formulas to effect transformations in the material and spiritual worlds. Consistent with the Congo focus on communications with spirits, practitioners of both Regla de Ocha and Palo Monte "borrow" techniques from Cuban spiritualism for their dealings with the dead. This latter tradition, we note in passing, has been strongly influenced by the European spiritualism popularized by Allan Kardek

(SMD 36). Still, despite such borrowings and adaptations, the center of the Bantu practice remains the nganga and the magic done with it.

Crossing the Center

Anthropologist Mischa Titiev has proposed a dichotomizing contrast between magic and religion applicable to the classification of the above mentioned Afro-Cuban practices. For Titiev, religious practice may be defined as communal and calendrical; magic, on the other hand, as individual-oriented and occasional. Calendrical ceremonies function by bonding individuals into a cohesive social unit, whereas magic comes to the aid of the client, resolving crises and fulfilling desires. In religion as Titiev defines it, problem-solving critical practices may still be performed at the behest of individuals but are considered nonetheless to serve the interests of the group (284–88). Yoruba-based religious practice in Cuba, as distinguished from the "magic" practiced in Palo Monte, accordingly tends to emphasize the communal or social aspects of worship, which fall into the category of the recurrent and calendrical mode of temporal organization. In this sense, religious practice relies on the institution such as it exists as an organization of mutually supporting practitioners. Magic as practiced in Palo Monte, on the other hand, tends to respond to problems, needs, or emergencies of a more personal nature. It involves manipulating or compelling the spirits to carry out, on request and through ritual formulas, the will of priest and client. It may also degenerate into formulaic conjurations lacking in religious content in disregard of its communal context.

In the subjectivist, magical view of the palero, the image of the center and of centering inscriptions may function as a mirror to an image of the monadic individual. What is centered in this relation is a perspective of the individual as set on the path of the cycle of life, death, and rebirth. This larger framework replicates the rising and setting movement of the sun, a movement the Kongo saw symbolized in the spirals of the Kodya shell (FS 104, 106). The imaging of the center also brings to mind the memory of the ancient Bakongo capital, Mbanza Kongo, built on a hilltop. In Cuba, this site of origins was reestablished, in Creole speech, by the Bantu renaming of Havana as *Mbansa Bana* (CA 3:130 n. 3).

The historical or nostalgic center of Bantu culture is homologous to a metaphysical center recalled into being by a form of writing on the ground, the design called the *tendwa nzá kongo*, upon which the nganga may be placed in rituals. This pictogram of Kongo and Angolan origin resembles the Haitian *vèvès* configured about the central post, or *poteau mitan*, supporting the roof

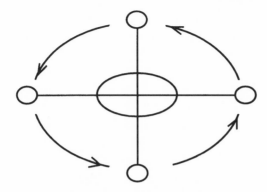

12. The *tendwa nzá kongo,* or Bantu-Kongo cosmogram.

of the Vaudou temple, the *houmfort.* The design also has affinities to the Lucumí grafias, the anaforuana of the Ñáñigos, and to the pontos riscados of Bahian Candomblé in Brazil. Like these other graphic emblems, the nucleating lines in the Palo Monte ground-designs represent the pulling of spiritual forces inward to the center while extending outward toward the four cardinal points of the universe, as Thompson explains in his *Flash of the Spirit.* For, in the beginning in Mbanza Kongo, "images of centering prevailed. It was a world profoundly informed by a cosmogram—an ideal balancing of the vitality of the world of the living with the visionariness of the world of the dead. Charms and medicines were constantly produced in the search for the realization of a perfect vision in the less than perfect world of the living" (FS 189, 102).

The Bantu-Kongo cosmogram, given to humans by the Supreme Deity Nsambi Mpungu, takes the form of a cross, the *yowa,* on the ends of which are drawn little circles that together symbolize the four moments of the sun, or the four cardinal points: noon is at the top, midnight at the bottom, dawn and sunset at the right and left ends. The revolving arrows trace a path around the intersection of the axes (FS 108).

Directed in counterclockwise motion, the arrows of the tendwa nzá kongo show the sun revolving about the body of the inner ellipse of earth's water. Those arrows also symbolize the path of reincarnation. The horizontal line divides the upper from the lower: above the line the earth is "the mountain of the living," *ntoto;* beneath the line is "white clay" or "the mountain of the dead," *mpemba.* The vertical axis is the path linking the two worlds. The zenith therefore signifies north, God, and the male principle. The nadir signifies south, the dead, and the female principle. Thompson adds that the ground drawings and nkisi markings often include symbols from Yoruba iconography. The elliptical tendwa nzá kongo inscribes a vision of wholeness: the totality life and death and the cycle of reincarnation (FS 108–9).

The ritual act of drawing the cosmogram, as traza or nganga-marking, is accompanied by the chanting of sacred songs, mambos, intended to bring down the divine power in the form of a spirit, simbi (EQT 10). With song, the centering cosmogram is inscribed in two instances: outside, on the ground where one takes an oath; and within, in the centerpiece of the Bantu system of magic and medicine, the aforementioned nkisi or nganga charm, whose construction I will elaborate on in the next section. This Kongo custom of "singing-and-drawing" (iyimbila ye sona) aims at activating the spirit-controlling charm (FS 108–10, 110–14).

Containing the Center

Nganga designates the fundamento or fundament of the Bantu religion in Cuba. As noted previously, the name nganga refers either to the small cauldron that holds the spirit or to the spirit itself. Kongo myth recalls the first nkisi or nganga, named Funza. From this nkisi, represented afterward in the twisted roots included in some magic cauldrons and bundle sacks, issued all the minkisi of the world. Afterward, the nkisi served as refuge or prison to the soul of a returned ancestor or of some spirit attached to this world. The Congo nganga itself is therefore a figure of "multiple representation." All told, it represents: the spirit it calls or controls; the first nganga named Funza; its own objective being as a cauldron full of magic objects; its interior graphic sign, drawn on the bottom of the cauldron; and its exterior graphic sign, the cosmogram signifying the nganga's centering force (SMD 18–19). The synonyms and metonyms of the nganga are manifold as well: in Cuba and the United States, it is also known as prenda, suggesting a pawn or guaranty and its related economic obligations, or a jewel, or some other valued article. Alternatively, the nganga spirit may be kept in a sack called jolongo or macuto (EQT 82–83). Nkisi means "charm" but also "positive magic," as opposed to "negative magic" or ndoki. Positive magic is usually the work of the nganga cristiana or so-called Christian nganga, which is "mounted" or formed with holy water as one of its ingredients. A ndoki on the other hand proceeds from the nganga judía—the so-called Jewish nganga (CA 3:144, 146). Finally, the powerful Cuban nganga called Zarabanda, associated with Oggún, Ochosí, and Elegguá, derives its name from the Kongo nsala-banda, the cloth used by Bakongo in their minkisi. Bastide identifies Zarabanda as a form of "magic" originating in Havana from the convergence of Yoruba and Congo practices. The Zarabanda concentrates this magic in a metal cauldron holding bones, plants, and the prayer to Oggún, who is known as Zarabanda in Congo culture (FS 110, 112, 118, 121, 131; CA 3:183).

The nganga furthermore may "engender" other ngangas, its "nganga hijas" or "daughters" made from materials or powers drawn from the madre nganga, the mother. Relying on the "curious mechanism" that James Figarola curiously names "retroalimentation," the "mother" in her turn draws sustenance from the "daughters" when these are fed the expected amount of sacrificial blood (SMD 19). A fascinating, complex lore of "making the nganga" has been recorded by Cabrera, Thompson, González-Wippler, Castellanos and Castellanos, and García Cortez. For the purposes of the following reconstruction I will rely mainly on Cabrera's and Thompson's writings.

Cabrera's informant Baró (one of a number in El monte) revealed that to build a powerful nganga one must go to the cemetery and obtain pieces of a corpse because a spirit, or fumbi, adheres to its body, even after death. The skull, called kiyumba, is especially prized because it is the seat of intelligence, "substancia espiritual." A synecdochic logic obtains here. When the kiyumba is lacking, another piece of skeleton will serve, even one as small as a phalange, because "it represents and 'is worth' the totality of the body" (M 121). The ceremony of the removal as narrated by Baró merits closer reading for its metaphoric implications: "Once in the cemetery, the padre [or Palo Monte priest or ngangulero], sprinkling cane liquor in a cross over a grave, will take away, 'if he can,' the head, the kiyumba of a cadaver, 'with a brain, where the fumbi thinks things, fingers, toes, ribs and long leg bones [canillas] so he can run.' With these remains wrapped in a black cloth, the ngangulero goes to his house to 'make the deal with the deceased' since it is not so easy to make it in the cemetery itself." This procedure is best carried out in the light of a new or full moon due to the close connection between the dead souls and the moon, Ochukwa: the two come into their fullest "vital energies" during those lunar phases. Conversely, it should be kept in mind that the vital forces are weakest in the declining phases, the dwindling crescent called Ochukwa aro. Children born under a full moon, it is known, are "strong," but those born under a waning moon will be expected to be "slow." Furthermore, children presented to the new moon some forty days after birth are strengthened by the ritual (M 118, 119–20, 122).

The ngangulero, having obtained those prized remains from the cemetery, returns home to create a nganga by combining the bones with other prescribed specific ingredients. First, however, "the *padre nganga*, followed by the godson and also attended by the mayordomo, stretches out on the floor. The mayordomo covers him with a sheet, and between four lighted candles, next to the remains, invokes the spirit that takes possession of the *padre* and speaks." Around the supine padre nganga, seven small mounds of gunpowder are lit; if they explode simultaneously, this is a sign that the dead spirit accepts the offer to speak. The ngangulero then writes the spirit's name on a piece of paper, which he places at the bottom of the inscribed cauldron with several coins. These coins constitute the "payment" to the spirit for his or her "sale" to the ngangulero. The priest then either cuts a vein in his own arm to "feed" the spirit some blood, or else sacrifices a rooster for the purpose. Then begins the process of constructing the nganga. Into the cauldron go the cemetery remains and four handfuls of earth taken from the four corners of the deceased's grave, along with other things (M 122–23).

The nganga-cauldron—itself a synecdochic representation of the nganga components, a metonymic representation of its contents—becomes charged with the superterrenal power of its combined ingredients. These include rooster blood, the Cuban ant called *bibijagua*, feathers from the *aura tiñosa* or turkey buzzard, and stones (SMD 19, 63). The ngangulero or ngangulera may also introduce Spanish coins called *reales*; sticks from twenty-seven different species of tree; chili peppers, ginger, garlic and other spices; a hollow piece of sugarcane, in which is sealed amounts of sand, seawater and mercury; the skull of a woodpecker or buzzard; possibly the body of a black dog (M 123). Another principal ingredient is the aché-filled branches of the *siguarraya*, sacred tree owned by Changó, the "Siete-Rayos" ("Seven Lightning-Bolts") of the Palo Monte pantheon (EQT 24). "The brains, which have already become a hard black paste, [go] to one side of the dog's head and the jaw bone" (M 123).

Once constructed, the nganga has to be buried in an anthill, where the characteristics of the ants will be "absorbed" into the charm and bring out its power. A transfer of qualities, following a metonymic logic of signification, operates once again in this step. As Cabrera writes, "Our blacks attribute to these destructive, laborious and indefatigable ants supernatural intelligence and wisdom. 'Bibijagua never rests, doesn't sleep, from night to day: bustling about at all hours. For her there's no Sunday or feast day.' With the industrious bibijagua—ntiawo—the nganga acquires the same extraordinary aptitude for work, assimilating her qualities of laboriousness and perseverance. It learns to demolish and to construct. To demolish what is another's, in order to construct its own" (M 130).

Strengthened by the bibijagua's strength and the nganga's potent ingredients, the muerto or kiyumba spirit contained and controlled within the nganga will come to resemble the Levi-Straussian "mana," the privileged signifier of Polynesian magic available to attach itself to the visible or palpable signifier manipulated by the shaman (see Tempels 53). Like mana, the Afro-Cuban nganga-spirit serves the priest's intention, whether to bring blessings or curses upon another, through a manipulation of symbols. This effect is possible due to the totalizing impulse evident in and expressed by the furnishing of the nganga-cauldron, the kiyumba's home. González-Wippler explains it in these terms: "The [Palo Monte] mayombero believes that his nganga is like a small world that is entirely dominated by him. The kiyumba rules over all the herbs and the animals that live inside the nganga with it. The mayombero in turn rules the kiyumba, who obeys his orders like a faithful dog. The kiyumba is the slave of the mayombero and it is always waiting inside the cauldron or the macuto to carry out his orders" (S 129).

In a similar vein, James Figarola calls the nganga a "scenic space" for magic operations because it is the screen on which is projected the imagined contact of powers and entities, the stage on which the Palo Monte priest meets with the spirit of the dead he would control or direct (SMD 19–20). The Kongo nkisi named Nsumbu, reports Thompson, "is believed to represent the world in miniature," but any nkisi is "informed by this metaphor of cosmos miniaturized." In all its diverse forms, the nkisi mirrors and gathers in the macrocosm, as does the name of a famous nganga of Marianao, called "Tree-of-the-Forest-Seven-Bells-Turns-the-World-Round-the-Midnight-Cemetery" (FS 119, 123). Castellanos and Castellanos' informant confirms the microcosmic aspect of the nganga, where "all the forces of nature join, a 'nature in sum'"; it is indeed "'the whole world in miniature and with which you dominate'" (CA 3:145). Object of power and dread, the nganga, one could say, to quote Zizek's words from a different but comparable context, functions as theater, phantasmic space or screen that serves "for the projection of desires" (Zizek 8–9).

What is generally desired are effects produced in other people. In Santería's *panaldo* cleansing, which shows definite Congo characteristics, malign spirits may be exorcised with the passing of a rooster over the body of the afflicted individual. The rooster, now thought to carry the contagion in its own body, is placed inside the Palo Monte *macuto* sack, in which it is buried in the ground (SR 105–6). If on the other hand harm or malice is intended toward others, the nganga or macuto may be called upon for effecting the spell, called bilongo or *kelembo*. The victims themselves, unconsciously subjected, by belief or psychic "self-alienation," to the dominion of the magic signifier, will confer power upon the malediction and act accordingly, whether by falling ill or suffering an "accident" or otherwise causing harm to themselves. They take the nganga seriously, and their belief often produces results.

A not-so-serious play on nganga-description appears in the section of Cabrera Infante's *Tres tristes tigres* titled "The Death of Trotsky Related by Various Cuban Writers, Years Later—or Before." The section consists of a series of clever parodies of Cuban writing styles. By these parodies, Cabrera Infante exaggerates and thus bares the artifice by which celebrated Cuban authors have achieved particular verbal effects. The targets of his parodies include Carpentier, Lydia Cabrera, Novás Calvo, and others. In Cabrera Infante's hands, their styles are made to report on the death of the Russian advocate of internationalist revolution. Relevant to our discussion of Bantu-based religion in modern narrative, the section dedicated to Lydia Cabrera is titled "El indisime bebe la moskuba que los consagra bolchevikua" ("The Abakuá neophyte drinks the moskuba liquor that the Bolshevik consecrates"). The narrative of the parody, concerned with a nganga, begins with the following paragraph replete with italicized exologisms presented in apposition or parenthesis, after Cabrera's manner:

> She had already forgotten the refusal of Baró, the babalocha of old Chacha (*Caridad*), his mother from Santiago, when she asked to borrow his *nganga* to do him a <<spell [*trabajo*]>> à la <<guámpara [or *uemba*, a kind of spell]>>, the day than the chief of the potencia or *orisha* arrived bringing nothing less that the sacromagic and terrible cauldron (*olla walabo*) hidden inside a black sack—*mmunwbo futi*. The spirit (*wije*) that dwelled in it had manifested to her that it was all right (*tshévere*) because the <<moana mundele>> (white woman, Chachita Mercarder, in this case) had asked him to please protect her son and the mission (*n'oisim'a*) she had before her. The old man hurried to fill that request (*o f'aboru*) because his *nganga* was also in agreement (*sisibuto*). The sorcerer was calmly authorizing her to be consecrated—<<with permission from the *prenda*>>—if she so desired. *Burufutu nmobutu!* (Cabrera Infante, TTT 235)

What was arcane or awkward in Cabrera becomes riotous wordplay in Cabrera Infante. The plethora of italicized Bantu or Lucumí words enriches or clutters the Spanish language, the tangled thicket of bilingual references and insider allusions rendering the passage unintelligible to the noninitiate or aleyo. References to the nganga or prenda fetish are incongruous with the historical account of Trotsky's assassination in Coyoacán but convey the sense of poly-glossia and code-switching customary to Cabrera's Afro-Cuban discourse.

A glossary full of nearly useless definitions and mutually referring cross-references completes Cabrera Infante's parody of Cabrera. But whereas that parody performs a certain demystification of religious and politicoreligious value, it also expresses a certain pleasure in the exuberant productivity of language. Despite its close resemblance to nonsense at times, Cabrera's language is displayed as a tour de force of multilingual musicality, an amalgam of magic and rationalism, of syntactic rhythms and lexical color. Cabrera Infante's parody is also a tribute to Cabrera.

A Hierarchy of Spirits

As stated earlier, the Reglas Congas lack a complex pantheon of their own due in part to the centrality of nganga-worship and in part to their relation of dependency to the Regla Lucumí for its mythological structure. Bantu-based religion nonetheless sustains a transculturated hierarchy of spirits, each called mpungu or santo, and collectively known as the kimpungulu. The kimpungulu is variable in its composition and organization and adaptable to different social and personal circumstances, but it includes spirits of ancestors, spirits of the dead, and spirits of nature. The name of one kind of ancestor-spirit is kinyula nfuiri-ntoto; a ghost or specter is named Musanga; a dead spirit, returned after dying twice is a simbi; one who protects, ndundu. The nature spirits are said to dwell in the bodies of trees, animals, and water. The water-spirit is Nkita-Kunamasa, and the river-spirit is Mburi. In the snake called majá dwells Nkisi Mboma (CA 3:137).

Reinforced by its syncretization with the set of Lucumí orishas, that hierarchy begins at the top with the supreme deity of the Kongos, the creator called Nsambi or Nzambi, Insambi, or Sambia Mpungu. The doctrine and myth of Nsambi, as Castellanos and Castellanos note, were influenced by the monotheism of Portuguese missionaries who succeeded in converting Bakongos of the Gold Coast in the fifteenth century. The Kongo king, Nzinga a Knuwu, and his son were among the converts, and the Kongo capital, Mbanza, was renamed San Salvador. As the supreme god, Nsambi became omniscient: he "sees a little ant in the darkest night" (RNV 9). The anthropogonic myths recount the way that Nsambi, like God of the Old Testament, created the first man and woman directly by his own powers, unlike the Lucumí Olodumare who entrusted the creation of humanity to his intermediaries, Obatalá and Oduddua. These aspects and developments explain why Bantu religion already displayed characteristics of Catholicism upon its arrival in Cuba (CA 3: 130–31).

As mentioned earlier, contact and intercommunication with the Lucumí religion established correspondences between the orishas and the Congo kimpungulu, giving the latter more definition and more affinity with the Catholic saints. Beneath Nsambi in the hierarchy of mpungus, but above humankind, one finds the Congo Nkuyo Watariamba, equated with Ochosí, who is San Norberto. Nkuyu Nfinda or Lucero Mundo is the Lucumí Elegguá as well as the Catholic Niño Jesús de Atocha and San Antonio de Padua (CA 3: 138). Given these numerous crossings, it is not surprising that many mayomberos, nganguleros, or paleros are also initiated in Regla de Ocha, as santeros or babalorishas, with the exception of those chosen by Obatalá and Oduddua, orishas who do not allow this sort of ecumenism among their children (M 122).

Isabel Castellanos lists the Lucumí orishas next to their equivalents in the list of the kimpungulu, to which I have added Castellanos and Castellanos' short list:

Olodumare	Nsambi, Sambia
Obatalá	Tiembla-tierra
Changó	Nsasi, Siete Rayos
Babalú-Ayé	Tata Kañén, Tata Fumbi
Ochosí	Nkuyo, Watariamba
Yemayá	Baluandé
Ochún	Chola Wengue
Oyá	Centella, Mamá Wanga, Kariempembe
Oggún	Zarabanda
Elegguá	Tata Elegua, Quicio-Puerta, Nkuyu Nfinda
Orúnmila	Tata Funde, Cuatro Vientos, Tondá (EQT 74)

Despite the appearance of direct correspondences given by this table, the Reglas Congas, refusing merely to imitate the orisha-worship of Regla de Ocha, relegate the mpungus to a subordinate position in their system: "in this process of synthesis," write Castellanos and Castellanos, "there is matching but not a complete identification. The mpungus are not the object of a special cult, like the Lucumí orishas. One respects them, one names them, they help the faithful, but their role is relatively secondary in the Congo religions where what is fundamental is the cult of the dead" (CA 3:140).

In the presence of the nganga, that which calls the dead, the mpungu-orisha may descend to mount his or her human "horse," *nkomo.* So mounted, the nkomo may perform extraordinary feats. Among her observations of Mayombe ritual, Cabrera reports instances of possessed individuals who eat fire and handle burning coals, and she tells of one nkomo who, mounted by Nsasi-Changó, grabbed the burning candle lying next to the nganga and put its flame up to his eyes, chest, and sides without burning himself (M 264).

Lower than the kiyumbas, simbis, mpungus, and orishas is the Congo ndoki, *endoqui,* or *guindoqui.* Bearing the name of bad magic, he is descended from the Angolan *nyaneka.* A malicious spirit, the ndoki goes out at night— sometimes flies, sometimes runs at lightning speed—to perform grisly bits of mischief on his victims. Sent out by the palero through the nganga's mediation, the ndoki has been known to drink blood and eat human flesh. The Lucumí fear him too (PQ 247).

Dramas of Power

In her article on the initiation in Regla de Palo, González Bueno records observations and testimonials made in Santiago de Cuba. Initiation into the religion is called *rayamiento en palo,* the "marking" central to the regla's rite of passage. The novices, initiates, and mayombero arrive in a room containing a collection of seven, fourteen, or twenty-one scorched sticks. Each participant kneels before the nganga, then takes sips of aguardiente from a gourd. Each takes turns spraying the nganga with a mist of this liquor. The neophyte must then sip the liquor, throw down the gourd, take up a lit cigar, put the burning end into his or her mouth, and blow smoke on the nganga. If the initiate is male, a padrino carries out the following ritual acts (a madrina does them for a female initiate): The initiate is stripped of clothes, which will be disposed of after he tramples them, and he is then bathed with leaves and herbs, blindfolded, and led into the sanctuary of the ngangas. There the padrino cuts the ends of his hair and puts them in the nganga cauldron. The padrino sprinkles aguardiente on some branches, and with them he purifies by aspersing the initiate. At this point, the latter may fall into a trance.

The marking rite proper can take place after the novice returns from the trance. For the marking, he is wrapped up to the neck in a big scarf and told either to lie down or to remain standing. The padrino proceeds to mark incisions in the novice's chest with a thorn from the *ayúa* bush. González Bueno narrates this part of the marking rite as follows: "Three small vertical incisions are made on each side of the chest, though some *paleros* do a fourth oblique incision across the vertical ones; the wounds are dusted with powdered wood and crushed egg shell scorched by fire; sometimes the powdered bones of the nfumbi (the dead spirit of the nganga) and then wax on top. First the nbele (ceremonial machete) and then the ceremonial cowhorn are placed over the wounds. Afterwards, the tongue is marked in the same way as the chest, and the powder put on the wounds must be swallowed with blood" (González Bueno 119).

Next comes a ceremonial test before the nganga. The still blindfolded novice must identify first a candle held up by the padrino, then a crucifix. Once this step is done, the padrino takes the nbele and strikes each side of the novice's back and the sole of each foot. The padrinos can now greet the initiate with the ritual words, "sala maleco," and administer the oaths of the order.

Sacrifices of animals, usually black cockerels or chickens, are made now to provide blood to the nganga-spirit. Some of this blood will be mixed with the aguardiente and given to the novice to drink. The sacred mambos are sung. The ceremony is concluded with the washing of the knife over the nganga with brown sugar water. The festivities may continue (González Bueno 120).

Just as the Lucumí believers may seek a registro or consultation with babalaos or iyalorishas concerning their destiny, the Cuban Congos go to a ngangulero, whose oracular power issues from the prenda. A ngangulero, as stated at the beginning of this chapter, may transmit messages while possessed by the mpungu or nganga, thus becoming the medium through which the spirit speaks. Outside of possession states, nganguleros may also perceive the "truth" through special techniques and powers of clairvoyance. Like santeros and santeras, the ngangulero knows how to cast four coconut pieces, which he calls ndungui in Congo rather than by the Lucumí biagué or obí, interpreting the configuration of white and dark sides that face up. The Congo practice of casting four sea shells or chamalongos relies on a method of interpretation similar to that of the ndungui, but in both forms of divination the primary channel of communication and source of power remains the nganga. In addition to reading coconut pieces and shells, the ngangulero uses the method of putting himself into a "mystical trance" during which, with the help of the nganga, his spirit leaves his body, communes with the spirits, and returns to this world with their message. Finally, an oracle called vititi mensu makes use of a horn in whose opening is placed a small mirror; this peephole into another world is called the mpaka nganga. Holding a lighted candle above the nganga in one hand and the mpaka, with opening facing down, in the other, the ngangulero allows the smoke to obscure the mirror. Then the same diviner, sometimes singing mambos, reads the signs written by the spirits in the sooted glass (CA 3:173–74).

The individualistic and problem-solving magic practiced in Palo Monte, aside from the uses to which the nganga itself can be put, is set in motion by the making of a bilongo. Lachatañeré writes that the Bantu *bilongo*—meaning spell, charm, hex—comes from the priests of the *Nganga-Bilongo* line, from the Mayombe region in what is today Zaïre. Also called *burundanga* and kelembo, the bilongo spell can work beneficent or maleficent magic (CA 3:388). The bilongo has at least three categories of application according to Lachatañeré: to secure, or amarrar ("tie up") the love of another by enchantment; to "curse" another, to spoil—*salar*, literally "to salt"—another's situation; and to attract, "*atraer*," or to distance, "*alejar*" another (by the "turning way," or apotropaic function). By making this last bilongo, then, one may repulse another's love, as in wishing impotence on the intended victim (MS 69, 70). In order to inflict impotence, one may resort to a bilongo consisting of tranquilizing herbs, soil from a cemetery, and the name of the victim written on a piece of paper (OC 28).

The branches of the magic tree called *palo mulato* (*Excothea paniculata*) are used by mayomberos to make bilongos that will despoil even a beautiful woman of her appeal or allure, her *sandunga*. A logic proper to the simile prevails in this bilongo. For its production, one requires the eyes and brains of beautiful animals such as the horse and the peacock. For *despojos*, or spiritual cleansings, mayomberos will use the "noble" *palo caja*, boxwood (*Allophyllus cominia*), and an infusion of boxwood is effective for stopping hemorrhages or aborting fetuses (M 501, 507).

The desire for power and protection ensures the continuation of such practices, serving as they do to give some compensation for the deprivations and hardships of the black underclass. "Magic is the great preoccupation of our blacks," observes Cabrera in an already quoted passage; "and the obtainment, the control of powerful occult forces that obey them blindly has not ceased to be their great desire" (M 16). In his essay "El arte narrativo y la magia" (Narrative art and magic, 1932), which I believe illuminates the principles of verbalization implicit in Bantu magic, Jorge Luis Borges drew out affinities between narrative causality and magical causality. Borges refers to examples of a modern fantastic literature that avails itself of the devices of realist verisimilitude to foster belief in the fantastic descriptions or events included in that narrative. In this realist context, Borges asserts, the "lucid, atavistic" order of magic, with its "primitive clarity," seems real and plausible. Magic operates by the law of sympathy explained by Frazer, that is, by imitation or homeopathy on the one hand, or by contact, contagion, on the other, both of them being varieties of analogy. In prescientific belief as in fantastic narrative, magic is "the coronation or nightmare of the causal, not its contradiction"; that is, miracles operate as the extension of natural causality. In narrative as in the prescientific belief to which we all subscribe at some psychological level, magic links disparate events by means of "a precise game of watchfulness, echoes and affinities." All narrative foreshadowings and prefigurations work like omens and belong to this lucid category of the magical, whose logic and simplicity are more appealing than the "infinite and uncontrollable operations" of normal causality (Borges 88–89, 90, 91). Schematizing a certain verbal thaumaturgy, Borges thus uncovers the magical thinking underlying the *vraisemblable* or verisimilitude of both narrative and the bilongo. The reductionist causality of narrative magic is the magic causality of the Congo narrative, whose functors correspond to a concept of humans as spiritual-material unities.

Spirits Embodied and Disembodied

The human being created by Nsambi is a complex whole composed of spirit and body, corresponding to internal and external aspects of the person. For the Bakongo, the soul inside, called *nsala*, animates the body; it is also identified with breath and shadow, but the nsala is centered in the heart (unlike the eledá spirit of Lucumí religion, seated in the head) and has the ability to leave and establish itself elsewhere. The belief in the nsala's mobility supports the belief that souls of the departed may be summoned through the work of a nganga-cauldron. Also residing within the body is the *mooyo*, focused in the stomach or belly, charged with feeding the rest of the body. The body proper is conceived of as a "shell" (*concha*) or "bundle" (*envoltorio*) called *vuvundi*. In death, the vuvundi remains and rots away while the nsala passes on to its next station.

The Kongo biometaphysical anatomy has been further elaborated in Cuba under the influences of Catholicism and Spiritualism, as detailed by Castellanos and Castellanos. All human beings, *bantus*, are again composed of a biological and a spiritual entity. The material shell is the body, *ntu-bantu*, and the "unintelligent shade," *sombra no inteligente* or *nkwama-bantu*. The Creole equivalent for the nsala-soul seems to be the *nfuiri*, the body-animating spirit, itself composed of three components: the "intelligent shade" called *nkwama-ntu*; the "intelligence" of the individual called *ntu*; and personality, with "the gift of speech," the *ndinga*. In death, again, the *ntu-bantu* decays and disappears, but the components of the spirit transform into the nfuiri-ntoto or "dead spirit."

The Bantu nkwama-ntu, the "intelligent shade," may slip away from the vuvundi, the nsala, and the mooyo. Many Cubans combine the belief in the sombra inteligente with the Spiritualist doctrine, propounded by Allan Kardek, of the periesprit, named after the analogous perisperm surrounding the seed germ; that is, the Kardekian periesprit usually protects the body but sometimes departs from it. In Congo philosophy, the nkwama-ntu surrounds the body during the waking hours, holding together its constituent parts; when one dreams, this spirit force goes forth to travel and experience but remains attached to the body by a cordón de plata, a "silver cord." Hence the name of the popular espiritismo de cordón. Even after death, the nkawama-ntu (intelligent shade) allows the nfuiri-ntoto (dead spirit) to retain his or her integrity and personality, bound up in the ndinga, the personality identified with the gift of language (CA 3: 131–33).

The Kongo bisimbi are the dead, or, more exactly, their spirits, nkwama-ntu, which speak in possession and divination through the agency of the nganga (FS 127). In an illuminating comparative study of funeral rites among the Bakoko-Bantu and the Afro-Dominicans, the Zaïrean anthropologist Muamba Tujibikilo finds that similarities between the rites reveal a common view toward death and the deceased. For both the African and the Dominican groups, the soul indeed departs from the body at death, absenting itself from family and familiars. Death does not however signify a complete break in the relationship between the living and the dead, insofar as the dead are thought to maintain communication with the living. They are therefore not so much one's deceased as one's ancestors who continue living in a certain sense, for the living continue to speak with their dead and will invite them back into the "circle of the living," offering their ancestors food and other gifts, calling on them for guidance and support. Such postmortem survival entails an extended concept of the family (Tujibikilo 47).

Not only do living and dead eat and speak with one another; the injustices that the departed have suffered must be borne and redressed by the living as well. Tujibikilo writes, "Living and dead are strongly united in a dialectic of fortification, because the ancestor nourishes himself with the gifts of the living, while the living find in the ancestor a protector, the assurance and the guarantee of the continuity of the lineage. They come to him to obtain blessing, fecundity, the fertility of the earth and the abundance of the harvest." This death-transcending coexistence, assuming a continuity on which the Afro-Dominican "ancestral logic" is founded, means that there is more to the self than one's self; namely, other selves. Those who believe in this continuity recognize that death is a threshold, not a limit, across which the living and the dead can nurture the ties of sociability and solidarity. Those other selves in Tujibikilo's "dialectic of fortification" shore up the self's own will to resist and challenge oppressive social structures. "Ancestral logic" is therefore a "dialectic of the struggle for the dignity and the rights of the Caribbean man or woman" (Tujibikilo 48, 54, 53).

The Colombian novelist Manuel Zapata Olivella derives a related African concept of language from Bantu ontogeny, that of the *kulonda*. Kulonda is defined as the engendering of offspring in the womb by the act of an ancestor. As with the ancestor who guides and protects the offspring, the word as kulonda marks another connection to the past through lineage and consanguinity: "In this legacy of powers is inscribed the word as giver of life and intelligence" ("Ancestros" 51; see Tempels 159). As an alternative to European phonocentrism, which sees the "letter" as a parasitic presence within the body of the organism that speaks (see D 128), the Bantu doctrine of kulonda as "inscription" supposes a language that flows within the body and through the bodies of all the generations.

The ancestral as the force of kulonda figures prominently in Zapata Olivella's novels, especially in *Changó, el gran putas*, set in part in the Caribbean. In an early scene of the novel, the historically based character of Father Claver attempts to instill the fear of eternal damnation into a recalcitrant slave. The slave, a babalao, responds: "You are mistaken, my indefatigable persecutor, the only eternity is in the Muntu." *Muntu* means "hombre," "man," its plural is *Bantu*, and Zapata Olivella's glossary—called "Cuaderno de bitácora" or shipboard "logbook"—explains that "Bantu" designates not only the human being but all the living and the dead and all that sustain that life so conceived. Accordingly, the word *Bantu* "alludes to the force that unites humans in a single knot with their forebears and posterity immersed in the universe, present, past and future" (Zapata Olivella, *Changó* 271, 731; see Tempels 55). By extended analogy, the novel *Changó* unfolds an expanded notion of character as linked by communication with deceased characters who continue life as sombras, or nkwama-ntu. The African Americans of today join hands with the African Americans of years past. The history of slavery takes on a significance beyond that of suffering and victimage in this omnitemporal framework. Zapata Olivella's multigenerational saga thus proposes a restorative, militant fiction of a collective racial subject engaged in an ongoing dialogue with spirits of the past. This sort of elaboration on the idea of kulonda does not to my knowledge appear in Afro-Cuban narratives.

Kutuguangos and Other Narratives

The traditional, sacred narratives of the Cuban Congos are called kutuguangos. The kutuguangos resemble the pataki of Lucumí tradition, although they are not as numerous, in forming a complete "canon" of folkloric stories that explain the origins of natural phenomena, the behavior of the spirits, the human condition, the existence of evil, and the inevitability of death. Castellanos and Castellanos retell ten of the kutuguangos they have gleaned from interviews with informants and from other authors. Some of the stories account for the tragic separation of humans from Nsambi, the Congo God.

In one of these stories, Nsambi in heaven, or muna-nsulu, created the earth, or muna-ntoto, and had the custom of climbing up or down between the worlds by way of the sacred ceiba tree, nkunia-ungundu, called Iroko by the Lucumís. Next, Nsambi created humans—the Bantu. To these he said that the nkunia-ungundu is sacred and should never be chopped down. Then Nsambi taught the Bantu to dance and sing so that they might beguile their boredom. Here is where the trouble starts: to dance and sing, the Bantu needed drums, and once they had carved out some drums they had to have a bigger drum, and what better source of a trunk for a bigger drum than the nkunia-ungundu? Foolishly, the Bantu cut down the sacred tree and made their giant instrument. Not pleased, Nsambi sent down the buzzard, the aura tiñosa, to retrieve the drum, on which Nsambi henceforth blasted out the thunder from the heavens. By committing their sacrilege, humans have lost their immunity from strife, disease, suffering, and death (CA 3:175–76).

Humans lose this divine privilege again in the second kutuguango of Castellanos and Castellanos' collection. Nsambi had the custom of descending to the earth to collect his favorite food, yams, ñames, at the side of a river, and then return to heaven. There he pronounced, "In heaven there is plenty of food. You can eat whatever you like of it, except for these yams, which I reserve for myself." Nsambi, drowsy after eating so many yams, fell asleep. The animals then saw their chance to eat up the tasty yams: the ox, the cow, the dogs, the goats; each animal had one. When only one yam was left, el hombre (the man) went up to the pot to take it but hesitated; his wife, la mujer (the woman), unfortunately urged him on. Nsambi woke up hungry, discovered that all his yams had been eaten up, then called all the creatures to announce: "You have disobeyed your God. Now leave heaven, to live on the earth with pain, work, sickness, death! I separate myself from you. I'm going far, far away. . . . Goodbye!"

Two other kutuguangos recorded by Castellanos and Castellanos relate other versions of the original sin. In the first of these narratives, the expulsion is motivated by a misunderstanding. Nsambi had given a calabash as food to a woman, but another woman had exchanged it for a rotten one. Believing that Nsambi had given them an unsatisfactory gift, all the women rebelled against the Almighty and received their punishment. The other kutugungo explains why heaven is so far away from earth: an ill-tempered woman, tickled by mischievous clouds one day while she is sweeping, chases them away. She scares the clouds so much that they fly to the sky, taking heaven away with them (CA 3:176–77). All four of these summarized narratives acknowledge, in cosmogonic myth, the condition of destitution, the sense of a lost birthright and plenitude never to be recovered but somewhat compensated for in dealings with the mediating mpungus. One also notes the spirit of misogyny in those kutuguangos, which assign to "woman," resembling Eve in Judeo-Christian tradition, the greater part of the blame for mankind's primordial loss.

Castellanos and Castellanos present other kutuguangos that blame woman again, this time for the curse of mortality. One day la Muerte, Death, "an old woman dressed in black," escaped from Nsambi and sought refuge on earth. Nsambi comes hunting with two dogs; Death runs to a house and knocks on the door, asking for a hiding place. A woman answers, and Death gains entry into her house after giving her a golden chain. Soon thereafter, Nsambi comes and knocks on the door. The woman answers. No Death here, she says. Nsambi returns to heaven without his quarry, and we are left to conclude that woman's venality and duplicity are responsible for Death's dominion over life (CA 3:179).

Of greater elaboration and complexity are the stories of Cabrera's Por qué . . . Cuento negros de Cuba (Why . . . black stories from Cuba, 1948) that feature Kongo-based elements of myth and ritual. In her morphological study of Cabrera's stories, many of which do draw from kutuguangos, Mariela Gutiérrez employs the Proppian model of narrative analysis that was adapted by Claude Bremond. Gutiérrez also bases her analysis on the premise of a Bantu cosmovision that perceives a reality that constantly regenerates itself, striving continually to reestablish a universal harmony that some see incarnated in the image of the bosque, the forest or jungle imaged as the Earthly Paradise. All parts of this unity are irreplaceable and integral, establishing a balance among themselves. They are joined by the spiritual-cosmic force called ntu in Kikongo: the previously discussed divine intelligence, "the original point of Creation" popularized by the Belgian writer Placide Tempels. In this expanded conception, ntu forms the basis of a kind of Kongo monism, the *"unique and pristine formula from which all creation proceeded," "matter and spirit, unified in one point where they cannot separate."* All creation, penetrated and united by ntu, continually undergoes the transition through creation-death-resurrection, the self-renewing pattern that corresponds to the narrative design of equilibrium-disequilibrium-equilibrium that Gutiérrez discerns in Cabrera's Afro-Cuban stories. Underlying all disorder, this vision maintains, is a discernible if complex order. All antagonism is a divine harmony working itself out. In Gutiérrez's reading of Cabrera's trickster stories, the cyclical pattern of life and death is translated into the narrative acts of an antagonist who dispossesses a protagonist (or attempts to do so) through cunning, only to be outwitted in his or her turn by the protagonist, who reestablishes his claim on the recovered possession (Gutiérrez 10, 11; see Tempels 49–53).

Although not a trickster story, Cabrera's "Tatabisako," one of the *Cuentos negros*, features rituals with Kongo elements set into the cycle of equilibrium-disequilibrium-equilibrium. In the story, apparently set in an African context by its cultural references, a woman identified only as "la mujer" works daily in a plot of land beside a lake. Seeing that she must carry her crying baby son on her back as she labors, the god Tatabisako, the "Master of the Lagoon Water," takes pity on the boy, rises from the water and offers to care for him while the woman performs her daily task. The arrangement works out well, relieving the woman of her extra burden, until one day when she decides to thank the Water Lord with an offering of a goat. Unable to find the right words, she offends the Water God by ineptly saying, "<<Coma chivo con hijo tó>>," which means, roughly, "Eat goat all with son." The consequences of the woman's breach of decorum are catastrophic. Tatabisako, angrily misunderstanding the woman's intent, withdraws into the water with the boy; the bulrushes of the shore turn into venomous black snakes; rocks become enormous crocodiles; the evil spirits called *güijes* cast sharp pebbles in her direction. "The black lagoon boiled, red with blood." So great is the inarticulate woman's grief that at home, in the presence of her husband, she can only scream and roll in the dirt. Confused and as yet unaware of the tragic loss, the husband opens a casserole in which the woman has cooked a calf's head; he rushes to the conclusion that it is his child's head that she has served for dinner. Grief and horror spread through the village; the chief may have to punish the husband with death for the alleged infanticide (CN 17–18, 119, 120).

Fortunately, however, the *babá* or babalao of the village can perform a divination rite to ascertain whether the boy has been killed. The babalao possesses—and here enters the Congo element—a prenda or nganga, which he calls Aire Grande ("Big Air"), and a deer's horn he calls Aire Chico ("Little Air"). "Aire Grande would bring him all the words that were said; Aire Chico would tell him all he had seen." Aire Chico also tells him that Tatabisako threatens to flood the land and destroy the crops. In the propitiatory rite he orders done, the babá first floats a calabash into the center of the lake, then twelve he-goats, and then twelve she-goats. Tatabisako accepts the offerings and reappears with the child asleep on his shoulder, "cradled in the great night." Tatabisako offers the child to his mortified mother, but she is too ashamed to receive him; the father, instead, takes the child. The story concludes by telling us that the humiliated woman hides herself and runs away, never to return (CN 120, 122, 123). The story is a paradigm of tribal morality, a sort of a social charter relegating human sacrifice and cannibalism to the "animal" realm of the socially other to which the improperly behaving and speaking woman has been exiled. In order for the community to restore the equilibrium she has upset, the woman must be separated, reviled, and cast out.

As in other traditions, some anthropogonic stories explain the Congo rationale for ritual. In Cabrera's *Por qué* . . . , Yácara, the first man, worked and scratched and turned over the soil of the earth, Entoto. The man cries out, "I am the King, the King of the World!" Wanting to know the identity of her torturer, Entoto asks Cheché-Kalunga, the hill, who it might be. Entoto then confronts Yácara, but Yácara justifies himself: "Nsambi sent me!" Yácara's presumptuous argument holds no weight for the earth, who closes herself up. Yácara must then appeal to Nsambi. The Almighty, not wanting to get too involved, tells Yácara to work out the problem between himself and Entoto (the earth). Entoto and Yácara meet and confer; the man agrees to the earth's condition: "You will sustain me with your children day by day and I, finally, will pay you with my body, which you will devour when Nsambi, our father, authorizes you, and may it be He who delivers me to you when he sees fit." The pact made, the story concludes with an epilogue telling that Man came to an understanding with Fire, the Spirits, the beasts, the Mountain, and the River but not with the Sea or the Wind (PQ 63–65). The story thus recalls the origins of cultivation and culture, reconciling their opposition to the natural world. Nsambi adjudicates in heaven, but humans must renew their contract with the earth, depicted here as the sentient and intelligent planet as well as the source of life and sustenance.

Another kutuguango rewritten by Cabrera, titled "Time Battles the Sun, and the Moon Consoles the Earth," tells of the day on which Time, King Embú, goes out in search of a woman who can bear him children, since his wife at home, the Ceiba, cannot. This departure will soon lead to another disruption and conflict. In Tángu-Tángu, King Embú (Time) finds a fecund Moana-Entoto ("Young Earth") who, despite having borne many star-children already, cries because her children's father, the Sun or King Tángu, will burn them all. Besides that, the cruel Sun spends his time up on the plain with his concubine named Ensuro, the Moon. Embú engages in battle with Tángu and defeats him, sending the sun down into a dark abyss. A new order is established: as victor in that inaugural confrontation, Time may now lay down with fertile Earth; the Sun must disappear at night, when the Moon pours her beneficent light on the mother of the stars, and yet the Sun will rise again to renew "the eternal struggle" with Time (PQ 66–67).

A devil called Indiambo appears in Cabrera's story "Cundió brujería mala," whose title promises to explain how "Bad magic spread" and whose narrative once again illustrates the importance of magic in the Congo universe. The woodcutter Brakundé passes daily in front of the devil Indiambo's hut on his way to work. When he does so, the devil regularly calls out to Brakundé, "Who rules?," to which the godly woodcutter regularly replies, "¡Inzambi!" (Nsambi). It turns out that Indiambo covets Brakundé's wife, Diansola, and plots to take her away from her husband. He prepares the bad magic in the form of a uemba, or ebbó—a spell—and then ties up an amarre charm by putting three knots in a scorched strip of corn husk. The first uemba charm succeeds in sending Brakundé to jail, but Diansola remains inaccessible; she is protected by Inzambi and by the dog Bagarabundi, and everyone knows that devils do not get along well with dogs.

The day arrives when Brakundé is to be released, but since Indiambo has not yet secured the love of Diansola, he abducts her as she is walking to the jail to meet Brakundé. Now wifeless, Brakundé returns home alone, but his hatchet follows the devil and his captive, cutting through to Indiambo's hiding place. Bagarabundi then leads his master there, and Brakundé hacks the devil into many little pieces. So that the pieces of Indiambo will not reunite, Brakundé and Diansola scatter them around the world, "each piece in a different country." By the same act, however, they unwittingly spread the evil in those pieces throughout the world (PQ 30–34).

Virtue and piety are good, but sometimes magic is stronger. The uemba (or wanga) consists of a powder called empolo, which is sprinkled near a door so that the intended victim may step on it, thus absorbing its potency into his or her body (PQ 253). Magic disrupts the equilibrium of conjugal order, but it takes a magic hatchet, a faithful dog, love, and belief to destroy evil and restore that equilibrium.

Bakongo Memories

Dora Alonso, folklorist, has two collections that include Afro-Cuban stories. *Ponolani* (1966) gathers together fragmentary narratives of devils and enchantments. With *Ponolani* and the subsequent collection *Cuentos* (1976), one story from which I will discuss in chapter 7, Alonso reveals an interest in preserving the Bantu heritage and especially the religious core of its values.

The fragments of *Ponolani* include sketches, vignettes, evocative descriptions and some short, very slim stories. Their style is minimalist in the extreme. As the narrator indicates, these bits and pieces came from the Bakongo with Ponolani, a "negrita macúa" from the village of Sama Guengení. Ponolani is the grandmother of Emilia, the black woman who nursed and raised Alonso's child. The grandmother's thin narratives evoke the distanced mythical epoch remembered by slaves and their descendants, in whose storytelling the voice cannot recuperate the seeming fullness of that closed, organic world. Ponolani, chained and carried away from her native land by the slave traders, survived the Middle Passage across "[e]l mar azul de Yemayá." Yet the blue sea of Yemayá, apparently indifferent to Ponolani's fate, barely sustains the reminder of the storyteller's continuing presence after her death: "All that remained floating adrift on the wave and the breeze and in the phosphorescent fish, were the stories of her village of Sama Guengení" (Alonso, *Ponolani* 11, 19, 22).

Like Cabrera's stories, Ponolani's are populated by the characters of myth and legend, including devils, *diablos*. As such, they offer another glimpse into aspects of the Bantu folklore that religious practice in itself does not convey. In one narrative fragment from the collection, Emilia's son Lilo is described as having one turned-in eye and knowing how to "dance on one foot like the Devil Donkine." In a longer narrative, the orphan girl of "La huérfana" (The orphan), leaves her adoptive father's house and claims her birthright from Palicé the devil, whom she calls "padre." Instead of eating his own daughter, Palicé gives her a palace and her own pig. Later on, he allows her to see her siblings on the condition that she not allow them to embrace her. After Palicé dies, she inherits everything.

Another of Alonso's devils appears in the two-page story titled "Lorenzo." The protagonist of the same name, seeking his fortune, arrives at the house of a devil who allows the boy to enter but only so he can eat him. Lorenzo isn't fooled by his hungry host. On the pretense of going to sleep outside, Lorenzo goes to the devil's shed, finds a drum and begins to play it. The enchanted "¡babiquindumba!" of Lorenzo's drumming arouses the devil, who cannot help but dance, such is his nature. The clever drummer will then put the devil to work to his own advantage (Alonso, *Ponolani* 36–58).

Other stories in *Ponolani* communicate an intent to distinguish the human world from the animal—and the possible difficulty of doing so in an animated or humanized universe. Pedro Animal is "half human and the rest of his body something strange." Yet Pedro Animal laughs at *Perro*, "Dog," for trying to disguise himself as a human. In "La mona," the female monkey of the title tricks a man into marrying her. Their little son betrays his mother's secret, but the truth will out when the man plays his *bandurria* (similar to a fiddle), and the maternal simian cannot help but sing and dance and turn into her true monkey self. No one doubts what should be done next: "Right there they cut off her head" (Alonso, *Ponolani* 64, 68).

In the story "Panga Maleka, cazador," the hunter Panga marries a woman who has eaten up every one of her previous suitors. She will not eat up her husband just yet, however: she sends him to the grove to gather mangos, knowing that devils await him there. But Panga sings a song that brings his dogs to the rescue. Self-confident, master of his dogs, and musically gifted, Panga vanquishes the devils. End of story (Alonso, *Ponolani* 86).

"Lilo," more a vignette than a story, tells of Emilia's son Lilo, the same one who could dance on one foot like the Devil Donkine at the reunions and bonfires. Lilo sings, and from his mouth, the narrator tells us, "would come out devils and spells and evocation of faraway Africa of his ancient blood, dead on the island by the hand of the slave trade; but resuscitated in a thousand secret and beautiful lives; in long, long, long flights of music and fire beetles" (Alonso, *Ponolani* 90).

Donkine is a one-legged devil who, when his drums play themselves, can do nothing but dance on his single foot. This occurs in the story "Donkine bailador" (Donkine, Dancer). The mischievous twins, the Jimaguas known to Lucumí tradition, want to put a stop to this dancing and call Donkine by blowing on a calabash whistle. His happy dance interrupted, the angry devil grabs the impertinent twins by the ears but finds no whistle, for the little *pícaros* (rogues) have hidden it under their animal skins (Alonso, *Ponolani* 89, 90, 124).

The story "El hijo del diablo" (The son of the devil) tells of an herbalist's widow who boils and eats up a large egg she finds in a bush of Guinea grass. Already pregnant, she becomes doubly impregnated because the egg belongs to the devil's wife, *la Diabla*. At the end of nine months, the widow gives birth as expected to a set of twins: one of them normal, the other with "long, long fingernails, teeth like pins, eyes like a boa." While she nurses them, the diablito bites and scratches her nipple. The mother continues to nurse and love both her sons, despite the bad twin's mischief. One day, the two boys go out to cut firewood; the good son climbs up a tree, and the bad son, instead of handing the hatchet to his half brother, enlists the aid of all the devils to chop down the tree. The good son calls his dogs, who come to the rescue, but prevents them from killing his brother: "After all," he explains, "the two of us were together in the heart of my mother!" (Alonso, *Ponolani* 94, 96)

With time and transculturation, as the previous "devil stories" and the preceding good twin/bad twin story illustrate, the devils of the Congo narratives appear as humanized versions of Lucifer-Satan. In "Juanillo jugador," Juanillo "the gambler" loses big in one game, falling so deeply into debt that he must become the slave of the devil don José, who secretly plans to eat up the improvident young man after subjecting him to a series of trials. It turns out that the devil's wife is a Christian (sic), and so is their good daughter Juanita, who falls in love with Juanillo and secretly performs the tasks that her father has assigned him. Juanita and Juanillo can then be married by a priest. Religious doctrines continue to intercross as Juanita gives Juanillo the means for them to escape her father, who quickly approaches on horseback. She says to her husband, "Throw this grain of salt. Papá doesn't step on Yemayá's sea." The devil cannot pass the grain of salt and must turn back (Alonso, *Ponolani* 115).

Images of centering once again dominate in the last story of *Ponolani*, "Cuento de marido bonito" (Story of the handsome husband), which is remarkable for its intricate construction and suggestive imagery. In the story, a young man goes searching for his sister, who has married a devil, the "handsome husband" of the title, and from whom he seeks to release her. At the outset of his journey he kills an ox and shares the meat, successively, with a lion, an eagle, and an ant. Each grateful animal gives the generous youth the ability to take on his form when the youth utters the words, "God is a lion!" "God is an eagle!," and so on. The gifts serve him well in helping him find the devil's palace and then find the means to kill the devil. Once the brother has arrived, it is the sister who draws the essential information out of the devil as he talks in his sleep: "My life is so hard and never ends. And there is only one way to take it from me: in the river there is a very bad animal called porcupine. That animal eats sheep. It is necessary to fight with him, beat him and pull out a little box from his craw. Inside that box there is a dove, inside the dove an egg. In that egg is the center of my life; if you break it on my forehead, my time will come." With this information, the resourceful brother, by transforming himself into an eagle, lion, and ant at the appropriate times, can locate the egg (in the dove in the box in the stomach of the porcupine), and the sister will smash the egg on the devil's head, thus ending his life (Alonso, *Ponolani* 130).

The story conforms to the familiar pattern of equilibrium-disequilibrium-equilibrium. The hero seeks the object, his sister, and thus seeks to reestablish the familial unit. The means or agency for attaining that object, the egg, is endowed with a nganga-like power inasmuch as it holds the life or nkwama-ntu of the devil. The opponent is the sister's husband, a devil akin to the demons of the kutuguangos. The word as nommo not only names the real things of the story but, in naming them, creates them: the brother says he is an animal, and he is that animal. Less apparently, when the devil describes the whereabouts of the egg containing his life, the story confirms its own self-referring reality. With the devil out of the way, moral order is restored, good triumphs. The story's narrative patterns of communication, centering, desire, and assistance all contribute to affirming the values of generosity, cunning, fraternal love, persistence, and magic methods. Not coincidentally, the devil's unconscious speech recalls the words of the palero who parrots the word of another—that is, the word of an absent authority or dead father.

6

⬧ Versions of Vaudou

Yet for himself Wes *was moved by the certainty that his* Fa *had not yet been acted out, and he sought to discover what it would be. This poised moment in the point of the horn, perhaps it was merely a place where Mawu had paused to rest in the writing of the story, which remained unfinished.*

Harold Courlander, *The African*

A passage in Carpentier's ¡Ecue-Yamba-O! reveals an early stereotypical view of the Vaudou practiced by the Haitians in Cuba. In that novel, the character Usebio Cue, returning home through an old sugar mill after a cyclone, peeks into an abandoned *barracón* or slaves' quarters and catches a glimpse of Haitian workers performing secret ceremonies, in the company of a feared *bruja* named Paula Macho, known for casting spells and the evil eye. The sight of their altar—adorned with a skull, "a rosary of molars," a femur, and other bones—and the thought of Haitians in the cemetery, stealing the dead, give a panicked Usebio reason enough to turn heels and run (EYO 62). The scene suggests the manner in which Haitians and their "magic" represented a threatening otherness within the Cuban society of the Republican period. Vaudou belief and practice have been surrounded by negative stereotypes outside of Cuba as well. Novels, movies, television, and comic books have popularized a kitschy-exotic image of Vaudou, evoking a slave island of "witch doctors," spells, possessions, zombies, and frenzied dances to the beat of the tom-tom.

As for more ethnologically responsible studies and interpretations of the religion, Vaudou themes and motifs have appeared in the Caribbean-based narratives of Jacques Stephen Alexis, Alejo Carpentier, Antonio Benítez Rojo, Pierre Clitandre, Maya Deren, Zora Neale Hurston, Wilson Harris, Alfred Métraux, Jacques Roumain, Patrick Taylor, Robert Farris Thompson, Manuel Zapata Olivella, and Wade Davis, even if a rather lurid movie was based on this last author's study of zombification. These authors make for fascinating reading on an intriguing and as yet little understood topic within the field of Afro-Caribbean narrative.

The Cuban religion known as the "Regla Arará" traces its African origins back to Dahomeyan or Ewe-Fon, Yoruba, and Kongo cultures by way of Haitian *Vaudou*. (I use the common "French" spelling since it evokes Creole pronunciation and defamiliarizes what has been stereotyped under other spellings in English and Spanish writing.) The name *Arará* itself is a cognate of the Haitian-Dahomeyan *Rada*, which derives from the name Allada, a town in Dahomey (FS 274–75n. 5). Cabrera observes that Arará "enjoys great prestige" in Cuba, and its *bokonos* (*bokors*) or priests have charged higher "fees" or *derechos* than their Lucumí counterparts for comparable services (M 22 n). Cuban practitioners of Arará, usually reluctant to reveal the secrets of their cult, are more numerous in the cities of Matanzas and Santiago de Cuba than in Havana for historical reasons that I will examine shortly.

A syncretic Creole religion of the Antilles—like Obeah, Myalism, Pocomanía, Gagá, Shangó, Candomblé, Umbanda, Regla de Ocha, Regla Abakuá, Palo Monte, and other layers of the Caribbean religious palimpsest—Vaudou emerged from a fusion of beliefs and practices related to the worship of West African gods. Like the other neo-African religions of the region, Vaudou kept alive such practices as possession, sacrifice, initiation, sacred music, religious dance, ethnomedicine, and the investing of objects with supernatural powers. Since Vaudou combines elements from Catholic, Dahomeyan, Yoruba, Kongo, and other religions, Thompson calls it an example of "Africa *reblended*" (164). As with the Afro-Cuban religions discussed in previous chapters, the ritual, mythology, and doctrine of Vaudou comprise a sign system that has maintained an identity distinct from the Regla Lucumí, the Regla Abakuá, and the Regla Conga.

Although the similarities between those religions and Vaudou are noteworthy, the distinguishing characteristics of the Afro-Haitian recombination include the following: the belligerent and sometimes militant nature of loa-worship, whose inherent aggressivity arguably motivated anti-French resistance in the Haitian Revolution; the close though variable and ambiguous relationship that Vaudou has had with national politics after independence; and the expressive primacy in Vaudou of singing, dance, and ritual over storytelling. Yet despite Vaudou's underestimation of narrative in its own signifying system, Vaudou's signs have been recoded in literary narrative. Its ritual, doctrinal, and artistic narratizations in texts that incorporate Vaudou signs can be understood within an adequate interpretive framework informed by history and semiotics.

Afro-Cuban culture's strong connection with Haiti begins at the end of the eighteenth century when the outbreak of the Haitian Revolution on Saint Domingue forced numerous planters and their slaves to relocate in southeastern Cuba and especially in the city of Santiago. Fernando Ortiz incidentally remarks in his foreword to ¡¡Oh, mío Yemayá!! that the name of its author, Rómulo Lachatañeré, probably derives from the Franco-Haitian Lachataignerais and links his family's establishment on the island with the event of the French colonial exodus ("Predisposición" xii–xiii). As Carpentier's La música en Cuba recounts it, many plantation owners fleeing from the Haitian Revolution disembarked in Santiago de Cuba with their domestic slaves. Those who had the means to do so traveled on to New Orleans. Others remained, some of whom, grateful to have escaped the bloodbath, sang both the "Marseillaise" and the "Hymne á Saint Louis" (128). In his study on Sarduy, González Echevarría refers to the Haitian-Cuban migration in affirming a continuity between the histories of the two islands. This continuity is evidenced today in the Afro-Cuban dances called danzón, cha-cha-chá, and salsa: these originated in the contredanse that was brought over by the French planters from Haiti (and made famous by Bizet's Carmen) and which had previously originated in the English country dance (RSS 76).

The same history of ruptures and transplantations includes the narrative of how Vaudou became vodú or vodún on the Spanish isle. Dathorne characterizes a process of disintegration and reintegration by which African-based religions, "recollected in a dismembered form" on one island, such as Haiti, are transported and "evolved into a secondary synthetic form," such as the Regla Arará of Oriente Province (28). In that transfer of discourse and practices, the process of transculturation continued, as heteroclite mythologies and liturgies merged and mixed, producing a new religious synthesis.

In contrasting Haitian with Cuban and Brazilian religious syntheses, Bastide argues that those produced by the latter two were also subject to a process of "cultural fossilisation," by which faith served as a defense of self-identity and dignity against continuous onslaughts from the social environment. A "preserved" or "fossilised" religion exhibits another culture's more conservative tendency to "cristalis[e]" and "remov[e] it from the flux of history." On the other hand, a continually evolving and self-adapting religion such as Bastide finds in Haitian Vaudou merits qualification as a "living" religion (131). The perception of Afro-Cuban and Afro-Brazilian religions as "fossilised" cultural spheres separated from history overlooks, in my view, their evolving, adaptive character in daily life, and possibly their intrinsic historicity. I believe that Bastide is nonetheless correct in accentuating the closer connection between Vaudou and historical processes, a connection that distinguishes it from most Afro-Cuban religions. Given its characteristic historicity, Vaudou nonetheless lacks a historical consciousness that would make it an authentic agent for progressive social change. Taylor has found in Vaudou an "example of the mythical encoding of experience," but he observes, from a more rationalist perspective than that of Vaudou's apologists, that Vaudou does not escape its mythical closure nor achieve the degree of self-conscious understanding that would allow it to engage in effective social critique (98).

Among its sympathetic interpretations, Maya Deren's account of Vaudou in *The Divine Horsemen* sees it as both a belief system and a survival mechanism appropriate to the impoverished milieu in which it is practiced. For the urbanized peasants, its cognitive schemes serve the function of providing "a familiar and stabilizing pattern, a comforting echo of the known past in an otherwise confusing and frightening new world" (87n.). In her affirmative definition of the religion in *Tell My Horse*, Zora Neale Hurston offers a suggestive reading of Vaudou as a "religion of creation and life"; furthermore, "[i]t is the worship of the sun, the water and other natural forces, but the symbolism is no better understood than that of other religions and consequently is taken too literally" (137). To be better understood, Hurston seems to be suggesting, Vaudou is to be interpreted in a nonliteral fashion, through a certain poetics or metaphorics. In this chapter, which will examine Vaudou from both the "critical" and the "sympathetic" perspectives, an exposition of the history, institution, ritual, and myth of the Vaudou religious system will precede a reading of Carpentier's *El reino de este mundo* (The kingdom of this world) and Benítez Rojo's story "La tierra y el cielo" (Earth and heaven), both of them Cuban narratives that focus on mythical and historical aspects of Vaudou. The Vaudou subtext to those narratives is multifaceted and as complex as the religion itself, but a brief reconstruction of Vaudou's history and system will help to define the Afro-Caribbean dimensions of Carpentier's novel and Benítez Rojo's short story. We will begin with some comparisons between Afro-Haitian and Afro-Cuban religions.

As contributors to "slave ideology," Vaudou and Santería, writes Lewis, "became . . . active protagonists in the war against the system" in Saint Domingue and Cuba. They became active protagonists in two ways. First, slave religion provided a medium of "religious compromise" whereby distinct African traditions could combine and mesh to produce the basis of an ideological unity among the rebelling slaves. Second, both syncretic religions initiated an "assimilationist compromise" with the official Catholicism and thus blunted or avoided potential opposition from the clergy. Yet of the two Vaudou was always more of a "unifying force . . . that nurtured the revolutionary drive" (Lewis 193). Vaudou is especially significant to Caribbean history and narrative because its believers, as Laguerre asserts, "became the first organised foci of open resistance to slavery" (33). Afro-Cuban religions, on the other hand, could make only an ambiguous and minor contribution to Cuban history. This weakness may account for the turn to Vaudou tradition within some Afro-Cuban narratives concerned with the possibilities of historical change in the Caribbean.

There were certainly significant similarities in the experience of slaves on the two sugar-producing islands. The runaway slaves were *cimarrones* in Cuba and *matiabo* in Haiti (FS 125). In both Cuba and Haiti, Laguerre notes, Saturday evening gatherings for dance and worship were also the occasion for organizing slave revolt (14). Lewis however attributes the weaker contribution of slave religion in Cuba to "the very ethnic heterogeneity" of the Cuban population in the nineteenth century. At that time, distinct racial and social groups vied for ascendancy. In addition to this lack of unity, the slaves' desire for emancipation clashed with the racist sentiment of the anti-Spanish revolutionary party, which feared the creation of "another Haiti" and for that reason moved but slowly toward abolition. Distancing themselves from the black slaves, the class of mulattoes, some of whom owning land and even their own slaves, felt that "the national interest" held priority over abolition, and it was from this group that the revolutionary leaders Maceo and Gómez emerged. These domestic factors deflecting the force of slave religion in Cuba kept it from having the impact that Vaudou had in Haiti, although that did not prevent some Cubans from becoming *serviteurs* and organizing their own Vaudou-inspired insurrections in the southeast end of the island (Lewis 194). Laguerre records, incidentally, that the Vaudou priest Padréjean, one of the leaders of the anticolonial revolt in Saint Domingue, was a maroon who may have arrived in Port-de-Paix by way of Santo Domingo or Cuba (29).

Serviteurs of the Gods

Some 85 percent of the Haitian population is said to practice Vaudou today. Like the Cuban Regla de Ocha, the Sociedad Secreta Abakuá, and Palo Monte, Vaudou teaches that believers can call upon the deities to intervene in their affairs and problems. As a worldview that mediates the relation between the human and the divine, Vaudou suffuses everyday life with its significations. Within its sign-world, order is found in chaos, and everything is related to everything else and has a reason for being so. "Within Vaudou society," writes

Davis, "there are no accidents. It is a closed system of belief in which no event has a life of its own" (77).

In Deren's previously summarized view, Vaudou serves the practical function of developing familiar patterns, controlling an environment, and creating meaning. A practical order of abstraction is implicit in Vaudou worship: the believer gives devotion to *les Invisibles* acting behind phenomena, contrary to the simplistic fetishism or animism wrongly attributed to the cult. "*To worship the loa,*" Deren emphasizes, "*is to celebrate the principle, not the matter in which it may be momentarily or permanently manifest*" (89). This principle informs matter as an indwelling spirit but corresponds to an incorporeal will and essence.

Haitian peasants who practice the religion say they "serve," as serviteurs, the *vaudoux* or loas. These latter designations mean "gods" or "spirits" and come from the Fon language spoken in Benin (formerly Dahomey and Togo). Since "one either 'serves the loa' . . . or one does not," the word *Vaudou* does not exactly name the religion but rather the ritual events specific to this service (Davis ii). The serviteur does not for all that renounce Catholic beliefs or practices but rather accommodates them into a system dominated by West African-based signs. Vaudou devotees do continue to uphold the sacraments, for baptism, communion, and extreme unction "have magical properties" for the serviteur, and for this reason "Vaudou" works as a name for the religious system, its customs of service and social organization included (Métraux 59).

One leader in Vaudou society is the *houngan*, the high priest of the cult. The houngan works as theologian, interpreter, diviner, storyteller, musician, and herbalist-healer. His religious training has given him *connaissance*, the special knowledge of the cures and rituals by which he commands the supernatural. Female figures within the hierarchy are the *hounsis*, female temple initiates robed in white, and the *mambos*, priestesses of the cult. Other personnel include the *commandant la place*, or master of ceremonies; and the *houguenicon*, the female director of the hounsis (Simpson 68).

The diviner of the Regla Arará-Dajomi is the previously mentioned bokono or bokor, "one who serves the loa with both hands" and practices magic. The divination system the bokor practices is called Fa, which descends from the Yoruba Ifá and is often identified with the idea of destiny itself, which is conceived as the text written by Mawu and lived out by humans. These reflections anticipate some recent critical theories on the operations of a primordial inscription involved in the constitution of experience.[1] The belief in Mawu's writing encourages a certain fatalistic, although not quietistic, trust in the divine. Fa also names the composure that the Fon admire in the bokor:

the quality of keeping cool, poised, staying fresh. As Zuesse observes, Fa sets the bokor apart and above the world of passion represented by the *vaudousi* followers. The Vaudou deities matter little in the more transcendent levels of Fon teachings because "Fa, in short, works as a depersonalization of the Fon cosmos," an idea consonant with Deren's concept of principles higher than their temporal manifestations (Zuesse 210). It should be noted that a parallel relation persists in Lucumí society between Santería proper and the Ifá cult, which overlap on many counts but constitute different orders within the religion.

With certain similarities to the Congo biometaphysics, Vaudou doctrine teaches that all human beings are made up of certain invariant components. The *corps cadavre* is the physical body, a living corpse. Several "souls" are said to reside in this "cadaverous" body destined for death. The ti *bon ange* or "good little angel" is the spirit of individuality that leaves the body in dreams. Also called ti-*z'ange*, or *non-ange*, this soul may be captured by the bokor in conjurations. (Simpson says however that witches and bokors in Haiti work on the separable *gros-bon-ange* [68].) The *gros-bon-ange*, as Davis defines it, is the energy that gives life and sentience to the body. This soul coincides with the intangible spirit that in Yoruba doctrine gives life and animation to the body: *èmi*, a personal force identified with the breath and breathing (Idowu 169). In Vaudou belief, on the other hand, the n'*âme* or "spirit of the flesh" gives form to the body; and the *z'étoile* is the individual's heavenly counterpart and the holder, or "star," of destiny, similar to the Lucumí orí chosen in the Yoruba heaven by the soul prior to birth. Zombification deprives the person of a ti bon ange and therefore of personality; a shell of his former self, the Zombi is only corps cadavre, gros bon ange, and n'âme, and a mambo may hold the ti bon ange captive in a jar, pot, or other receptacle (Davis 218–19; Simpson 68). This preoccupation with capturing souls does not appear in Afro-Cuban literature with the frequency that it does in Vaudou lore.

Orishas or Loas

Many of the Yoruba orishas are said to have their *caminos ararás*, that is, a Vaudou aspect or incarnation. The babalao Samba confirms as much in telling Hwesuhunu, in Courlander's The African, "Your Fon vodoun, they the same as the orisha, only they got different names" (173). Cabrera's Arará informant Salakó identifies "Naná Bulukú" (in Haiti, she is "Nananboulouku") as both a Lucumí and Arará avatar of Obatalá, who is also known as Akkadó in Pinar del Río. Salakó also names Mabú and Freketé as Obatalás of Dahomeyan provenance (M 307, 313).

Among other correspondences, the Lucumí Babalú-Ayé or San Lázaro, according to some, came from Dahomey as Sagpata or Chankpana; others say that he originated in Yorubaland but traveled to the west during his exile, to return later to his birthplace. The Arará call Eleggúa by the names Afrá, Ogguiri élu, Makénú, or Keneno, and they do not, as do the Lucumí, spray him with *jan*, or cane liquor (M 35, 71, 73, 96, 232). Like the Lucumí orishas, the loas are identified with natural phenomena and the elements, and yet, as mentioned before with reference to Deren's account, resist strict identification with them, unlike the more earthbound orishas. Nor are the loas set into an unchanging Olympus: "No one knows the name of every loa because every major section of Haiti has its own local variation," and that means that certain loas worshipped by one zone's populace may be unknown to another's (Hurston 138).

Although there may have existed more than seven pantheons or classes of loa on Haiti, nowadays each loa falls into one of two groups, corresponding to the two major traditions. The loa originating in Dahomey or Yorubaland are the Rada, so-called after the Dahomeyan port city of Arada, the name derived from that of the holy city Allada. The other major tradition, the Petro-Lemba, traces its double name to don Juan Felipe Pedro, the early Vaudou leader famed for his violent dancing, and to the Kongo trading center known as Lemba, belonging to the Kikongo (Hurston 139; Deren 328, 335). Rada and Petro therefore designate two "classes" of deities. One looks to the gentler Rada loas, led by the oldest god or ancestor "Dambala Ouedo Freda Tocan Dahomey," to bring peace and do "good" work. Rada is thus identified with the "cool" qualities of peace and reconciliation, and Rada serviteurs wear the all-white clothing and head scarves symbolic of this branch's ideal of purity. Carpentier in *El reino de este mundo* identifies the rebel leader Mackandal as a houngan of the Rada rites (REM 29). On the other hand, the loas in the Petro-Lemba branch are willing to do harmful magic in ceremonies allegedly inspired by the original Carib and Arawak inhabitants of Hispaniola.

At the head of the Petro branch is the trinity of Baron Samedi, Baron Cimetière, and Baron Crois, the lords of the graveyard. Petro is identified with spells and protection against evil and therefore with personal attributes considered "hot." Some loas, such as the Haitian Ogoun, have aspects or avatars in both Rada and Petro groups (Simpson 65). In Davis's interpretation, "the Rada have come to represent the emotional stability and warmth of Africa, the hearth of the nation" (46). On the other hand, as Thompson reports, the gun-powder–charged Petro altar of the houmfort temple itself expresses a "notion of salvation through extremity and intimidation."

Whereas the Rada vaudoux dress in cool white, the angry Petro spirits blaze in the red of fire and blood (FS 164, 181).

The loas worshipped by Vaudou society are also called *les esprits*, *zanges*, and *les mystères*, and their list includes hundreds of names, of both African and Haitian origin (Simpson 65). Of these names for the vaudoux, both loa and mystère derive from the Yoruba l'awo, "mystery," which forms part of the name *babalawo*—the Ifá diviner known as "father of mysteries." From this Yoruba word also derives the Haitian Creole name for priest, *papaloi* (FS 166). Like the orishas and mpungus of Cuba, the loas tend to syncretize with the Catholic saints. As Melville Herskovits states, the saint's image in Haiti constitutes an "outward symbol of the psychological reconciliation" between the Catholic saints and African deities, and that reconciliation has occurred even in West Africa (*Life* 278). Hurston also recognizes this syncretization between the Catholic hagiography and the Ewe-Fon and Kongo pantheons, evident in the practice of purchasing and displaying lithographs of the saints to represent the loas. She notes however that "even the most illiterate peasant knows that the picture or the saint is only an approximation of the loa" (Hurston 138).

Simpson reports three distinct interpretations he gathered in the Plaisance region concerning the relationship of loas and saints. One group believes that the loas, who live "under the water," communicate with saints, who reside in heaven. This vision is consonant with the schema of the Bantu-Kongo cosmogram examined in chapter 5. The loa are said to meet with the saints midway, between earth and heaven, conveying the concerns of humans to the saints, who then may communicate those concerns to God. A second school of thought holds that each loa corresponds to a saint. According to a third view, "the saints and the loa are bitter enemies" (Simpson 65).

The following series of brief profiles will characterize the most prominent loas of northern Haiti and include mention of their personality traits, attributes, and, when appropriate, syncretizations. The profiles are drawn primarily from Simpson (66–67, table 3.1); from Thompson (FS 166–67); and from Hurston, Deren, and Métraux, passim.

Above both the Rada and the Petro deities sits *Mawu*, or in Creole, *Bondieu* or *Grand Met*. In the beginning, Mawu (or Mahou), created the universe, upon which he would write the narrative of human destiny. Like his Yoruba equivalent Olodumare, he is the supreme god who knows all and can do all, but he prefers to remain distant from the creation he authored. Mawu is an androgynous deity who becomes feminine in order to join with a masculine aspect, Lisa; together, Mawu and Lisa are symbolized by the moon and the sun (FS 176). After creating the universe, a weary Mawu bestowed wisdom and power to the subordinate spirits named vaudoux, loas, esprits, or mystères: those who master the natural elements and control the lives of mortals. Their connection with Mawu explains the Dahomeyan expression recorded by Price-Mars: *"Vodoun e gui Mahounou," "The Spirit is a thing (a creature) of God"* (97). Serviteurs at any rate prefer intercourse with the more personable loas who, like the Afro-Cuban orishas, deign to come down to earth and mingle with the faithful through the rite of possession in which the work of "the hand of divine grace" is seen.

It will be recalled that the loas of the Rada class are headed by Damballah and those of the Petro by the Vaudou triumvirate of Baron Samedi, Baron Cimetière, and Baron Crois. All good things flow from *Damballah*, the beneficent and powerful. Damballah, represented as the Great Serpent, is "Li qui retti en ciel (He who lives in the sky)." Damballah gives permission for ceremonies dedicated to the other spirits. Worshippers hold him in awe, they supplicate him and render "service" to him as to his representatives. Unlike the Afro-Cuban Olofi, whom he resembles, Damballah has few stories in which he figures as a character (Hurston 139, 141, 143, 170). He is often identified with St. Patrick because the saint's icon displays a snake, and the iron snake-totem of Damballah, Carpentier notes, is often found on Vaudou altars (MC 292). Yet Damballah is more commonly identified with Moses, whom the Old Testament associated both with a serpent and with certain miraculous powers.

Damballah drinks rum and cures grave illnesses. As the Great Serpent, he is often depicted as embraced with his mate Ayida Hwedo or Uedo, symbolized by the rainbow or a smaller coiled snake, in a union of male and female principles (Simpson 176). Damballah merged with Ayida Hwedo is therefore the great serpent-rainbow who stretches out in a great arc across the sky after the rain. Deren writes that Damballah and Ayida even coil around the cosmos; our world is an egg offered to this supreme serpent god (115–16). In addition to doubling the rainbow of Ayidah Hwedo, the snake also serves as Damballah's "maid servant," his *bonne*. For the serviteur, Damballah is "the highest and most powerful of all the gods"; he is "good," "the *great source*." In sacrifices he prefers offerings of the white hens or cocks and also accepts sweet wine and white pigeons. His day is Wednesday (Hurston 139, 141–43).

Agasu has no Yoruba equivalent for he is the legendary ancestor of all the Fon. In tracing the genealogy proceeding from this euhemeristic deity, Thompson writes that Agasu's descendants founded Allada. After the throne of Allada passed to his eldest son, Agasu's younger sons went on to rule the cities of Ajase-Ipo and Abomey (FS 165).

Papa Ogoun, like the Fon Gu and the Yoruba Oggún, is master of the forge and a fierce deity of war. The saber-wielding Ogoun Feraille is often identified with the militant, authoritarian Saint Jacques, or Saint James the Greater (the Spanish Santiago), depicted in lithographs as an armored knight (Métraux 61). The ritual slashing of the air with Ogoun's gubasa blade signifies a cutting through the material world. Deren describes Ogoun as a violent revolutionary hero: "Intense, ready to fly into a rage, he periodically shouts: 'Foutre tonerre!' (By thunder!) which is his special epithet, or announces: 'Grains moin fret!' (My testicles are cold)—his particular way of demanding a drink of rum" (133). To invoke Ogoun is to fire up the warrior in those who serve him (Hurston 177). Taylor describes the iron-god in similar terms: "A strong protector, Ogoun provides immunity against attack, and weapons for war." The Haitian Ogoun has absorbed attributes that further identify him with the Fon Hèbyosso and the Yoruba Shango, who gives Ogoun his association with fire and lightning. Indeed, the former has become a "manifestation" of the latter, as the Haitian "Ogoun-Shango" (Taylor 116, 117).

One aspect of Ogoun, named Loco Atissou, possesses knowledge of herbs and medical treatments; he helps the houngan to diagnose diseases and to prescribe cures. In this incarnation he seems to correspond to the Yoruba Osaín. Saint Joseph is his Catholic double; his day, Wednesday. Loco Atissou, like Ogoun, is fond of rum (Hurston 152–53).

Papa Legba is already familiar as the Vaudou counterpart of the Lucumí trickster Eshú-Elegguá and as the Catholic Saint Peter. In Haiti as in Cuba he guards doorways and crossroads. He is descended from the Fon Legba, whose ascendancy over the other vaudoux springs from his connection with divine wisdom, the transcendental center of the knowledge-reality that holds sway over the passions of the gods (Zuesse 208).

Because Legba allows or facilitates communication between realms, it is appropriate that the temple-patio's center post, the poteau-mitan along which the loas are said to descend between worlds, also bears the name of poteau-Legba (Deren 97). Like Eshú-Elegguá in the Cuban Regla de Ocha, Papa Legba Attibon ("Legba of the Good Wood"; that is, of the poteau-mitan) enjoys the privilege of receiving the first prayers and first offerings in Vaudou ceremonies because he is the one who watches all entrances and calls on the other deities. Legba customarily stands at the gate of the houmfort, or "holy of holies," and at the entrance to the cemetery. Because he also stands watch over the crossroads, he is also called Baron or Maître Carrefour. Not usually identified with the childish prankster of Lucumí myth, for the Haitian peasants Papa Legba is more apt to appear as an aged man who limps and supports himself with a cane, often carrying both a straw pouch, the *sac paille* or *macoute*, and an exaggeratedly large phallus. Also syncretized with John the Baptist, Legba eats only roasted foods, offered to him in a macoute slung from a tree branch. These foods include the "zinga" rooster (with white and black specks), and "corn, peanuts, bananas, sweet potatoes, chicken, a tobacco pipe for smoking, some tobacco, some soft drinks" (Hurston 151).

The mulatta loa *Erzulie* is the Fon Aziri and the Yoruba Oshún. She is the river goddess, present in the sacred falls of Saut d'Eau, who intervenes in matters of love. For this reason her archetype resembles that of the Greek Aphrodite. She is also associated with the moon and prosperity. Hurston characterizes Erzulie Fréda as a "perfect" object of desire, promising erotic bliss by all her bodily signs and accoutrements. Her appearance and attributes are listed in Hurston's account:

> Erzulie is said to be a beautiful young woman of lush appearance. She is a mulatto and so when she is impersonated by the blacks, they powder their faces with talcum. She is represented as having firm, full breasts and other perfect female attributes. She is a rich young woman and wears a gold ring on her finger with a stone in it. She also wears a gold chain about her neck, attires herself in beautiful, expensive raiment and sheds intoxicating odors from her person. To men she is gorgeous, gracious and beneficent. She promotes the advancement of her devotees and looks after their welfare generally. She comes to them in radiant ecstasy every Thursday and Saturday night and claims them. (145)

Simpson adds that those possessed by Maitresse Erzulie are "[t]ranquil, aristocratic, and coquettish"; she "[p]ersonifies gentleness, sensitiveness, and health"; in addition she "[s]peaks several languages" (67). Many in Haiti know the love song dedicated to the possessive, alluring loa. Like the Cuban Ochún, Erzulie is syncretized with the Blessed Virgin, but in her other selves she can turn "maliciously cruel, for not only does she choose and set aside for herself, young and handsome men and thus bar them from marriage, she frequently chooses married men and thrusts herself between the woman and her happiness" (Hurston 45). Erzulie's vèvè symbol is a heart. In the houmfort room kept for this goddess, there are "pink and white dresses" and, on a dressing table, "a wash-basin, towel, soap, comb, lipstick, nailbrush and orange-stick." Another of her avatars is Erzulie ge-rouge, or "the red-eyed": an old, frightening woman belonging to the Petro branch who is called upon by harm-intending bokors. Generally, though, Erzulie shows affection and loves eggs, rice flour, white pigeons, and Madeira wine (Métraux 64, 80).

The Fon Sakpata was adopted by the Yoruba as Chankpana or Shokpana, by the Afro-Cubans as Babalu-Ayé, and by the Haitians as *Sabata* or *Sousous Pannan*. The god of smallpox has skin covered with ulcers and favors pork and red cocks. In Haiti he is seen as malicious and cruel, unlike the "Lord of the World" of Lucumí religion, whose syncretization with San Lázaro has softened his image in Cuba.

The identifying signs of *Agwé-Taroyo*, loa of the sea and ships, include shells, small boats, paddles, *madrepore* corals, and little fish made of metal. Agwé-Taroyo, resembling the Lucumí Olokun, likes to drink champagne and eat sheep and fowls.

The apparent equivalent to the Lucumí Orisha-Oko among the vaudoux is *Zaka*, lord of agriculture. Called "cousin" by those who know him, he wears the peasant's straw hat, carries the macoute satchel and smokes a clay pipe (Métraux 63).

The *Guédé* or *Gédé* family have been identified above as the Haitian loas of death, often invoked in spells. In portraits, the Guédés look dead, wear black, and carry a knife. Guédé himself, in the singular, is also the loa who idealizes or deifies the character of the Haitian peasant. When he comes down, he smokes a cigar, drinks a clairin mixed with fresh nutmeg and hot peppers and speaks in nasal tones (Hurston 232–33). The Guédé who presides over the cemetery and the entire grim family is Baron Samedi, paired with his female consort, Madame Brigitte. Baron Samedi dresses like an undertaker, in black suit complete with top hat and cane. His emblems are the skull and crossbones and the gravedigger's tools. Also known for his "lascivious sensual gestures," the clownish sovereign of the cemetery also symbolizes eroticism and debauchery, according to Deren, for he embodies not only the death drive but sexual desire. He is the loa the bokors invoke to change their shape, to mix a poison, to bind up a paquet-congo charm or to create a zombi (Deren 112–13; Métraux 66, 104). The zombi-making bokors in fact look to Baron Samedi for support: when bringing a corpse "back to life," they call on him to "hold that man [*quembé n'homme na*]" (Taylor 105).

The Fon Hohovi and the Yoruba Ibeyi became the *Marassa* twins of Haitian myth, corresponding to Kaínde and Taewo, the jimaguas of Lucumí myth. In the northern part of Haiti, the Marassas, along with the dead, are invoked in every Vaudou ritual (Simpson 68, 297).

The Fon market god Aizan merged with the sea goddess Avrekete to form the Haitian loa known as *Aizan-Velekete*. Similar fusions of identities and absorptions of characteristics account for the absence of Yemayá and Ochosí in the Haitian pantheon (FS 167).

The Vaudou serviteur lives a life amidst these loas, recognizing Agwé-Taroyo in the sea, Erzulie Fréda in love, Legba in communication, Ogoun in fire and metallurgy, and Guédé in death (Davis 206). The loas impose taboos and require offerings and sacrifice from the whole hierarchy: serviteur, mambo, hounsis, bokor, and houngan. In exchange for this service, the vaudoux will grant them health, protection, and assistance. Denied these offerings, they can also bring down misery in the form of crop failure, illness, and even death (Simpson 68).

It has been pointed out that many of the loas correspond to the orishas of Cuba. Agwé-Taroyo, to give another example, is the loa of the seas who resembles Olokun; he is syncretized with Saint Ulrich and depicted with the emblems of armor and a fish. Then there are others that seem to have no exact correspondence. Of local origin is Baron Samedi, the lord of the dead. As these predications may suggest, the loas like the orishas may be further divided into the deities of earth, air, fire, and water, and they give the model and pattern for human passions. They are supplemented by the local gods that dwell in trees, stones, and other natural objects.

Rites and Writing

The principal mode of signification in Vaudou is ritual, especially that of dance and possession. Earlier I described ceremonies as complex forms of communication among members of the group, giving the context and gathering members together for communication, mirroring thereby the phatic function in the communicative act. Despite Vaudou's relative lack of narrative, the talk of Vaudou society, its *langage*, is already imbued with divinity, for the sacred tongue is said to have descended from Damballah's cosmic hissing (Taylor 99). Essential knowledge in Vaudou society is transmitted mainly in the ceremonies, and there are many.

Some Vaudou ceremonies take place before the altar, called *pe*, which bears similarities to the Lucumí or Mayombe altar in Cuba. One places chromolithographs of the saints on the pe, as well as attributes, such as Damballah's iron snake or beads, and plates of food, sacred stones, flags with images of the saints, rattles, liquor, and candles (Simpson 68). Offerings are placed in niches of the tiered altar. Other sacred objects may include soul-containing *govis* jars, or jars containing crucifixes; cards, rattles, a Kongo charm (nkisi), and perhaps a human skull (FS 182–83).

Collective ritual takes place in the Vaudou temple's covered courtyard or patio, the aforementioned peristyle, reserved for dancing and possessions. The peristyle's central post or poteau mitan, raised upon its circular socle and embellished with symbols representing Papa Legba, Damballah, and Ayida Hwedo, constitutes a kind of *axis mundi* connecting the upper and lower worlds. It therefore functions as the kind of concrete centering "metaphor" that focuses the personal energies of the serviteurs when the drumming and dancing heat up. Vèvè ground-signs drawn around it reinforce the centering, gathering function of the sacred post (FS 181).

Carpentier reconstructs some Vaudou elements of musical culture in colonial Saint Domingue in his *La música en Cuba*. The beating *bamboula* drums of the Rada ritual could be heard in the slaves' houmfort along with the shaking of the belt rattles called *bran-bran sonnette*. The serviteurs would sing Creole songs of Fon origin, including the *yanvalous* and the *dahomé-z'epaules*. In the presence of the ceremonial drum named *tambor assotor*, the believers invoke Erzulie, Papa Legba, and Ogoun Ferraille (MC 124). Other ceremonial drums include the *boulatier*, the *sirgohn*, and "the thundering hountah, which controls the mood and the movement of the dancers" (Hurston 173). The *ascon* gourd, filled with seeds or covered in a network of rattling beads and snake vertebrae, resembles the Afro-Cuban *shekeré*. The ascon is played to the chant that calls on Papa Legba to open the doors and thus permit the other loas to enter the houmfort; in such ceremonies it is often accompanied by a small bell. *Chachas* (rattles) are shaken and *ogans* (iron bars) are beaten as well (Hurston 152; Deren 325; Simpson 297).

Certain gestures, endowed with sacred or profane meaning, signify in the language of bodily movement. Commenting on the gestural language of Vaudou society, Henry Drewall explains that "[g]iving with both hands signifies . . . the union of social and spiritual worlds, for the left is used in greetings by *orisa* (that is, possessed worshippers) to mortals. Thus it is a *sanctified* gesture of giving" (FS 272n. 16).

Charms or fetishes add their poetic power to the Vaudou practice. The Haitian practice of tying up magic charms with ribbons or silk bindings originated in Kongo culture. Cousins to the Cuban *nkangues*, the wound-up charms called pacquets-congo are adorned with sequins, beads, and feathers. Their construction itself signifies, by analogy, the magic that "ties up" a lover, ensuring that he or she does not stray. Fittingly, the word *nkangue* in Kongo means "one who arrests." Famous pacquets-congo remembered by Thompson include one called *Simbi makaya*, "simbi-of-the-leaves," and *Reine Kongo*, "Queen of the Kongo" (FS 126–28).

Other ceremonies or ritual practices of Vaudou society resemble Afro-Cuban rituals from the Lucumí, Abakuá, and Bantu traditions. A special mass or a drumming ceremony, like the Cuban misa espiritual or the güemilere, respectively, may be held for a specific loa. Haitians say that certain stones belong to the loas or that they are loas or have loas themselves. "The way to tell whether a stone has a loa or not," writes Hurston, "is to cup it in the hand and breathe upon it. If it sweats then it has a spirit in it. If not, then it is useless." The right stone for a certain loa will have the right color and quality, and it will be consecrated and set upon a white place where it will be worshipped. Such a stone may be passed on from generation to generation (Hurston 158). Like practitioners of Santería, serviteurs will "feed" the loas inhabiting the stones of their altars with offerings of blood (Simpson 297).

All Vaudou ceremonies begin with homages to a number of loas and in the proper order: first, one prays to Papa Legba, opener of doors and opportunities; second, to Ogoun Loco Attison, "[m]ystère of work and knowledge"; third to Mah-lah-sah, guardian of the threshold. Appeals to these loas, preceding the greeting to Damballah, will increase the chances that the petition in question will be heard. Last in order of appeals is Guédé, Lord of the Dead (Hurston 142; Deren 93n.).

Through drumming, singing, and dancing, in the light of candles or torches, the participants in the Vaudou ceremony prepare a physical and psychological atmosphere propitious for a possession, which, as in Afro-Cuban rituals, is the centerpiece of Vaudou ritual and the aim of dancing and entrancement. This possession can arguably be read as a performance as well, for a subject possessed by a loa in effect acts out gestures and movements "chosen" from a repertoire of coded behaviors. Like the believers of Regla de Ocha with their orishas, "[f]ollowers of the loa know how their loa dress, talk, act, and even eat; they know their ritual symbols and sacred drawings, the music and songs to which the loa respond" (Taylor 99). As the prime objective of worship, possession consists in "hav[ing] loa in the head." Giving life and embodiment to the loa, possession thus allows the spirit to "mount" the serviteur, who for this purpose is called *cheval* or "horse" (Deren 101n.).

Extraordinary things happen during possession. Davis reports seeing one hounsi who, mounted by her loa, grabbed burning sticks, licked them, and ate the fire. She then released the brands and fell back, caught by the mambo. That hounsi had held the hot coal in her mouth for three minutes without inflicting apparent harm to herself (46–47). Thompson describes a repeated drama of possession in which the cheval of Ogoun grasps a red-hot iron bar with bare hands. Although, as Thompson comments, this feat could indicate a "[d]eep mastery of self" (FS 172–73), one also notes in possession an undeniable dispossession of the subject's own self, or a trance-induced self-alienation by which mastery is ceded to the possessing loa. A possessed Maman Loi in Carpentier's *El reino de este mundo* shows such ambiguous mastery when she runs to the kitchen, immerses both her arms in boiling oil, and withdraws them, unscathed (REM 21). The apparent passivity or intransitivity on the part of the possessed with relation to the loa translates, paradoxically, into the cheval's transitive "mastery" over fire, heat, and pain.

The nature of possession remains a mystery nonetheless. Past observers have interpreted the possession ritual as a manifestation of psychoneurosis and for that reason negative; as a socially acceptable form of insanity in a harsh environment; or as a normal spiritual expression in the Haitian context (see Lewis 191). Explained as a holy act of descent or mounting, possession is also said to open communications between humans and the divinities. Writing of this mediumistic possession, Zuesse observes that the ritual is structured like a marriage, turning the possessed into a *vaudousi* or "mate of the god" through whom the god will speak. In this way, desire is channeled toward the unifying identification with divinity (Zuesse 206).

In a typical ceremony, the mambo priestess invokes these spirits first by an act of writing: that is, the aforementioned drawing of graphic symbols called vèvès on the floor of the peristyle. In the vèvès, designs representing specific loas, are drawn at the ends of rays that branch out toward the four cardinal points from the poteau-mitan (FS 189). The vèvè of Legba as Maître Carrefour displays a cross and that of Baron Cimetière, a coffin, to give two examples. This ground-writing, constituting a scriptural foundation for the ceremony, calls the loas into attendance and prepares the stage or map on which the devotees will sing and dance. Yet the straight or curvy lines of the vèvè are not literally inscribed or scrawled on the ground. Instead, the mambo (or houngan) pours the lines in varied materials, whose ingredients could be cornmeal, tafia (raw rum), gunpowder, or syrup (see Simpson 68). Other ingredients could include "wheat or maize flour, crushed bricks, coffee grounds or ash," but they are chosen according to the requirements of the divinity that would be invoked (Métraux 80). Each of the diverse mystic signs belongs to a cryptographic system that recalls the Efik nsibidi and the Bakongo yowa cosmograms.

The system of the vèvè is complex and deserves future study. For now we may note the import of vèvès that have been printed or alluded to in works of Caribbean literature, where the vèvè has often taken on new symbolic values apart from its exact signification in Vaudou ritual. In Pierre Clitandre's *Cathédrale du mois août* (Cathedral of the month of August, 1982), vèvès precede the beginnings of the novel's major sections and thus invite a divine will to manifest itself in action culminating in the mass insurrection of the novel's conclusion. In Edward Kamau Brathwaite's poem "Vèvè," the sacred writing, escaping the toils of Eurocentric thinking and philosophic systems, connects the visible and the invisible, the human and the divine. The "broken ground" on which Brathwaite's griot-houngan-speaker inscribes a new tradition is hallowed by the slave's sacrifice and controlled by a crippled Legba-Elegbara: that ground is a gathering space for fragments of memory, potsherds of the shattered vessels of a community. The broken ground is also the soil of the New World prepared for a new sowing of the divine Word, the vèvè:

> For on this ground
> trampled with the bull's swathe of whips
> where the slave at the crossroads was a red anthill
> eaten by moonbeams, by the holy ghosts
> of his wounds
> The Word becomes
> again a god and walks among us
> ("The Arrivants" 266)

By mythopoetic vision, writing is reinvested with the centering and ingathering power of vèvè and thus bridges the distance between heaven and earth. In writing on the ground, the slave descendants rewrite the ground of community itself, refiguring the foundations of identity, history, and worship in a metaphor of divine inscription.

In Vaudou ceremony, once the vèvès are drawn, the mambo goes on to pour libations of holy water, flour, corn, and liquor at the four cardinal points and on the poteau mitan. The three major drums play the particular rhythm of the loa to which the ceremony is directed, accompanied by the shaking of chachas (rattles) and the beating of ogans (iron bars). After some singing and praying, sacrifice is made to Legba; the initiates are led into the houmfort. The dancing and drumming go on and can continue for hours, with a number of possessions taking place (Davis 43). The houngan ends the ceremony by leading more prayers and singing, leaving offerings of food for the loa and distributing the remaining food to the hungry devotees (Simpson 69, 297).

As alluded to earlier, the Vaudou dance performed around the poteau mitan has itself been called a form of "writing" executed over the already inscribed vèvè, recalling the "palimpsest," calling the divine into presence and making the present divine. Serviteurs have referred to their dancing itself as a way of "writing" with their feet, as if to underscore the kinetic, gestural mode of expression fundamental to their religion. A subsequent act of erasure is what allows the divine to manifest itself: "These signs, these vèvè are then erased by the dancing feet of devotees, circling around the pillar, even as, in spirit possession, the figures of these deities are redrawn in their flesh" (FS 191). By the act of putting the sacred pictograms *sous rature* (under erasure), an arche-writing disappears but enters and reinscribes itself again in the body of serviteur who may then speak the divine word of the vaudoux.

Other Vaudou rituals address the dead, who matter to the serviteurs as they do to the Cuban Lucumís and Congos. The *manger des morts*, or feast of the dead, is also called *wete' loa non tete yum mort*. This ceremony centers on the offering of birds and libations to one's departed. Its purpose is to remove the spirit from the head of the deceased serviteur, for otherwise the spirit would go to the bottom of the water and wait there until the manger des morts is celebrated (Hurston 162–63). Courlander's *The African* reconstructs another slave ceremony of Fon origin for the dead in its Georgia plantation setting. The character Samba reminds the gathered devotees that the living should help the dead if the dead are to help the living. Samba then guides Hwesuhunu ("Wes"), the novel's young Fon protagonist, in leading the invocation. Hwesuhunu pours water on the ground and "calls the role": "Legba, carry the word for us, ago-é! Respect to all the vaudoux, ago-é! Mawu, the grandfather of all, respect! Ogoun, who lives in this house, and all his kin, respect! Nananbuluku, Sobo, Obatala, Damballa, Hevioso, Azaka, respect!" Samba then adds the call to the "Nago" (Yoruba) orishas: "Oya, Orula, Panchagara [Oshún], Yemaya" (Courlander, *African* 107).

As these accounts of ritual suggest, Vaudou is a beautiful and poetic lived religion, founded on a mystical, mythical, histrionic attitude toward the real. Its "medicine" is that of transcendence, but the same medicine can be turned against those it would harm. With its myth, ritual, doctrine, and pharmacopeia, Vaudou constructs a self-sufficient cultural world, a mythic-existential domain that affirms identity as it at the same time subjects that identity to appropriation by a variety of causes and programs, as examples from history and literature will demonstrate in the sections to follow. For as it is inserted into history, Vaudou remains trapped within its own vision of fatality and magical causation in which evil is seen as a perennial and metaphysical force rather than as the product of historical forces. Its signs are dazzling, but it still lacks an historicocritical perspective from which to assess or challenge the objective conditions of unfreedom (see Taylor 122, 125).

Vaudou in History

Vaudou's history can be traced back to the African wars between Dahomey and the Yoruba kingdoms, which contributed to the decline of the Yoruba and the expansion of the West African slave trade. For many from the Yoruba and other neighboring peoples were sold in exchange for European goods and exported through the southern kingdoms of Allada and Ouida (Law 226). The Dahomeyans, desirous of carrying on a coastal trade with the European armies as Widah and Ardra did, found it necessary first to conquer the competition: Great Ardra in 1724 and Widah shortly thereafter. Yet Dahomey's geographical position left it open to westward Yoruba invasions and migrations. Oyo would restore its dominance over Dahomey in campaigns between 1730 and 1750, exacting a tribute, and by relocating trade to non-Dahomeyan ports including Badagry, Lagos, and Porto Novo. Claiming to come to the aid of Widah but in effect protecting its commercial ties with the Europeans, the Yoruba thus attacked the Dahomeyans and conquered them. When Gezo ascended to the Dahomeyan throne in 1818, he freed his people from Yoruba imperial rule. Yet Dahomey continued to pay a tribute to the Alafin of Oyo until 1827, when Oyo was engaged in war with Ilorin and when the pressure of Dahomeyan slave wars was doubled by other wars between Yoruba kingdoms (Eades 20). The kingdom restored some of its might by attacking Ketu in the year of the French Revolution (1789), taking some two thousand as captives and, presumably, as slaves. The Yoruba-Dahomey wars ended, not with a victory of one side over another, but with the Dahomeyan defeat by the French in 1892 (YSN 12).

These wars and the westward migrations of Yorubas in this period allowed the orishas to travel and undergo syncretizing metamorphoses into the loas of the Ewe and Fon nations of Dahomey, a process that Thompson describes as a "[f]usion and refusion of Yoruba spirits." The Yoruba occupations in Dahomey thus began the transculturation process that, interrupted by the French slave trade, recommenced in Haiti (FS 166).

In the "European cockpit" that was the Caribbean, France in the meantime had acquired, in 1697, the western third of the island of Hispaniola through the Treaty of Ryswick. The approximately fifty thousand African slaves brought to the island at the beginning of the eighteenth century included peoples originating from Dahomey and Senegal; from the Yoruba, Ibo, Bamana, and Mande territories; and from the Kongo and Angolan civiliza-tions. The majority of slaves in French Saint Domingue came from the Kongo and Angola. As in Cuba, these "Bantu" slaves developed a religion based on the belief in the intercession of the dead in human affairs and on a depen-dence on charms to influence events. Ewe-Fon ideas emphasized a polytheis-tic doctrine of the loa-orishas founded on an underlying monotheism that considered Mawu-Lisa to be the supreme god. These ideas gained ascendancy within a system of diverse and superimposed codes. Catholicism contributed images and figures from its liturgy, particularly those related to the interces-sion of the saints (Simpson 64; FS 164). Thus developed the religion of the serviteurs, elaborating and widening its pantheon of neo-African deities and adding its layer to the Caribbean religious palimpsest.

The manner in which Vaudou traveled to Cuba helps to explain its signifi-cance to Afro-Cuban culture and literature. As mentioned earlier, the religion crossed with the black servants of those French planter families who, to avoid the vengeful violence unleashed by their erstwhile slaves, fled westward to the neighboring island in the 1790s. It is to their experience that Alejo Carpentier devotes the chapter "Santiago de Cuba" in El reino de este mundo (63–67). In more recent times, Bastide notes, Haitians arrived in record numbers in 1913–25 as part of a wave of immigrant sugar workers coming in from various West Indian islands. Some 145,000 came from Haiti and an addi-tional 107,000 from Jamaica. Eight thousand more Haitians arrived in 1941 (Bastide 146).

The intermittent influx of Haitians bred the fear, among white or Creole Cubans at various times, of the "Haitianization of Cuba"; that is, of a situa-tion in which black masses would predominate and overthrow the power structure as they did in Haiti, which would lead to Cuba's isolation by other nations and cause further exoduses and impoverishment (Pérez Sarduy and Stubbs 5). If the existence of Vaudou in Haiti "has always been an embar-rassment to the Western-oriented and educated elite," in Cuba too African-inspired religion proved an embarrassment—a stigma, a sign of backward-ness—to the dependent bourgeoisie of this largest of Caribbean islands (Laguerre 19).

The depiction of Haitians in Cuban writing, exemplified in the references to ¡Ecue-Yamba-O! that opened this chapter, indicates from an external per-spective the way in which the experience of migration has strengthened the faith of the migrants themselves. Serving the loa becomes an emblem of personal identity and a mechanism of defense after the passage westward to Oriente Province, as James Figarola points out. Uprooted, impoverished, and exploited as *braceros* or laborers in the cane fields, transplanted Haitians have often practiced Vaudou more actively than they did in Haiti in order to maintain a sense of themselves as a unique and proud minority—a minority within a minority—in a foreign land (SMD 22).

Inasmuch as Vaudou culture played an active role in forming an antislavery ideology in Saint Domingue prior to the migration and contributed to the outbreak of the revolution on Saint Domingue, an overview of that history will help to frame the subsequent discussion of religion's role in the confrontation and in the period afterward. On the eve of the revolution, in 1791, some 465,429 slaves were dominated by some 30,836 whites and 27,548 free colored. The colony was tremendously productive: its nearly half a million slaves produced two-thirds of the value of France's total overseas trade (Laguerre 29).

Inspired by their vaudoux-spirits, the Haitian peasantry rose to defy the imposition of forced labor on the plantations, fighting their revolution to overthrow their masters with machetes and other farming implements. Davis confirms that the slaves, armed with "knives and picks, [and] sticks tipped in iron," could challenge the bayonets and artillery of the French in the belief that their loas protected them or that in death they would return to their African homeland, *Guinée*. The Revolution lasted twelve years and turned back incursions not only by Napoleon's troops, led by the emperor's brother-in-law Leclerc, but by the Spanish and the British as well (Davis 68, 67). Modern history's first successful slave revolt overthrew the colonial hold on the island and led to the founding of the second republic in the Americas and the first black republic in the world. For these reasons, Haiti became a symbol, although an ambiguous one, for anticolonial revolt.

For with its triumph, the Haitian Revolution opened the doors to black despotism and terror. The state became the new slave master, with the military as overseer. In his effort to compel peasants to stay on the plantations, Dessalines ordered mass executions or had "criminals" buried alive. The revolutionary elite led by Toussaint L'Ouverture fought to reconstruct the plantation system, believing that the success of the revolution would have to be measured both by the continued freedom of the people and by their prosperity, and that these could be ensured only by continued agricultural productivity. After emancipation, the former slaves were forced to leave their private plots and return to the plantations. So that Haiti could become strong enough to resist recolonization by France and other powers, Toussaint in fact dictated that former slaves be assigned to plantation work gangs (Ott 161). Henri Christophe, both tyrant and benefactor to the nation, imposed a ten-year regime of forced labor that produced crops for export and filled the coffers of the treasury of the Northern Kingdom, allowing him to build the impressive palace of Sans-Souci and the Citadelle La Ferrière by 1820, when he was deposed (Davis 69–71; Ott 161).

The Haitian Revolution, having deposed the white planters, then gave itself over to rule by a mulatto aristocracy, and this change brought no improvement to the lives of the former slaves, who made up some 85 to 90 percent of the total population of the newly renamed country. In the wake of the revolution, L'Ouverture's and Christophe's fears appeared to be well founded: agricultural productivity was low. Few were the opportunities for social mobility among this majority of peasants and urban poor, who found themselves undereducated, unemployed or underemployed, afflicted by poverty and diseases (such as tuberculosis and malaria), and lacking in adequate doctors, hospitals, and health programs. In the continued climate of abject dispossession, many Haitians, deprived of the necessities of health care, would turn to traditional African-based practices for treatments or at least for relief from anxiety. Lacking nearly everything that would be necessary for a life worth living, the Haitian peasant even today finds some compensation in Vaudou, which continues to offer "meaningful explanations of reality and a basis for relationships with others" (Simpson 63).

The roll call of Haitian leaders who may have practiced Vaudou in some form or another after the revolution indicates the manner in which the cult has been employed for partisan, antidemocratic ends. Stories concerning Vaudou's role in politics abound. General Faustin Solouque, later Emperor Faustin I (1847–59), was reputed to have held Vaudou rituals in the national palace "in order to legitimate his own regime in the eyes of his black subjects" (Taylor 118). President François Antoine Simon (1906–11) did likewise.

Hurston retells the stories surrounding the mambo Celestina, daughter of General Simon. A figure of mystery and awe in her own right, Celestina kept company with a consort, a pet goat named Simalo. It was rumored that Celestina was "married" to Simalo. It was commonly known that Simalo and Celestina's presence at the vanguard of Simon's troops made the rebelling soldiers invulnerable to enemy charges, and their victory under Alexis at Ansa-a-veau brought Simon to the presidency. The story went that Celestina had called on Ogoun Feraille to protect her father's supporters, who marched from Aux Cayes to Port-au-Prince carrying the sign of the loa, namely, "their coco macaque sticks to which had been tied a red handkerchief." For her prowess and power in that struggle, she became known as a "black Joan of Arc." Meanwhile, the Haitian upper classes chose to ignore or deny the presence of Vaudou in their society rather than acknowledge publicly a religious practice they called primitive and barbaric. Yet to the chagrin of these elites, it was said that Vaudou rituals were taking place in the national palace, not to mention the Sect Rouge ceremonies that were rumored to take place in the Mountain House, summer palace of the president. Another spate of stories told of a "divorce" between Celestina and her consort, after which Simalo soon died and was buried with pomp and honors in the cathedral of the capital. Celestina never remarried (Hurston 116–21).

These anecdotes confirm the thesis that, although the Saint Domingue slaves could create an identity for themselves in a neo-African cultural code focused on Vaudou worship, that cultural code could be "co-opted" by oligarchies to serve ends opposed to the needs and interests of the masses. Although Vaudou inspired slave insurrection and even the Caco (or mercenary) uprising during the American occupation (1915–34), "the history of Vaudou in the postindependence period," as Taylor writes, "is largely a legacy of accommodation with oppressive neocolonial regimes" (117).

Some twenty years after the fall of Simon's regime, Dr. François Duvalier participated in creating a black nationalist cult of négritude of a specifically Haitian kind. Davis reports that the journal called Les Griots (The storytellers), to whose editorial staff the young Duvalier belonged, espoused a new Haitian nationalism in reaction to the American occupation of the island. One significant platform of Les Griots was the demand that Vaudou be recognized as the official religion of Haiti, paving the way over the years for Duvalier to manipulate it for his own demagogic ends after winning the 1957 election.

Duvalier, or "Papa Doc," made himself premier houngan of Haiti and declared himself the heir of the founders L'Ouverture, Dessalines, Pétion, Christophe, and Dumarsais Estimé. In public, Papa Doc dressed in black, and many identified him with the vaudou of death, Guédé, or the loa of the cemetery, Baron Samedi. He surrounded himself with a coterie of houngan priests and sponsored the association of a dreaded secret police, the Ton Ton Macoute, with the dreaded Bizango secret society. This was the same Bizango society, named after the loup-garou or werewolf said to prey upon children, that was infamous for carrying out zombifications against its enemies (Davis 316–17). Duvalier himself reputedly turned the corpse of a political opponent into a zombi (Taylor 118–20). This approach actually succeeded in bringing some stability to Haiti. Through his circle of priests, some of them recruited into his administration, the elder Duvalier exercised dominion over the Haitian culture and its populace during seven years of arbitrary rule, then declared himself president for life in 1964. Jean-Claude, or "Baby Doc," availing himself of the same sort of political magic, carried on the family tradition under "Jean-Claudismus" for fifteen years more, until his ouster in 1986. Recently, in May of 1994, Emile Jonaissant, the nominal head of the military junta that had ousted Jean-Bertrand Aristide from the presidency, invoked the principle of Haitian national sovereignty and the protection of Agwé-Taroyo in defiance of rumors that a U.S. invasion was imminent.[2]

Trapped as it was in the circularity of its own mythico-magical representations, Vaudou, as these periods of collusion with dictators suggest, had no critical perspective on the sociohistorical context, no viable alternative to Enlightenment reason, no agenda for emancipation. "There was nothing intrinsic to the Vaudou narrative order that demanded that the believer enter into a struggle for liberation" (Taylor 118). Carpentier's novella of the Haitian Revolution delivers the same verdict on the impotence of Vaudou to save the Revolution. At the same time, as we will see, Carpentier's version of Vaudou in history reiterates at another textual level the mythopoetic power of Vaudou's signs in order to shake apart the metaphysical scaffolding of the postcolonial world.

The Worlds of This Kingdom

Patrick Taylor's distinction between the "mythic narrative" and the "liberating narrative" illuminates the ideological implications of Vaudou for both popular culture and literature, although Taylor's distinction must be both expanded and problematized if it is to do justice to the complexity of Afro-Caribbean religion. For Taylor, popular culture from its beginnings in the West Indies has always been a political culture of resistance: "African-based, European-influenced religious and aesthetic symbolism unified the community in opposition to slavery and oppression" (xi). Narrative is one cultural means of transmitting tradition, producing communitarian cohesion, group identity, and social consciousness. Yet narratives distinguish themselves according to the two divergent functions of narrative. First, mythic narrative, of which the Anancy tales are a prime example, may celebrate the cunning of the slave in outwitting his masters, but its mode of storytelling tends to fix the master/slave relationship into static, archetypal, and falsely universal terms. "There is no narrative imperative demanding the fundamental transformation of the master-slave relationship itself" (Taylor 2). As such, mythic narrative depicts an atemporal, no-exit situation. Furthermore, inasmuch as it lacks an imperative for restructuring an unjust social order, it may be co-opted, exploited for the ends of oppression and exploitation, a process for which Vaudou's "unliterary" narratives of mythic ritual provide a case study.

On the other hand, liberating narrative, the second of Taylor's categories, engages authentic historical temporality and calls for a real overcoming of oppressive social structures. Refusing the mythic affirmation of the status quo, liberating narrative "makes a decisive break with mythical narrative when it goes radically beyond the latter to assert the necessity of freedom. It attacks mythical and ideological categories for sustaining oppressive situations that restrict and hide human freedom" (Taylor 3). In Taylor's view, Carpentier's narrative of Vaudou would be considered liberatory in affirming the slave's right to freedom, but it would have to break with Vaudou's mythical, mystifying narrative by revealing Vaudou's tendency toward regressive complicity with the powers that be once it has played its liberating historical role.

Vaudou appears as just such a double-edged sword in Carpentier's *El reino de este mundo* (1949). The novel's narration makes it clear that the loas are on the side of the slaves in the struggle. Sylvia Carullo has argued that Vaudou, as "protagonist" and "epicenter" of the novella, "serves as a pillar for the political-ideological infrastructure" of the novel" (3). Yet the progressivist ideals of the Enlightenment, I would hasten to add, are for all that not discarded. One could say more accurately that the narrative of *El reino* is double-coded—for the meaning of its signs depends on their European and Afro-Caribbean interpretive frameworks—and indeed the novel, similar in this respect to Carpentier's ¡*Ecue-Yamba-O!*, is about the double-coding that makes historical and literary meaning a transculturative matter.[3]

From a double perspective informed both by written histories and by the viewpoint of slaves who are serviteurs, the novel presents a peculiar reconstruction of the period encompassing the Haitian Revolution. As Speratti-Piñero has plotted it, the action spans some eighty years: from the 1750s, with Mackandal's escape from the plantation to the mountains, to the early 1830s and the departure of Henri Christophe's family for the baths of Karlsbad (*Pasos*, 4).[4] The narrative consists of a series of vignettes presenting impressions of events comprising that history, some peripheral or seemingly irrelevant to the revolution. Many of the impressions are filtered through the consciousness of the protagonist Ti Noël, slave of the plantation owner Lenormand de Mezy. The vignettes are organized into twenty-six loosely connected chapters recounting sometimes miraculous occurrences linked with the insurrections. These chapters are themselves distributed into five sections presenting the major phases of the novella's action. The most explicit references to Vaudou occur in the first two of the five sections.

The first section of the novel details Ti Noël's observations of colonial life, his apprenticeship to the Mandinga *brujo* (sorcerer) and storyteller Mackandal, Mackandal's injury in the *trapiche* or sugar mill and subsequent flight from the plantation, his reported metamorphoses into a series of animal shapes, his supervision of mass poisonings of colonists and their animals, and his public execution at the hands of the whites. In the beginning of this section, Ti Noël recalls the stories told by Mackandal. Contrary to the stereotype of a nonnarratistic Vaudou culture, Mackandal is a houngan storyteller—his Mandinga origins may justify his association with orality—and his voice is the very creative force of nommo so named by the Bakongo: he creates worlds in his words, evoking the figure of Kankán Muza, Muslim founder of the Mandinga empire (1297–1332), remembered for bringing writers to his court and for building mosques in his kingdom (Price-Mars 71). Mackandal's voice evokes other kingdoms: those of Adonhueso and those of the Nago, Popo, and Arada. His voice brings the myth of Damballah and the rainbow to life. Mackandal, we also learn, is an herbalist who becomes the cimarrón leader of the secret campaign to poison the planters of the Plaîne du Nord and their animals. After Mackandal loses his arm in the sugar mill and escapes from the plantation, he becomes a magical shape-changer, sometimes appearing at night "beneath the black goatskin with red-hot coals on his horns" (REM 33).

In the Haitian national mythology, C. L. R. James confirms, the houngan "Makandal" is remembered as possessing immortality and supernatural powers of transformation (86). Thanks to the strength of the slaves' faith, sustained by their talk and tales, Mackandal can "transform" himself into a series of animal forms, creating in this way the unifying and emboldening legend of his own figure: "Now, his powers were unlimited" (REM 33). In explicating the text, Carullo underscores the role of language in the novel's Vaudou occurrences, asserting that Mackandal's metamorphoses are not only referred to in words but realized in them: "the word in itself is 'nocturnal butterfly,' 'pelican,' 'green iguana,' 'unknown dog'" (5). That is to say, magic occurs in the very naming (nommo) of the thing. Mackandal even "escapes" execution "by the power of the word. His salvation becomes real through the cry that announces it" (Carullo 5).

The cry Carullo cites is the "¡*Macandal sauvé!*" of the African spectators, brought to Cap Haitien to witness the spectacle, who believe that their leader has succeeded in flying from the bonfire in the shape of a butterfly (Carullo

5–6). Mackandal thus becomes an inspiring multivalent symbol for the slaves, yet synecdochically incarnating in his own person the power they possess as a group: "One day he would give the signal of the great uprising, and the Lords of Over There, headed by Damballah, by the Master of the Roads and by Ogoun, Master of Iron, would bring the lightning and the thunder, to unleash the cyclone that would complete the work of men" (REM 33). Mackandal's narrative, both mystical and liberating, furnishes Ti Noël and the other slaves with a protective knowledge of the loas, including Baron Carrefour or Elegba, powerful mystère of interpretations, who in effect authorizes the slaves' reinterpretation of their conditions.[5]

The sense of collective identity and direction, founded on consensually validated interpretation, guides the slaves of Saint Domingue to turn the philosophical idea of independence into reality. Referring to the Haitian blacks galvanized by their Vaudou beliefs, Carpentier said on one occasion, "[I]t is going to be this pariah, this man situated on the lowest rung of the human condition, who will give us no less than the concept of independence" (Novela, 182–83). Slave religion indeed translates the Enlightenment abstractions into practice, as in the midst of the first great uprising on the island Père Labat is quoted as mentioning something the slaves call "vaudoux," and the plantation owners realize that it was this "secret religion that encouraged and brought them together [los solidarizaba] in their rebelliousness" (REM 62). Vaudou thus serves as a kind of "ideología secreta" that raises the abstract ideals of the bourgeois French Revolution to a higher dialectical level (Volek 158).

Returning to Ti Noël's activities in the first chapter of El reino, we see the slave scrutinizing the chromolithographs, hung in a bookseller's shop, of kings both European and African. In Ti Noël's ensuing reverie, the slave recalls Mackandal's genealogical tales of the virile African kings, superior to the effeminate, faro-playing dandies of the French court. The African kings include the Dahomeyan King Da, the euhemeristic Da or Damballah, who is also the "incarnation of the Serpent, which is [an] eternal principle, neverending, and who romped mystically with a queen who was the Rainbow, mistress of the water and every childbirth" (REM 12). In "reading" the chromos, the slave of course grasps a symbol of his own group's identity in the myth of the wise Damballah Hwedo, the serpent merged with his consort the rainbow, Ayida Hwedo (Speratti-Piñero, Pasos, 130). In their mythic union, as referred to here and elsewhere, their love created the heavens, made the earth fecund, and infused spirit into blood so that sacrifice could bring humans into the Great Serpent's wisdom (Davis, 213–14, 330, 332).

Other Vaudou-informed readings are performed in Carpentier's text. A talking head entertains Ti Noël during a remembered visit to a fair; it furthermore suggests the Afro-Haitian belief that spirits may possess the head of a deceased, a ghostly presence that the ritual called *déssounin* (or *déssouné*) serves to exorcise (DALC 162). Other portents hint at the coming cataclysm. The calves' heads mounted in the butcher's window are juxtaposed with the wax heads of the wig display in the barber's window; the metaphor of an "abominable feast" in which those "white masters' heads" are served may anticipate, in Ti Noël's mind, sacrificial beheadings to come (REM 10–11).

The second chapter of the second section, "El Pacto Mayor" (The great pact), tells of the legendary meeting of the Plaîne du Nord slaves in the Caïman Woods. Significantly, this chapter follows on the one entitled "The Daughter of Minos y Pasiphäe," in which the theme of drama and theatricality is established in Mademoiselle Floridor's performance of Racine's *Phaedra* before an uncomprehending, literally captive audience of slaves (REM 48–49). By this juxtaposition of performances, Carpentier's rendition of "the great pact" foregrounds the theatrical element of a subsequent performance in which history and histrionics converge. First, the night sky as backdrop is filled with chilly rain, wind, and foreboding thunder, "breaking itself on the craggy profile of the Morne Rouge" (REM 52). Once again the narrative emphasizes the power of the voice's presence, but this time the speaker is Bouckman Dutty, the Jamaican, in whose words "[t]here was much of invocation and incantation" (REM 51). The ceremony led by Bouckman in the Bois Caïman, according to an account recorded by C. L. R. James, included the Vaudou elements of dance, invocation of the loa, and sacrifice (86). In his speech, indirectly delivered in Carpentier's narration, Bouckman mixes discourses. He refers to the latest developments of France (the *Declaration of the Rights of Man and Citizen*, and the Decree of Pluviôse that emancipated the slaves) and to the monarchical intransigence of the planter aristocracy. This he interweaves with talk of a pact between the initiates on Saint Domingue and the "great Loas of Africa, so that the war may begin under the propitious signs." The signs already say that the war is between "our gods" and the God of the whites, who "orders the crime." Another sign to revolt is the dance to the war god "Fai Ogoun" by a "bony negresse" blandishing the god's characteristic *gubasa* sabre (REM 52). The narration translates the Creole language of the Rada invocation, which names Ogoun's aspects or *caminos*: "Ogoun of iron, Ogoun the warrior, Ogoun of the forge, Ogoun field marshal, Ogoun of the lances, Ogoun-Changó, Ogoun-Kankanikán, Ogoun-Batalá, Ogoun-

Panamá, Ogoun-Bakulé." What follows is the sacrifice of the black pig, in whose blood all the participants will wet their lips (REM 53). (More will be said on Carpentier's Ogoun in an upcoming section devoted to Benítez Rojo's story.)

Other historical sources and informants confirm the veracity of Carpentier's poeticized account and fill in some of its gaps. On the famous night of August 14, 1791, on top of the Bois Caïman, the Maroon leader named Bouckman Dutty did, according to those accounts, speak above the thunder, or he mixed his words with the thunder, and delivered the word of freedom to the hundreds of slaves gathered there. Among the leaders in attendance were Jean François, Jeannot, and Biassou, all of whom Bouckman embraced after the sacrifice sealed the pact. A slave of the same Plantation Lenormand where Ti Noël and Mackandal labored, Bouckman understood the need for a cross-cultural agenda. Mindful of Mackandal's abortive attempt to lead a mass poisoning of the plantation owners, Bouckman continued the effort to channel religious feeling in the direction of revolt, with positive results: "Loas were called upon to make known their will, and a pact was made between the slaves and Vaudou spirits. By coming to supplicate Vaudou loas before the opening struggle, the slaves continued an old African tradition. Vaudou loas agreed not only to increase their force tenfold, but also to cover their enemies with all sorts of curses" (Laguerre, 61). With the ceremony completed, the burning and looting of plantations and the massacre of whites were not long in following. One of the testimonials recorded by Davis suggests the persistence of a certain cult of hero worship associated with the "Bwa Caiman" and other locales: "They fall within the same empire of thoughts. Our history, such moments, the history of Mackandal, of Romaine La Prophétesse, of Bouckman, of Pedro. Those people bore many sacrifices in their breasts. They were alive and they believed! We may also speak of a certain Hyacinthe who as the cannon fired upon him showed no fear, proving to his people that the cannon were water. And what of Mackandal! The one who was tied to the execution pole with the bullets ready to smash him but found a way to escape because of the sacrifice he did" (Davis 245–46, 304). Although some of the speaker's details diverge somewhat from Carpentier's version (REM 33–34, 79–80), they evince the manner in which the Haitian Revolution lives on in collective memory as a heroic narrative protagonized by Vaudou.

Besides representing the collective subject of revolt in Carpentier's plot, Vaudou provides an infrastructure or subtext to which doubly coded Afro-

Haitian signs, whether pivotal or ancillary to the main narrative action, may refer. As Speratti-Piñero rightly asserts, Vaudou "intertwines itself closely in *El reino* with events and circumstances. The divinities are not for decoration but active presences, whose secret mills—slow, effective, implacable—function without stopping until the appropriate time. All of this begins to impose itself when the reader enters into the Vaudou beliefs and into the character and attributes of the loas. Only then does one reach the most profound and significant level of the work" ("Noviciado" 113). Yet the loas in the text are actively "present" as names whose invocation suggests their absence as much as their presence. Their "secret mills" turn in a space of sacralized signs transmitted in the song, storytelling, talk, iconography, speech making, and even "drumming" of the narrative. The reader experiences the absence of the loas, displaced by their substitutionary signs, as a gap between historical reality and an ideal, mythical supplement.

Portuondo affirms that "[t]he novel gives us the vision of a germinal reality described by a prescientific, underdeveloped mentality, which appeals to mythological fabulation to explain what is hidden or escapes by rational means" (87). Fiction, Portuondo's "fabulation," complements historical science by providing the empowering narrative knowledge necessary to grasp history and one's place in it. Yet the novel does not exclusively valorize this prescientific mentality, for it shows how the culture of Vaudou, while offering an alternative or corrective to the European epistème, later sanctions the despotism of Henri Christophe and all of his "heirs" to autocratic power.

Another treatment that would vindicate Vaudou's role in the Haitian Revolution presents a revealing contrast to Carpentier's. In the novel *Changó el gran putas* (1983) by Colombian author Manuel Zapata Olivella, the loas and the dead play their role in guiding the Haitian leaders. They appear in the third part of Zapata Olivella's novel, "The Rebellion of the Vaudoux," in order to pass on their experience to others along what amounts to a dynastic chain of command. Under the aegis of the Vaudou gods, history can be conceived as cyclical, recursive, and progressive at the same time. The vaudoux and the dead themselves are "rebels," "rebeldes," opposed to the religious institution that sanctions slavery (Zapata Olivella, *Changó* 283).

The cyclical motif of rebirth is the key: the life force, called *kulonda* in Kikongo (see chapter 5), is the spirit-word reincarnated in the succeeding generations of Zapata Olivella's black protagonists. Mackandal, immolated by the French for leading some of the first uprisings, returns in spirit to acknowledge his death, but he declares, "my ekobios [comrades, in Abakuá], know that I, transformed into the serpent of Damballah, will be reborn triumphant in the rainbow after every storm." Toussaint L'Ouverture, conspicuously absent from Carpentier's Vaudou-focused account, appears as an offended shade, resenting the defaming of his revolution as a massacre by blacks when it constituted a just war against the genocide sponsored by the plantation owners. Yet Toussaint must previously appear before Henri Christophe and confess, remorsefully, that he attempted to reinstitute slavery on Saint Domingue. On the same island, it is Baron Samedi, Lord of the Graveyard, who handed Bouckman his bullet of gold, perhaps the same bullet that the Guédé gives to Henri Christophe with which to shoot himself, an act preordained on the Ifá Board. In his turn, Bouckman will also pass the keys of Elegba to Toussaint, who after his death will truly become his name— L'Ouverture, "the Great Opening of Liberty." Against the attack of Napoleon's fleet, the deified Ancestors become the slaves' "compass," without which the defenders of the republic "would have lost the road to liberty" (Zapata Olivella, Changó 290, 314, 279, 320–21, 354, 326, 324).

The Haitian saga of Zapata Olivella's novel comes to an open-ended conclusion when Henri Christophe, ambivalently treated in Carpentier's narrative, justifies his coronation as absolute monarch. With this royal act, he claims, he is sending the message to Napoleon that the French emperor is dealing not with some petty colonial governor but with a peer among statesmen. Christophe's monumental statement of black defiance is "the citadel of Ogoun Ferrière" (Zapata Olivella, Changó 346; 307, my emphasis).

Zapata Olivella thus presents a more sophisticated, multisided rendering of the Haitian Revolution than Carpentier's by reconstructing and including the "Black Jacobins'" perspective (i.e., that of Toussaint, Dessalines, and Pétion, among other statesmen-generals studied by C. L. R. James) without overlooking the power of the mythic dimension projected by Vaudou religion and aesthetics. More completely than Carpentier as well, Zapata Olivella rebuilds a cosmos in which the orisha-loa archetypes can take an active and personalized role in political action. Yet in both narratives, the mythopoetics of history and the history of mythopoesis, both loaded with African-based symbols, cross and conflate. In literature and history alike, the legend of the Great Opening became poetry and reality.

Yet for all its liberatory capability, Vaudou sanctions a form of mythic and fetishistic thinking caught in the spell of the (sacralized) image, a spell that overpowers perceptions of sociohistorical conditions. Thought in Carpentier's novel is shown as enchanted by the image of loas, omens, royal emblems, the monumental architecture of Sans-Souci and the Citadelle la Ferrière. Such mystification demonstrates Adorno's insight that "[w]hat clings to the image remains idolatry, mythic enthrallment" such that "[t]he totality of images blends into a wall before reality" (205). In mystifying the motives for class struggle, the Vaudou image enthralls, blocking the insight needed to organize resistance to the power of the mulatto elite under Jean Pierre Boyer. Thus, the anticolonial, antislavery revolution ushers in the reinstatement, in 1820, of colonial structures (see Davis 71).

The novel's representation of Vaudou fetishism, on the other hand, makes a valid critique of "Enlightenment culture" itself by mirroring a fetishism inherent to Enlightenment. Before "succumbing" to the temptations of tropical languor and Vaudou ritual, Pauline Bonaparte, married to General Leclerc, already appears enslaved to the image and therefore to magico-religious patterns of thought associated with her Corsican upbringing. Pauline masters her slave Solimán, not only commanding him to carry out her every whim but also taunting him by allowing him to massage her body and kiss her legs: in one scene, Solimán is "kneeling on the floor, with a gesture that Bernardin of Saint-Pierre would have interpreted as a symbol of the noble gratitude of a simple soul before the generous undertakings of the Enlightenment" (REM 73). Imaged as such, Enlightenment becomes a legitimating ideology of colonialism and makes domination over into a matter of noblesse oblige for the benefit of the subjugated, the colonizer's gift to the colonized. The Enlightenment faith in reason becomes a sort of Vaudou rationalism. Yet this imagistic ideology will have its revenge: the European Pauline will have no choice but to surrender to the magic of Vaudou when, desperate, she seeks a cure for her husband's, Leclerc's, fatal case of yellow fever. "One morning, the chambermaids discovered, with fright, that the black man was executing a strange dance around Pauline, kneeling on the floor with loosened hair." A rooster with its throat slit and images of the saints hanging from the rafters completes the scene of the cure (REM 77–78).

Idolatrous imagery will play a mean joke on Solimán later on, when, reveling in Rome during Carnival time, he suddenly discovers, inside the Borghese Palace, a statue of a nude woman holding out an apple—the Venus of Canova. Drunkenly mistaking the statue for the body of his former mistress, Solimán begins to massage it in the accustomed fashion, "moved by an imperious physical remembrance" because "[a]n unbearable feeling of nightmare remained in his hands" (REM 129–30). Then follows the mad scene in which Solimán, bereaved or malaria-stricken, tries to "revive" the statue and falls into a feverish dream. In that dream, "he was trying to reach a God who was in faraway Dahomey, at some shady crossroads, with his red phallus resting on a crutch that he carried with him for that purpose" (REM 131). In his delirium, Solimán finds an exit from the colonial history that has twisted his desire and distanced him from the loas. In Papa Legba, patron saint of crossroads and interpreters, the former masseur seeks a messenger to the loas: he calls to the guardian of a heritage in which he identified himself. On this "night of the statues," the reminder of Pauline's body provokes a hysterical attack, bringing to mind the sounds of the song (one also imagines drumming) that would invite the loa to open up the door between worlds and possess the serviteur: "*Papa Legba, l'ouvri barrié-a pou moin, agó yé, / Papa Legba, ouvri barrié-a pou moin, pou moin passé*" (REM 131). The whole enigmatic scene could be construed as one showing Solimán's continued "psychical" subjugation to magical thinking in the postindependence period. The former slaves still cling to myth and image. Solimán's "madness" in Karlsbad constitutes a doomed attempt to restore a psychic wholeness.

Much of the narrative of the novel's third section recounts the tyrannical reign of Henri Christophe. Christophe's ascent to the throne of the Northern Kingdom demonstrates that the renascent spirit of monarchy—his blazon is the phoenix—and the recourse to violence exist in even the most rational-sounding programs. The motto on Christophe's cannon appropriately declares itself to be Ultima Ratio Regum, or The Last Argument of the King (REM 113, 112). Even though Christophe is said to have "always kept himself at the margin of the Africanist mystique of the first caudillos of the Haitian independence," he uses Vaudou signs as means of obtaining power and interpreting his experience (REM 112). The emperor allows bulls to be sacrificed so that their blood may be added to the mortar of the Citadelle la Ferrière (REM 97, 98). Just prior to the ghostly appearance of Corneille Breille and the onset of Christophe's paralysis, Christophe "suspects" that "there would be an image of him stuck with pins or hanging in a bad way with a knife shoved into its heart. Very far away, at times, arose a palpitation of drums that were probably not playing in supplication for his long life" (REM 106).

I have noted the accent that the novel places on the powers of speech and verbal performance. Mackandal was said to charm, seduce, and create a mythical African world by his storytelling; Bouckman's voice invoked both the loas and the French Declaration; and Solimán's incantations, it was hoped, would save the dying Governor Leclerc from the yellow fever. In the Christophe episodes, the talking drums, which convey news and signal the start of the revolt, pattern their messages on the verbal formulas that circulate in the slave community. By these means, as stated by Carullo, "The drums produce the 'nommo,' 'the magic word,' here prediction of the revolutionary movement of this Afro-American community" (8). Vaudou is above all a language, or a congeries of distinct idioms that communicate worship, identity, protection, as demonstrated in Carpentier's narrative. Vaudou as language also functions as an instrument of interpretation whose potential, it could be argued, has not been exhausted by Haitian history. The character of père Labat is cited as saying, "[T]he blacks were acting like the Philistine, adoring Dogón inside the Ark" (REM 61), and indeed it is a certain kind of allegorical interpretation, a cross-cultural "misreading," that produces this form of worship. The slaves, rude philosophers, interpret the world before changing it. Such interpretation constitutes another contribution to transculturation, as when the novel demonstrates how Spanish colonial culture would have appeared to a serviteur of the loas. Once in Santiago de Cuba in the company of his expatriate master, Ti Noël hears the contrapuntal music of Esteban Salas in a Cuban cathedral. There he finds a Baroque sensuality and spirituality agreeable to his Vaudou sensibilities:

> a Vaudou heat that he had never found in the Saint-Sulpician temples of the Cap. The Baroque golds, the human hairs of the Christs, the mystery of the confessionals heavily decorated with mouldings, the dragons crushed by holy feet, the swine of Saint Anthony, the broken color of San Benito, the black Virgins, the Saint Georges with the coturni and corselets of French tragic actors, the pastoral instruments played on festival nights, had an enveloping force, a power of seduction, through presences, symbols, attributes and signs, similar to that given off by the altars of the houmfort consecrated to Damballah, the Serpent God. In addition, Saint James [Santiago] is Ogoun Fai, the field marshal of storms, at whose entreaty [or incantation—conjuro] the men of Bouckman had risen up. (REM 67)

Ti Noël's reading of the Baroque music, architecture, and iconography—and our reading of (the narrator's reading of) his reading—makes the church over into a Vaudou temple, a houmfort on a grand scale. The attendance at mass is doubled by the presence of loas masked by Catholic images. Mystery, theatricality, iconography, hagiography, and embellishment, all touchstones of the Baroque style, are made for Vaudou, just as the ritual and symbols of Cuban Catholicism were reinterpreted by slaves in an Afro-Cuban context (SAS 114). For Ti Noël, a way of seeing is a way of thinking. In the light of this cross-cultural reading, I do not fully agree with Carullo's estimation that "Carpentier demonstrates that Vaudou presides over the life of this people of

America; that its people, king, governors and governed, oppressors and oppressed, find themselves subject to its supernatural and divine laws, the only means of liberation" (9). Carpentier's text does demonstrate the manner in which the European powers and European versions of truth and history are overthrown by the forces of Haitian Vaudou. Vaudou does preserve a cultural tradition and foster the rise of a rebellious subject. Yet Vaudou reaches its interpretive limits when it attempts to read the text of history. The arms of liberation impose their own form of blindness, subjecting the Haitians to a new harvest of poverty, illiteracy, isolation, and dictatorship. Returning to his old plantation in the Plaîne du Nord after his exile in Santiago de Cuba, Ti Noël walks through a sterilized, hostile countryside, reading "signs": goats hang from spiny trees; Legba's crutches lie amidst the "gnarled" roots of a tree. Ti Noël is glad to be back in "the land of the Great Pacts": "For he knew—and all the French blacks from Santiago de Cuba knew—that the triumph of Dessalines was indebted to a tremendous preparation, in which had intervened Loco, Petro, Ogoun Feraille, Brise-Pimba, Marinette Bois-cheche and all the divinities of powder and fire" (REM 85).

But from the broader historical perspective, this wasteland indicates more: the consequences of Christophe's tyranny, the refusal to work, the coup of the republican mulattoes. These readings tragically contradict the utopian image painted by Vaudou ideology. What Ti Noël cannot comprehend, nor has the means to comprehend, is that the mulattoes distinguished themselves from the blacks by fighting for equality with the whites. In the midst of the conflict, some 10 percent of the land and some fifty thousand slaves were the property of the mulatto class in 1789 (Hurston, 94). Once they ascended to power, the mulattoes put down and exploited the black insurrectionaries, who had made it possible for them, the mulattoes, to replace the white aristocracy in power. Ti Noël recognizes both the horsemen of the mulattoes' troops and the surveyors sent to reparcel the land, but he lacks the kind of narrative knowledge that would make sense of these developments.

Vaudou, as I have argued, was a means of both empowerment and mystification in the Haitian Revolution. This double path crosses itself in the concluding chapter of El reino, "Agnus Dei," where the narrative makes an appropriately open-ended statement on the laws of Vaudou. A dispossessed Ti Noël in that chapter has transformed himself into a gander in an attempt to join a goose clan. The geese reject him. He feels a "cosmic weariness" at this, yet another in a series of disempowering exclusions in a lifetime of negations. Then comes the epiphany: Ti Noël realizes, according to the narrator, that one must suffer and work to improve things, for "the greatness of man is precisely in wanting to be better than what he is" (REM 144). As an apocalyptic storm brews up, Ti Noël disappears, or else he has metamorphosed himself into the "wet vulture," whose extended wings form a cross before he plunges in flight into the Bois Caïman (REM 145). The saga of Bois Caïman, whose name gives us the last words of the narrative proper, has for a colophon the symbol of death or transcendence, the buzzard or vulture known as *aura tiñosa*, or, in Lucumí, *Kanákaná*, a sacred scavenger who, like the Lamb of God, mediates between heaven and earth in bringing the message of humans to the Almighty (APA 35, 195–96).

Vaudou symbolism has triumphed in Carpentier's novel, not in history but as slave ideology, religious mystification or artistic, marvelously real fetish. As in ¡*Ecue-Yamba-O!*, Carpentier projects in *El reino* a world in which neo-African religion is but one conspicuous piece in the transcultural mosaic alongside other texts of tradition and culture. Apart from the historical failure of Vaudou, the manner in which cultural practices from diverse origins converge and transform one another in ways subversive of the dominant Eurocentric discourses; perhaps he agreed with Lezama Lima's apparent parody of Ti Noël's moment of *anagnorisis* when the narrator of *Paradiso* declares: "[T]he greatness of man consists in being able to assimilate what is unknown to him" (265). The apparently "centerless" quality of *El reino*, composed of a series of vignettes loosely and inconsistently bound by Ti Noël's assimilative viewpoint, allows the text to foreground the continuing significance that Vaudou has for Caribbean culture while emphasizing its limitations when confronted with other forces and discourses. Vaudou, thus redefined and reframed in Carpentier's text, is recodified and restored to its ambiguous, subjectivist, and subversive drift.

Between Heaven and Earth

The stories of Antonio Benítez Rojo's *El escudo de hojas secas* (1969) depict prerevolutionary Cuba as a country in need of regeneration. The book's title translates as "The Coat-of-Arms of Dry Leaves," alluding to a Spanish escutcheon that the bourgeois family of the title story purchases for itself. Afro-Cuban religious practices, especially divination and the family's devotion to San Lázaro, the Chankpana or Babalú-Ayé of Dahomeyan tradition, gives the main characters the luck they need to win the national lottery. With these developments, the story satirizes the search for the symbols of prestige and power on the part of a Cuban middle class whose position in Cuban society before the Revolution was always tenuous, based not on dominance in industrial or agricultural wealth so much as on the vagaries of a market dominated by foreign capital. The title story also targets the nouveau-riche's superficial spiritualism through abundant references to palm readers, card readers, fortune tellers, mediums, santeros, and astrologers, and thus alludes to a generalized crisis of orthodox religion in modern society. Nouveau-riche occultism here signifies a commodified transcendentalism, but it also remits to a world of ritual and mystic significations only vaguely sensed by the story's acquisitive protagonists.

Benítez Rojo's story "La tierra y el cielo" (Earth and heaven), from the same collection, on the other hand, brings Afro-Cuban religion, and specifically Vaudou or Arará, into the narrative of liberation and on the side of radical change. The story can be placed in Taylor's category of the liberating narrative, for it critiques a dominant ideology and addresses real issues in Cuban history. Yet the juxtaposition of historical and mythical visions in the story works to reveal a bicultural, polysemic construction of experience that admits the two worldviews in a complementary fashion. Julio Miranda confirms that Benítez Rojo's stories in the anthology belong to the category of Carpentier's *lo real maravilloso*, "generally orienting him in the same sense of a critical grasp of history and with a similar Baroque brilliance, only now often directed toward the present: residues of a magical mentality in the Revolution—*La tierra y el cielo* . . . etc." (102).

These "residues" in the story convey mythological and doctrinal content from Arará tradition. Possession and divination play a significant role in the narrated experience of its central characters, serving as metaphors of identity and of ideological and group allegiance throughout. Yet despite the story's explicit relegation of Afro-Cuban beliefs and practices to a prehistory of the Cuban Revolution, we may question the apparent closure of the story's plot if we take, as readers, the more ambivalent viewpoint suggested by the story's text.

Concretely, "La tierra y el cielo" immerses the reader in the world of the loas as experienced in the lives of Haitian characters transplanted in Camagüey province. Pedro Limón, Pascasio, and Aristón are three impoverished Haitian workers who, threatened with deportation by Batista's government, see no alternative but to join the anti-Batista resistance in the Sierra Maestra. Through the teachings and guidance of an old Haitian houngan named Tiguá, the young men believe that the loas will protect them in battle. Tiguá's grandson

Aristón in particular puts his faith in "Oggún Ferrai": "That night Tiguá assured that Oggún Ferrai had mounted Aristón, that he had conversed with the god and the latter is very happy to have been able to move about and fight inside the muscles of his grandson" (Benítez Rojo, "tierra," 13). The story follows the divinely inspired Aristón and his *compañeros* through their participation in the fighting and explores the consequences of their loa worship as well. Throughout the narrative, Oggún, as Ariston's divine double, plays a key role as a narrative functor in the story and merits here a brief "background check."

A literary precedent for this use of Oggún can be found in Carpentier's *El reino de este mundo*, to which we momentarily return. In that novel, Oggún in some aspect or other appears and reappears in the context of the Haitian Revolution. When the fighting becomes especially brutal under the government of Rochambeau, the gods of both sides become involved. "Now, the Great Loas smiled upon the Negroes' arms. Victory went to those who had warrior gods to invoke. Ogoun Badagrí guided the cold steel charges against the last redoubts of the Goddess Reason" (Carpentier, *Kingdom* 103). The passage brings to mind an earlier intervention into the struggle by Oggún Ferrai, who with other loas becomes intertwined with the living legend of the houngan Mackandal: "One day he would give the signal of the great uprising" (REM 33). Later on in the ceremony of the famous pact of the Bois Caïman, during which the Bouckman calls on the Saint Domingue blacks to rise up, a Rada priestess is said to invoke the presence of Ogoun Badagrí, addressed as "*Général sanglant*" (bloody general) (REM 53).

The Ogoun Badagrí of Carpentier's novel is the owner of the secret of iron and the warrior god who leads the charges of the rebelling slaves. Carpentier and Benítez Rojo refer to Ogoun Feraille, again patron of warriors and of blacksmiths. Other Afro-Haitian manifestations include the red-eyed Ogoun Jérouge; Ogoun Laflambeaum, a god of fire; and Ogoun Panamá, a guardian against sunstroke. This last one wears a panama hat (DALC 358–59). Ogoun is also the path breaker, he who cut through the primordial thicket to clear a way for orishas and humans on earth. He symbolizes justice, as evidenced in the Nigerian courtrooms where Yoruba witnesses will swear upon Ogoun in the form of a piece of iron (SR 47–48).

Thompson remarks that the Papa Ogoun of Vaudou often appears as a hot, truculent god of the Petro side, the one known in Dahomey as Gu: "the personification of iron's cutting edge" and the gubasa blade, who is further syncretized in the Caribbean with the militant saints of Catholicism (FS 167,

169, 172). Fables and pataki in the Regla de Ocha canon emphasize Oggún's violent rivalry with Changó, but in Vaudou these two are syncretized, fused together, in the figure of Papa Ogoun, sometimes seen, as mentioned before, in the form of Ogoun Changó (SMD 34–35; REM 53).

Let us return to Benítez Rojo's story. Its story begins near the end of its plot: the Revolution has triumphed, and Pedro Limón is returning to Camagüey, after a long absence, to work as a teacher. On the way back home, Pedro has stopped by the ingenio or sugar mill to greet Pascasio. From the free, indirect discourse relating the scene of their reunion, the reader learns that Limón has spent time in the hospital for reconstructive surgery after a mortar explosion destroyed his face and that he belonged to the group of Afro-Haitians and speaks their Creole. We also learn that someone named Tiguá continues to converse with the loas and to criticize Fidel for appropriating the farmlands in the Agrarian Reform, that something significant concerning Pascasio's brother remains unsaid between them, and that Leonie, once beloved by Pedro, has been living with Pascasio for six years and they now have a son (TC 5–6). This overview serves to frame the rest of the story, which concerns events leading up to Pedro's return.

Next we learn that Pedro, separated from his parents in Cuba during a forced repatriation of Haitian immigrants, was raised like a brother to Pascasio and Aristón by their mother. In the present tense, Pedro narrates the memory of nights when he lay awake in bed listening to the prayers of Tiguá, the grandfather of his adoptive brothers. Tigua's Afro-Haitian religion, as Tiguá re-creates it, is beautiful and comforting. Pedro tells of his happiness in Guanamaca when, seated next to his sweetheart Leonie, they would listen to Tigua's fireside stories: "Through the crack in the board I hear Tiguá speaking with the gods and the dead. Tiguá is a powerful houngan who even knows Cuban brujería. He also transforms into a snake and eats the chickens of the tenant farmers. I respect him a lot. Tiguá loves Aristón more than all of his grandsons. He says that he will make an houngan out of him, that he is going to teach him leave his skin and become an owl, or a boa." The loving grandfather, reminiscent of Mackandal in his shape-changing and storytelling, does teach Aristón, and well. Thanks to an herbal mixture prepared by Tiguá to strengthen his grandson's arm, Aristón can cut more cane than anyone else ("the machete is like a thunderbolt in his hand"), and he can defeat a fellow cane cutter in a machete fight, slashing open the opponent's abdomen. Aristón welcomes the training in religion and his possession by Oggún with a declaration that resembles the Vaudou praise-songs: "I will be an houngan greater than Tiguá. Oggún Ferrai protects me, Oggún the marshal, Oggún the peasant, Oggún of iron, Oggún of war. I am Oggún!" So empowered by the belligerent god of the forge, Aristón forces Pedro to accompany him to the Sierra Maestra to fight Batista as Aristón's *resguardo*, his talisman, or else die at Aristón's hand. Pedro, "choosing" to fight alongside Aristón, realizes that "we were going to war because Oggún had ordered it, to fight against the tanks and cannons of Batista." As it did for the slaves in Carpentier's novel, a belief in the loas produces confidence and courage in the anti-Batista guerrillas, for the rite of possession is actually said to bring down the "will" of Oggún into Aristón's body. This son of Oggún even defies an airplane of Batista—"he was even going to cut off its wings." When the airplane drops a bomb near the Haitian fighters that does not explode, the apparent miracle convinces Pedro that Oggún is indeed protecting them, and it convinces the Oriente rebel band to accept the two Haitians into their troop (TC 11–12, 14, 17, 18).

From his viewpoint in the postwar present, Pedro also recalls how Oggún would take complete possession of Aristón, without Aristón's awareness of it, right before entering combat. As Oggún Ferrai, Aristón thinks and fights and strides as the orisha does, with audacity enough to kill an enemy soldier with his machete once his ammunition has run out. But possession means a loss of both self and self-control. Aristón's rash action forces the Haitians to retreat, which provokes a spate of racially tinged criticisms from a rebel soldier from the plains. Instantly, Aristón raises the machete and cracks the soldier's skull open with one blow. We see in the ensuing confrontation between Aristón and his materialist comrades a clash of rival codes. Yet judgment belongs to the Revolutionary Tribunal, and Aristón is sentenced to execution. But he doesn't care, confident that, with Pedro present as his resguardo, nothing can harm him. Pedro must, nonetheless, form a part of the firing squad that executes him. Aristón is stood before a sacred ceiba tree, and his colored handkerchiefs do not avail him, nor his seed necklaces nor the proxmity of Pedro (TC 19, 21, 22).

After the officer from Havana gives Aristón the coup de grace, Pedro believes he sees something like a snake, sliding away from Aristón's body under the cover of smoke. A question arises in Pedro's mind: has Aristón taken the animal's form and escaped? Whatever the case, the officer from Havana does not include that bit of interpretation into his record. But as he writes, he tells Pedro to go "decide" because, Pedro reflects, "in life men always had had to choose between the earth and heaven, and for me the time had come" (TC 24).

So ends the story, explaining therewith the reasons that Pedro has chosen "the earth," renouncing the path of the loas and taking up the path of the Revolution as one of its rural teachers. The story is "liberatory" on this level. Yet the denouement does not completely ensure the narrative's closure: does Pedro's decision, we wonder, amount to renouncing Vaudou's vision of salvation? For Cuervo Hewitt, the answer to the question is no, for the moment of Aristón's execution becomes a "mythical vision": "It is the instant of a crossing of perspectives, and at the same time, a reality with neither center nor borders, fragmented and moving." And as this example demonstrates, "the African presence in the work of Benítez Rojo leaves reality suspended on the threshold of a profound crack that opens up within the objective. The fragmentation [of two cosmovisions] is an illusion as much as is [their] unity" (APA, 221, 223). Juxtaposing such "simultaneous readings," Benítez Rojo's text seems to argue against attributing epistemological priority to one or the other cosmovision, for his narrative also declares that the same "spirit" that fired the Haitian Revolution reemerged in the Cuban Revolution. Yet the text takes a relativist stance in acknowledging that the Vaudou cosmovision that proved empowering in the Haitian Revolution would lose legitimacy in another context, under the eyes of the official culture of the Cuban Revolution.

The crossed perspectives of this last scenario of transformation indicate the adjacency of incommensurable discourses that come into conflict, especially in moments of crisis. Mythic narrative and liberating narrative converge in certain revolutionary struggles but diverge and oppose one another in other battles. Aristón's possession signals the manner in which Vaudou eschews scriptural, historicocritical forms of signification, relying instead on the "physical remembrance"—inscription on the body—that Mackandal and Tiguá speak, that Solimán and Aristón act out, that the serviteurs in general dance. Unlike the orishas in Cuba, the loas' historicity distinguishes them as functors in the grand and incomplete narrative of Haitian independence, a narrative implicitly continued on into other anticolonial, antiimperialist struggles. Carpentier and Benítez Rojo offer versions of Vaudou in narratives that scrutinize both its liberating myths and its mythical liberations. Neither makes a final verdict on Vaudou, as if to confirm that Mawu's writing is not just the script of life but life itself as an interplay of truth and fiction: an unfinished story.

1

❖ Religion and Revolution

*Candela alumbra y mamba apagá (Fire illuminates
and water extinguishes).*
Lydia Cabrera, *Refranes de negros viejos*

When Enrique, protagonist of Carpentier's *La Consagración de la Primavera* (The
rite of spring, 1978), returns home to a postrevolutionary Havana after a
long absence, he is greeted by Camila, a black maid who is wearing all-white
clothing in the fashion of the devotees of the Virgen de las Mercedes (Obatalá).
Enrique asks her why, and Camila answers: "The Revolution has not prohib-
ited anyone from believing in whatever they feel like, and less now that all of
us, blacks and whites, are equal" (Carpentier, *Consagración* 527). Her statement reveals the degree of acceptance that Afro-Cuban religion had won by
about the mid-1970s: officially tolerated and even recognized as an ingredient of what could be called a national culture. Yet Camila's statement also
conceals the story of how, before this point, the revolutionary regime had
waged a war of repression, silence, harassment, and attrition against Afro-
Cuban religion and its practitioners. It was only after an initial period of
governmental intolerance toward the religion that agencies of the official
culture attempted a new strategy, that of managing and containing the varieties of Afro-Cuban religious expression by a variety of means. The changing
attitudes and policies toward Afro-Cuban religion in post-1959 Cuba can be
traced through the cultural history and literary narratives of the period. In
this chapter I will examine that history and these narratives, considering the
specific paths of affirmation and resistance that an Afro-Cuban religious culture has taken in its confrontations with the reasons of state.

Throughout the preceding discussions of literary backgrounds and treatments of Afro-Cuban religions—Regla de Ocha, la Sociedad Secreta Abakuá,
Palo Monte, and Regla Arará—it has been the idea of "fiction," conceived as
a sign system productive of its own reality, that has served to foreground the

means by which Afro-Cuban narrative reconstructs the signifying dimensions of Afro-Cuban religion. By recodifying that religion's myths, institutional forms, ritual, doctrine, and patterns of experience as text, narrative has made it accessible to analysis and critique, revealing in the process the possible element of fictionality inherent in the religion's own systems. When that text comes into dialogue with the discourse of power authorized by the Cuban Revolution, Afro-Cuban religion takes on new sociohistorical significations, as I will illustrate in this last chapter.

Postrevolutionary Cuban literature has described, narrated and cited Afro-Cuban religion in a variety of ways, such that, at different moments after 1959, it has symbolized an ethnic difference within the culture of the nation-state, a legacy of past resistance against colonial domination, or an enlivening contribution to an integrated national culture. In the first decade and a half of the Revolution, however, the official culture chose to see in that religion's subculture an alternate or competing economic activity that negated the centralized planned economy of the state. Afro-Cuban religious practice was therefore actively discouraged. Intolerance ceded to a tolerance toward the end of the 1970s, when the cultural ministries decided that if they couldn't beat Afro-Cuban religion, they could at least in a sense invite it to join them. Under these circumstances, Afro-Cuban religion became a governmentally approved "folklore." Yet the promotion of folklore as the alternative to outright prohibition entailed subtle and not-so-subtle forms of negation since "folklorization" not only consisted of a process of simplifying and secularizing religious expression but also subjected Afro-Cuban religious values to a materialist critique. This strategy of containment—for that is what it amounted to—resulted in the assessment of Afro-Cuban religion as an irrational, barbaric, and mystifying, although admittedly beautiful and colorful, body of antisocialist tendencies. Those tendencies, in the official view, had to be mastered by new historical forces of the Revolution, whose collective voice would drown out the small voices of myth and folklore. Regla de Ocha, la Sociedad Abakuá, Palo Monte, and Regla Arará were thus stigmatized as subcultures belonging to a legacy of ignorance and to memories of underdevelopment. A brief overview of the Revolution's literary-cultural politics with relation to African-based religions will serve to contextualize my subsequent discussion of Afro-Cuban narratives after the Revolution.

In his *African Civilizations in the New World* (1971), Roger Bastide refers to the forms of syncretic religion that have been "violently attacked" in Cuba, Haiti, and Brazil, by both capitalist and communists alike: "It is charged with being a non-productive form of economy, an obstacle to the country's progressive development in that it maintains pockets of restricted circulation currency, which thus cannot be capitalised or ploughed back into industry" (123). Simpson also writes in 1978 that the practice of Santería, like that of all other religions in Cuba, was discouraged under Castro's regime (94). Reports concerning Afro-Cuban religion's situation in recent Cuban history lend support to these charges. Cabrera has referred to repressions of African cults in Cuba and in particular to incidents in the airports in which officers have confiscated eleke necklaces from those about to embark on so-called freedom flights. Government officers have even confiscated the kofá bracelets of green and yellow beads, worn by the babalao, that bring protection from Orúmila (YO 126). The attitude expressed in such prohibitions stands in curious contrast to the various attitudes that prevailed in the literature and culture of capitalist Cuba.

Prior to 1959, Afro-Cuban religion, as I have argued in previous chapters, often provided literature with an alternative viewpoint from which to reveal and criticize the contradictions of a Cuban society under U.S. hegemony and dependent dictatorship. Whereas Carpentier in ¡Ecue-Yamba-O! attempted to reconstruct Abakuá religion from a putative "inside" viewpoint, he also elaborated the ideological implications of its belief and practice from a sociohistorical perspective. Ramos reconstructed the religious worldview of a runaway slave in colonial Cuba in order to critique the failings of a republican Cuba. Del Valle in his Ñáñigo stories attempted to unmask the erotic and political desire within what he perceived to be a world of Afro-Cuban religious illusion. Whereas these writers included Afro-Cuban discourse in the narratives of social critique, Lachatañeré, Cabrera, and, for the most part, Ortiz published many texts affirming the complexity, dignity, beauty, and integrity of Afro-Cuban religious cultures, whose values, they believed, could contribute to the making of an authentically national culture. As this study's earlier chapters have shown, Afro-Cuban literature sometimes occupied itself with re-creating the entire "other world" of orishas, mpungus, vaudoux, and saints, sometimes examining the architectonics of their systems, sometimes analyzing the mechanisms of their religious practices. In the prevailing bourgeois opinion prior to 1959, however, that religion and its associated culture, despite their literary treatments, represented a stage of barbarity that the "modern" republic would soon outgrow.

Yet, strangely, Afro-Cuban religion and Cuban politics in the twentieth century have often occupied the same bed. We have examined the links between Havana politicians and Ñáñigo confraternities and recalled anecdotes concerning Castro and his supposed links to Santería. By some accounts,

Machado was an *Omo-Changó* who wore a red kerchief around his waist to ensure protection from his orisha (SR 69). Lachatañeré tells the story of how Machado in 1928 inaugurated a park during the Sixth Panamerican Conference in Havana. In the center of that park he had ordered the planting of a sacred ceiba tree in a plot in which had been placed soil from the twenty-one republics in attendance. Two palm trees—the favorite refuge of Changó— had been planted there too. The presence of these two trees sent out the message that Machado's orisha had told him to hold the ceremony. It was not uncommon thereafter to find offerings placed between the roots of the ceiba and at the foot of the palm trees. Some thirty years later, Batista was considered a "son of Orúmila," and his rise to power was credited to this devotion, which he expressed in the revolution against Machado, on September 4, 1933, by choosing a banner for the army that bore the green of Orúmila and the yellow of Ochún (MS 37–39).

Fulgencio Batista, it is also said, made contact with many Afro-Cuban priests and diviners. Before he abandoned the Cuban capital in December of 1958, a Jamaican obeahman and a Haitian houngan predicted that the end was near for the dictator. In a last-ditch attempt to hold on to power in September 1958, Batista had assembled hundreds of Afro-Cuban religious leaders together. Their mission: "to summon the gods of Africa to his aid and 'to appease the demons of war'" (CBA 12).

After 1959, when culture and intellectual production had to be harnessed in service to the agendas of the socialist state, Afro-Cuban religion would provide its followers with a refuge from the pressures of the economy and an alternative to the culture of politics. Yet the state had its own ideas about that alternative.

In *Castro, the Blacks, and Africa* (1988), Carlos Moore, referring to Afro-Cuban religion as "the repository of Cuba's most powerful cultural distinctiveness," has criticized the socialist government's repressive treatment of their practices (98). Moore's sociohistorical analysis illustrates that repression by referring to the reception of Walterio Carbonell's *Crítica: Cómo surgió la cultura nacional* (Critique: How the national culture arose, 1961), a book that, as we have seen in earlier chapters, defended the preservation and promotion of Afro-Cuban culture, arguing that it has expressed the core of nationalist and anticolonialist sentiments throughout Cuba's history. Religion for a people such as the Afro-Cubans was not, in Carbonell's view, the "opiate" of Marx and Engels's manifesto but an "instrument for investigating natural and social phenomena," one offering supernatural explanations that, although "vitiated at their origins," provided a "social sense" of said phenomena.

Carbonell's book had been published for three months when it was withdrawn and banned and Carbonell relieved of duty in the foreign ministry (CBA 99, 109).

Jorge I. Domínguez has called Castro's policy toward Afro-Cuban culture a "negrophobic" one, charging that it has suppressed political movements emphasizing the issues concerning blacks. In addition, "[i]t has sought to extirpate Afro-Cuban religions, by fighting them directly or by seeking to transform them into artistic folklore." With repression or neutralization went the tendency in post-Batista Cuba to exclude blacks from positions of authority, to silence discussions on racism, and to acknowledge only the process of assimilation. It appears that Castro instituted a battery of measures to discourage the practice of Afro-Cuban religion in the early 1960s. The regime restricted public drumming, central to Afro-Cuban rites and fiestas, by requiring prior authorization from the local Committee for the Defense of the Revolution. Castro, writes Moore, even considered banning carnivals and starting up bullfights as an alternative to the street celebrations. Members of Afro-Cuban fraternities were barred from membership in the Communist Party. Foreign visitors were discouraged from attending Santería ceremonies (CBA xi, 100, 131).

Exclusions, arrests, and other forms of prohibition discouraged participation in the Afro-Cuban brotherhoods during the first decade of the regime's power. The response, writes Moore, relying on interviews with informants including dissidents Gilberto Aldama and Esteban Cárdenas, was a series of Abakuá-organized counterattacks in 1969. They occurred "in reprisal, it seems, for the uncovering of an all-black underground movement called the Movimiento de Liberación Nacional (MLN). Although there was no conclusive evidence that the Abakuá as such was involved, the indiscriminate arrests of known Ñañigos were carried out. As the repression continued into 1970, the Abakuá brotherhood took an action that frightened the government even more. For the first time since Fidel Castro came to power, a successful twenty-four-hour strike was carried out, paralyzing the entire port of Havana" (CBA 306).

The "bulldozer" approach of the 1960s thus backfired, producing "the opposite of desired results: Afro-Cuban religions had gone deeper underground and grown in size." This forced clandestinity and involution provoked a more subtle, diffuse campaign of subversion directed against Afro-Cuban community groups and especially against the secretive Abakuá potencias. Moore cites the final declaration of the 1971 National Congress on Education and Culture, which associated "mental backwardness" and "school retardation" with "[t]he incidence of problems arising from some religious sects, especially some of African origin (Ñáñigo and Abakuá)." The National Congress also raised the concept of socialist revolution to the status of "highest expression of Cuban culture" with the concomitant degradation of Abakuá brotherhoods to expressions of "criminality" and "juvenile delinquency." In 1971 as well, a campaign was launched to infiltrate, expose, and thus undermine Abakuá brotherhoods (CBA 304, 102).

The government's attitude of intolerance and suspicion was soon to relax in response to internal and external developments. The 1970s were to be Cuba's "Africa Decade," during which the interventions in Angola and Ethiopia exposed Cubans to the cultural practices of their anti-imperialist comrades in arms. Contact with African soldiers had occurred even earlier, preparing Cubans to embrace a more tolerant attitude at a later time. For Simba fighters in the Congo under the leadership of Ernesto "Che" Guevara, it would be "unthinkable . . . to go into battle without special anti-bullet charms and amulets (gris-gris); or without seeking the advice of elderly wise men." Guevara viewed such practices as primitive and atavistic, contradictory to the "scientific communism" he sought to propagate in Africa. He viewed with disgust the Simbas' practice of taking away organs from the bodies of the fallen mercenaries for the making of amulets, and he even suspected Congolese guerillas of cannibalism (CBA 368).

Despite such anti-African ideas emerging from Cuba's involvement in African independence movements, other developments seemed to invite the orishas back into the public purview. The Black Power movement in the United States had affirmed African-based religion as a part of its identity politics since the 1960s, and the economic setbacks of the Revolution moved many to turn to the same religion as a refuge and an escape valve. The U.S. continued to impose its embargo, the CIA sponsored terrorist acts, the 1970 sugar harvest failed to meet the ten-million-ton goal set by the regime, and tropical storms wreaked havoc. The boat lift from Mariel, with the exodus by September 1980 of some 125,000 Cubans, sent out a clear message of discontent. In this climate of scarcity and instability, the regime had to lift most overt repressions of Afro-Cuban religion by the early 1980s, when it was permitting private "farmers' markets" to operate and inviting some foreign corporations to invest on the island. And Afro-Cuban religion seemed a good selling point for the tourist industry (CBA 340).

The state's policy toward Afro-Cuban cults definitely took a more sophisticated accommodationist approach later on in the 1980s with the appointment of Afro-Cuban specialist José Carneado Rodríguez to survey religious

activity on the island. Carneado is reported to have attended initiation
ceremonies and organized meetings between officials of the regime and Cuban babalaos. The great coup of Carneado's administration of religions was
to arrange the visit to Cuba, in June 1987, of the Oni of Ife, his Majesty
Alaiyeluwa Oba Okunade Sijuwade Olubuse II, supreme spiritual leader of
the Nigerian Yoruba. During his visit, the Oni met with top-ranking officials
of the Politburo, including Armando Hart Dávalos. After the meeting between Castro and the Oni, it was decided that the Fourth International Congress on Orisha Tradition and Culture would be held the following year in
Cuba (and not in Haiti, as originally planned) and that Cuba would install a
"José Martí Cultural Center" right in Ife. The government also received com-
mendations, reported in *Granma Weekly Review* (June 29, 1987), from the Oni
and his cultural adviser for its progress in eliminating racial discrimination
(CBA 343).

Despite the disincentives to doing so, some 85 percent of the Cuban population practices one or another Afro-Cuban religion, according to Monsignor
Carlos Manuel de Céspedes, the secretary general of Cuba's Catholic episco-
pate interviewed by Moore in 1985. African-inspired religions could no
longer be ignored, and their popularity and rootedness, Moore asserts, account for Castro's gestures of rapprochement with the Catholic Church in
1985 and 1986 as part of an attempt at "counterbalancing the Afro-Cuban
religions" (CBA 344).

To counterbalance Moore's virulent attacks against Castro's Afro-Cuban
policies somewhat (for we will not engage in a full-blown debate in these
pages; see Pérez-Sarduy's "Open Letter" for a rebuttal to Moore), one could
argue that culture—whether religious, artistic, or literary—has a special function in an embattled third world nation-state that must organize its citizenry
to do what is necessary to survive. Cultural production is not carried out in a
sociohistorical vacuum. In Cuba, the writer is not only an intellectual but
also, like it or not, an ideologue, one helping to create a feeling of commitment and solidarity among the Cubans. In the exiguity of resources and coun-
tenancing the threat of invasion and terrorism, the Cuban leadership has not
often permitted the kind of market-dominated "freedom of expression" en-
joyed by intellectuals and artists in the more developed capitalist countries.
Some have called this limitation "censorship." It means that Cuban writers
concerned with getting published and making a living have had to deal with
official constraints on discourse, including the occasions when they would
address the question of Afro-Cuban religion.

The Afro-Cuban Difference

When justifying the government's reason for prohibiting the screening of the movie P.M., whose screenplay was written by Guillermo Cabrera Infante, Fidel Castro, in a speech that would be published as *Palabras a los intelectuales* (Words to the intellectuals, 1961), stressed that some intellectual or artistic manifestations indeed "have an importance with regard to . . . the ideological formation of the people, superior to other types of artistic manifestations." In fulfilling its responsibility to "direct the people," the government claims the right to promote, regulate, and fund those works that it finds most contributory to the common welfare. What is at stake here is the question of legitimacy: at bottom, the revolutionary government has the right to decide who gets published and who doesn't, and no one has the right to dispute or question that right, for "it has not given reason to put in doubt its spirit of justice and equity" (Castro 17, 18).

Before he wrote the screenplay for P.M., Cabrera Infante had fulfilled his responsibility to direct the people by writing a story that depicted an Afro-Cuban scene while defending the right of the Revolution. The story appears among those written through the 1950s and collectively published under the title *Así en la paz como en la guerra* (In peace as in war, 1960). A kaleidoscopic vision of prerevolutionary Havana and its terrors unfolds in these pages, in which two different kinds of narrative alternate in the order of presentation. Vignettes of about a page in length depict the unromanticized violence of the era: oppressive poverty, machine gunnings, torture. These vignettes come before and after the longer stories of protagonists who, in their struggle to get by in an environment of urban decay and dispossession, remain indifferent to, although undeniably connected with, the violence of the vignettes. In the introduction to *Así en la paz*, Cabrera Infante signals the themes of the story—"En el gran ecbó" (In the great ecbó)—that concerns us here: "the loss of virginity, adultery, racial discrimination" as well as the mindset of the Cuban bourgeoisie, in whose members the contradictions of society "appear most obvious" (AP 10). The hedonistic, carpe diem atmosphere of nightclubs, television, and tourism seems to distance Cabrera Infante's bourgeois characters from the political violence depicted in the vignettes.

The intratextual relations implicit in such juxtapositions help to situate "En el gran ecbó," whose title refers to the Afro-Cuban ceremony witnessed by a young couple involved in an adulterous relationship. The story's inclusion of Afro-Cuban elements demonstrates a certain acceptance of difference and incommensurability within the space of Cuban culture, with a clear decentering of European or colonial cultural values.

Cuervo Hewitt and Luis have noted that "Ebó, ecbó, egbo or, pronounced in Cuba even with the Yoruba sound, ebbó, is a rite of purification in which offerings are made to the saints or orishas. It is commonly known as a cleansing [limpieza]" (16n. 2). Cuervo Hewitt has also noted that the story's depiction of the purification ceremony constitutes an exception to the trend among modern Cuban narratives to ironize, demystify, or even secularize Afro-Cuban religious expression (APA 278).

The adulterous couple of the story rides in the man's MG to a stadium, where, in one of its buildings, the *gran ecbó* is taking place. As they enter, the woman feels that "she ha[s] penetrated a magical world." The narrative evokes this magic by various means. First, typographically: the part of the story devoted to the ceremony is indented some five spaces for five and a half pages. The diegesis of the ceremony itself lacks capital letters and normal punctuation, creating a run-on, stream-of-consciousness effect. Second, the man and woman see "one hundred or two hundred blacks dressed in white from head to feet." They are orisha worshippers, probably devotees of Obatalá, and, chanting Congo verses in call-and-response format to the beating of drums, they dance in a circle, invoking Olofi, praying to the dead, and calling down the saint (AP 127–32).

Although the entire ritual is seen from the perspective of two white Cubans who are slumming about in Old Havana, some mysterious power issues from the ritual to touch and change their lives. First, the man explains that the ceremony is preparing a mulatto to receive the saint. The woman asks, "And can I receive it too?" The narrative cites the chanting, which includes the following phrases: "*tendundu kipungulé*"; "*naní masongo silanbasa*"; "*olofi maddié maddié olofi bica dioko bica ñdiambe olofi olofi.*" In that chant, we hear the invocation of the supreme god Olofi (Olorun, Olodumare); the call to the *kipungulé* (kimpungulu) or Congo spirits; and the exorcism of *ñdiambe* or *ñdiambe* and *dioko* (ndoki?), the evil spirits. The uncomprehending couple stays to watch and listen, enchanted. For the man, the language of the invocations is "damn theater slang," and the ceremony itself, "something barbarous and remote and alien like Africa." The woman on the other hand feels that something truly spiritual is taking place: "They don't seem ignorant to me. Primitive, yes, but not ignorant. They believe. They believe in something that neither you nor I can believe and they let themselves be guided by it and they live by its rules and die for it and afterwards they sing to their dead in accordance with its songs. I think it's marvelous" (AP 128, 130, 131).

The strangeness of the ritual and the opacity of its language, with the suggestions implanted by the man's "interpretation," work themselves into a scenario of transformation that disrupts the course of the woman's life. She reveals this change after an ancient black woman, dressed in the white of Obatalá's purity, has approached her to say, "Daughter, stop living in sin. That is all." The words have an oracular effect. The woman leaves the great ecbó; she cries; she hands the man the photograph of his wife and son (AP 133, 134–35).

For Cuervo Hewitt, the young woman's change of heart signals the presence of Obatalá as a cultural fact: "with the epiphany of a new personal alternative, the young woman in Cabrera Infante's story saw a road open up, purified, that adultery had covered over beforehand" (APA 126). Although she does not chant and dance in the ritual, and although she has been neither versed in the doctrine nor initiated into the order, the young woman at least believes in the belief she sees expressed in the ceremony. Julio Miranda confirms the view that the woman undergoes a crisis while witnessing the ecbó, "vacillating between the mystery of the black rites and the cynicism of the seduction that she has just undergone" (81). With the companion's "voiceover" translation, the event becomes a poetic turning point in the woman's life. And by its translation of the Afro-Cuban liturgy, the narrative itself performs a new literarization of Afro-Cuban culture.

Yet the story's anagnorisis and peripateia must be understood as well in terms of its theme of incomprehension. Cultural difference provides the catalyst for changing the woman's life. The relation between cultural universes staged within the story remains indeterminate and open-ended, but the story of the couple frames the display of Afro-Cuban signs and makes them over into symbols of renewal in a society distressed by the violence of the Batistato. That kind of "misreading" of Afro-Cuban religion was one that the Revolution could accept.

The Consecration of the Prime Directives

Fidel Castro pronounced as early as March of 1959, according to Salvador Bueno, that one of the Revolution's goals was to "put an end to that injustice that is racial discrimination," inaugurating with those words a national program of cultural revalorization and reformulation that has led to the founding of the Institute of Ethnology and Folklore and the National Folkloric Troupe (NNH 22).

In such official gestures, Cuban writers have read the mandate to rework Afro-Cuban religion in such a way as to make it a part of the official culture. The prologue entitled "Antes de empezar" (Before beginning), of Excilia Saldaña's Kele kele (Lucumí: Softly, softly, 1987), for instance, locates this anthology of retold patakís in the category of "Nuestro folclor afroespañol" (Our Afro-Spanish folklore) before acknowledging the transculturation that created the ethnic mixtures of Cuban society. As Saldaña puts it, "Cuba is a new and authentic product, born of Spain and Africa. To look in the mirror of that past is to see our face of today. Our Commander-in-Chief Fidel Castro already said the word: 'We are Latinoafroamericans.'" The African contribution matters as one of the three traditions in the national blend, if one counts the indigenous heritage, not only because Africanity gave Cuban society its distinctive character, but also because blacks supported and fought in the wars for independence in 1868 and 1895 (Saldaña 7, 8, 9).

Yet the same African contribution, continues Saldaña's prologue, has to be seen in a correct historical perspective. The black masses, brutalized by slavery, discrimination, and deprivation, "searched for a way out of their problems in esotericism and magic." This escape is understandable but offers no real solution to the problems created by racism or their root cause, the structure of economic inequality. In the postrevolutionary era, reasons Saldaña, it is necessary to let go of African-based religion but hold on to "the wisdom of the people" and to the elements of an autochthonous culture associated with the African presence in Cuban society. This means that the patakí-based narratives of Saldaña's collection may refer to Ochún and Oggún but must allegorically tell the story of real humans: "Because the *pataki* is addressed to men, and these are, in their daily simplicity, or sublimated to deification, the true protagonists." Humanizing the mythology of the divination narratives, Saldaña's stories are contributions to the enrichment of a national culture. Afro-Cuban culture thus gains in official recognition and legitimation what it loses in its power of mystification over erstwhile believers. The same prologue prescribes the alternative to esoteric escapism, namely, a new way of looking at Afro-Cuban religion appropriate to the historical moment:

> Contemporary reality is something else. Dispossessed of the sacred elements, the African universe of which we are beneficiaries shows itself to us in all its splendid beauty, in all its wisdom, in all . . . its universality. To ignore it is to ignore ourselves; not to know it, not to know ourselves. Many are those who have perfectly learned the Greek Olympus, but not that there exists another Olympus, tropical and their own, at the top of the hill; they know that Aphrodite "provoked," *with the apple of discord*, the war of the *Alafín of Oyo*, only by loaning him her braids. . . . "May the world be grafted onto our republics, but the trunk should be our republics," said Martí.

The rewritten patakís that Saldaña offers in *Kele kele* are now to be regarded only as literature, as aesthetic objects, as a part of mythology or of the world that should be grafted, as Martí said in the famous metaphor, to the trunk of the Cuban republic. Afro-Cuban religion forms a part of what "we" are and of what "we" should know in order to know "ourselves" once it has been taken out of the ile ocha and relegated to the archives of folklore and comparative mythology (Saldaña 10, 11).

Once the narrative of a life among the saints reaches the text of Fernández Robaina's *Recuerdos secretos de dos mujeres públicas* (Secret remembrances of two public women, 1983), Afro-Cuban religion belongs to the world of "superstitions." For Consuelo la Charmé or Violeta, who have wised up since the triumph of the Revolution, that religion is a sham consisting of an endless series of "porquerías," of worthless tricks or trifles assigned by the santero for the purpose of collecting *derechos*, his spiritual payments (RSD 56). Lourdes López's "reformed" babalao-informant, Gabriel Pasos, admits that Santería and its special branch of Ifá divination served to mystify and console the members of its marginalized believers, Pasos included. The Revolution changed all that: "The revolution," writes López, "brings this individual the solution to his material necessities, and now he begins to question the powers of the orishas as his economic problems are being resolved." Once the Revolution had triumphed, López tells us in an afterword, Pasos underwent a process of "defanatization" with the help of fellow party members from his work center (López 12, 69). Now rehabilitated, Pasos feels free to disseminate the secrets of the priestly caste to which he once belonged. And this he does in telling all for López's book.

Carpentier's aforementioned *La Consagración de la Primavera* takes a more approving, affirmative approach to Afro-Cuban religion than López and Pasos by incorporating the myths, doctrine, and ritual of the Abakuá Society into an epic vision of the twentieth-century Hispanic revolutions. Seymour Menton has compared *La Consagración* with César Leante's *Los guerrilleros negros* (The black guerillas, 1976), which depicts the struggles of runaway slaves in colonial Cuba to resist recapture and to survive in their mountain encampments or palenques. Both history-based novels, judges Menton, affirm the Communist orthodoxy and in effect add a racial dimension to the revolutionary agenda (Menton, "Novela" 917–20). Carpentier's novelized statements on Afro-Cuban religion attempted another rapprochement between Afro-Cuban religion and history-based narrative of the kind that ¡*Ecue-Yamba-O!* and *El reino de este mundo* had previously presented. Salvador Bueno characterizes *La Consagración* as a novel based on an "ecumenical conception of culture" that marks the extent to which Carpentier has evolved since the "localist limitations" of ¡Ecue-Yamba-O! (NNH 21). Within its ecumenical conception, La Consagración at the same time vindicates Afro-Cuban religion in the name of cultural particularity and authenticity within the postrevolutionary context. Carpentier's Enrique ponders the African contribution to Cuban society as he grows accustomed to the idea that his maid is an omo-Obatalá. Enrique concludes, after a period of reeducation, that the ending of racial discrimination and inequalities in Cuba has in itself justified for the Revolution, especially "since the black, despite his many miseries and humiliations, ha[s] enriched our tradition with his creative presence, contributing powerfully to giving us our own physiognomy" (Carpentier, Consagración 528).

The plot of La Consagración concerns the story of Vera, a Russian ballerina of conservative and even aristocratic ideas. Vera immigrates to the Cuba of Batista and develops her own sense of a Cuban national identity amidst the events leading up to and following the Revolution. The novel's virtual Cubanization of Vera mirrors a process of cultural hybridization occurring in the narrative itself.[1]

Vera's art of ballet itself figures in the novel as a symbol for the novel's theme of modern Hispanic revolutions: these revolutions belong to a world-historical "rite of spring," a ceremony of historical sacrifice and rebirth performed by revolutionaries of the modern age. The narrative likens their acts to those of the "original" clan, envisioned by Stravinsky and Roerich, of pagan and prehistoric Russian ancestors whose ceremonial sacrifice was intended to propitiate the earth (Carpentier, Consagración 12). (The title of the French translation, incidentally, is La Danse sacrale, 1980). In her search for the artistically new, Vera conceives the idea of choreographing Stravinsky's Le Sacre du Printemps with Afro-Cuban dancers from Guanabacoa, with motifs taken from the rites of Santería and the Abakuá. In the realizing of this plan, the avant-garde would recover the authentic gestures of a tribal past. In Vera's envisioned rewriting of Stravinsky's ballet, we could add, the meaning of "consecration" would be enriched by the Afro-Cuban sense of invoking the saint and inviting the orisha's presence into objects of ceremony or the head of the dancer. "Through the consecration," states Cabrera, "which is to say, through the transfer of a superhuman force to an object, the latter takes on personality, acquires the power, the aché of the god or of the spirit who pays attention to him" (YO 156).

Invoking that divine force in the manner of a Lucumí or Ñáñigo, Carpentier's narrative also evokes the ritual surrounding the central symbols of Abakuá faith, the speaking drum called Ecue, and the silent drum called

Seseribó, whose prototype was the drum made with the skin of Sikanecua. The narrative attempts to reconcile Abakuá myth with official culture by suggesting a number of universalizing comparisons and substitutions in the restaging of Sikanecua's sacrifice. In Vera's mind, that sacrifice, "with its mechanism of substitution, . . . was the same as Iphigenia's, offered by Agamemnon in holocaust to the Gods, and snatched away at the last moment by Artemis, while a white doe—*there* it was a doe and not a goat—whose throat was cut by the sacrificer." The black dancers of Guanabacoa, Vera reflects, will give the ballet a new interpretation in an Afro-Cuban key, making it seem, more than ever before, "truly submitted to elemental, primordial impulses." What was before an evocation of prehistoric rites has now a new frame of reference, for the "Danse sacrale" itself, says Vera to Enrique in reference to a movement in the ballet, "should resemble what you describe when you speak of women possessed by a *Santo*: ecstatic and gestural hysteria brought to paroxysm" (Carpentier, *Consagración* 261, 262). With the metaphor of possession, Vera further reworks her mythical subtext of the dance to transform it from an apotheosis of violence into a ritual of reconciliation between the natural order of the feminine with the cultural order of the masculine, an interpretation confirmed in Efik myth by Sikanecua's ascent to the kingdom of heaven to become the bride of Abasí. Consecration becomes a question of devotion, mediation, and union; it need not imitate the ritual mysogynistic violence exalted by Roerich and Diaghilev. Vera therefore plans to conclude the rite not with the sacrifice of the Virgin Elect but instead with the marriage of the divine couple (Carpentier, *Consagración* 312).

Analogously, in the marriage of Vera with Enrique, and in the progressive politicization and radicalization of both, we see the gradual reconciliation of aestheticism with revolutionary commitment. It is the vicious murder of her black dancers by Batista's gunmen that finally causes Vera to hate the regime and wish for the success of the guerrilleros in the Sierra Maestra; it is Enrique's heroism and near fatal injury at Playa Girón (the Bay of Pigs) that reunites the once estranged husband and wife in a new Cuba. Carpentier's or Vera's rewriting of the Efik myth, suggesting the symbolic resolution of tensions implicit in the novel's plot, thus proposes a mutual accommodation of politics and religion. But in their novelization, Santería and the Abakuá culture become aestheticized when viewed as material for artistic reframing and reinterpretation. They lose some of their soul, much of their mystery. Carpentier's narrative makes an analogous gesture when José Antonio, the future publicist, takes Vera on a walk past various shops representing the diverse cultures of old Havana. As they stroll along, he shows Vera a *botánica*, or religious herbal shop, in which the amulets, stones, hatchets, and other "objects of syncretic sorcery" are sold. José Antonio remarks, "Here, you find surrealism in its brute form" (Carpentier, *Consagración* 336). Whether Carpentier's novel finds more surrealism in Santería than Santería in surrealism is a moot point.

La letra con sangre (y fuego) entra

One year before Carpentier's characters in *La Consagración* would seek *le merveilleux* in Afro-Cuban ritual and myth, Manuel Cofiño's characters discovered the beauty and power of Lucumí and Abakuá religion in *Cuando la sangre se parece al fuego* (When blood looks like fire, 1977). This second novel by Cofiño follows the precedent of his *La última mujer y el próximo combate* (The last woman and the next battle, 1971) in its fragmentary style of collage and in its elaboration of the "novel of the Revolution and Reconstruction," adding a folkloric element of apparitions, brujas, and bilongos to *Cuando la sangre*. Like Manuel Granados's earlier *Adire y el tiempo roto* (Adire and the broken time, 1967), a chaotic novel that I will not examine in these pages, *Cuando la sangre* features an Afro-Cuban protagonist named Cristino, who as a revoltionary does his part in the making of modern Cuba. Yet before he commits to the cause, the Abakuá religion ties Cristino to the culture of poverty and the marginal world of the *solar habanero*, the Havana tenement. Numerous episodes in the novel refer to the Afro-Cuban religion of the solar residents, a religion that one of the novel's narrative voices identifies as a part of a past that the protagonist must overcome and forget with the help of therapy and rehabilitation. Cristino, by undergoing this regimen, subjects himself to a process of personal recentering and restructuring.

The solar in which the marginalized lives of Cristino and his neighbors take center stage, in whose central patio African culture is reborn in the singing and dancing of bembés, sustains a reminder of the plantation compound, the space in which the slaves could hold social intercourse, perform rituals, and also establish a sort of a modern "anti-plantation," where the self-employed and spiritual guides could "set up shop" (IR 239). There in the solar, in defense against hardships and calamities, it is Cristino's grandmother, Abuela, who keeps alive the old faith in the orishas.

Abuela's way of speaking makes her a mysterious, sacred being. Her religion sounds like poetry. She talks with the trees along the road in Regla. She even asks permission of a ceiba before stepping in its shade. In a spontaneous burst of synesthesia, Abuela tells a young Cristino, "Tinito, the flamboyant has heat inside the trunk and fire blows it up and it comes out through the flowers. That tree has music. Music of the wind enters through the ears, that of the flamboyant enters through the eyes." Abuela's prestige and power are enhanced when her osain, "the feathered gourd that Abuela had hanging in the backyard," is carried by the wind and left hanging in the branches of a sacred ceiba nearby (Cofiño, *Cuando* 28–29, 37). The coincidence is really a miracle within Abuela's universe, in which the supernatural is natural. Cristino recalls Abuela's words with a nostalgia for the sense of meaning, wholeness, and harmony that they produced and that subsequent events in his life would shatter.

The first paragraph of the text sets up the oppositions of past versus present, of who one was then versus who one is now. It is Cristino who now "is other," who now realizes that once, "He lived in a world of gods. Surrounded by misery, blood and dreams. In the blink of danger. In the change of one time for another. He lived in the world of saints, kings and warriors, gluttons and dancers, lechers and virgins, good and bad" (Cofiño, *Cuando* 21).

Within this retrospective frame of reference, from the perspective of a reeducated Cristino, Cofiño's narration evokes the Afro-Cuban cosmology by intercalating, between the episodes of Cristino's experience and "testimonies" provided by other characters, a series of italicized vignettes that describe the principle orishas of the Lucumí pantheon. One narrative "voice" delivers those vignettes. Its descriptions bear no direct relation with the events of the plot, but they provide an entry into the Lucumí-Ñáñigo thought-world. Beautiful unto themselves, capturing the mythopoetic allure of Afro-Cuban religion, the eighteen vignettes each profile an orisha (including the Olofi and the Jimaguas). The following is a list of the orishas profiled in the vignettes (with the corresponding page numbers):

Olofi (25)	Orisha Oko (127)
Yemayá (33–34)	Elegguá (133–34)
Osaín (38–39)	Obbá (145)
Obatalá (48–49)	Osun (168)
Ochosí (65)	los Jimaguas (179–80)
Oshún (78–79)	Oggún (186–87)
Inlé (92–93)	Babalú Ayé (200–201)
Changó (100–101)	Oyá (206–7)
Yewá (106–7)	Argayú Solá (209–10)

Alvarez rightly observes that "the vignettes about the orishas as much as the psychology of the grandmother, who is the antithesis of the new that is Cristino, her historical negator, turn out to be a swan song, a lovely

crespuscular dimension, the transmutation of a mythology based on superstition into a poetry suggestive of deep syncretic roots" (112).

The vignettes, with their impressionistic, disjointed style, contradict the
historical reason of the "realist" narrative. Yet at times they illuminate aspects
of Cristino's life in the language of myth, if we are willing to make intratextual
connections. The description of Yemayá follows shortly upon Cristino's recollection of crossing the Bay of Havana (of which Yemayá/la Virgen de Regla
is the patron saint) and the mention of Abuela's crossing herself when she
saw anything floating on its waters. The orishas are symbolic manifestations
of natural phenomena as well as psychological archetypes. The vignettes are
juxtaposed with references to other characters. Roli, the streetwise young
black who becomes a devoted disciple of Abuela, serves the revolutionary
cause as a messenger, intelligence gatherer, and bomb maker. His profile is
followed by a poetic profile of Osun, who "keeps people from trembling before death.
Without him, life is afraid of the journey without shores. Messenger of the great god and his son,
he warns of the end, and gives the final instant. Spy of the gods." In similar fashion, a
second-person characterization of Cristino as the haunted revolutionary
fighter bears some resemblance to the third-person poetic evocation of the
angry warrior Oggún: "He goes through life furious. He has never been happy" (Cofiño,
Cuando 33–34, 29, 163–64, 166–67, 168, 187). The Afro-Cuban archetypes
thus clarify the characters' experience by presenting its fictional double and
pattern.

At other times, the vignettes run counter to the realist narrative: just before the report of Cristino's impressions upon revisiting the solar in which
he lived his youth, the description of Yemayá tells us that "She reins in blue
eternity with ribbons of foam. She governs the mysteries of the salt waters" (Cofiño, Cuando
3). This Yemayá belongs to a beautiful world apart, a utopia of the spirit, and
not to the run-down apartment complex.

Both Deschamps Chapeaux and Cuervo Hewitt note that Cristino's
Náñiguismo constitutes a major obstacle that he must surmount as he joins
in the revolutionary movement initiated by Castro and his followers on July
26, 1953. Deschamps Chapeaux observes in his prologue to Cuando la sangre
that the novel gathers together cultural remnants of the past, "remainders of
yesterday," which include "religious beliefs in permanent collision with reality, people who marginalize themselves, in short; ballast tied to the heels of
the Revolution, which is being worn away into nothing by the irrepressible
force of events." For Cuervo Hewitt, the narrative demonstrates Cristino's
need to shed the encumbering beliefs in Afro-Cuban religion that have done
nothing to alleviate his family's suffering. Nor does the Lucumí-Abakuá sys-

tem, in this view, offer its believer any viable means of understanding the sociohistorical situation or of changing the living conditions of its believers (APA 279, 282). Ñañiguismo is little more than a "memory of underdevelopment," to cite the title of Edmundo Desnoes's novel. When the Revolution begins to build momentum, Cristino, like the narrator of Benítez Rojo's "La tierra y el cielo," must decide once and for all to abandon the religion and join in the struggle. Lucumí and Ñáñigo belief, lest it block the process of personalization in solidarity with the anti-imperialist struggle, must be reprocessed into folklore and become "mere" poetry—or exorcised like a ghost. "The revolutionary ideology, always in ascent, defeats the ancestral beliefs" (Deschamps Chapeaux 7).

The chiasmus of the novel's title signals both the rhetorical structure of the narrative and the form of Cristino's conversion. When Cristino was a child, his father showed him how "the fire looks like blood" when he used it to harden the wickers on the baskets he wove or to burn leaves. But Cristino knows otherwise, as the second-person narrator confirms: "You see the flames again and you think that blood looks like fire, which changes everything, destroys, creates everything and makes it born, pure and eternal, new forever and ever" (Cofiño, *Cuando* 234). Chiasmus is an antithetical repetition in which a balanced second phrase of a sentence repeats the two terms of the first phrase, but reversing them. Analogously, the general overturning of the paternal (Afro-Cuban) word and paternal order heralds the emergence of Guevara's "new man of socialism." Fire moreover constitutes a mark of Cristino's identity, linked with the word of the father, ironically foreshadowing Cristino's assignment, after the triumph of the Revolution, to the Ministry of Industries, where he designs matchboxes. (Cofiño, *Cuando* 234, 235).

In the narrative's dominant materialist perspective, Santería, like Vaudou in Carpentier's *El reino de este mundo*, is shown to lack a critical capacity to judge history, as when Abuela tells her proud story of being received in the Presidential Palace by none other than the First Lady herself, la señora Batista. "She was blinded," remarks Cristino, "by her saints, not capable of seeing nor of comprehending bitter reality. My anxieties, my uneasiness, my struggle, were alien to her." Later on, Abuela's divinations with the obí, or coconut pieces, and with the cowries of the diloggún—combined with her supplications to Ochosí, "god of prisons," and to Elegguá, "of paths and destinies"—do nothing to reveal the identity of Cristino's father's murderer. In the end, it seems to be the Department of State Security, and not Abuela's oracles, that reveals the murderer's identity: the ex-Captain Aracelio González, known as the Tiburón (Shark), his capture representing a triumph of rationalism over the failed magic arts of Abuela. In an earlier passage referring to the same event, the narrative voice tells Cristino, "what the gods could not do, humans could" (Cofiño, *Cuando* 165, 44, 239, 186).

Cuba under Castro is to be disciplined, no-nonsense, postwar, practical, and myth-poor. The change of consciousness requires a change of attitude toward language: with the Revolution, language is to become concrete, objective, unequivocal. This changeover is registered in Cristino's consciousness, confirming the assertion of the early Barthes that "myth on the left" is *"inessential"* precisely because "[R]evolution excludes myth" (*Mythologies* 146–47). For the new Cristino, now is the time to study the texts of Marxism; there is no time for orishas, those "beautiful but useless gods," who have now become "exiles in agony." In addition to his studies in the Basic School of Revolutionary Instruction and his work in the Ministry of Industries, Cristino's sessions with the psychiatrist Dr. Gutiérrez help him through a painful process of "adaptation." Cristino struggles to overcome a "personality conflict," a "situational neurosis," as documented by Gutiérrez, since Cristino is "[s]ubmitted to the pressure of the epoch and a human essence that forced him to negate his upbringing" (Cofiño, *Cuando* 225, 226, 218, 235, 202).

Yet something is lost in this deprogramming, as the narrative suggests in celebratory descriptions of the beauty and pleasure that the orishas bring into human existence. Myth is a vital component of everyday talk and provides the consensual basis of a community, as dialogues among the neighbors and family illustrate. A particular woman who "look[s] naked" even when dressed, one who rubs palm oil on her body and initiates Cristino into the mysteries of carnal love, is compared by the neighbors to Ochún. As a vignette will later illuminate, Ochún is *"the holygoddesswhore and carouser"*; and *"[w]ith a hammer she drives in love and desire in the hearts of people"* (Cofiño, *Cuando* 59–60, 78, 79). By these intratextual connections, the two worlds, of the solar and of Lucumí myth, intersect and interilluminate. The latter gives perspective and poetic depth to the former.

In addition to mythical narratives from the religion, Cofiño includes interesting examples of bilongos and cures that Abuela performs for her family. Cristino recalls the failed ritual with which Abuela attempted to discover her son's murderer: "At twelve midnight we went to the Luyanó River. She grasped a piece of black cloth, crumpled it, tied knots in it and threw it into the river. 'There I throw the life of the one who killed my son.' She took out a black hen from the bag and opened it up with the knife. She took out its intestines and threw them into the river. Afterwards she ran the hen through with the knife and left it fixed in the ground. 'As this hen rots, so will rot the one who killed my son'" (Cofiño, *Cuando* 58). The setting at the riverside recalls numerous Yoruba river gods—Yemonjá, Erinle or Inle, Yewá, Ondo, Oba, Oshun, Are—and suggests their divine intervention in the revenge plot (YSN 87–90). The knotted cloth and the black chicken, by a substitutive or metaphoric logic, stand in for the unidentified killer.

By the novel's dominant rationalist logic, Abuela's bilongo comes to no avail, for it does not operate within the Revolution's narrative of liberation. Within another narrative framework, however, it could be said that Abuela's bilongo does work nonetheless. The killing of the black and white hens by the river does at least precede the discovery of the murderer by state security (Cofiño, *Cuando* 58, 238). It would be presumptuous to say that the ritual does not work simply because the state was the agency of that vengeance: the desired event did, after all, come to pass. At this level of *post hoc* narratization, the novel does give some credence to Abuela's magical conflation of causality with sequentiality rather than simply allowing the scientific, rationalistic explanation to prevail unchallenged.

In the end, however, the orishas are defeated by the goddess Reason. After massacring her animals, destroying her cane, and smashing her saints, a devastated Abuela is forced by her profound disillusionment to swallow her own tongue, painfully committing suicide in a manner once practiced by slaves during the colonial period. Yet Afro-Cuban practices continue after Abuela's death. In the funeral ceremony or ituto dedicated to her, Abuela is buried with her cowries, with corn, smoked hutia, and fish; she is dressed in the same blue dress she wore as an initiate in Abakuá; a black cock is killed. And her followers continue to look to Abuela for guidance even after her death. Cristino comments, "The site where she was buried became a place of pilgrimage. For a long time they said that Abuela was making prodigies and miracles. They said that a seagull fluttered above the cross, that at night a blue fire was seen, and if you came close, a smell of the sea came from the earth. And I don't know who planted leadworts around her tomb." The evocative passage indicates how faith continues to find the signs that validate faith in a way that finds and makes poetic beauty on the occasion of the santera's death. Nonetheless, it is Abuela's suicide—along with the later revelation that Abuela's grave has been opened, desecrated, her bones used in ngangas and amulets—that seals the novel's condemnation of Abuela's Afro-Cuban magic (Cofiño, *Cuando* 228–29, 230, 231, 242).

There is no happy synthesis or crossing of cultural universes here; incommensurability and conflict are accentuated, not smoothed over, as they are in

Carpentier's balletic vision. Since the dominant code of Cofiño's novel obeys the imperative of the Revolution, orisha-worship comes to appear at best an irrelevance, at worst, an impediment to needed social change. An epigraph by Marx at the opening of the novel already anticipated the competition between rival interpretations: "Every mythology subdues, dominates, molds the forces of nature in the imagination; and therefore disappears when those forces are truly dominated" (Cofiño, *Cuando* 19). The explicit message seems clear enough: that mythology belongs to "mere" imagination and can be dispensed with once the forces of nature have been brought under scientific, "real" control.

Yet I would insist that another reading of the epigraph, one subversive of the novel's explicit message, is tenable: the "forces of nature" that can be dominated, "realmente dominadas," are none other than "las fuerzas de la naturaleza en la imaginación," that is to say, those forces conceived mythologically, forces "in the imagination" that periodically requires the formation of another "mythos" (for example, the "mythos" of enlightenment reason, science, progress, dialectical materialism, or official history) to subjugate and mold the forces of nature, such that one narrative paradigm can be said to overpower and subsume another. *Cuando la sangre* does not so much discredit Afro-Cuban religion as demote it in favor of the myth of materialism, legitimizing the revolutionary ethos at the expense of other, less "scientific" versions of the truth. That is to say, the secular myth of the Revolution displaces and devalues the sacred myth of the Ecue and the orishas. Yet the metalanguage used to demystify the Ñáñigo cult, even to wrest legitimacy from it in calling it a "cult" rather than a bona fide religion, must itself become subject to demystification and analysis. Socialist ideology, like Santería, has its limitations and blindnesses, and so the text of the novel pushes against the totalizing and historicizing monism preached by the narrative voice of officialdom. With its kaleidoscopic shifting of perspectives, this multivoiced narrative projects a view of reality that is more pluralistic than that valorized by the explicit narrative. Yet by Cristino's conversion to the revolutionary program, the narrative's voice of reason is allowed to drown out the minoritarian voices of religious myth and doctrine. Orisha worship, after all, does not cut the sugar cane or defend the Revolution against its enemies.

If, as Cofiño's novel illustrates, Afro-Cuban religious culture comprises a body of narrative knowledge opposed to the materialist culture sanctioned by the state, the menace of Afro-Cuban religion so conceived must be managed, reworked, sometimes tamed, sometimes refitted and rechanneled, deterritorialized and reterritorialized to serve the common good as defined by the state. Although the practice of Afro-Cuban religion was suppressed or discouraged from 1959 to the 1970s, a revised Afro-Cubanism could function to promote nationalist values and denounce imperialism. Beginning around 1977, Afro-Cuban myth and scholarship in Afro-Cuban religion thus underwent a certain museumizing folklorization, as evident in exhibitions of Afro-Cuban culture in old Havana, in the small museum adjoined to the cathedral of Regla, and in the cultural centers of Santiago de Cuba. As an alternative to outright prohibition, an overall strategy of containment, secularization, aestheticization, and possibly commodification has become the preferred method.

In the Folklore Museum

Folklorization serves to relegate a vital, lived cultural form to the category of the artistic and picturesque, thus neutralizing its ideological power. Barnet looks on this process of aestheticization with approval: "From Santería, from the wealth of its songs and dances, of its mythology, will remain those permanent values in the purely aesthetic order. The allegory to its philosophical and cosmogonic models will also be valid in artistic and literary creation" (FV 197). Moore disapprovingly argues on the other hand that the Cuban government has attempted to folklorize Afro-Cuban religion in order to send out a deceptive message that it was promoting both its growth in particular and black ethnic expression in general. In December 1961, Moore states by way of illustration, the National Institute of Ethnology and Folklore, led by Argeliers León and Isaac Barreal, was commissioned to study all aspects of Afro-Cuban culture, including music, mannerisms, and customs. Of the Afro-Cuban religions especially targeted, according to an announcement at the opening of the Institute, were "those sects which have come into conflict with the Revolution" (CBA 99–100).

Folklorization is not necessarily an unhealthy development, however, as some materialist theory suggests. In his essay "Observations on Folklore," Antonio Gramsci writes, in a manner anticipating James Figarola's defense of a "mulatto culture," that "folklore" should be studied seriously as the artistic and religious expression of the popular masses. For folklore in this view is a multifaceted reflection of a popular consciousness and often articulates concepts of "natural right" that coincide with official concepts, as was the case with French Catholicism and the liberal ideology of the French Revolution. In so politicizing folklore and recognizing its antihegemonic potential, Gramsci values what Raffaele Corso has called the "contemporary pre-history" sustained in its multilayered, heterogeneous genres. At the same time, folklore and the art of the dominant class do not necessarily represent opposed values, for they sustain an interrelationship analogous to that of the artisanal "arte menor" with the higher and more prestigious "arte mayor." Popular verbal art has always drawn upon the art of the elites but remains "fragmentary" and "unstable": "folklore has always been tied to the culture of the dominant class and, in its own way, has drawn from it motifs which have then become inserted into combinations with previous traditions. . . . It deals, in any case, with a relative and disputable 'pre-history' and there could be nothing vainer than to try to find the different stratifications in a single folklore area." By recombining motifs "with previous traditions," art promises a positive redefinition or regeneration of the national culture. Because the sources of this stratified folkloric content are usually difficult to trace and because folklore "is much more unstable and fluctuating than language and dialects," folkloric taxonomies must for the most part remain conjectural and analyses of form and content for the most part semantic (Gramsci, *Cultural Writings* 194–95). By affirmation or negation or both, it has been the function of cultural politics in Cuba to deal with the indeterminacy of folklore, to manage its freeplay with elements of tradition and with the official culture.

Although the Cuban revolutionary regime once attempted to suppress or extirpate Afro-Cuban religion, it seems to have shifted its attitude to accommodate a concept of folklore similar to Gramsci's. Various treatments of Afro-Cuban "folklore," such as those by Carpentier and Cofiño that we have discussed, exhibit this integrating impulse to categorize, contain, and control it such that it "does its part" for the social whole. Sacred narratives lose their authority, but they are refunctioned to participate in a broader narrative of self-determination. Barnet refers to the process of by which myths are secularized: "They are beginning to lose that religious core [*médula*, marrow] in order, without weakening, without losing their original beauty, to transform themselves into an accepted and even functional popular history. Functional because, although myth serves as a religious background, the people use it to explain many things" (FV 159). The explanatory, illustrative or instrumental function of myth designates the use that the realist postrevolutionary writer would make of it. Another way to make myth serve politics is to preserve it and publish it while avoiding comment on the political implications it might have.

The fourteen pataki-based narratives of Martínez Furé's collection *Diálogos imaginarios* (Imaginary dialogues, 1979) are included in the article titled "Patakín: literatura sagrada de Cuba" (Patakís: sacred literature of Cuba).

Martínez Furé's versions of the patakís, like their oral "originals," exemplify the procedures that the clients of the babalao should follow in order to solve their problems. Within the "imaginary dialogues" of which they form a part, the divination stories legitimate the divination ritual itself, by illustrating the consequences of carrying through—or not carrying through—the instructions of Ifá. In addition, the stories display their own "packaging" as artifacts for folkloric consumption, complete with classifications, glosses, and footnotes.

The patakís have been divided into myths and fables. The myths tell of the lives and exploits of the orishas, recounting the creation of the world and humans and often explaining the origins of practices or prohibitions. The fables, on the other hand, feature animals as characters and serve to teach a moral value, often castigating antisocial behavior motivated by greed, envy, sloth, and pride (DI 213–14). Martínez Furé lists a number of features of this oral literature, of which an abbreviated version follows:

1. Simple and direct style.
2. Magical realism.
3. Reiteration as a stylistic element.
4. Insertion of songs within narrations.
5. Shifts in verbal tense from past to present and vice versa.
6. Didacticism and moralizing, explicit in the end proverb.
7. Propaganda exalting the priestly caste.
8. Universal symbolism; exaltation of human and social values.

In addition to listing these features, Martínez Furé briefly characterizes the three "levels of development and antiquity" of his patakís: the oldest, of strictly Yoruba "content"; the intermediary, presenting a mixture of African and colonial cultures; and the most recent, developed in Cuba on the Yoruba model (DI 216–17). Through his presentation of myths and folktales, Martínez Furé resumes the work of compilation initiated by Ortiz, Cabrera, and Lachatañeré in the first half of the century and thus maintains a safe distance from political agendas and exigencies.

A Poetry Out of Orbit

Explicit references to Afro-Cuban religion in the postrevolutionary era, especially to the Ñáñiguismo of Regla and Marianao, appear in Dora Alonso's "Los ojos de Simón" (Simon's eyes, from Cuentos [Stories], 1976). The story expresses skepticism toward the beliefs of its Ñáñigo characters yet sympathy for their plight and understanding for their desire to find solace in the orishas. In elegiac tones, the narration recreates the mythical Afro-Cuban world as a "desorbitada poesía"—an uncommon, out of proportion, "out-of-orbit" poetry—whose beauty is comforting yet useless.

The story's narration tells us that Simón Valdés is a dwarf. The story opens with reference to the death of Simón's santera mother and of Simón looking through her cuarto fambá, which he has inherited, "with the hope of finding something more than the adorned canopied altar, dressed up with indigo blue satin, where the Virgin of Regla, covered with necklaces, looked with knowing eyes." The text evokes childhood impressions of drums, attributes, mysteries. "Iremes danced between vegetable beats of bitter broom, and the men came to be initiated before the ceiba and the royal palm" (Alonso, *Cuentos* 197). The text prepares us for the appearance of orishas.

Yet the invocations of his parents and the "Morúa Yansa" of the Abakuá potencia have no power to cure Simón of his dwarfism. The narrative goes on to interweave citations of the Lucumí hagiography into a history of Simón's growing mental alienation as Simón's parents attempt other cures. A rooster passed over Simon's body, by a logic of metonymy, should have taken away the evil or poetic cause of Simón's defect, but this cure fails, as does a purification invoking the Ireme Encánima and a streaking with *yeso*, chalk, or *efún* (ground eggshell) (Alonso, *Cuentos* 198–99). The allusion to Obatalá as Simón's "godfather" is apt because he is the orisha credited with fashioning human bodies, and so he bears the blame for creating human deformities.

In Simón's eyes, the zoo where he obtains employment provides ample opportunity for reestablishing the *desorbitada poesía* of his own orisha-worship. Because here, for Simón, the gods are present. "He couldn't help but notice that the place where so many animals and plants were gathered together was inhabited by the black gods and presided by Osaín, the owner of the Mountain. Simón takes refuge in the zoo. He feels at home there, especially after disturbances take place around the university involving a cadaver, police, and tear gas. As a zoo attendant and feeder, Simón can continue to make offerings to the orishas of their favorite foods: "And to Eleggua he would bring mice and cane liquor; tomatoes to Changó, saving for Obatalá, all white of starch and jasmines, the sweet pulp of the custard apples." The narrator does not fail to mention that some orishas arrived dressed up as Catholic saints, "in the symbiosis imposed by the white slaveholders" (Alonso, *Cuentos* 200, 202, 203). Simon's adherence to the Abakuá ways even after the triumph of the Revolution constitutes not so much a counterrevolutionary stance as an adjacent and complementary way of interpreting reality. It does not interfere with revolutionary politics as usual at any rate. As Cuervo Hewitt notes, "Simón defers to the presence of a mythological dimension, anachronistic, contiguous to the political events of a Revolution, from which the socio-political situation is perceived as one more manifestation of the invisible natural forces that live with man and are never used up because they are always eternal" (APA 94).

Yet some awareness of that sociopolitical situation is registered in the arrival, at the zoo, of a new group of hybrids—composite creatures, monstrosities combining animal and human parts, including centaurs and merpeople: all in all, "[a] group that mixed horns, manes, feathers and scales in a single anguish." The newcomers join the company of the zoo animals and the black gods, "who perhaps would be able to understand their different form, perhaps disposed by Olofi, the only one, he who knows why things are that nobody understands, the Olorun who doesn't come down to the world to fix it" (Alonso, *Cuentos* 204, 205). The creator allows the suffering of this world, epitomized by Simón's suffering, to continue without surcease. In the eyes of Simón, the world and zoo become a bestiary of sad and fantastical creatures. Although the disorbited poetry of the orishas once created a *schöneWelt* of illusory transcendence, the uneasy awareness of the orisha's makeshift construction intensifies Simón's feelings of alienation and absurdity. "Los ojos de Simón" thus sings an elegy of Afro-Cuban religion as only religion, or as an errant satellite orbiting around an anxious planet.

From Where the Singers Would Be

What could be paradoxically called the "classic" postmodern treatment of Afro-Cuban religion in Cuban prose fiction succeeds in evoking the desire for unification and centering of religious discourse as it simultaneously displays a secularizing impulse to deflate religious claims to transcendence. A double tendency implicit in the verbal aspect of religion itself, one that tends toward both centering and decentering, characterizes Severo Sarduy's *De donde son los cantantes* (Where the singers are from, 1967), which was written in Paris under the influence of the "Tel Quel" group of structuralist-poststructuralist theorists, far from the scrutiny of Cuban culture ministers and their Union of Writers and Artists.[2] Rather than attempt to unearth the deep symbols of religious meaning, as Cofiño's novel does with a certain solemnity, Sarduy's "telquelian" narrative careens irreverently through the extensive regions composed by religion's networks of signifiers. The novel's treatment of Afro-Cuban religion is "superficial"—in the sense of "shallow" but also in the sense of scanning signifying surfaces producing the illusion of depth. What matters is not the search for the meaning but following a map of consciousness, with the understanding that the terrain through which the map guides the traveler very much resembles a torn and possibly crumpled map (of maps) in itself.

Julio Miranda describes *De donde son los cantantes* as "a sort of dynamic collage, continually superimposing new elements in a discourse situated on the level of metaphor" (92). The characters of that dynamic collage are more narrative functions than characters, for they put on and take off personalities like so many masks, and they embark on a phantasmagorical journey beginning in republican Cuba, going back to medieval Spain, and then returning to Cuba. Undergoing those transformations and translations, they pass through the three immigrant cultural worlds that together sum up the ethnic mix of *la cubanidad*: the Chinese, the African, and the Spanish. The African elements appear in what Miranda calls "a heavily ornamented procession of pseudomiracles from Santiago de Cuba to the capital." The crossing from east to west, from Santiago to Havana, gives some structure to an otherwise chaotic narrative as it also suggests the parade of the comparsa of the carnival group, whose activities in Epiphany or Holy Week street celebrations hark back to Kongo and Yoruba ritual processions (Miranda 92, 123–24; see Thompson, "Recapturing" 19–20).

Selfhood in this extroverted world of simulacra and appearance is not essence but artifice, or "self-service," to use the narrative's term. For after applying wig, eyeshadow, and beauty marks, Socorro does not forget to put on her "Yoruba necklaces," the elekes whose colored beads probably include in this instance the yellows of Ochún and the blues of Yemayá. The general who lusts after Socorro's "twin," Auxilio, wears a uniform and medals and invokes "the invincible Changó." The mutating, name-changing Mortal Pérez, obsessed with the Chinese opera singer Flor de Loto (Lotus Flower) or Cenizas de Rosa (Rose Ashes) becomes el Matarife (the Butcher) and el Libidinoso (the Libidinous one), and Flor de Loto turns into Chola Angüengue, the *Ochún conga* whom the text perhaps erroneously identifies as "the queen of arms," an epithet perhaps more appropriate for Changó as Santa Bárbara (Sarduy, *De donde* 14, 19).

Yet these identifications are not fixed indefinitely nor does the archetypal reading reveal any "secret" fundament of identity. True to their names, Socorro and Auxilio are no one in themselves but both give help and cry out for it. As mutually duplicating twins they are themselves as lacking in essence as

Cabrera Infante's starstruck Arsenio Cué and Silvestre. In the already cited chapter titled "A New Version of Events: Parca and General," the desire-driven pursuit is underway, and the narrator says that "the Pyrrhic invoked the patroness of artillerymen, the invincible Changó, to which she responded by appealing to the queen of river and sky, her antidote and *detente*: you don't know anything yet." Counterbalancing the General's invocation of Changó/ Santa Bárbara, the epithet "queen of the river and the sky" again refers to Ochún, and the *detente* is the painted or embroidered image of the saint worn, like a talisman, on the chest. Yet the object of the General's desire is but the mirage projected narcissistically by his self's own need: the image of La Ming pursued by "G" is therefore nothing more than "a pure absence, she is what she is not," such that the conquest of La Ming would indeed constitute a costly, Pyrrhic victory for the other-centered self. The image in the mirror of the self-service café, while suggesting this specular interplay of self and other, evokes the number four, sacred number of completion or totality, although this described vision may be purely "imaginary": "So it is that, seen from above, from an imaginary mirror that we can situate for example above the cash register of the self-service . . . the whole is a giant four-leaf clover, or an animal that looks toward the four cardinal points, or a Yoruba sign of the four roads" (Sarduy, *De donde* 19, 61, 38, 20–21). The four-leaf clover mirrors the quadripartite concept of Cuban culture as a blending of the Spanish, African, Chinese, and the virtually extinct Indian cultures. It also emulates the Bantu *tendwa nzá kongo*, charting the daybreak, noon, sunset, and midnight: the four points of the sun's revolution around the world of the living and the world of the dead. Those four cardinal points of the cosmos are repeated again in the crossroads of Elegguá and the four corners of the Board of Ifá, which symbolizes the world and whose four cardinal points are called *ati guoro, ati guale, ati gualone,* and *ati cantari* (see Sánchez-Boudy 34, 21). Before setting off on her journey toward Havana and literary immortality, Dolores Rondón recalls having offered fruits to the saints of her altar, "asking then that they open up the four roads to me" (Sarduy, *De donde* 82). The sacred number four also refers to the four days that it took Oddudua or Ochanla to create the world. In Sarduy's text, the four—itself a doubled double—thus constitutes the symbol that refers to all other symbols, or a metasymbol, figured here by the metaphor of the doubled reflection and the schema of the doubled self facing its doubled other.

The implication is that there is no religious transcendence except in specular doublings and shifting symbolizations, which are implied in the very being of literature and its (non)relation to some nonlinguistic reality. In pedantic reply to Narrator One's equating literature with an emetic, Narrator Two confirms that writing induces disgorgement or at least works a nontranscendent spewing-forth of words on words and things, for all words and things, if they are and mean anything, are part of everything and grounded ultimately upon nothing: "everything returns to everything, that is to say to nothing, nothing is everything" (Sarduy, *De donde* 58). Language, that is to say, and literature as its test case have no ultimate referent in either empirical or transcendental "reality." The ambiguous divine absence is related to the "sixty-four-thousand-dollar question, the definition of being," or, which is the same question, the ground of being itself.

In an illuminating gloss on Heidegger, Kenneth Burke has reasoned that the ground of being can only be Nothing, the ultimate context and counterpart of being (RR 25). In the first chapter of the "Curriculum Cubense" section of the novel, Auxilio has already given Socorro the contradictory word on being and nonbeing: "This is the situation: we have remained and the gods left, they took the boat, they went in trucks, they crossed the border, they shit in the Pyrenees. They all left. This is the situation: we left and the gods remained. Seated. Lying low, taking a siesta, enchanted by life, dancing the Ma Teodora, the initial *son*, the repetitive *son*, turning the air, as if they were hanged." Identity is left hanging in the void by the departure of the transcendent; but then again, that void is filled by sacred/secular song or the repetitive force of the orishas' personality within the realm of culture, or by the layering of signifying surfaces in the palimpsest of Cuban religious cultures. The *son* or Afro-Cuban song that is repeated is the figure that fills the void, giving the illusion of depth to the palimpsest, which is after all only sedimented writing(s). In this twilight, the idols are but a flickering phantasmic presence, a part of popular culture, as observed in the narrative's "Sexteto habanero": "The gods / went away, they stayed, / those who died with Beny Moré who hallucinated with him, / or still live in the Havana orchestras" (Sarduy, *De donde* 12, 98).

By thus equivocating with its impudent double-talk, Sarduy's text rehearses the interplay of divine being and absence in the modern world. The transvestites Auxilio and Socorro are mirror images of each other's appearance but also reflections of the images of femininity handed down by cabaret culture and orisha worship. Socorro, as much as Auxilio, is judged as "[i]nesencial" outside the "Domus Dei," but then again, their inessentiality is the "essence" of the human. Their Cuban identity has no core but relies on a series of specular (mis)identifications with each other or with the orishas. In a later section, Dolores Rondón, the "*mulata wifredolamesca*" (Wifredo Lamesque mulatta) described as "steeped [*calada*] in saints," will in reiterative fashion declare herself "legitimate daughter of Ochún, the queen of the river and heaven" (Sarduy, *De donde* 13, 60–61). Like an Ochún of the patakís, Dolores will journey in search of her fortune, but not from the river to Olofi's hill; she will make her way from Camagüey toward Havana, where she will join Senator Mortal Pérez and make her debut.

Artifice—in the form of makeup, clothing, transvestitism, ritual, language, and art—fills in the lack of this "female" inessentiality. In the chapter "Orquestica sivaica" (Little Shivaic orchestra) of the section "By the River of Rose Ashes," Auxilio and Socorro have been transformed into the semblance of the Hindu deity of destruction, or into the Bald Divinities, and they are seated and riding on their motor scooters. A description of their movements prompts the following comparison: "As on a Yoruba altar the heads of the saints shine in the chalice, surrounded by rotten fruits and roosters with their throats cut, so among horns and levers, emerge the heads of the Dead-Alive (*Muertas-Vivas*): white eyes on white faces, hairs of mint crowned by flames, broken eyelids from which roll two little threads that divide their faces into fringes, Byzantine coins" (Sarduy, *De donde* 36). On the altar desecrated by the remains of offerings, the dead chickens lie in a jumble of symbols signifying nothing but their own drained symbolicity. The passage consists of one extended simile likening the iconic image of santos to the reincarnated jimaguas, now both dead and alive, the appropriate dual condition for textual bearers of texts. The two transvestites are "Byzantine coins," both displaying the formalized, colorful figures of Byzantine religious subjects in gold or mosaic and embodying the doubleness-duplicity symbolized in the two sides of a coin. It is appropriate that Shiva the destroyer should preside over the sacrifice, a symbolic act joining death with life in a single two-sided gesture reinscribing the difference. The immortality that religion promises is neither the one of heavenly salvation nor the other of enchainment to the wheel of life and death: it is instead the endless recurrence of a figural language, the self-reproduction of the signs and symbols that betokens transcendence but delivers instead the endless relay of their deferred meaning.

By foregrounding the self-referring facts of language and artifice in the manner just described, Sarduy in *De donde son los cantantes* and other texts displays the hallowed but hollow signifier of the Afro-Sino-Hispanic religious system(s). Philip Barnard, translator of Sarduy's *Para la voz* (For voice, 1978), corroborates our judgment that Sarduy's work "exemplifies a displacement of literature onto a negative, plural, empty movement of language, rather than repressing that movement, suppressing literature (in other words rhetoric) in favor of its ostensible aesthetic or ideological value" (10). Yet this "empty" rhetoric, in signifying nothing, signifies its own self-replenishing creative power of signification and/or signification of creative power. Brahma creates and Vishnu upholds and Shiva destroys what Brahma creates, and so on. Upon a layer of recodified Hindu signs, the signs of Afro-Cuban religion reinscribed in Sarduy's textual palimpsest trace out a possible route through fragments of rites and myths—scenarios of transmogrification—by which the reading subject vicariously experiences the alternating creation and destruction of the already "vicarious" self.

Journey Back to the Source

By its refusal of transcendental signifieds, the postmodern discourse of signifying surfaces, polysemy, masking, fragmentation, and self-recursive verbal play exhibited in *De donde son los cantantes* does not simply destroy religious meaning but foregrounds the aesthetic mechanisms working toward building coherence, continuity, order, community, and effects of meaning in religious signification. In contrast to Sarduy's novel, Eugenio Hernández Espinosa's drama *María Antonia* (1979) presents those mechanisms from the perspective of belief. The drama defies dessicating analysis in entertaining the possibility that the Lucumí "metaphors of divinity" are somehow divine metaphors "in truth," and not only metaphors of other metaphors. The play appeared at a time when folklorization under the government's auspices was the official policy, but it has a reputation in Cuba for fidelity to the language, ritual, and myth of Lucumí religion.

The play's protagonist is María Antonia, beautiful and sensuous daughter of Ochún; in Sergio Giral's movie based on the play, she wears diaphanous yellow. More exactly, María Antonia emulates Ochún Shekeshé Afígueremo, the happy one who lives at the river's mouth and tempts the surly Oggún to come down from his forest retreat (Hernández Espinosa 116). María Antonia thus embodies a Cuban archetype, the passionate mulatta who steals away husbands. And María Antonia believes in the saints, although she does not always obey them.

The opening scene of *María Antonia* presents the character of the Madrina conducting a limpieza or cleansing with Cumachela and the protagonist. The

Madrina departs from the normal protocol, first invoking "Baba Orúmila," or Ifá, and then praying for protection from the great evils of this life: "kosí aro, kosí ikú, kosí eyé, kosí efó, kosí iña, kosí achelú, iré owó"; that is, "Grant that there be no sickness, nor death, nor blood, nor curse, nor dishonor, nor quarrel, nor trouble with justice, with a blessing of money" (see Cabrera, AVL 194, 288). Next, the Madrina continues the ceremony in Lucumí, praying to Ochún, María Antonia's orisha, that she lead and not abandon her daughter. *Moforibale*, or respectful greetings, go to Elegguá, Olofi, Changó, and Yemayá. With the registro or consultation of the babalao, María Antonia learns that someone has thrown her a curse ("Le han echado un daño"), and that she has lost her aché ("lo ha perdido"). To restore María Antonia to happiness, it will be necessary to cleanse her thoroughly. Madrina tells the babalao, "Erase her inside. Pull her out by the roots and sow her again" (Hernández Espinosa 7–8, 9, 10). Thus with metaphors that invoke replanting and writing (or more precisely, its negation, as in "Bórrela"), the divination scene demonstrates the manner in which the Afro-Cuban oracle introduces a new narrative into the subject's construction of the real, such that the individual may comprehend "life" as a coherent narrative. If a goal is wished for within the context of the new narrative, the reality to which the client aspires, as James Figarola puts it, "does not substitute factual reality but rather rises up inside it, and within it emphasizes the attitude and even the struggle for a better situation" (SMD 76). Through divination, imagination serves the ends of self-perfection or of self-fulfillment, through the imagining of a new configuration of facts. Yet the individual must take the initiative—by performing sacrifice and making an effort—to change the basic situation. This María Antonia refuses to do.

The second babalao warns María Antonia of the disaster her disobedience invites. He throws the ekuelé necklace and gives this counsel: "Hum, if you don't know the law by which you have to live here, you will learn it in the other world. . . . Look, the sailor is the son of the sea, exposed to whatever the sea wishes. You like putting yourself above other people. So you understand me better, you had wanted things that don't belong to you." A "bad woman," a "homewrecker" who has already twisted the path of more than one man, María Antonia does not heed the law of her community. Others disapprove of her behavior, call her a troublemaker, and throw water out into the street to dispel her disruptive influence (Hernández Espinosa 12, 68). Her offense is "bravuconería," insolence—but she, like the sailor subject to the law of the sea, will suffer the consequences of misbehavior.

María Antonia does indeed "twist the path" of the boxing champion Julián—fighting son of Oggún—by performing a "tying" ritual, an amarre, to bind up his desire. That ritual consists of calling a personal "ánima" and all other souls or spirits of earth and sea. Then María Antonia verbalizes the the desired outcome: that Julián follow behind her "like the dead man behind the cross and the live one upon the cross." Julián's desire is finally "tied" when María Antonia pronounces the formula, "with two I measure him and with three I tie him, the blood of his heart I drink and his heart I snatch away." The surrounding chorus of iyalochas comments by uttering Yoruba-Lucumí proverbs: "Cabeza tiene mala cosa"—"Head has something bad"—and the saying that corresponds to Okana sode and Ofún: "¡La fosa está abierta!," "The grave is open!" Disregarding the babalao's warning in acting on her passion for Julián, María Antonia puts a magic powder in his chequeté, a drink popular in Santería. Unexpectedly, the potion kills him (Hernández Espinosa 58, 89).

The play comments on that action and declares its own "thesis" in the scene of its tenth "cuadro" or frame, where the Madrina delivers a lengthy monologue while possessed by Yemayá, who speaks through her. Yemayá laments the lot of her children, delivered over to crimes of blood and destructive passion. "Man, look at man!," she cries; "you offer sacrifices in vain if you don't clean your house which is my house. The day will come when you learn to walk with a strong and tranquil step." Yet that day never comes for María Antonia. The proverb from a second Ifá reading ominously reveals that she has turned things upside down: she should have remembered that "the head is what leads the body." Repulsed and sickened by her destructive irresponsibility, she attempts to renounce men and reject the overtures of her former lover, Carlos. Angered by the rebuff, Carlos thrusts a knife into her groin (Hernández Espinosa 100, 105, 107–9).

María Antonia dies, the victim of her destiny, an Afro-Cuban destiny foretold in the odu figures of the Lucumí religion to which she subscribed. Hernández Espinosa's Afro-Cuban play and the divination ritual that it stages rehearse mutually reflecting scenarios of narrative transitions from structure to structure, crystallizing as they contemplate the "world of desire" (see Frye 184). By her dependence on divination and magic, María Antonia exemplifies the subject's empowering-disempowering accession to the Afro-Cuban sign-world of desire, a signifying web that generates the desire it must inevitably frustrate. The inexorable force that attracts her toward her tragic end is the same hipertelia de la inmortalidad (hypertelia of immortality) that draws Lezama Lima's José Cemí through the labyrinth of forms toward a center in which awaits death or the *paradiso* (Lezama Lima 288). In this fashion, Afro-Cuban religion mediates the subject's, María Antonia's, desire as it constitutes the very subject of that desire.[3]

For all its personal satisfactions, whether real or imagined, however, Afro-Cuban religion, like Haitian Vaudou, and like Brazilian *Candomblé* for that matter, cannot lay a strong claim to achieving the public good. Hernández Espinosa's play demonstrates some of the psychological benefits offered by Afro-Cuban religion, but reforming land distribution, nationalizing industries, and building schools are simply not on the religion's agenda, for it has no plan or program of its own to speak of. In an illuminating text comparable with the ones examined in this book, the *pai de santo* named Jubiabá, in Jorge Amado's novel of the same name (1935), plays no effective part in the Bahian labor movement. The novel's protagonist, Antônio Balduíno, comes to realize the priest's uselessness for the social struggle: "He is amazed that Jubiabá knows nothing about the strike. Jubiabá knows stories of slave days and things about spirits; he is free, yet he has never taught the enslaved people of the hill anything about the strike." As this quote indicates, Jubiabá's function in Amado's novel is to provide its characters with spiritual guidance, with cures and spells, and with a sense of history in stories of slave revolt and marronnage such as that of Zumbi of Palmares. Above all, Jubiabá provides the magical means of solving life's difficulties, as when Antônio thinks that Jubiabá would be able to save a certain woman from prostitution by casting a spell on the man who exploits her (Amado 272, 197). Jubiabá, Antônio concludes, will take care of the workers' spiritual welfare, but the business of changing history remains for the workers to take into their own hands.

A similar agreement to disagree, to settle for the complementary coexistence of incommensurate sign systems, seems to have been struck in Cuba. The Revolution is no longer the water that extinguishes the fire of religion. It may even see itself fanning the flames a bit in the near future, if the travel ban on the isolated and impoverished island is lifted and waves of tourists and scholars, "tempted by folklore," to cite one of Willy Chirino's song lyrics, decide to make that ninety-mile journey to the source.[4]

⬦ Notes

Chapter One: Afro-Cuban Religion in Narrative

1. See Burke, *The Rhetoric of Religion*, 7–8, on this economic circulation of supernatural and secular terms.

2. On the primacy of "iterability," see Derrida, "Signature Event Context," 179–80.

3. Castellanos and Castellanos, *La cultura afrocubana* 1:25. The figure is extrapolated from Philip D. Curtin's estimate of 702,000 slaves brought to Cuba, D. R. Murray's 820,000, and Manuel Moreno Fraginals's 1,012,386.

4. For a more extensive discussion of Cartesianism's ideological consequences, see Matibag, "Reason and the State."

5. See Descombes, *Modern French Philosophy*, 85–87, on basic concepts of "structural analysis."

Chapter Two: The Lucumí Sign System

1. The following section was adapted from my "Yoruba Origins of Afro-Cuban Culture."

2. The works to which I refer most frequently in this section on the diloggún include the following: García Cortez, *El Santo*; Cabrera, *Yemayá y Ochún*; Bascom, *Sixteen Cowries*; Rogers, *Los caracoles*; Cros Sandoval, *La religión afrocubana*; de la Soledad and Sanjuan, *Ibo*; González-Wippler, *Introduction to Seashell Divination*; and Castellanos and Castellanos, *La cultura afrocubana* 3.

3. See Lyotard, *The Postmodern Condition*, xxiii–xxv. Lyotard's pragmatics of language games accounts for a particular externalization and technification of knowledge comparable to those of other informational systems: "Data banks," writes Lyotard, "are the Encyclopedia of tomorrow. They transcend the capacity of each of their users. They are 'nature' for postmodern man" (51). As I imply by my choice of terms throughout the foregoing discussion of the diloggún, computers and divination systems have certain similarities and differences deserving of further study.

Chapter Three: The Orishas in Republican Cuba

1. See Aguilar, "The Revolution of 1933."

2. Bakhtine's concept of novelistic "carnivalization" supports some of the following discussions of references to Afro-Cuban religion in the literature of the period. See Bakhtine, *L'oeuvre de François Rabelais*, 202–3, 218–19.

Chapter Four: A Is For Abakuá

1. See also Ortiz, *Los negros brujos*, 18–21, 240–41, on the aura of criminality surrounding the Ñáñigo practitioners.

Chapter Five: Re-marking the Bantu Center

1. The commands of the poem translate as follows:

Hit him with the hatchet, and he dies!

Hit him now!

Don't hit him with your foot, he'll bite you,

don't hit him with your foot, he'll go away!

Chapter Six: Versions of Vaudou

1. The Vaudou metaphor of Mawu's writing suggests that neither speech nor meaning preexists "writing": writing is not merely the transcription of spoken thoughts nor the mere recording of those thoughts but that complex activity of differentiation and supplementation that makes speech and meaning possible. This concept of an impersonal or nonhuman inscription prior to speech and meaning lies behind Derrida's claim that "writing is *inaugural*" (WD 10, 11).

2. See French, "Is Voodoo the Weapon to Repel the Invaders?" *New York Times* (late New York edition), June 24, 1994, A4.

3. González Echevarría, in "Socrates Among the Weeds: Blacks and History in Carpentier's *Explosion in a Cathedral*," 545–50, develops the concept of conflicting interpretations and multiple codings in Carpentier's narratives.

4. For a detailed historical background to the novel, see Speratti-Piñero, "Noviciado y apoteósis de Ti Noël en *El reino de este mundo*" and *Pasos hallados en "El reino de este mundo,"* passim.

5. For an extended discussion of Eshú-Elegbara's role as African-American interpreter, see Gates, 5–11.

Chapter Seven: Religion and Revolution

1. See Matibag, "Carpentier's Consecration of Stravinsky: The Avant-Garde after the Avant-Garde" for an expansion of the following comments on *La Consagración de la Primavera*.

2. See Barthes, "La face baroque" (The baroque face); Barthes and Sollers, "Severo Sarduy"; and Sarduy, "Tanger" for more on the *Tel Quel* influence on Sarduy's works.

3. See Girard, 2, 5, 9, 13, and Lacan, 286–87, on the theory of desire as mediated by signifiers.

4. Willy Chirino, "Mister, Don't Touch the Banana," in *Oxígeno* (sound recording).

⬧ Works Cited

Abimbola, 'Wande. "African Culture in the Americas." Paper presented at Iowa State University, April 5, 1990. Sound recording in Parks Library Media Center, Iowa State University.

———. *Ifá: An Exposition of Ifá Literary Corpus*. Ibadan, Nigeria: Oxford University Press, 1976.

———. *Ifá Divination Poetry*. Lagos: NOK, 1977.

———. "The Literature of the Ifa Cult." In *Sources of Yoruba History*, edited by Saburi Olademi Biobaku, 41–62. Oxford: Clarendon Press, 1973.

Adesanya, Adebayo. "Yoruba Metaphysical Thinking." *Odu* 5 (June 1958): 36–41.

Adorno, Theodor W. *Negative Dialectics*. Translated by E. B. Ashton. New York: Seabury, 1979.

Aguilar, Luis E. "The Revolution of 1933." In *The Cuba Reader*, edited by Philip Brenner and others, 19–24. New York: Grove, 1989.

Alonso, Dora. *Cuentos* [Stories]. Havana: Unión de Escritores y Artistas de Cuba, 1976.

———. *Ponolani (Cuentos)* [Ponolani (stories)]. Havana: Ediciones Granma, 1966.

Alvarez, Imeldo. *La novela cubana en el siglo XX* [The Cuban novel in the twentieth century]. Havana: Editorial Letras Cubanas, 1980.

Amado, Jorge. *Jubiabá*. 1935. Translated by Margaret A. Neves. New York: Avon, 1984.

Anonymous. "El cuarto fambá" [The fambá room]. In *La enciclopedia de Cuba: Poesía*. [The encyclopedia of Cuba: poetry], edited by Vicente Báez, 1:384. San Juan, P.R., and Madrid: Enciclopedia y Clásicos Cubanos, 1973.

Argüelles Micet, Ercilia. "Oricha, mito y color" [Orisha, myth and color]. *Del Caribe* 13 (1989): 10–22.

Arozarena, Marcelino. *Canción negra sin color* [Black song without color]. Havana: Ediciones Unión, 1966.

Bakhtine, Mikhail M. *The Dialogic Imagination: Four Essays*. Edited by Michael Holquist; translated by Caryl Emerson and Michael Holquist. Austin: University of Texas Press, 1981.

————. *L'oeuvre de François Rabelais et la culture populaire au Moyen Age et sous la Renaissance* [The works of François Rabelais and the popular culture of the Middle Ages and under the Renaissance]. Translated by Andrée Robel. Paris: Editions Gallimard, 1970.

Bal, Mieke. *Narratology: Introduction to the Theory of Narrative.* Translated by Christine van Boheemen. Toronto: University of Toronto Press, 1985.

Barnard, Philip. Translator's preface. In *For Voice (The Beach, Fall, Re-cite, The Ant-Killers)*, by Severo Sarduy. Translated by Philip Barnard. Pittsburgh: Latin American Literary Review Press, 1985.

Barnet, Miguel. *Akeké y la jutía. Fábulas cubanas* [The scorpion and the hutia: Cuban fables]. Havana: Ediciones Unión, 1978.

————. *Biografía de un cimarrón* [Biography of a runaway slave]. Barcelona: Ediciones Ariel, 1968.

————. *Canción de Rachel* [Song of Rachel]. 1967. Madrid: Alianza Editorial, 1988.

————. *La fuente viva* [The living fountain]. Havana: Editorial Letras Cubanas, 1983.

————. "Función del mito en la cultura cubana" [The function of myth in Cuban culture]. *La gaceta de Cuba* 178 (1979): 11–13.

————. *La piedra fina y el pavorreal* [The precious stone and the peacock]. Havana: Ediciones Unión, 1963.

————. *La sagrada familia* [The holy family]. Havana: Casa de las Américas, 1967.

Barreda, Pedro. *The Black Protagonist in the Cuban Novel.* Translated by Page Bancroft. Amherst: University of Massachusetts Press, 1979.

Barry, Tom, Beth Wood, and Debra Preusch. *The Other Side of Paradise: Foreign Control in the Caribbean.* New York: Grove Press, 1984.

Barthes, Roland. "La face baroque" [The baroque face]. *La Quinzaine littéraire* 15 (May 1967): 13.

————. "From Work to Text." In *Textual Strategies: Perspectives in Post-Structuralist Criticism,* edited by Josué Harari, 73–81. Ithaca: Cornell University Press, 1979.

————. "Introduction to the Structural Analysis of Narratives." In *A Barthes Reader,* edited by Susan Sontag, 251–95. New York: Hill and Wang, 1982.

————. *Mythologies.* Translated by Annette Lavers. New York: Hill and Wang, 1977.

Barthes, Roland, and Philippe Sollers. "Severo Sarduy." In *Severo Sarduy,* edited by Julián Ríos, 107–12. Madrid: Editorial Fundamentos, 1976.

Bascom, William. *Ifá Divination: Communication Between Gods and Men in West Africa.* Bloomington: Indiana University Press, 1969.

————. "The Relationship of Yoruba Folklore to Divining." *Journal of American Folklore* 56 (1943): 127–31.

————. *Sixteen Cowries: Yoruba Divination from Africa to the New World.* Bloomington: Indiana University Press, 1980.

————. "Verbal Art." *Journal of American Folklore* 68, no. 269 (1955): 245–63.

————. *The Yoruba of Southwestern Nigeria.* New York: Holt, Rinehart, and Winston, 1969.

Bastide, Roger. *African Civilizations in the New World.* New York: Harper and Row, 1971.

Beckford, George. "The Continuing Influence of the Plantation." In *Readings in Caribbean History and Economics: An Introduction to the Region*, edited by Roberta Marx Delson, 58–64. New York: Gordon and Breach Science Publishers, 1981.

Beier, Ulli. *The Return of the Gods.* Cambridge: Cambridge University Press, 1975.

———. *Yoruba Myths.* Cambridge: Cambridge University Press, 1980.

———. *Yoruba Poetry.* Cambridge: Cambridge University Press, 1970.

Benítez Rojo, Antonio. *El escudo de hojas secas* [The coat-of-arms of dry leaves]. Buenos Aires: Aditor publicaciones, 1969. Includes the title story and "La tierra yel cielo" [Earth and heaven].

———. *La isla que se repite. El Caribe y la perspectiva posmoderna* [The repeating island: The Caribbean and the postmodern perspective]. Hanover, N.H.: Ediciones del Norte, 1989.

Bolívar Aróstegui, Natalia. *Los orishas en Cuba* [The orishas in Cuba]. Havana: Ediciones Unión, 1990.

Borges, Jorge Luis. *Discusion* [Discussion]. 1957. Buenos Aires: Emecé Editores, 1982. Includes the essay "El arte narrativo y la magia" [Narrative art and magic].

Brathwaite, Edward Kamau. "The African Presence in Caribbean Literature." In *Africa in Latin America: Essays on History, Culture, and Socialization*, edited by Moreno Fraginals, 103–44. Translated by Leonor Blum. New York: Holmes and Meier, 1984.

———. *The Arrivants: A New World Trilogy.* London and New York: Oxford University Press, 1973.

———. *Contradictory Omens: Cultural Diversity and Integration in the Caribbean.* Mona, Jamaica: Savacou Publications, 1974.

———. *The Development of Creole Society in Jamaica, 1770–1820.* London: Oxford University Press, 1971.

Brushwood, John S. *The Spanish American Novel: A Twentieth-Century Survey.* Austin: University of Texas Press, 1975.

Bueno, Salvador. "Aproximaciones a la vida y la obra de Fernando Ortiz" [Approaches to the life and work of Fernando Ortiz]. *Casa de las Américas* 19, no. 113 (March–April 1979): 119–28.

———. *Historia de la literatura cubana* [History of Cuban literature]. 3rd edition. Havana: Editorial Nacional de Cuba, 1963.

———. *El negro en la novela hispanoamericana* [The negro in the Hispanoamerican novel]. Havana: Letras Cubanas, 1986.

Burke, Kenneth. *A Grammar of Motives.* Berkeley and Los Angeles: University of California Press, 1969.

———. *Permanence and Change: An Anatomy of Purpose.* 3rd edition. Berkeley and Los Angeles: University of California Press, 1984.

———. *The Philosophy of Literary Form: Studies in Symbolic Action.* 2nd edition. Baton Rouge: Louisiana State University Press, 1967.

———. *The Rhetoric of Religion: Studies in Logology.* Berkeley and Los Angeles: University of California Press, 1970.

Cabrera, Lydia. *Anagó: vocabulario lucumí* [Anagó: Lucumí vocabulary]. Miami: Ediciones Universal, 1986.

———. *Cuentos negros de Cuba* [Black stories from Cuba]. 1938. 2nd edition. Madrid: Ediciones CR, 1972.

———. *Koeko iyawo: aprende novicio. Pequeño tratado de Regla Lucumí* [Koeko iyawo: Learn, novice. Small treatise of Regla Lucumí]. Miami: Ediciones Universal, 1980.

———. *La lengua sagrada de los Ñáñigos* [The sacred language of the Ñáñigos]. Miami: Collección CR, 1988.

———. *El monte: Igbo, finda, ewe orisha, vititi nfinda* [The mountain: stones and herbs of the orishas]. Miami: Collección del Chicherekú, 1971.

———. *Por qué . . . (Cuentos negros de Cuba)* [Why . . . black stories from Cuba]. Madrid: Colección del Chicherukú, 1972.

———. *Refranes de Negros Viejos* [Proverbs of old blacks]. Miami: Editorial CR, 1970.

———. *La sociedad secreta Abakuá* [The Secret Abakuá Society]. Miami: Ediciones Universal, 1970.

———. *Yemayá y Ochún.* Madrid: Ediciones CR, 1974.

Cabrera Infante, Guillermo. *Así en la paz como en la guerra* [In peace as in war]. 1960. Barcelona: Editorial Seix Barral, 1975. Includes the story "En el gran ecbó" [In the great ecbó].

———. "La confundida lengua del poeta." *Primera Plana,* January 14–20, 1969, 64–65.

———. *Tres tristes tigres* [Three sad tigers]. Barcelona: Editorial Seix Barral, 1974.

Canet, Carlos. *Lucumí: religión de los yorubas en Cuba* [Lucumí: religion of the Yorubas in Cuba]. Miami: Editorial A.I.P, 1973.

Canizares, Raúl. *Walking with the Night: The Afro-Cuban World of Santería.* Rochester, Vt.: Destiny Books, 1993.

Carbonell, Walterio. *Crítica: cómo surgió la cultura nacional* [Critique: how the national cultural arose]. Havana: Ediciones Yaka, 1961.

Carpentier, Alejo. *Concierto barroco* [Concerto barroco]. 2nd edition. Madrid: siglo veintiuno, 1974.

———. *La Consagración de la Primavera* [The rite of spring]. 1978. 12th edition. Mexico and Madrid: siglo veintiuno editores, 1981.

———. *La danse sacrale* [The sacred dance.] Translated by René L. F. Durand. Paris: NRF, Gallimard, 1980.

———. *¡Ecue-Yamba-O!* [Ecue be praised!]. 1933. In *Obras completas,* vol. 1. México: siglo veintiuno, 1983.

———. *The Kingdom of This World.* 1949. Translated by Harriet de Onís. New York: Noonday Press, 1989.

———. *La música en Cuba* [Music in Cuba]. 1946. 2nd edition. México: Fondo de Cultura Económica, 1980.

———. *La novela latinoamericana en vísperas de un nuevo siglo y otros ensayos* [The Latin American novel on the eve of a new century and other essays]. Mexico and Madrid: siglo veintiuno editores, 1981.

———. *El reino de este mundo* [The kingdom of this world]. 1949. 7th edition, Barcelona: Seix Barral, 1978.

———. *El siglo de las luces* [The century of lights]. 1962. Caracas: Ayacucho, 1979.

———. *Tientos y diferencias* [Gropings and differences]. Mexico: Universidad Nacional Autónoma de México, Dirección General de Publicaciones, 1964. Includes the essay "De lo real maravillosamente americano" [On the marvelously American real].

Carullo, Sylvia. "El vaudoux como protagonista en *El reino de este mundo*" [Vaudou as protagonist in *The Kingdom of This World*]. *Afro-Hispanic Review* 9, nos. 1–3 (1990): 3–10.

Casals, Lourdes. "Cultural Policy and Writer in Cuba." In *The Cuba Reader*, edited by Philip Brenner, 506–13. New York: Grove Press, 1989.

———. *Elegua quiere tambo: cosmovisión religiosa afrocubana en las canciones populares* [Elegua wants a drum: The Afro-Cuban cosmovision in popular songs]. 2nd edition. Cali, Colombia: Universidad del Valle, 1983.

Castellanos, Jorge, and Isabel Castellanos. *La cultura afrocubana 1: el negro en Cuba, 1492–1844* [Afro-Cuban culture 1: The negro in Cuba, 1492–1844]. Miami: Ediciones Universal, 1988.

———. *La cultura afrocubana 3: las religiones y las lenguas* [Afro-Cuban culture 3: Religions and languages]. Miami: Ediciones Universal, 1992.

Castillo, J. M. *Ifá en tierra de Ifá: manual de recitaciones para santeros y babalaos de las reglas lucumíes* [Ifá in the land of Ifá: manual of recitations for santeros and babalaos of the Lucumí religions]. N.p., 1976.

Castro, Fidel. *Palabras a los intelectuales* [Words to the intellectuals]. Havana: Ediciones del Consejo Nacional de Cultura, 1961.

Césaire, Aimé. *The Collected Poetry*. Edited and translated by Clayton Eshleman and Annette Smith. Berkeley and Los Angeles: University of California Press, 1983.

———. "The Responsibility of the Artist." In *The African Reader: Independent Africa*, edited by Wilfred Cartey and Martin Kilson, 153–61. New York: Vintage, 1970.

Chatman, Seymour. *Story and Discourse: Narrative Structure in Fiction and Film*. Ithaca: Cornell University Press, 1978.

Chirino, Willy. *Oxígeno* [Oxygen]. Miami: Sony Discos, 1991. Sound recording. Includes the song "Mister, Don't Touch the Banana."

Clitandre, Pierre. *Cathédrale du mois d'août* [Cathedral of the month of August]. Paris: Syros, 1982.

Cofiño, Manuel. *Cuando la sangre se parece al fuego* [When blood looks like fire]. Havana: Editorial de Arte y Literatura, 1977.

———. *La última mujer y el próximo combate* [The last woman and the next combat]. 1971. Havana: Editorial Letras Cubanas, 1984.

Coulthard, G. R. *Race and Colour in Caribbean Literature*. London: Oxford University Press, 1962.

Courlander, Harold. "Abakwa Meeting in Guanabacoa." *Journal of Negro History* 29 (1944): 461–70.

————. *The African.* New York: Holt, 1993.

————. *A Treasury of African Folklore: The Oral Literature, Traditions, Myths, Legends, Epics, Tales, Recollections, Wisdom, Sayings, and Humor of Africa.* New York: Crown Publishers, 1975.

Cros Sandoval, Mercedes. *La religión afrocubana* [Afro-Cuban religion]. Madrid: Playor, 1975.

————. "Thunder Over Miami: Changó in a Technological Society." In *Thunder Over Miami: Ritual Objects and AfroCuban Religion*, program notes for exhibition at University Gallery, University of Florida, September 7–October 17, 1982. Center for African Studies, University of Florida.

Cuervo Hewitt, Julia. *Aché, presencia africana: tradiciones yoruba-lucumí en la narrativa cubana* [Aché, African presence: Yoruba-Lucumí traditions in Cuban narrative]. New York: Lang, 1988.

————. "Yoruba Presence: From Nigerian Oral Literature to Contemporary Cuban Narrative." In *Voices from Under: Black Narrative in Latin America and the Caribbean*, edited by William Luis, 65–85. Westport, Conn.: Greenwood Press, 1984.

Curtin, Philip. *The Atlantic Slave Trade: A Census.* Madison: University of Wisconsin Press, 1969.

Dalton, Roque, René Depestre, Edmundo Desnoes, Roberto Fernández Retamar, Ambrosio Fornet, and Carlos María Gutiérrez. *El intelectual y la sociedad* [The intellectual and society]. 5th edition. Mexico: siglo veintiuno, 1988.

Dathorne, O. R. *Dark Ancestor: The Literature of the Black Man in the Caribbean.* Baton Rouge: Louisiana State University Press, 1981.

Davis, Wade. *The Serpent and the Rainbow.* New York: Warner Books, 1985.

Deikman, Arthur J. "Deautomatization and the Mystic Experience." In *The Nature of Human Consciousness: A Book of Readings*, edited by Robert E. Ornstein, 216–33. San Francisco: Freeman, 1968.

Delano, Chief I. O. "Proverbs, Songs, and Poems." In *Sources of Yoruba History*, edited by S. O. Biobaku, 77–86. Oxford: Clarendon Press, 1973.

del Valle, Gerardo. *1/4 fambá y 19 cuentos más* [Fambá room and 19 more stories]. Havana: Ediciones Unión, 1967.

Deren, Maya. *Divine Horsemen: Voodoo Gods of Haiti.* New York: Dell, 1970.

Derrida, Jacques. *Dissemination.* Translated by Barbara Johnson. Chicago: University of Chicago Press, 1981.

————. *Positions.* Translated by Alan Bass. Chicago: University of Chicago Press, 1981.

————. "Signature Event Context." In *Glyph*, edited by Samuel Weber, 1:172–97. Baltimore and London: Johns Hopkins University Press, 1977.

————. *Speech and Phenomena and Other Essays on Husserl's Theory of Signs.* Translated by David B. Allison. Evanston: Northwestern University Press, 1973.

————. *Writing and Difference.* Translated by Alan Bass. Chicago: University of Chicago Press, 1978.

Deschamps Chapeaux, Pedro. "Prólogo" [Prologue]. In *Cuando la sangre se parece al fuego*, by Manuel Cofiño, 7–15. Havana: Editorial de Arte y Literatura, 1977.

Descombes, Vincent. *Modern French Philosophy.* Translated by L. Scott-Fox and J. M. Harding. Cambridge, London, and New York: Cambridge University Press, 1980. First published as *Le Même et L'Autre,* 1979.

Desnoes, Edmundo. *Memorias del subdesarrollo* [Memories of underdevelopment]. 1965. Mexico: Joaquín Mortiz, 1975.

Devisch, Renaat. "Perspectives on Divination in Contemporary Sub-Saharan Africa." In *Theoretical Explorations in African Religion,* edited by Wim van Binsbergen and Matthew Schoffeleers, 50–83. London: KPI/Routledge and Kegan Paul, 1985.

Díaz Fabelo, Teodoro. *Olórun.* Havana: Ediciones del Departamento de Folklore del Teatro Nacional de Cuba, 1960.

Donato, Eugenio. "The Idioms of the Text: Notes on the Language of Philosophy and the Fictions of Literature." *Glyph* 2 (1977): 1–13.

Draper, Theodore, *Castroism: Theory and Practice.* New York: Praeger, 1965.

During, Simon. "Postmodernism or Post-colonialism Today." In *Postmodernism: A Reader,* edited by Thomas Docherty, 448–62. New York: Columbia University Press, 1993.

Durkheim, Emile. *The Elementary Forms of the Religious Life.* Translated by Joseph Ward Swan. New York: Free Press, 1965.

Eades, J. S. *The Yoruba Today.* New York: Cambridge University Press, 1980.

Eco, Umberto. *Tratado de semiótica general* [Treatise of general semiotics]. Translated by Carlos Manzano. México and Barcelona: Editorial Nueva Imagen and Editorial Lumen, 1978.

Ellis, A. B. *The Yoruba Speaking Peoples of the Slave Coast of West Africa.* London: Chapman and Hall, 1894.

Eshleman, Clayton, and Smith, Annette. "Introduction." In *Aimé Césaire, the collected poetry,* edited and translated by Clayton Eshelman and Annette Smith, 1–28. Berkeley and Los Angeles: University of California Press, 1983.

Fage, J. D. *An Introduction to the History of West Africa.* Cambridge: Cambridge University Press, 1969.

Fagg, John Edwin. *Cuba, Haiti, and the Dominican Republic.* Englewood Cliffs, N.J.: Prentice-Hall, 1965.

Fanon, Frantz. *The Wretched of the Earth.* Translated by Constance Farrington. New York: Grove Press, 1968.

Fatunmbi, Awo Fá'lokun. *Iwa-pèlé, Ifá Quest: The Search for the Source of Santería and Lucumí.* New York: Original Publications, 1991.

Fernandez, James W. "Afterword." In *African Divination Systems: Ways of Knowing,* edited by Philip M. Peek, 213–21. Bloomington: Indiana University Press, 1991.

Fernández Retamar, Roberto. *Calibán: apuntes sobre la cultura en nuestra América* [Caliban: notes on the culture of our America]. Mexico: Diógenes, 1971.

Fernández Robaina, Tomás. *El negro en Cuba, 1902–1958: Apuntes para la historia de la lucha contra la discriminación racial* [The black in Cuba, 1902–1958: notes for the history of the struggle against racial discrimination]. Havana: Editorial de Ciencias Naturales, 1990.

————. *Recuerdos secretos de dos mujeres públicas* [Secret remembrances of two public women]. Havana: Editorial Letras Cubanas, 1983.

Foner, Laura, and Genovese, Eugene D., eds. *Slavery in the New World: A Reader in Comparative History.* Englewood Cliffs, N.J.: Prentice-Hall, 1969.

Fossey, Jean-Michel. "Severo Sarduy: máquina barroca revolucionaria" [Severo Sarduy: revolutionary Baroque machine]. In *Severo Sarduy,* edited by Julián Ríos, 15–24. Caracas: Editorial Fundamentos, 1976.

Franco, Jean. *Historia de literatura hispanoamericana: a partir de la Independencia* [History of Hispanoamerican literature: since independence]. 2nd edition. Barcelona: Seix Barral, 1979.

French, Howard W. "Is voodoo the weapon to repel the invaders?" *New York Times* (late New York edition), June 24, 1994, A4.

Frobenius, Leo. *The Voice of Africa.* Vols. 1–2. London: Hutchinson, 1913.

Frye, Northrup. *Anatomy of Criticism: Four Essays.* Princeton: Princeton University Press, 1972.

García Cortez, Julio. *Patakí: Leyendas y misterios de Orishas Africanos* [Patakí: legends and mysteries of African orishas]. Miami: Ediciones Universal, 1980.

————. *El Santo (La Ocha): secretos de la religión Lucumí* [The saint (the orisha): secrets of the Lucumí religion]. Miami: Ediciones Universal, 1983.

Gates, Henry Louis, Jr. *The Signifying Monkey: A Theory of Afro-American Literary Criticism.* New York: Oxford University Press, 1988.

Genette, Gérard. *Narrative Discourse: An Essay in Method.* Translated by Jane E. Lewin. Ithaca: Cornell University Press, 1980.

Girard, René. *Deceit, Desire, and the Novel: Self and Other in Literary Structure.* Translated by Yvonne Freccero. Baltimore: Johns Hopkins University Press, 1965.

Gleason, Judith. *Orisha: The Gods of Yorubaland.* New York: Atheneum, 1971.

Gleason, Judith, with Awotunde Aworinde and John Olaniyi Ogundipe. *A Recitation of Ifa, Oracle of the Yoruba.* New York: Grossman, 1973.

Gómez de Avellaneda y Arteaga, Gertrudis. *Sab: novela* [Sab: a novel]. Havana: Consejo Nacional de Cultura, Editorial Nacional de Cuba, 1963.

González Bueno, Gladys. "An Initiation Ceremony in Regla de Palo." In *AfroCuba: An Anthology of Cuban Writing on Race, Politics, and Culture,* edited by Pedro Pérez Sarduy and Jean Stubbs, 117–20. New York: Center for Cuban Studies/Ocean Press/Latin America Bureau, 1993.

González Echevarría, Roberto. *Alejo Carpentier: The Pilgrim at Home.* Ithaca: Cornell University Press, 1977.

————. "Criticism and Literature in Revolutionary Cuba." In *Cuba: Twenty-Five Years of Revolution, 1959–1984,* edited by Sandor Halebsky and John M. Kirk, 154–73. New York: Praeger, 1985.

————. "Literature of the Hispanic Caribbean." *Latin American Literary Review* 8, no. 16 (Spring–Summer 1980): 1–20.

————. *La ruta de Severo Sarduy* [The route of Severo Sarduy]. Hanover, N.H.: Ediciones del Norte, 1987.

————. "Socrates among the Weeds: Blacks and History in Carpentier's *Explosion in a Cathedral.*" *Massachusetts Review* 24, no. 3 (Autumn 1983): 545–61.

González-Wippler, Migene. *Introduction to Seashell Divination*. New York: Original Publications, 1985.

———. *Santería*. New York: Doubleday Anchor, 1975.

———. *The Santería Experience*. Englewood Cliffs, N.J.: Prentice-Hall, 1982.

———. *Santería: The Religion. A Legacy of Faith, Rites, and Magic*. New York: Harmony Books, 1975.

———. *Tales of the Orishas*. New York: Original Publications, 1985.

Gramsci, Antonio. *Selections from Cultural Writings*. Edited by David Forgacs and Geoffrey Nowell-Smith. Translated by William Boelhower. Cambridge, Mass.: Harvard University Press, 1985.

———. *Selections from the Prison Notebooks of Antonio Gramsci*. Edited and translated by Quintin Hoare and Geoffrey Nowell Smith. New York: International Publishers, 1971.

Granados, Manuel. *Adire y el tiempo roto* [Adire and the broken time]. Havana: Casa de las Américas, 1967.

Greenwood, R., and S. Hamber. *Arawaks to Africans*. London and Basingstoke: Macmillan, 1979.

Greimas, A. Julien. "The Interpretation of Myth: Theory and Practice." In *Structural Analysis of Oral Tradition*, edited by Pierre Maranda and Eli Köngas Maranda, 81–121. Philadelphia: University of Pennsylvania Press, 1971.

———. *Structural Semantics: An Attempt at a Method*. Translated by Daniele McDowell, Ronald Schleifer, and Alan Velie. Lincoln: University of Nebraska Press, 1984.

Greimas, A. Julien, and F. Rastier. "The Interaction of Semiotic Constraints." In *Game, Play, Literature*, edited by Jacques Ehrman, 86–105. Boston: Beacon Press, 1971.

Guevara, Ernesto "Che." *El socialismo y el hombre nuevo* [Socialism and the new man]. Edited by José Aricó. 3rd edition. Mexico: siglo veintiuno, 1979.

Guillén, Nicolás. *Sóngoro cosongo (Motivos de son, West Indies, Ltd., España)* [Sóngoro consongo (Motifs of son, West Indies, Ltd., Spain)]. 1930–34. 7th edition. Buenos Aires: Editorial Losada, 1976.

Guiraud, Pierre. *La semiología* [Semiology]. Translated by María Teresa Poyrazian. 8th edition. Mexico: siglo veintiuno editores, 1979.

Gutiérrez, Mariela. *Los cuentos negros de Lydia Cabrera: estudio morfológico esquemático* [The black stories of Lydia Cabrera: a schematic morphological study]. Miami: Ediciones Universal, 1986.

Habermas, Jürgen. "The Entry into Postmodernity: Nietzsche as a Turning Point." In *Postmodernism: A Reader*, edited by Thomas Docherty, 51–61. New York: Columbia University Press, 1993.

Hall, Gwendolyn M. "The Slave's Life in Cuba." In *Readings in Caribbean History and Economics: An Introduction to the Region*, edited by Roberta Marx Delson, 98–102. New York: Gordon and Breach Science Publishers, 1981.

Hanley, Elizabeth. "With the Saints." *Mother Jones* (September–October 1990): 83, 85.

Harnecker, Marta. *Indígenas, cristianos y estudiantes en la revolución* [Indians, Christians, and students in the revolution]. 2nd edition. Lima: Editorial en Imprenta DESA, 1988.

Harrison, Lawrence E. "Voodoo politics." *Atlantic* 271 (June 1993): 101–7.

Hernández Espinosa, Eugenio. *María Antonia*. Havana: Editorial Letras Cubanas, 1979.

Herskovits, Melville J. "African Gods and Catholic Saints in the New World Negro Belief." *American Anthropologist* 39 (1937).

————. *Life in a Haitian Valley*. New York and London: Knopf, 1966.

————. "The Study of African Oral Literature." In *Cultural and Social Anthropology: Selected Readings*, edited by Peter B. Hammond, 361–67. New York and London: Macmillan, 1964.

Huberman, Leo, and Paul M. Sweezy. "Background of the Revolution." In *The Cuba Reader*, edited by Philip Brenner and others, 5–19. New York: Grove Press, 1989.

Hurston, Zora Neale. *Tell My Horse*. Berkeley: Turtle Island, 1983.

Idowu, E. Bolaji. *Olodumare: God in the Yoruba Belief*. London: Longmans, Green, 1962.

Ijimere, Obotunde. *The Imprisonment of Obatala and Other Plays*. Translated by Ulli Beier. London: Heinemann Educational Books, 1968.

Jackson, Richard L. *The Black Image in Latin American Literature*. Albuquerque: University of New Mexico Press, 1976.

Jahn, Janheinz. *A History of Neo-African Literature*. Translated by Oliver Coburn and Ursula Lehrburger. New York: Faber and Faber, 1968.

————. *Muntu: An Outline of the New African Culture*. New York: Grove Press, 1961.

Jakobson, Roman. "Closing Statement: Linguistics and Poetics." In *Style in Language*, edited by Thomas A. Sebeok, 350–77. Cambridge, Mass.: MIT Press, 1960.

————. "Two Aspects of Language and Two Types of Aphasic Disturbances." In *Fundamentals of Language*, by Roman Jakobson and Morris Halle. 'S-Gravenhage: Mouton, 1956.

James, William. *The Varieties of Religious Experience: A Study in Human Nature*. New York: Modern Library, 1929.

James Figarola, Joel. *Sobre muertos y dioses* [On the dead and gods]. Santiago, Cuba: Caserón, 1989.

Jameson, Fredric. "World Literature in an Age of Multinational Capitalism." In *The Current in Criticism: Essays on the Present and Future of Literary Theory*, edited by Clayton Koelb and Virgil Lokke, 139–58. West Lafayette, Ind.: Purdue University Press, 1987.

Jules-Rosette, Benetta. "The Veil of Objectivity: Prophecy, Divination, and Social Inquiry." *American Anthropologist* 80, no. 3 (September 1978): 549–70.

Klein, Herbert S. *Slavery in the Americas: A Comparative Study of Virginia and Cuba*. Chicago: University of Chicago Press, 1967.

Knight, Franklin W. "How to Compare Slavery Systems." In *Readings in Caribbean History and Economics: An Introduction to the Region*, edited by Roberta Marx Delson, 65–69. New York: Gordon and Breach Science Publishers, 1981.

Kubayanda, Josephat B. "On Discourse of Decolonization in Africa and the Caribbean." *Dispositio* 14, nos. 36–38 (1989): 25–37.

Lacan, Jacques. *Ecrits: A Selection*. Translated by Alan Sheridan. New York: Norton, 1977.

Lachatañeré, Rómulo. *Manual de Santería: el sistema de cultos "Lucumís"* [Manual of Santería: the system of the "Lucumí" cults]. Havana: Editorial Caribe, 1942.

————. *¡¡Oh, mío Yemayá!!* Manzanillo, Cuba: Editorial El Arte, 1938.

————. "El sistema religioso de los lucumíes y otras influencias africanas en Cuba"

[The religious system of the Lucumís and other African influences in Cuba]. *Estudios Afrocubanos* 3, nos. 1–4 (1938): 27–38.

Laguerre, Michel S. *Voodoo and Politics in Haiti.* Houndmills and London: Macmillan, 1989.

Law, Robin. *The Oyo Empire, c. 1600–1836.* Oxford: Clarendon Press, 1977.

Leante, César. *Los guerrilleros negros* [The black guerillas]. Mexico, Madrid, Bogotá: siglo veintiuno editores, 1979.

Lévi-Strauss, Claude. *Structural Anthropology,* vol. 1. Translated by Claire Jacobson and Brooke Grundfest Schoepf. New York: Basic Books, 1963.

Lewis, Gordon K. *Main Currents in Caribbean Thought: The Historical Evolution of Caribbean Society in Its Ideological Aspects, 1492–1900.* Baltimore: Johns Hopkins University Press, 1983.

Lezama Lima, José. *Paradiso.* 1966. 8th edition. Mexico: Biblioteca Era, 1987.

Lloyd, P. C. "The Yoruba of Nigeria." In *Peoples of Africa,* edited by James L. Gibbs, Jr., 547–82. New York: Holt, Rinehart, and Winston, 1965.

López, Lourdes. *Estudio de un babalao* [Study of a babalao]. Havana: Departamento de Actividades Culturales, Universidad de La Habana, 1978.

Luis, William. "History and Fiction: Black Narrative in Latin America and the Caribbean." In *Voices from Under: Black Narrative in Latin America and the Caribbean,* edited by William Luis, 3–32. Westport, Conn.: Greenwood Press, 1984.

————. *Literary Bondage: Slavery in Cuban Narrative.* Austin: University of Texas Press, 1990.

Luis, William, and Julia Cuervo Hewitt. "Santos y santería: conversación con Arcadio, santero de Guanabacoa" [Saints and Santería: conversation with Arcadio, santero of Guanabacoa]. *Afro-Hispanic Review* 6, no. 1 (January 1987): 9–17.

Lumsden, C. Ian. "The Ideology of the Revolution." In *Cuba in Revolution,* edited by Rolando Bonachea and Nelson P. Valdés, 529–44. Garden City, N.Y.: Anchor Books, 1972.

Lyotard, Jean-François. *The Postmodern Condition: A Report on Knowledge.* Translated by Geoff Bennington and Brian Massumi. Minneapolis: University of Minnesota Press, 1984.

Macherey, Pierre. *A Theory of Literary Production.* Translated by Geoffrey Wall. London: Routledge and Kegan Paul, 1978.

Martínez Furé, Rogelio. *Diálogos imaginarios* [Imaginary dialogues]. Havana: Editorial Arte y Literatura, 1979.

Masó, Fausto. "Literatura y revolución en Cuba" [Literature and revolution in Cuba]. *Mundo Nuevo* (February 1969): 50–54.

Matibag, Eugenio D. "Carpentier's Consecration of Stravinsky: The Avant-Garde after the Avant-Garde." *Journal of Interdisciplinary Literary Studies* 5, no. 2 (1993): 299–322.

————. "Reason and the State: The Enlightened Dictator of Alejo Carpentier's *El recurso del método* [The recourse of the method]" *Dispositio* 18, no. 44 (1993): 153–73.

————. "Self-Consuming Fictions: The Dialectics of Cannibalism in Modern Caribbean Narratives." *Postmodern Culture* 1, no. 3 (May 1991).

————. "The Yoruba Origins of Afro-Cuban Culture." *Journal of Caribbean Studies* 10, nos. 1–2 (Winter 1994–Spring 1995): 50–65.

Menton, Seymour. "La novela de la Revolución cubana, fase cinco: 1975–1987" [The novel of the Cuban Revolution, phase five]. *Revista iberoamericana* 152–53 (July–December 1990): 913–32.

———. *Prose Fiction of the Cuban Revolution.* Austin: University of Texas Press, 1975.

Métraux, Alfred. *Haiti: Black Peasants and Their Religion.* London and Toronto: George G. Harrap, 1960.

Metz, Diana K. "Syncretism and Symbiosis: Santería and Afro-Cuban Culture." Unpublished manuscript in author's possession, 1992.

Mintz, Sidney W., and Richard Price. *An Anthropological Approach to the Afro-American Past: A Caribbean Perspective.* Philadelphia: Institute for the Study of Human Issues, 1976.

Miranda, Julio E. *Nueva literatura cubana* [New Cuban literature]. Madrid: Taurus Ediciones, 1971.

Montes Huidobro, Matías. "Lydia Cabrera: observaciones estructurales sobre su narrativa" [Lydia Cabrera: structural observations on her narrative]. In *Homenaje a Lydia Cabrera* [Homage to Lydia Cabrera], edited by Reinaldo Sánchez, 41–50. Miami: Ediciones Universal, 1977.

Moore, Carlos. *Castro, the Blacks, and Africa.* Los Angeles: University of California Center for Afro-American Studies, 1988.

Morales, Jorge Luis, ed. *Poesía afroantillana y negrista* [Afro-Antillean and Negrista poetry]. 2nd edition. Río Piedras, P.R.: Editorial Universitaria, 1981.

Morúa Delgado, Martín. *Sofía.* Havana: Instituto Cubano del Libro, 1972.

Murphy, Joseph M. "Lydia Cabrera and *La Regla de Ocha* in the United States." In *En torno a Lydia Cabrera* [About Lydia Cabrera], edited by Isabel Castellanos and Josefina Inclán, 246–54. Miami: Ediciones Universal, 1987.

———. "Santería." In *The Encyclopedia of Religions,* edited by Mircea Eliade, 13:66–67. New York: Macmillan, 1987.

———. *Santería: African Spirits in America.* Boston: Beacon Press, 1993.

Nietzsche, Friedrich. *Twilight of the Idols, or, How One Philosophizes with a Hammer.* In *The Portable Nietzsche,* edited and translated by Walter Kaufmann, 463–563. New York: Viking Press, 1974.

———. *The Will to Power.* Edited by Walter Kaufmann. Translated by Walter Kaufmann and R. J. Hollingdale. New York: Random House/Vintage Books, 1968.

Norris, Christopher. *Deconstruction: Theory and Practice.* London and New York: Methuen, 1982.

Novás Calvo, Lino. *Pedro Blanco, el negrero* [Pedro Blanco, the slaver]. 5th edition. Madrid: Espasa-Calpe, 1973.

Nuñez, Benjamin, with the assistance of the African Bibliographic Center. *Dictionary of Afro-Latin American Civilization.* Westport, Conn.: Greenwood Press, 1980.

Olatunji, Olatunde O. *Features of Yoruba Oral Poetry.* Ibadan, Nigeria: University Press Limited, 1984.

Ortega, Julio. *Relato de la utopía: notas sobre narrativa cubana de la revolución* [Tale of utopia. Notes on Cuban narrative of the revolution]. Barcelona: La Gaya Ciencia, 1973.

Ortiz, Fernando. *Contrapunteo cubano del tabaco y el azúcar* [Cuban counterpoint of tobacco and sugar]. Prologue by Bronislaw Malinowski. Barcelona: Editorial Ariel/Esplugues de Llobregat, 1973.

———. "Los factores humanos de la cubanidad" [The human factors of Cubanity]. *Islas* 70 (September–December 1981): 71–78.

———. "La fiesta afro-cubana del 'Día de Reyes'" [The Afro-Cuban fiesta of the "Day of the Three Kings"]. *Revista Bimestre Cubana* 15, no. 1 (January–June 1920): 5–26.

———. *Hampa afrocubana: los negros brujos* [Afro-Cuban underworld: the black sorcerers]. Miami: Ediciones Universal, 1973.

———. "Por la integración cubana de blancos y negros" [For the Cuban integration of whites and blacks]. *RBNH* [Revista de la Biblioteca Nacional de la Habana] 23, no. 3 (September–December 1981): 21–36.

———. "La tragedia de los ñáñigos." *Cuadernos americanos* 9, no. 52 (1950): 79–101.

Ortiz, Fernando. "Predisposición del lector" [Predisposition of the reader]. Rómulo Lachatañeré. ¡¡Oh, mío Yemayá!! Manzanillo, Cuba: Editorial El Arte, 1938.

Ott, Thomas O. "Toussaint's New Order." In *Readings in Caribbean History and Economics: An Introduction to the Region*, edited by Roberta Marx Delson, 158–64. New York: Gordon and Breach Science Publishers, 1981.

Pageaux, Daniel-Henri. "Alejo Carpentier devant Haïti: *Le royaume de ce monde*" [Alejo Carpentier before Haiti: *The kingdom of this world*]. In "Alejo Carpentier et son oeuvre" [Alejo Carpentier and his work], *Sud* 4 (1982): 131–47.

Peek, Philip M. "African Divination Systems: Non-Normal Modes of Cognition." In *African Divination Systems: Ways of Knowing*, edited by Philip M. Peek, 213–21. Bloomington: Indiana University Press, 1991.

Pemberton, John, III. "A Cluster of Sacred Symbols: Orisha Worship among the Igbomina Yoruba of Ila-Orangun." *History of Religions* 17, no. 1 (August 1977): 1–28.

Pérez Firmat, Gustavo. *The Cuban Condition: Translation and Identity in Modern Cuban Literature.* Cambridge and New York: Cambridge University Press, 1989.

Pérez Sarduy, Pedro. "Open Letter to Carlos Moore." *Afro-Hispanic Review* 3, nos. 1–3 (January–May–September 1990): 25–29.

Pérez Sarduy, Pedro, and Jean Stubbs. "Introduction: The Rite of Social Communion." In *AfroCuba: An Anthology of Cuban Writing on Race, Politics, and Culture*, edited by Pedro Pérez Sarduy and Jean Stubbs, 3–26. Melbourne, Aust., and New York: Center for Cuban Studies/Ocean Press/Latin America Bureau, 1993.

Portuondo, José Antonio. "Alejo Carpentier: creador y teórico de la literatura" [Alejo Carpentier: creator and theorist of literature]. In *Recopilación de textos sobre Alejo Carpentier* [Abridged texts on Alejo Carpentier], edited by Salvador Arias, 83–96. Havana: Casa de las Américas, 1977.

———. *Bosquejo histórico de las letras cubanas* [Historical outline of Cuban letters]. Havana: Dirección General de Cultura, 1960.

Price-Mars, Jean. *So Spoke the Uncle.* Translated by Magdaline W. Shannon. Washington, D.C.: Three Continents Press, 1983.

Propp, Vladimir. *Morphology of the Folktale.* 2nd edition. Revised and edited by Louis A. Wagner. Translated by Laurence Scott. Austin: University of Texas Press, 1968.

Ramos, José Antonio. *Caniquí.* 1936. Havana: Editorial Arte y Literatura, 1975.

Rimmon-Kenan, Shlomith. *Narrative Fiction: Contemporary Poetics.* London and New York: Methuen, 1983.

Rivera, Francisco. "*La consagración de la primavera* de Alejo Carpentier" [The rite of spring by Alejo Carpentier]. *Vuelta* 3, no. 32 (July 1979): 35–37.

Rogers, Andrés R. *Los caracoles: historia de sus letras* [The shell: story of their letters]. 2nd edition. Washington, D.C.: Librería Latinoamericana, 1973.

Saldaña, Excilia. *Kele kele* [Softly, softly]. Havana: Editorial Letras Cubanas, 1987.

Salzmann, Isidro. "Pasividad y vacío ideológico en *Ecue-Yamba-O* de Alejo Carpentier" [Passivity and ideological vacuum in *Ecue-Yamba-O* by Alejo Carpentier]. *Revista de literatura hispanoamericana* 10 (January–June 1976): 69–119.

Sánchez, Julio. *La religión de los orichas: creencias y ceremonias de un culto afro-caribeño* [The religion of the orishas: beliefs and ceremonies of an Afro-Caribbean cult]. 3rd edition. Hato Rey, Puerto Rico: Colección Estudios Afrocaribeños, 1991.

Sánchez-Boudy, José. *La temática novelística de Severo Sarduy (De donde son los cantantes)* [The novelistic thematic of Severo Sarduy (Where the singers are from)]. Miami: Ediciones Universal, 1985.

Sarduy, Severo. *Big Bang.* Barcelona: Tusquets Editor, 1974.

———. *De donde son los cantantes* [Where the singers are from]. 1967. 2nd edition. México: Joaquín Mortiz, 1970.

———. *For Voice (The Beach, Fall, Re-cite, The Ant-Killers).* Translated by Philip Barnard. 1978. Pittsburgh: Latin American Literary Review Press, 1985.

Sarduy, Severo. "Tanger." *Tel Quel* 47 (1971): 86–88.

Sheridan, Richard B. "The Plantation Revolution and the Industrial Revolution." In *Readings in Caribbean History and Economics: An Introduction to the Region,* edited by Roberta Marx Delson, 44–51. New York: Gordon and Breach Science Publishers, 1981.

Shklovski, Victor. "El arte como artificio" [Art as artifice]. In *Teoría de la literatura de los formalistas rusos* [Literary theory of the Russian formalists], edited by Tzvetan Todorov, 55–70. Translated by Ana María Nethol. 3rd Spanish edition. México: siglo veintiuno, 1978.

Simpson, George Eaton. *Black Religions in the New World.* New York: Columbia University Press, 1978.

Skidmore, Thomas E., and Peer H. Smith. *Modern Latin America.* 3rd edition. New York and Oxford: Oxford University Press, 1992.

Smart, Ninian. *The Phenomenon of Religion.* New York: Herder and Herder, 1973.

———. *The Religious Experience.* 4th edition. New York: Macmillan, 1991.

Smith, Robert. *Kingdoms of the Yoruba.* 2nd edition. London: Methuen, 1976.

Smith, Robert Freeman. "United States Businessmen in Cuba." In *Readings in Caribbean History and Economics: An Introduction to the Region,* edited by Roberta Marx Delson, 190–96. New York: Gordon and Breach Science Publishers, 1981.

Soledad, Rosalía de la, and M. J. San Juan. *Ibo: Yorubas en tierras cubanas* [Ibo: Yorubas in Cuban lands]. Miami: Ediciones Universal, 1988.

Sommers, Joseph. "¡Ecue-Yamba-O!: semillas del arte narrativo de Alejo Carpentier" [¡Ecue-Yamba-O!: Seeds of the narrative art of Alejo Carpentier]. In *Estudios de literatura hispanoamericana en honor a José J. Arrom* [Studies of Hispanoamerican literature in honor of José J. Arrom], edited by Andrew Peter Debicki, 227–38. Chapel Hill: University of North Carolina Press, 1974.

Souza, Raymond D. *Major Cuban Novelists: Innovation and Tradition.* Columbia: University of Missouri Press, 1976.

Speratti-Piñero, Emma Susana. "Noviciado y apoteósis de Ti Noël en *El reino de este mundo* de Alejo Carpentier" [Novitiate and apotheosis of Ti Noel in *The Kingdom of This World* by Alejo Carpentier]. *Bulletin Hispanique* 80, nos. 3–4 (July–December 1978): 201–28.

———. *Pasos hallados en "El reino de este mundo"* [Steps found in *The Kingdom of This World*]. Mexico: El Colegio de México, 1981.

Taylor, Patrick. *The Narrative of Liberation: Perspectives on Afro-Caribbean Literature, Popular Culture, and Politics.* Ithaca: Cornell University Press, 1989.

Tempels, Placide. *Bantu Philosophy.* 1945. Translated by Colin King. Reprint, Paris: Présence Africaine, 1969.

Thompson, Robert Farris. *Flash of the Spirit: African and Afro-American Art and Philosophy.* New York: Vintage Books, 1984.

———. "Recapturing Heaven's Glamour: Afro-Caribbean Festivalizing Arts." In *Caribbean Festival Arts: Each and Every Bit of Difference*, edited by John W. Nunley and Judith Bettelheim, 17–29. Seattle and London: St. Louis Art Museum/University of Washington Press, 1988.

Timmerman, Jacobo. *Cuba: A Journey.* Translated by Toby Talbot. New York: Vintage Books, 1992.

Titiev, Mischa. "A Fresh Approach to the Problem of Magic and Religion." In *Cultural and Social Anthropology: Selected Readings*, edited by Peter B. Hammond, 284–88. New York and London: Macmillan, 1964.

Todorov, Tzvetan. *Introduction to Poetics.* Translated by Richard Howard. Minneapolis: University of Minnesota Press, 1981.

———. *The Poetics of Prose.* Translated by Richard Howard. Ithaca: Cornell University Press, 1977.

Tujibikilo, Muamba. *La resistencia cultural del negro en América Latina: lógica ancestral y celebración de la vida* [The cultural resistance of blacks in Latin America: Ancestral logic and celebration of life]. San José, Cuba: Editorial Departamento Ecuménico de Investigaciónes, 1990.

Turner, Victor. "Social Dramas and Stories About Them." In *On Narrative*, edited by W. J. T. Mitchell, 137–64. Chicago: University of Chicago Press, 1981.

———. "The Syntax of Symbolism in a Ndembu Ritual." In *Structural Analysis of Oral Tradition*, edited by Pierre Maranda and Elli Köngas Maranda, 125–36. Philadelphia: University of Pennsylvania Press, 1971.

Tynjanov, Jurij. "On Literary Evolution." In *Twentieth-Century Literary Theory*, edited by Vassili Lambropoulos and David Neal Miller, 152–62. Albany: State University of New York Press, 1987.

Ulloa, Justo C. "Contenido y forma yoruba en 'La Dolores Rondón' de Severo Sarduy" [Yoruba content and form in Severo Sarduy's "Dolores Rondón"]. In *Homenaje a Lydia Cabrera* [Homage to Lydia Cabrera], edited by Reinaldo Sánchez, 241–50. Miami: Ediciones Universal, 1977.

Valdés Bernal, Sergio. "Caracterización lingüística del negro en la novela *¡Ecue-Yamba-O!* de Alejo Carpentier" [Linguistic characterization of the negro in the novel *¡Ecue-Yamba-O!* by Alejo Carpentier]. *Anuar de Linguistica si Istorie Literara* 2 (1971): 123–70.

Valdés-Cruz, Rosa. "El mundo del folklore en Lydia Cabrera: su técnica narrativa" [The world of folklore in Lydia Cabrera: her narrative technique]. In *En torno a Lydia Cabrera* [Concerning Lydia Cabrera], edited by Isabel Castellanos and Josefina Inclán, 161–72. Miami: Ediciones Universal, 1987.

Verger, Pierre. "The Yoruba High God: A Review of the Sources." *Odu* 2, no. 2 (1966).

Vidal, Hernán. *Para llegar a Manuel Cofiño (estudio de una narrativa revolucionaria cubana)* [To arrive at Manuel Cofiño (study of a revolutionary Cuban narrative)]. Minneapolis: Society for the Study of Contemporary Hispanic and Lusophone African Revolutionary Literatures and Institute for the Study of Ideologies and Literature, 1984.

Volek, Emil. "Análisis e interpretación de *El reino de este mundo* de Alejo Carpentier" [Analysis and interpretation of *The Kingdom of This World* by Alejo Carpentier]. In *Homenaje a Alejo Carpentier: variaciones interpretativas en torno a su obra* [Homage to Alejo Carpentier: interpretive variations concerning his work], edited by Helmy F. Giacomán, 145–78. New York: Las Américas, 1970.

Vunda, Zola ni. "La función del proemio en *Changó, el gran putas*" [The function of the preface of Changó, the great "motherfucker"]. *Afro-Hispanic Review* 9, nos. 1–3 (1990): 18–24.

Webb, Barbara J. *Myth and History in Caribbean Fiction: Alejo Carpentier, Wilson Harris, and Edouard Glissant.* Amherst: University of Massachusetts Press, 1992.

Wynter, Sylvia. "Jonkonnu in Jamaica." *Jamaica Journal* 4, no. 2 (June 1970): 44.

Zapata Olivella, Manuel. "*Los Ancestros Combatientes*: Una Saga Afro-norteamericana" [The combating ancestors: an Afro-North American saga]. *Afro-Hispanic Review* 10, no .3 (September 1991): 51–58.

―――. *Changó, el gran putas* [Changó, the great "motherfucker"]. 1983. Bogotá: Rei Andes, 1992.

―――. *Las claves mágicas de América (raza, clase y cultura)* [The secret keys to America (race, class and culture)]. Bogotá: Plaza and Janes, 1989.

Zizek, Slavoj. *Looking Awry: An Introduction to Jacques Lacan through Popular Culture.* Cambridge, Mass., and London: MIT Press, 1992.

Zuesse, Evan M. *Ritual Cosmos: The Sanctification of Life in African Religions.* Athens: Ohio University Press, 1979.

✦ Index

nostalgia, 41, 241; Ochún and, 64; and
possession, 200; projection of, 165; in
Ramos, 107–8; and the signifier, 258
despojo, the, during *ituto*, 73
Dessalines, Jean Jacques, 205, 207, 219; in
Zapata Olivella, 215
déssounin ritual, 212
determinism, in del Valle, 142
devil(s): in Abakuá beliefs, 132; Alonso and,
180–83; in Bantu myth, 42; in Cabrera,
179; in del Valle, 144, 146; Eshú-Eleggúa
as, 61; in Havana, 1
diagnosis, and prognosis through diloggún,
82
dialectic(s): and *atributos*, 48; of fortification,
173; and the idea of independence, 211;
of inscription, xiv; of signs, 45, 90
dialogism: in Carpentier, 96; in narrative,
xiv; patakís and, 33; in Ramos, 102, 105,
108; in Zapata Olivella, 174
Diaspora, the African, xii, 41
didacticism: and parables in diloggún, 78;
in patakís, 249
diegesis, 234
différance: in signification, 3; and syncretism,
27
difference: Africanity and, 94, 227; in
Barnet, 121; and *fundamento*, 37; and
disruption, 91; gradient of, 17;
individuation as, in Ramos, 110; and
interpretation, xv; and signs, 16; in
structure, 3; and syncretic artifacts, 27
diloggún, 13, 73–84, 261n. 2; in *asiento*, 48;
Babalú-Ayé and, 68; Carpentier on, 96;
del Valle and, 143; and Ifá contrasted, 70,
78; Inle and, 66; and *mèríndínlógún*
contrasted, 79; patakís in, xiv
discontinuity, experience and, 29
discourse(s): and Africanity, xi; alternating,
in Carpentier, 98; free indirect, 223;
incommensurability of, 225, 233, 245;
orders of, 4; political, in del Valle, 146;
practices of, xv; and reiteration, 17;
religion and, xii, 6–7; of Vaudou, 214
diseases, Babalú-Ayé and, 67–68
dispersion, of Caniquí, 112
displacement: in Abakuá symbolism, 128;
meaning as, 46, 152; and metonymy, 14;

and negativity, 256; signification and,
3, 28
diversity, and dissension, 8
"divide-and-rule," *cabildos* and, 23
divine, the: polytheism and, 11; religion
and, 6
divination, 13; the bourgeoisie and, 220; in
Cofiño, 243; and *nganga* worship, 170; as
metaphor, 6, 85; and narrative, xiii-xiv;
and prediction, 84, 258; and signs, 44;
as strategy, 74; *vititi mensu* and, 170–71
documentation, of liturgy, xiv
dominance: of Lucumí religion, 38, 49, 88;
and encroachments, 39
doubling: in Cabrera Infante, 130; in
Sarduy, 253, 255
drama(s), social: in Carpentier, 136;
metaphor and, 46; ritual as, 6; Turner
on, 12
dream(s): in Carpentier, 216; Lachatañeré
and, 115; in Ramos, 107, 111; and the
quotidian, 27; in Vaudou, 190
drum(s): in Abakuá ceremony, 120, 122–
23, 126, 132–33; in Alonso, 181, 250;
in Cabrera Infante, 234; in Carpentier,
99, 136, 214, 217; in del Valle, 149; and
music, 15; and *nommo*, 218; and Rada
rites, 198; restriction of, 230; in Vaudou
ceremony, 201. *See also* Ekue; Seseribó
Dutty, Bouckman: in Carpentier,
212, 218; in Zapata Olivella, 215
Duvalier, François, 207–8
Duvalier, Jean Claude, 208

earth, the, in Cabrera, 178
ebbó(s): in Cabrera, 179; in Carpentier, 100;
definition of, 234; and diloggún, 76, 83;
in Guillén, 157; magic and, 13; Osaín
and, 67; and Caniquí, 111
eclecticism, as method, 8
economy: rationalization and, in Carpentier,
95; of signification, xiv, 28
Efik, the: and the Abakuá, 124, 128, 239;
the Carabalí, 18; language of, 19; and del
Valle, 141
efimeramaetacua, the, in del Valle, 142
Efor, the, and the Abakuá, 127